PENGUIN BOOKS

THE PENGUIN BOOK OF DIARIES

Ronald Blythe has written poetry, short stories, history and literary criticism, much of it reflecting his East Anglian background. His first book, the novel *A Treasonable Growth*, was published in 1960. *Akenfield*, his remarkable evocation of rural change, much of which he had himself witnessed, appeared in 1969. It was followed by *The View in Winter*, a study of old age. *The Age of Illusion* and *Writing in a War*, an anthology, contain further personal assessments of Britain's recent past. *From the Headlands*, Ronald Blythe's collected essays, was published in 1982. *Divine Landscapes* was published by Viking in 1986, and his latest book is *Private Words: Letters and Diaries from the Second World War*, also published by Viking. His work has been translated and filmed and has received a number of literary awards.

Ronald Blythe has also edited and introduced several volumes in the Penguin Classics, including *Emma* by Jane Austen, William Hazlitt's *Selected Writings*, *The Awkward Age* by Henry James and *Far From the Madding Crowd* by Thomas Hardy.

THE PENGUIN BOOK
OF
DIARIES

SELECTED BY
RONALD BLYTHE

PENGUIN BOOKS

PENGUIN BOOKS

Published by the Penguin Group
Penguin Books Ltd, 27 Wrights Lane, London W8 5TZ, England
Penguin Books USA Inc., 375 Hudson Street, New York, New York 10014, USA
Penguin Books Australia Ltd, Ringwood, Victoria, Australia
Penguin Books Canada Ltd, 10 Alcorn Avenue, Toronto, Ontario, Canada M4V 3B2
Penguin Books (NZ) Ltd, 182–190 Wairau Road, Auckland 10, New Zealand

Penguin Books Ltd, Registered Offices: Harmondsworth, Middlesex, England

This selection first published by Viking 1989
Published in Penguin Books 1991
1 3 5 7 9 10 8 6 4 2

Introduction and selection copyright © Ronald Blythe, 1989
All rights reserved

The moral right of the editor has been asserted

Printed in England by Clays Ltd, St Ives plc
Typeset in 10/12pt Lasercomp Sabon

For Charles Causley

CONTENTS

Contents

Contents

Contents

INTRODUCTION

'I wonder why I do it?' was what Virginia Woolf once asked herself as she raced down the events of yet one more day. To put a brake on Time's wingèd chariot? Most diarists question what is often their most compulsive daily activity. They sense that some kind of explanation or apology to themselves is due, they wonder about their powerful self-centredness, or whether diary-writing is their particular drug. Strong guilt builds up when a day or week is missed and they beg forgiveness of the neglected page. George Mikes said that although all writing was probably a manifestation of a neurotic need, diary-writing was more so, adding, 'Where does the diary-reader come in?' Another contemplator of the genre, Stefan Kanfer, suggested that a diary is 'a kind of looking-glass. At first it reflects the diarist. But it ends by revealing the reader.' The number of diaries which have been scrupulously kept for the diarist's eyes alone must be comparatively minute. Lurking in the most private journals is the tremulous thought that one day they will get into other hands. Then what?

Many diaries declare that they exist for posterity, some are clearly the result of a form of pleasure-seeking, or of a passion for secrecy, some are records of the inner life, a lot are outlets for gossip and tale-telling, some are confessionals and some, by their faithfulness to the humdrum, are major historical documents. All contain the magic of the frozen moment. Not even the arrival of the photograph album has been able to destroy the fascination of countless diary-days. The reason why diaries spellbind is that they admit us, not to a great many pasts, but to seemingly endless variants of the present. The diary-keeper is an interventionist, the transmuter of what would be normally perishable into what must last. Without a diary, almost everything we do or say or think or feel slips very quickly into oblivion. The born or natural diarist – he is a special being and not like the rest of us – cannot bear that this should be so. It cannot be egotism which makes him write, 'Saw Price the grocer uncrating oranges' or 'Rain shakes the line of poplars', but a kind of spiritual craving for holding such actions in his personal vision for ever, or until the final entry. Presumably, the non-diarist is indifferent to what the natural diarist would find an intolerable loss. Puzzled, too. Put down what you saw when the reservoir burst or what the P.M. told you, but why put down, 'Rose at 8. Kippers. *Hotel du Lac* where I left it . . .' The born or natural diarist cannot tell us why either, although he frequently feels the need to.

Here is a handful of would-be explanations.

Sir Henry Slingsby (1602–58): '[Montaigne's father] kept a journal Book, wherein he day by day registr'd the memories of the historys of his house; a thing pleasant to read, when time began to wear out the Remembrance of them . . . [my intention is] to sett down in this Book such accidents as befall me, not that I make my study of it, but rather a recreation at vacant times, without observing any time, method, or order in my wrighting, or rather scribbling.'

The Rev. James Hervey (1714–58) tells himself: 'Compile a secret History of your Heart and Conduct. Take notice of the manner in which your Time is spent & of the strain that runs through your Discourse, how often the former is lost in trifles, how often the latter evaporates in vanity . . . Register those secret Faults, to which none but your own Conscience is privy & none but the all-seeing Eye discerns. Often contemplate yourself in this faithful mirror.'

James Boswell (1740–95): 'I should live no more than I can record . . . There is a waste of good if it cannot be preserved.'

Anaïs Nin(1903–77): 'The period without the diary remains an ordeal. Every evening I want my diary as one wants opium.'

Benjamin Robert Haydon (1786–1846): 'I acquired in early life a great love of journals of others, and Johnson's recommendation to keep them honestly I always bore in mind. I have kept one now for thirty-four years. It is the history, in fact, of my mind . . . I hope that my journals, if ever they are thought worthy of publication, may give as much pleasure to others as other journals have given delight to me.'

John Byrom (1692–1763): 'When I consider that it is the most trifling things that help us to recover more material things I do not know that I should omit trifles; they may be of use to me though to others they would appear ridiculous, but as nobody is to see them but myself, I will let myself take any notes, never so trifling, for my own use.'

Lady Mary Coke (1726–1811): 'Lady Spencer came to see me and found me writing my journal. She desired I would let her read it. She wou'd be content with a single page, but as much as I love her I cou'd never consent. I felt ashamed thou' I told her some years hence I thought it might be an amusement, at least it would have one thing to recommend it – that everything that was found in it might be depended upon for truth.'

Mr Strother, draper's assistant (b. 1763): 'And now I have filled this book but perhaps shall not fill another. I have learnt by keeping this Journal that I have been discontented more than was profitable and that it is not proper for a Tradesman to keep a Journal without he has enough of time and plentiful fortune . . . I began Sunday 8 of August 1784 and now conclude 17 July 1785 at 7 o'clock in the evening.'

Richard Hurrell Froude (1803–36), whose diary was written in his mid-twenties: 'Have read my journal. I can hardly identify myself with the person it describes.'

John Addington Symonds (1840–93): 'Diary good for thoughts, not for things. Ordinary log book a poor affair. Useless to eliminate what others ought not to see. Danger of overdoing emotion.'

Tallulah Bankhead (1903–68): 'Only good girls keep diaries. Bad girls don't have the time.'

Published diaries frequently create panic in the diarist's circle. When Lady Charlotte Bury's *A Diary Illustrative of the Times of*

George the Fourth was published, the poet Tom Hood spoke for many of its victims when he wrote:

> When I resign the world so briery
> To have across the Styx my ferrying,
> O may I die without a DIARY
> And be interr'd without a BURYing!

Hubris is not entirely concealed by self-mockery and essays into naïvety. 'What will become of the world if my Annals are thus irregular?' asks Fanny Burney. 'Almost two months have elapsed without my recording one anecdote! I am really shocked for posterity! But for my pen, all the adventures of this noble family might sink into oblivion! I am amazed when I consider the greatness of my importance, the dignity of my task, and the novelty of my position!'

'I thought,' wrote Boswell, 'that my son would perhaps read this journal and be grateful to me for my attention about him ... My wife, who does not like journalizing, said it was leaving myself embowelled to posterity – a good strong figure. But I think it is rather leaving myself embalmed. It is certainly preserving myself.'

On the whole, and in spite of their daily self-staring and self-presenting, diarists tend to be non-narcissistic. They tackle the Self rigorously and the greatest of them, Pepys and Boswell, can proceed to what for most of us would be unthinkable – let alone compositional – lengths in their observation of its nakedness. Many are permanently intrigued by being alive and would set down their every breath were it possible. The measure of the true diarist is the loving attention which he or she will give to the minutiae of existence and the faithful chronicling of the day's *longueurs* as well as its peaks. Dull diaries can be very readable.

Some diaries provided sanctuary for their owners and the reader has to find his way around a bolt-hole. Some were written for the specific purpose of tying the diarist into history and it is mostly from these semi-public journals that we have gained a unique and brilliant set of portraits of some four centuries of celebrities. Monarchs, saints, actors, whores, artists, politicians, poets, soldiers, children, tyrants: it is in diaries that we experience our most intimate encounters with them. We also hear the way they spoke, for one of the first things the diarist knows he must get right is talk. The discipline of memorizing conversation and putting it down on the page hours later can help the diarist in other ways. Novelist-diarists are not necessarily best at it; their dialogue often gets carried away by art, by professional technique.

Diaries come in all sizes and are not to be judged by length. Some are a long life's length; Samuel Pepys's is nine years long. They could be kept for a special occasion, a war or a journey, or a love affair. They could be read to amuse friends, sent piecemeal through the post or locked up and hidden from sight, their secret existence being a large part of their importance to their owners. They could be a diarist's most valued possession. 'I am increasingly haunted by Horace Walpole,' wrote Sir Henry Channon, 'can I be his reincarnation? I am extraordinarily like him in many ways . . . Honor and I have decided to bury my diaries in the churchyard [at Kelvedon, Essex – it is 23 May 1940 and Hitler's invasion is expected]; Mortimer has promised to dig a hole tomorrow evening after the other gardeners have gone home: perhaps some future generation will dig them up.' Later: 'I collected two volumes of diaries dating from October 1940 until now and took them to the British Museum where I was received with deference and respect by the Director, John Forsdyke, the custodian of Manuscripts, and he led me through caverns measureless to man, where after unlocking many doors we came upon the tin boxes containing my older diaries . . .'

Many hundreds of English and American diaries now exist in print, and it has recently become the fashion for well-known people, especially politicians, to publish fat edited versions of their diaries in local libraries, national archives – and attics. As with any other subject, the anthologist has to include masters and minors, the expected and the unexpected, what the reader hopes to find and his own little-known favourites. A diary's individual flavour takes a few pages to catch, and a paragraph or two won't do. The masters themselves have had to be curtailed here in order to leave space for the many excellent or unusually interesting diary-writers I have enjoyed who cannot lay claim to genius. The 'I', needless to add, is the principal unavoidable factor in the making of an anthology. I cannot say that I am a diarist, being all fits and starts, inhibitions and sloth. Anyone reading my fragments would smell duty and effort at once. My addiction is to other people's diaries, and this book offers samples from the many that I have particularly remembered.

Robert Fothergill speaks of the diary as 'the passionately cherished Book of the Self, the essential imprint of a man's-being-in-the-world'. He is talking of Pepys, but every diary attains to this to some degree. Cautious or all-out, we can still sense the pull which drew their keepers to them day after day, year after year, appointments which in many cases took priority over most others. Is it vanity to transform so much of what is transitory into what could be permanent? Taken all in all, vanity in diaries is either on such preposterous display as to rob it of offence, or at a very low ebb indeed.

The first diarists wrote to bring some kind of systematizing to the rich muddle of their lives. What did they believe? What did they actually do? And what and who were they? The progress of ships and military campaigns was logged, so was weather, so were travels, the latter because it was essential to have first-hand facts about distant lands. The post-Reformation centuries made people more inwardly searching and outwardly inquiring. Spiritual mavericks like the Quakers, like John Bunyan, developed religious strengths and insights which required ordering and analysis. Bunyan's autobiographical masterpiece, *Grace Abounding to the Chief of Sinners* (1666), is really the pinnacle of puritan diary-writing. Such diaries have been described as 'journals of conscience', although I have always liked to think of them as Providence diaries. The notion that they took the place of the Catholic confessional has been much emphasized.

However, when all is said and done, we read diaries and journals because their keepers possessed a special literary ability. 'I believe,' says Robert Fothergill in his *Private Diaries,* 'that the major achievements in diary-writing have been produced out of a conscious respect for the diary as a literary form, and that the criteria which they explicitly aspire to meet are by far the most appropriate and rewarding to apply to all writing within the genre.'

6

Introduction

Diary = Latin *diarium*, the substantive of *diarius* – 'daily'.
Journal = Latin *diurnalem* – diurnal: 'daily'.
Journey = a day's travel.

Although diaries and journals became indistinguishable very early on, the latter retained some reputation for being of greater public importance, and the former always spelt privacy. The operative – and mystic – force in both was the *day*. Not a day without a line, advised the older Pliny.

Ronald Blythe

1. THE DIARIST AS EYE-WITNESS

JOHN EVELYN
(1620–1706)

Evelyn's is one of the longest and grandest of diaries. He adored spectacle, dress, gorgeous processions, architecture, gardens, trees, paintings, delicious fruit, jewels, rites, the ornate and the glorious, and his sumptuous cataloguing of such things contrasts with the primness of his emotions concerning other matters. He is a public diarist who conducts the reader towards the great happenings of his age. He was born in Wotton, Surrey, and after three years at Balliol College, Oxford, set out on what was an early version of the Grand Tour of Europe. There he married Mary Browne, the faithful wife who is never mentioned by name in his vast diary. She stays in the shadows, as do their many children, especially the daughter who (incomprehensibly to her father) eloped. We come closest to the Evelyns when they gather at frequent gravesides. The funerals of the children are appallingly numerous – almost an annual coffin for the armigerous vault at Wotton.

Evelyn was twenty-seven when he and his wife returned from abroad to a much changed England, with Cromwell assuming power. One day Evelyn slipped into the 'Painted Chamber' (Banqueting Hall) in Whitehall to listen unbelievingly as Bradshaw and Peters discussed the killing of the King. From this point on, the magnificently formal diary takes us to every major event from the time of Charles I to that of Queen Anne. It also includes rich accounts of the birth of modern science (he was a founder member of the Royal Society) and of art. Evelyn's prose is a consummate mixture of the domestic, the learned and the ornate, and is splendidly entertaining. The diary is a source-book of late seventeenth-century history and is full of astonishing portraits. Wren, Boyle, Burnet, Lancelot Andrewes, Grinling Gibbons, Charles II, Hobbes, Clarendon, William and Mary, Prince Rupert, Louis XIV, Nell Gwyn, Titus Oates, James II: each is given Evelyn's astute attention. It is history as a parade, with banners flying and trumpets blowing – and with sharp assessments of each character. That of Charles II is devastating.

Venice, June 1645. The next morning finding my-selfe extreamly weary, & beaten with my Journey, I went to one of their *Bagnias,* which are made, & treate after the Eastern manner, washing one with hot & cold water, with oyles, rubbing with a kind of Strigil, which a naked youth puts on his hand like a glove of seales Skin, or what ever it be, fetching off a world of dirt, & stretching out on[e]s limbs, then claps [on] a depilatoire made of a drug or earth they call *Resina,* that comes out of Turky, which takes off all the haire of the body, as resin dos a piggs. I think there is orpiment & lime in it, for if it lie on to long it burns the flesh: The curiosity of this Bath, did so open my pores that it cost me one of the greatest Colds & rheumes that ever I had in my whole life, by reason of my comming out without that caution necessary of keeping my selfe Warme for some time after: For I immediately began to visite the famous Places of the Citty. And Travellers do nothing else but run up & downe to see sights, that come into *Italy*: And this Citty, for being one of the most miraculously plac'd of any in the whole World, built on so many hundred Ilands, in the very sea, and at good distance from the Continent, deser[v]'d our admiration: It has neither fresh, nor any other but salt Water, save what is reserved in Cisterns, of the raine, & such as is daily brought them from *Terra firma* in boates: Yet it wa[nt]s nor fresh water, nor abboundance of all sorts of excellent Provisions, very cheape. 'Tis reported that when the *Hunns* overran all *Italy,* some meane fishermen & others left the Maine land, & fled to these despicable & muddy Ilands for Shelter, where in process of time, & by Industry, it is growne to the greatnesse of one of the most considerable states in the World, consider'd as a *Republique* & having now subsisted longer, than any of the foure antient Monarchies, & flourishing in greate State, welth & glory by their Conquests of greate Territories in Italy,

Dacia, Greece, Candy, Rhodes, Slavonia, & at present challenging the Empire of all the Adriatique Sea, which they yearly espouse, by casting a gold ring into it, with greate pomp & ceremony upon Ascension day: the desire of seeing this, being one of the reasons, that hastned us from *Rome*: First the *Dodge* or Duke (having heard Masse) in his robes of State (which are very particular & after the Eastern) together with the Senat in their gownes, Imbarkd in their gloriously painted, carved & gilded *Bucentoro,* invirond & follow'd by innumerable Gallys, Gundolas, & boates filled with Spectators, some dressed in Masqu[e]rade, Trumpets, musique, & Canons, filling the whole aire with din: Thus having rowed out about a league into the Gulph, the Duke at the prow casts into the Sea a Gold ring, & Cup, at which a loud acclamation is Echod by the greate Guns of the Arsenale, and at the *Liddo*: & so we returnd: Two days after taking a *Gundola* which are their Water Coaches, (for land ones many old men in this Citty never saw any, or rarely a horse) we rowed up & downe the Channells, which are as our Streetes; These *Vessells* are built very long & narrow, having necks and tailes of steele, somewhat spreading at the beake like a fishes taile, & kept so exceedinly polish'd as giues a wonderfull lustre: some are adornd with carving, others lined with Velvet, commonly black, with Curtains & tassals, & the seates like Couches to lie stretch'd on, while he who rowes, stands on the very edge of the boate, upright, and with one Oare (bending forward as if they would precipitate into the Sea) rows, & turnes, with incredible dexterity, thus passing from Channell to Channell, & landing his fare or patron, at what house he pleases: The beakes of these vessells are not unlike the Roman antient Rostrums: The first thing I went to see of publique building was the *Rialto,* celebrated for passing over the *grande Canale* with one onely Arch, so large as to admitt a Gally to row thro[ugh] it, built of good Marble, & having on it, besides many pretty shops, three stately & ample passages for people, without any incumbrance, the 2 outmost nobly balustr'd with the same stone, a piece of Architecture to be admir'd. It was Evening & the Canale (which is their Hide-park, where the Noblesse go to take the aire) was full of Ladys & Gent; & there are many times very da[n]gerous stops by reason of the multitude of Gu[n]dalos . . . .

Twas now *Ascention* Weeke, & the greate Mart or faire of the whole yeare now kept, every body at liberty, & jollie; the Noblemen stalking with their Ladys on *Choppines* about 10 foote high from the ground. These are high heeld shoos particularly affected by these proude dames, or as some say, invented to keepe them at home, it being so difficult to walke with them, whence one being asked how he liked the *Venetian* Dames, replyd, they were *Mezzo Carne, Mezzo Legno*; & he would have none of them: The truth is their Garb is very odd, as seeming allwayes in Masquerade, their other habite also totaly different from all Nations: The[y] wear very long crisped haire of severall strakes and Colours, which they artificially make so, by washing their heads in pisse, & dischevelling them on the brims of a broade hat that has no head, but an hole to put out their head by, drie them in the Sunn, as one may see them above, out of their windos: In their tire they set silk flowers & sparkling stones, their peticoates comming from their very armepetts, so high as that their very breasts flub over the tying place; so as they are neare three quarters & an halfe Apron: Their Sleeves are made exceeding wide, under which their smock sleeves as wide & commo[n]ly tucked up to the shoulder, & shewing their naked arme, through false Sleeves of Tiffany girt with a bracelet or two: besides this they go very bare of their breasts & back, with knots of poynts richly tagg'd, about their shoulders & other places, of their body, which the[y] usualy cover with a kind of yellow Vaile of Lawn very transparant. Thus attir'd they set their hands on the heads of two Matron-like servants or old women to support them . . .

The death and character of King Charles II

4 February 1685. I went to Lond, hearing his Majestie had ben the moneday before surpriz'd in his bed chamber with an Apoplectical fit, & so, as if by Gods providence, Dr King (that excellent chirurgeon as well as Physitian) had not ben accidentaly present (to let him bloud) (with his lancet in his pocket) his Majestie had certainly died that moment, which might have ben of direfull consequence, there being no body else with the King save this doctor & one more, as I am assured: It was a mark of the extraordinary dexterity, resolution & presentnesse of Judgment in the Doctor to let him bloud in the very paroxysme, without staying the coming of other physitians, which regularly should have ben don, & the not doing so, must have a formal pardon as they tell me: This rescued his Majestie for that instant, but it prov'd onely a reprieve for a little time; he still complain'd & was relapsing & often fainting & sometimes in Epileptical symptoms 'til Wednesday, for which he was cupp'd, let bloud againe in both jugularies, had both vomit & purges &c: which so relieved him, that on the Thursday hops of recovery were signified in the publique Gazett; but that day about noone the Physitians conjectur'd him somewhat feavorish; This they seem'd glad of, as being more easily alaied, & methodicaly to be dealt with, than his former fits, so as they prescrib'd the famous *Jesuits* powder; but it made his Majestie worse; and some very able Doctors present, did not think it a feavor, but the effect of his frequent bleeding, & other sharp operations used by them about his head: so as probably the powder might stop the Circulation, & renew his former fitts, which now made him very weake: Thus he pass'd Thursday night with greate difficulty, when complaining of a paine in his side, the[y] drew 12 ounces more of blood from him, this was by 6 in the morning on friday, & it gave him reliefe, but it did not continue; for being now in much paine and strugling for breath, he lay doz'd, & after some conflicts, the Physitians desparing of him, he gave up the Ghost at halfe an houre after Eleaven in the morning, being the 6 of Feb: in the 36t yeare of his reigne, & 54 of his age. [6 *February*] 'Tis not to be express'd the tears & sorrows of Court, Citty & Country: Prayers were solemnly made in all the Churches, especialy in both the Court Chapells, where the Chaplaines relieved one another every halfe quarter of an houre, from the time he began to be in danger, til he expir'd: according to the forme prescribed in the Church office: Those who assisted his Majesties devotion were the A: Bish: of Cant: of London, Durrham & Ely; but more especialy the B: of Bath & Wells. It is sayd they exceedingly urged the receiving the H: Sacrament but that his Majestie told them he would Consider of it, which he did so long, 'til it was too late: others whispered, that the Bishops being bid withdraw some time

13

the night before, (except the Earls of Bath, & Feversham), *Hurlston* the Priest, had presum'd to administer the popish Offices; I hope it is not true; but these buisie emissaries are very forewarde upon such occasions: He gave his breeches & Keys to the Duke, who was almost continualy kneeling by his bed side, & in teares; he also recommended to him the care of his natural Children, all except the D: of Monmoth, now in Holland, & in his displeasure; he intreated the Queene to pardon him, (nor without cause) who a little before had sent a Bishop to excuse her not more frequently visiting him, in reguard of her excessive griefe, & with all, that his Majestie would forgive it, if at any time she had offended him: He spake to the Duke to be kind to his Concubines the DD: of *Cleveland*, & especialy *Portsmouth*, & that *Nelly* might not sterve; I do not heare he said any thing of the Church or his people, now falling under the government of a Prince suspected for his Religion, after above 100 yeares the Church & Nation had ben departed from Rome: Thus died K. Charles the 2d, of a Vigorous & robust constitution, & in all appearance capable of a longer life. A prince of many Virtues, & many greate Imperfections, Debonaire, Easy of accesse, not bloudy or Cruel: his Countenance fierce, his voice great, proper of person, every motion became him, a lover of the sea, & skillfull in shipping, not affecting other studys, yet he had a laboratory and knew of many Empyrical Medicines, & the easier Mechanical Mathematics: Loved Planting, building, & brought in a politer way of living, which passed to Luxurie & intollerable expense: He had a particular Talent in telling stories & facetious passages of which he had innumerable, which made some bouffoones and vitious wretches too presumptuous, & familiar, not worthy the favours they abused: He tooke delight to have a number of little spaniels follow him, & lie in his bed-Chamber, where often times he suffered the bitches to puppy & give suck, which rendred it very offensive, & indeede made the whole Court nasty & stinking: An excellent prince doubtlesse had he ben lesse addicted to Women, which made him uneasy & allways in Want to supply their unmeasurable profusion, & to the detriment of many indigent persons who had signaly serv'd both him & his father: Easily, & frequently he changed favorites to his greate prejudice &c: As to other publique transactions and unhappy miscarriages, 'tis not here I intend to number them; but certainely never had King more glorious opportunities to have made himselfe, his people & all Europ happy, & prevented innumerable mischiefs, had not his too Easy nature resign'd him to be menag'd by crafty men, & some abandoned & prophane wretches, who corrupted his otherwise sufficient parts, disciplin'd as he had ben by many afflictions, during his banishment: which gave him much experience, & knowledge of men & things; but those wiccked creatures tooke him [off] from all application becoming so greate a King: the History of his Reigne will certainely be the most wonderfull for the variety of matter & accidents above any extant of many former ages: The [sad tragical] death of his father, his banishment, & hardships, his miraculous restauration, conjurations against him; Parliaments, Warrs, Plagues, Fires, Comets; revolutions abroad happening in his time with a thousand other particulars: he was ever kind to me & very gracious upon all occasions, & therefore I cannot without ingratitude [but] deplore his losse, . . .

The death of his friend Samuel Pepys

26 May 1703. This [day] dyed Mr Sam: Pepys, a very worthy, Industrious & curious person, none in England exceeding him in the Knowledge of the Navy, in which he had passed thro all the most Considerable Offices, Clerk of the Acts, & Secretary to the Admiralty, all which he performed with greate Integrity: when K: James the 2d went out of England he layed down his Office, & would serve no more: But withdrawing himselfe from all publique Affairs, lived at Clapham with his partner (formerly his Cleark) Mr Hewer, in a very noble House & sweete place, where he injoyed the fruit of his labours in g[r]eate propserity, was universaly beloved, Hospitable, Generous, Learned in many things, skill'd in Musick, a very great Cherisher of Learned men, of whom he had the Conversation. His Library & other Collections of Curiositys was one of the most Considerable; The models of Ships especialy &c. Beside what he boldly published of an Account of the Navy, as he found & left it, He had for divers years under his hand the History of the Navy, or, *Navalia* (as he call'd it) but how far advanced & what will follow of his, is left I suppose to his sisters son Mr Jackson, a young Gent: whom his Unkle had educated in all sorts of usefull learning, Travell abroad, returning with extraordinary Accomplishments, & worth to be his Heire: Mr Pepys had ben for neere 40 years, so my particular Friend, that he now sent me Compleat Mourning: desiring me to be one to hold up the Pall, at his magnificent Obsequies; but my present Indisposition, hindred me from doing him this last Office . . .

SAMUEL PEPYS
(1633–1703)

Pepys has suffered more than any other diarist from plums extraction. Both his achievement and his famous power to amuse have been falsified by early editors and anthologists. To know him we have to submit to the tenor of each page, each month, and not pounce and pick our way through his great book. It is in the often unsensational pace of his narrative that his genius is best seen. All diaries are intimate, but his draws us to him with a closeness that is almost palpable. How is this done? How too does he present himself to himself so roundedly when he isn't really self-analytical?

Pepys is the upwardly mobile young man of the Restoration. The sixteen-year-old who stood in the snow outside the new Banqueting Hall to watch with small regret the King's execution is at twenty-six the pragmatic, rather than ecstatic, observer of Charles II's flag being fixed to the maypoles. And on 17 May 1660 he is actually at The Hague chatting 'merrily' to the new monarch, 'a very sober man' (!). Only a month later he is made Clerk of the Acts to the Navy Board, and the astonishing career has begun. So has the diary. The latter would be written until he was thirty-six, when his eyes began to hurt and, for fear of blindness, he cut down on writing and reading. During this decade he worked hard and played hard, and was a celebrated figure at Court and in the highest cultural and scientific circles, became well-off and the very epitome of Late Stuart successful man. He loved and deceived his pretty wife, and she herself – unlike Mrs Evelyn – makes unforgettable appearances throughout the diary, which is of their heyday. After the abandonment of the diary and Mrs Pepys's early death there would be thirty years or more of chequered success, a big disaster, and life with Will Hewer, the rich bachelor who, when a lad, had begun his rise to prosperity as a clerk in Pepys's house. It was in this house on the banks of the Thames at Westminster, a delightful new building, that the diarist became a collector and brought together what is now the Pepys Library at Magdalene College, Cambridge.

The diary was written chiefly in Thomas Shelton's system of shorthand, which was very popular at the time, and which Pepys had learned when he was young in order to make reports and take down minutes – and once, Charles II's own account of his adventures when he was on the run. It was long popularly believed that (a) Pepys used shorthand for the sole purpose of secrecy and (b) that it prevented scholarly access to his diary for over a century following his death. But apart from keeping it in a locked drawer during the time he was writing it he seems later to have had it bound and placed with his other treasures in a glass-fronted bookcase in the normal way; and Shelton's shorthand was so well known – and so elementary – that there could never have been any difficulty in deciphering it. Less easy were the passages describing his love-life. These were written in his own contrived Spanish-based code, which itself exudes a charming mumbo-jumbo eroticism. The handwriting is beautiful, and all six volumes of the finely bound manuscript (by John Cade of Cornhill) indicate Pepys's own valuation of his diary, which was clearly very high. He took the greatest care of it during the dangers of the Great Fire and the Plague, and ran a considerable risk in not destroying it when he was arrested during the Popish Plot crisis of 1678–9, when its criticism of Charles II and his ministers might well have constituted treason.

The diary began to be mentioned in 1812, a time of great interest in all kinds of journal-keeping. When, six years later, John Evelyn's diary was published, speculation began to centre on the handsome set of volumes in the Pepys Library. They were translated well but laboriously by a scholar named John Smith, who was employed by Lord Grenville, the brother of the Master of Magdalene. None of

The Penguin Book of Diaries

these three, or the scholars who contributed the notes, knew about Shelton's famous book, *Short Writing*. Smith finished his excellent transcription in 1822 and a further editor, Lord Braybrooke, entered the scene to distort and bowdlerize it. Called the *Memoirs,* Pepys's diary made its first published début in 1825, to sniffy reviews and popular appreciation. There was little understanding of its historic importance as a work which covered everything from the growth of Britain's marine power to the development of the national language. And further editions fell hopelessly short of conveying what the diary actually was.

All these restrictions, ignorances and distortions were swept away by the 'New and Complete Transcription' edited by Robert Latham and William Matthews from 1970 on. Their eleven-volume Samuel Pepys, with its wonderful notes and near total understanding, has no equal in diary publication. In it the barriers of the years fall away and the reader enters late seventeenth-century England, town and country, easily and intimately.

The diarist, aged twenty-six, sails to Holland to help bring King Charles II home

13 May 1660. Lords. day. Trimmed in the morning; after that to the Cooke room with Mr Sheply, the first time that I was there this voyage.

Then to the Quarter Deck, upon which the taylors and painters were at work cutting out of some pieces of yellow cloth into the fashion of a crown and C.R. and put it upon a fine sheet, and that into the flag instead of the State's arms; which, after dinner, was finished and set up – after it had been showed to my Lord, who took physic today and was in his chamber; and liked it so well as to bid me give the tailors 20s. among them for doing of it.

This morn Sir J. Bois and Captain Isham met us in the *Nonsuch,* the first of whom, after a word or two with my Lord, went forward; the other stayed.

I heard by them how Mr Downing hath never made any address to the King, and for that was hated exceedingly by the Court, and that he was in a Duch ship which sailed by us then, going for England with disgrace.

18

And, how Mr Morland was knighted by the King this week, and that the King did give the reason of it openly, that it was for his giving him intelligence all the time that he was clerk to Secretary Thurloe.

In the afternoon a council of war, only to acquaint them that the Harp must be taken out of all the flags, it being very offensive to the King.

Mr Cooke came after us in the *Yarmouth*, bringing me a letter from my wife and a Latin letter from my brother Jo:, with both which I was exceedingly pleased.

No sermon all day, we being under sail; only at night, prayers, wherein Mr Ibbott prayed for all that were related to us in a spiritual and fleshly way.

We came within sight of Middleburg shore.

Late at night we writ letters to the King of the news of our coming, and Mr Edwd Pickering carried them . . .

14 May. Some masty Duchmen came on board to proffer their boats to carry things from us on shore &c., to get money by us.

Before noon, some gentlemen came on board from the shore to kiss my Lords hands. And by and by Mr North and Dr Clerke went to kiss the Queen of Bohemia's hands from my Lord, with a dozen of attendants from on board to wait on them; among which I sent my boy – who, like myself, is with child to see any strange thing.

After noon they came back again, having kissed the Queen of Bohemia's hand, and was sent again by my Lord to do the same to the Prince of Orange. So I got the Captain to ask leave for me to go, which my Lord did give; and I, taking my boy and Judge Advocate with me, went in company with them. The weather bad; we were soundly washed when we came near the shore, it being very hard to land there.

The shore is, as all the country between that and The Hague, all sand. The rest of the company got a coach by themselfs. Mr Creed and I went in the fore-part of a coach, wherein there was two very pretty ladies, very fashionable and with black paches, who very merrily sang all the way and that very well. And were very free to kiss the two blades that were with them.

I took out my Flagelette and piped, but in piping I dropped my rapier-stick; but when I came to The Hague, I sent my boy back again for it and he found it, for which I did give him 6*d*. but some horse had gone over it and broke the scabbard. The Hague is a most neat place in all respects. The houses so neat in all places and things as is possible.

Here we walked up and down a great while, the town being now very full of Englishmen, for that the Londoners were come on shore today.

But going to see the Prince, he was gone forth with his Governor; and so we walked up and down the town and Court to see the place; and by the help of a stranger, an Englishman, we saw a great many places and were made to understand many things, as the intention of the Maypoles which we saw there standing at every great man's door, of different greatness according to the Quality of the person. About 10 at night the Prince comes home, and we found an easy admission. His attendance very inconsiderable as for a prince. But yet handsome, and his tutor a fine man and himself a very pretty boy. It was bright Mooneshine tonight. This done, we went to a place we had taken up to sup in – where a sallet and two or three bones of mutton were provided for a matter of ten of us, which was very strange. After supper the Judge and I to another house to bed, leaving them there; and he and I lying together in one of their press-beds, there being two more in the same room, but all very neat and handsome; and my boy sleeping upon a bench by me, we lay till past 3 a-clock; and then rise and up and down the town to see it by daylight. [*15 May*] Where we saw the soldiers of the Prince's guard, all very fine, and the Burgers of the town with their arms and musquets as bright as silver; I meeting this morning a Schoole-Master that spoke good English and French, he went along with us and showed us the whole town. And indeed, I cannot speak enough of the gallantry of the town. Everybody of fashion speak French or Latin, or both. The women, many of them very pretty and in good habitt, fashionable, and black spots . . .

After that, the Judge, I, and my boy by coach to Scheveling again – where we went into a house of entertainment and drank there, the wind being very high; and we saw two boats overset there and the gallants forced to be pulled on shore by the heels – while their trunks, portmanteaus, hats, and feathers were swimming in the sea.

Among others, I saw the Ministers that came along with the Commissioners sadly dipped – Mr Case among the rest. So they came in where we was; and I being in haste, left my Copenhagen knife there and so lost it.

Having stayed here a great while, a Gentleman that was going to kiss my Lord's hand from the Queen of Bohemia and I hired a Duch boat for four Rix Dollers to carry us on board. We were fain to wait a great while before we could get off from the shore. The sea being very rough.

16 May. As soon as I was up, I went down to be trimmed below in the great cabin, but then come in some with visits; among the rest, one from Admirall Opdam who spoke Latin well, but not French nor English – to whom my Lord made me to give his answers and to entertain. He brought my Lord a tierce of wine and a barrel of butter as a present from the Admirall.

After that to finish my trimming; and while I was doing of it, in comes Mr North very sea-sick from shore, and to bed he go. After that to dinner, where Comissioner Pett was come to take care to get all things ready for the King on board.

My Lord in his best suit, this the first day, in expectation to wait upon the King. But Mr [Ed.] Pickering, coming from the King, brought word that the King would not put my Lord to the trouble of coming to him – but that he would come to the shore to look upon the fleet today; which we expected, and had our guns ready to fire and our Scarlett wastecloths out and silk pendants; but he did not come.

My Lord and we at nine-pins this afternoon upon the Quarter-deck, which is very pretty sport.

This evening came Mr John Pickering on board like an asse, with his feathers and new suit that he had made at The Hague. My Lord very angry for his staying on shore, bidding me a little before to send for him, telling me that he was afeared that for his father's sake he might have some mischief done him – unless he used the Generalls name.

To supper; and after supper to cards; I stood by and looked on till 11 at night; and so to bed.

This afternoon Mr [Ed.] Pickering told me in what a sad, poor condition for clothes and money the King was, and all his attendants, when he came to him first from my Lord – their clothes not being worth 40s, the best of them. And how overjoyed the King was when Sir J. Greenville brought him some money; so joyful, that he called the Princess Royall and Duke of Yorke to look upon it as it lay in the Portmanteau before it was taken out.

My Lord told me too, that the Duke of Yorke is made High Admirall of England.

17 May. Up early to write down my last two days observations. Then Dr Clerke came to tell me that he heard this morning, by some Duch that are come on board already to see the ship, that there was a Portugese taken yesterday at The Hague that had a design to kill the King. But this I heard afterwards was only the mistake upon one being observed to walk with his sword naked, he having lost his scabbard.

Before dinner, Mr Edward and I, W. Howe – Pim and my boy, to Skeveling, where we took coach, and so to The Hague, where walking, intending to find one that might show us the King incognito, I met with Captain Whittington (that had formerly brought a letter to my Lord from the Mayor of London) and he did promise me to do it; but first we went and dined – at a French house, but paid 16s for our part of the club. At dinner, in came Dr Cade, a merry mad parson of the King's. And they two after dinner got the child and me (the others not being able to crowd in) to see the King, who kissed the child very affectionately. There we kissed his and the Duke of Yorkes and the Princesse Royalls hands. The King seems to be a very sober man; and a very splendid Court he hath in the number of persons of Quality that are about him; English, very rich in habit. From the King to the Lord Chancellor, who did lie bed-rid of the goute: he spoke very merrily to the child and me. After that, going to see the Queen of Bohemia, I met with Dr Fuller, who I sent to a tavern with Mr Edwd. Pickering, while I and the rest went to see the Queen – who used us very respectfully. Her hand we all kissed. She seems a very debonaire, but plain lady.

After that to the Doctor, where we drank a while. And so, in a coach of a friend's of Dr Cade, we went to see a house of the Princesse Dowagers in a parke about half a mile or a mile from The

Hague, where there is one of the most beautiful room[s] for pictures in the whole world. She had her own picture upon the top, with this word, dedicating it to the memory of her husband:

Incomparabili marito inconsolabilis vidua.

Here I met with Mr Woodcock of Cambrige, Mr Hardye and another. And Mr Woodcock beginning, we had two or three fine songs, he and I and W. Howe, to the Echo, which was very pleasant, and the more because in a haven of pleasure and in a strange country – that I never was taken up more with a sense of pleasure in my life. After that we parted and back to The Hague and took a tour or two about the Forehault, where the ladies in the evening do as our ladies do in Hideparke. But for my life I could not find one handsome; but their coaches very rich and themselfs so too . . .

22 *May*. Up very early; and now beginning to be settled in my wits again. I went about setting down my last four days' observation this morning. After that, was trimmed by a barber that hath not trimmed me yet, my Spaniard being on shore.

News brought that the two Dukes are coming on board, which, by and by they did in a Duch boat, the Duke of Yorke in yellow trimming, the Duke of Glocester in gray and red.

My Lord went in a boat to meet them, the Captain, myself, and others standing at the entering Port.

So soon as they were entered we shot the guns off round the fleet. After that, they went to view the ship all over and were most exceedingly pleased with it.

They seem to be both very fine Gentlemen.

After that done, upon the Quarter Deck table under the awning, the Duke of Yorke and my Lord, Mr Coventree and I spent an houre at allotting to every ship their service in their return to England; which having done, they went to dinner, where the table was very full – the two Dukes at the upper end, my Lord Opdam next on one side, and my Lord on the other.

Two guns given to every man while he was drinking the King's health, and so likewise to the Dukes healths . . .

I took down Monsieur D'esquier to the great Cabbin below and dined with him in state alone, with only one or two friends of his.

All dinner the Harper belonging to Captain Sparling played to the Dukes.

After dinner, the Dukes and my Lord to see the Vice and Rere-Admirall; and I in a boat after them.

After that done, they made to the shore in the Duch boat that brought them, and I got into the boat with them. But the shore was so full of people to expect their coming as that it was as black (which otherwise is white sand) as everyone would stand by another.

When we came near the shore, my Lord left them and came into his own boat, and Generall Pen and I with him – my Lord being very well pleased with this day's work.

By the time we came on board again, news is sent us that the King is on shore; so my Lord fired all his guns round twice, and all the fleet after him; which in the end fell into disorder, which seemed very handsome.

The gun over against my Cabbin I fired myself to the King, which was the first time that he hath been saluted by his own ships since this change. But holding my head too much over the gun, I have almost spoiled my right eye.

Nothing in the world but going of guns almost all this day . . .

23 May. The Doctor and I waked very merry, only my eye was very red and ill in the morning from yesterday's hurt.

In the morning came infinite of people on board from the King, to go along with him.

My Lord, Mr Crew, and others go on shore to meet the King as he comes off from shore.

Where (Sir R. Stayner bringing His Majesty into the boat) I hear that His Majesty did with a great deal of affection kiss my Lord upon his first meeting.

The King, with the two Dukes, the Queen of Bohemia, Princesse Royalle, and Prince of Orange, came on board; where I in their coming in kissed the Kings, Queen and Princesses hands, having done the other before. Infinite shooting off of the guns, and that in a disorder on purpose, which was better then if it had been other-wise.

All day nothing but Lords and persons of Honour on board, that we were exceeding full.

Dined in a great deal of state, the Royall company by themselfs in the coach, which was a blessed sight to see.

I dined with Dr Clerke, Dr Quarterman, and Mr Darcy in my Cabbin.

This morning Mr Lucy came on board, to whom and his company of the King's guard in another ship my Lord did give three dozen of bottles of wine. He made friends between Mr Pierce and I.

After dinner, the King and Duke upon the   * altered the name of some of the Shipps, *viz.* the *Nazeby* into *Charles* – the *Richard, James*; the *Speaker, Mary* – the *Dunbar* (which was not in company with us) the *Henery* – *Winsby, Happy returne* – *Wakefield, Richmond* – *Lamport*, the *Henretta* – *Cheriton*, the *Speedwell* – *Bradford*, the *Successe*.

That done, the Queen, Princess Royall, and Prince of Orange took leave of the King, and the Duke of Yorke went on board the *London,* and the Duke of Glocester the *Swiftsure* – which done, we weighed Ancre, and with a fresh gale and most happy weather we set sail for England – all the afternoon the King walking here and there, up and down (quite contrary to what I thought him to have been), very active and stirring.

The King lands in England

25 May 1660. About noon (though the Brigantine that Beale made was there ready to carry him), yet he would go in my Lord's barge with the two Dukes; our captain steered, and my Lord went along bare with him. I went, and Mr Mansell and one of the King's footmen, with a dog that the King loved (which shit in the boat, which made us laugh and me think that a King and all that belong to him are but just as others are) went in a boat by ourselfs; and so got on shore when the King did, who was received by Generall Monke with all imaginable love and respect at his entrance upon

* ? 'quarter-deck table'.

the land at Dover. Infinite the Croud of people and the gallantry of the Horsmen, Citizens, and Noblemen of all sorts.

The Mayor of the town came and gave him his white staffe, the badge of his place, which the King did give him again. The Mayor also presented him from the town a very rich Bible, which he took and said it was the thing that he loved above all things in the world.

A Canopy was provided for him to stand under, which he did; and talked awhile with General Monke and others; and so into a stately coach there set for him; and so away straight through the towne toward Canterbury without making any stay at Dover.

The Shouting and joy expressed by all is past imagination. I seeing that my Lord did not stir out of his barge, I got into a boat and so into his barge, whither Mr John Crew stepped and spoke a word or two to my Lord; and so returned. We back to the ship; and going, did see a man almost drowned, that fell out of his boat into the sea but with much ado was got out.

My Lord almost transported with joy that he hath done all this without any the least blur and obstruccion in the world that would give an offence to any, and with the great Honour that he thought it would be to him.

Being overtook by the Brigantine, my Lord and we went out of our barge into it; and so went on board with Sir W. Battin and the Vice and Rear-Admiralls.

At night my Lord supped, and Mr Tho. Crew, with Captain Stoakes. I supped with the Captain, who told me what the King had given us. My Lord returned late and at his coming did give me order to cause the marke to be gilded, and a Crowne and C. R. to be made at the head of the Coach table, where the King today with his owne hand did mark his Highth – which accordingly I caused the painter to do; and is now done, as is to be seen.*

---

* The King had hit his head on a beam and had marked the place with his knife.

ELIZABETH SMITH
(1797–1885)

Elizabeth Smith, the Edinburgh-born wife of an Irish landowner, kept a diary for almost half a century, but its most enthralling and historically invaluable section is that which covers Ireland's Hungry Forties and the great migration. She wrote her journals for her second daughter, Annie. Elizabeth had met her future husband in India and returned with him to live at Baltiboy's House in Blessington, County Wicklow. (Her great-granddaughter, the dancer Dame Ninette de Valois, was born in this house.) The diarist had little understanding of the Irish or ever pretended otherwise, and it is due to her austere Highland commonsensical approach to their appalling problems, her lack of mysticism, and her racy humanity and bluntness, that we get such a direct view of what was happening. She is bossy and dogmatic, yet humble when she oversteps the critical or informational mark, taking it all back. She has no real insight or future vision, and this is her great virtue as a diarist: a plain statement of the facts at such a disastrous moment in a nation's existence carries with it all the prevailing attitudes of the decade. 'She had no self-doubt,' says David Thomson, 'but whenever we are startled by one of her outrageous statements, we must remember that she is writing a journal, not a reflective work looking back over these years with knowledge gained later, with the wisdom of one who can calmly review the past.' He sees her as a materialist, a lady of the Industrial Revolution, and so far removed from the feckless, religious peasantry, now starving at her gates, that she might belong to another millennium. She is a good writer and a very kind, if exasperated, woman, tough, practical and eternally busy. Irish society, its priesthood and politicians, and especially the Irish full-stop, all drive her mad. Nearly a century and a half later much that she fulminates about, often very amusingly, can still be seen in both the North and South, ineradicable, intact. She preserves a little order and authority in the midst of famine, chaos and flight to America, while running her big house, a farm and a school, and never quite comprehending the scale of the human disaster sweeping Ireland.

The potato famine

5 November 1846. Hal has just brought in two damaged potatoes the first we have seen of our own for on our hill few have been found as yet.

6 November. Another blustering day after a stormy night, however as there is no rain it will dry the potatoes finely.

11 November. Mr Darker much afraid of this second potato field. The first had hardly a bad potato so that he was unprepared for this.

13 November. Half the potatoes in this new field are tainted, some very badly.

16 November. This had been a regular rainy day, the river all over the meadows. The papers still occupied with the potato disease though Lady Odela Villiers and her well managed elopement has been a God-send to them the last few days . . .

30 November. Mr Robinson came down yesterday to collect the rents, the Tennants paid well, were in good spirits, made no complaints, not even of their potatoes, were well dressed, so that altogether it was a most comfortable gale day [rent day]. The potato failure has been much exaggerated, the disease is by no means so far spread as was supposed and the crop so over abundant that the partial failure will be less felt, particularly as the corn harvest was excellent. But people were much frightened and this caused a run on the Savings Bank which might have encreased the evil, that too is luckily over so that the prospects for the winter are brightening. John Robinson said nothing could more fully prove the encreasing prosperity of the country than the multitudes whom this panick proved to have been saving, the very poorest looking people drawing out their fortys, fiftys, hundreds. The crowds were so immense and so excited that horse and foot police were necessary to guard their lives.

12 January 1847. . . . we make daily a large pot of soup which is served gratis to 22 people at present. It is ready at one o'clock and I thought it quite a pretty sight yesterday in the kitchen all the workmen coming in for their portion, a quart with a slice of beef; half of them get this one day for dinner with a bit of their own bread; the other half get milk and the cheap rice we have provided for them. Next day they reverse the order. The Colonel is giving them firing too; so they are really comfortable; there are twelve of them and ten pensioners, old and feeble men and women, or those with large families of children; some of them no longer living on our ground yet having been once connected with us we can't desert them. So far well; but beyond our small circle what a waste of misery; how are we to relieve it? Such a dense population squatted here and there upon neglected properties, dying with want, wretched every year but ruined this. At the Relief Committee yesterday it was resolved to institute soup kitchens at proper stations for general relief, to be supported by subscription, each subscription to have a certain number of tickets. I think the gentlemen are doing this, the ladies must combine for a clothing fund. The rags are hardly coverings for decency; beds and bedding there are none, among the mob, I mean; such miseries crush hope, yet hope I will . . .

Landed property must be sold in those miserable parts of the country, where the landlords have been keeping up false appearances, living like wealthy men while drowned in debts. And the equally improvident tradesman must publish his insolvency, break and lie and cheat no more. The whole people, so to speak, have been existing on credit make believe, there was nothing real about far more than half of them.

16 January. . . . we called on Peggy Nary, who is going to turn her lodgers out of the house, having at last quarrelled with them. I don't on earth know what to do with her. She is going to white wash her kitchen! she says – herself – no one else would do it to please her. We then went on to Jem Doyle's. Most wretched it was, though very clean, he must go to the poor-house, he and his family. He has an ulcer on his leg, which will prevent his working for weeks and they will starve during this month, that there is no relief going. Widow Mulligan is also starving. So are the widow Quin and fifty more. They must be forced into the poor-house for they cannot otherwise be supported. They are the meanest feeling people ever were, they will accept of charity from anyone, live on it in idleness, but they won't go to the poor-house.

10 October. Sunday. Little in the papers but failures. Cattle dealers in Dublin have gone and caused immense distress, in fact paralysed the markets; not an offer for a beast of any sort at any of the late fairs. Banks, merchants, brokers, agents, all are bankrupt in all places. John Robinson has lost seven thousand pounds by bad debts, trusting people who have failed to pay; he must pay the millers who sent him the flour he so imprudently parted with out of his former profits, his capital, and learn wisdom by this shake. He hopes to recover about half this sum when the affairs of some of these firms are wound up. . .

17 October. Sunday again – the 17th – I hardly know how the week has gone – not a creature has entered the house but the Doctor. We have been as quiet as possible, indeed the country generally is very dull; people are oppressed by this frightful amount of bankruptcies, almost everyone either themselves or their friends affected by some of these numerous failures. Then the winter prospects look very gloomy. The destitution is expected to be wider spread than last year for the very poor will be nearly as ill off while the classes above which then relieved them are all this year in serious difficulties. No money anywhere; the little hoards of cash and goods all spent and nothing to replace either. The ministry says the land must support the people on it. Half the country having been left untilled for want of means to crop it while a million of money was squandered in destroying the roads, much of it finding its way into pockets full enough before. The Queen has ordered the begging box to go round all the English churches for us!

31 January 1848. 6 inches of snow lying evenly over the country. Except that it stops the outwork, we ought to be glad to see it to keep the ground warm, purify the air, and drive fever away. Spite of the worthlessness of our fine peasantry one can't help grieving for their sufferings. We in this district never would give out any out door relief while there were vacancies in the poor-house at any rate; at Ballymore they gave it and it was abused beyond idea. The Government Commissioners have put a stop to it, taken another house in Naas and refused all aid except under what the people consider imprisonment. A report got about that only the able bodied would be forced into the poor-house, that the aged, sickly, etc. would be relieved in their own homes; crowds therefore presented themselves to the Doctor to beg certificates of decrepitude, hale and hearty men and women assuring him they were suffering under every ill that flesh is heir to. This description of consciences last year when only the able bodied were accepted for certain relief works were equally anxious to make themselves out in the rudest health whatever infirmities they had. They are all again beginning to beg, of course, because some are so foolish as to give. We are little teased, we never refuse a bit of bread, we never give anything else, and they leave us in quiet, for it is money they want, pennies for tobacco and snuff and tea and whiskey.

THOMAS JONES
(1870–1955)

One of the finest political diarists of the twentieth century. Jones made the classic struggle from industrial Wales via the chapel and a hard-won education to become, at forty-six, First Assistant Secretary to the Cabinet. He was eventually to serve Lloyd George, Bonar Law, Stanley Baldwin and Ramsay MacDonald, the latter not without conflict. Later, among a vast mass of other activities, he was to found the Council for the Encouragement of Music and the Arts (C.E.M.A.), which itself was to establish the Arts Council, and help to set up the Gregynog Press. His political diaries were published in 1969, edited by Keith Middlemass, and followed *A Diary with Letters*, which he himself issued a year before his death. In the latter, Jones's introduction is extremely candid on the question of official secrecy:

When Sir Maurice Powicke learned that I was to join the War Cabinet Secretariat on its formation in 1916, and we met

31

shortly afterwards at All Souls, he urged me to help the historians of the future by keeping a diary ... Later I found another justification for keeping a record. I was sometimes involved in confidential exchanges with opposed parties during labour and other disputes, or in secret conversations with Ministers. I then felt the need for written proof that I had faithfully interpreted the instructions of my principals. Yet I wrote furtively until I learnt, as soon I did, that my immediate chief, Maurice Hankey, kept a diary in a stoutly bound locked book, the first I had ever seen. He could do no wrong.

... My diary has many blanks and much that it contains is unimportant. No day was in fact blank and empty of all significance, but there were many days when the chronicler was blind or deaf or indolent or fatigued ... A diary, by hypothesis, forbids complete self-effacement, but I hope I have also steered reasonably clear of self-glorification, the vice of this sort of book ...

Secrecy and suppression as instruments of policy have no chapters assigned to them in manuals of statesmen and have been much less studied than publicity and propaganda. Yet secrecy and suppression have moulded the arts of politics, diplomacy and war. Secret-aries, or keepers of secrets, have long been part of the machinery of Government, though it was only yesterday they were permitted to record the proceedings of British cabinets. Experience shows that they can be more safely trusted than many ministers.

A visit to Herr Hitler

17 May 1936. On Sunday morning at 9.30 we left Tempelhof and flew to Munich accompanied by the adjutant, two private secretaries, and the official interpreter, Dr Paul Schmidt. The weather was perfect and the flight most enjoyable. The plane had painted on it in large letters, D.Amyy, and inside carried the photograph of Wilhelm Siegert. It has 3 engines, two pilots, and a radio operator. We reached Munich at 11.45. On leaving Berlin and on arriving at Munich the ambassador saluted a small guard of honour drawn up

near the 'plane. It transpired that the Führer was to have received
me in Berlin, but owing to the sudden illness and death of his
chauffeur he had gone to Munich. We drove rapidly in an open
Mercedes car to the Führer's flat, 16 Prinz Regenten Strasse. There
were two stout guards posted outside, in bright uniforms, and we
walked up to (I think) the third floor and were received by Bruckner,
whose name I had seen in Gunther's *Inside Europe*. I was struck
with his height and he told me with pride that it was 1 metre
94 cm.

There were two other attendants. Schmidt and I were shown into
a spacious sitting-room with an alcove at one end lined with books,
many of them large illustrated quartos. The furnishing was solid
and Victorian. There was a small portrait of Wagner, and a half-
length of Bismarck by Lenbach. There were also pictures by Feuer-
bach, Cranach, Schwink, Zugel and Breughel. Nothing modern. We
might have been in Park Terrace, Glasgow, in a shipowner's
drawing-room in 1880.

At 12.15 the Führer entered, accompanied by Herr von Ribbentrop towering above him. Hitler then came up and shook me by the
hand, and we all sat down in four ample easy chairs. I started off
and Schmidt translated. The Führer replied and I had another
period, and then he spoke again with increasing animation as he
went along, tapping the table around which we all sat. He is a
complete contrast to Mussolini, and made no attempt whatever to
impress or 'aggress' his visitor. He is slender, of medium height; has
blue and slightly protruding eyes, hair brushed well down and with
a wisp reaching down to the left eyebrow, as in the photographs.
He looked dressed in his Sunday best, all fresh from the laundry;
brown drill jacket, pale gold buttons, white soft linen collar and
shirt, with tie to match jacket and badge stuck in it, scarlet armlet
with black swastika on white ground, black or very dark blue
trousers. We parted at 1.45 and motored to see the new Party
buildings on the Königsplatz before taking lunch at the Walterspiel
Restaurant in the Four Seasons Hotel. We left the aerodrome at
Munich at 3.40; at 4.40 we were 4,800 metres high and the moisture
on the windowpanes was frozen and I spread a rug over my knees.
Ribbentrop worked away at official papers. I slept for a bit, and
then scribbled three notes. By 6.10 we were having tea again at

Dahlem, and I was telling my host that in January 1922 I had dined quietly one evening at Cannes with Benito Mussolini and had entirely failed to divine his greatness only a few months before the march on Rome.

Secret

I saw the Führer in his flat in Munich on Sunday morning, 17 May 1936. The other persons present were Herr von Ribbentrop and the official interpreter. The interview lasted an hour and a half.

After I had thanked the Führer for honouring me with the invitation to meet him I pointed out that I was a private and unofficial person, but that as a former Civil Servant I had come much into contact with Mr Lloyd George, Bonar Law, Mr Ramsay MacDonald, and Mr Baldwin. I still saw Mr Baldwin from time to time, but when we met we talked of many things besides peace and war ...

20 May. Breakfast with P.M. at No. 10, and I delivered my message from Germany. He was all attention and interjected at one stage: 'Go on. This is like an Oppenheimer story.' Then at the end: 'We must talk all this out. Come to Chequers at the weekend.' He agreed that in my place he would have done as I had done.

SIR HAROLD NICOLSON
(1886–1968)

A diarist in the grand tradition. Two volumes of extracts from Nicolson's three-million-word diary were published in his lifetime, edited by his son Nigel, and they attracted enormous interest. The diarist himself was bemused by the fact that, having published forty books, he should be remembered only for those he had not realized he had written. Diarists who are professional writers do not usually regard their diaries as books; when they do so, they sometimes allow a non-diarist element to creep in which can often spoil the daily entry. Nicolson wrote his diary early each morning, 'an entertaining literary exercise,' as Nigel Nicolson called it, which no doubt primed the pump for his very considerable flow of memoirs and journalism.

Harold Nicolson was the son of Lord Carnock, head of the Foreign Office during the First World War. He married Vita Sackville-West just before the outbreak of war and himself became a diplomat. In every way possible his career and his private life fell between two stools; he said that he was seen by the bohemians as conventional and by the conventional as bohemian. He and his wife were in fact extremely happily married homosexuals, the parents of devoted sons, and radical traditionalists. He was knighted for his definitive biography of King George V. His diary is lodged in the library of Balliol College, Oxford, and only about a twentieth of it has so far been published. He kept it from 1930 to 1964 and it will always be essential reading for those with a need to understand mid-twentieth-century Britain. It is permeated with (and exploits) the old liberal cultural values. It is also a candid confession of ambivalence in many areas, and a severe self-scrutiny. The following extracts are taken from the single-volume edition (1984) edited by Stanley Olson from the original three-volume work which Nigel Nicolson published between 1966 and 1968.

Self-disillusion and the rise of Fascism

31 December 1931. Of all my years this has been the most unfortunate. Everything has gone wrong. I have lost not only my fortune, but much of my reputation. I incurred enmities: the enmity of Lord Beaverbrook; the enmity of the B.B.C. [Sir John Reith terminated his contract when H.N. praised James Joyce's *Ulysses* in a broadcast] and the Athenaeum Club; the enmity of several stuffies. I left the *Evening Standard*, I failed in my election, I failed over *Action*. I have been inexpedient throughout. My connection with Tom Mosley has done me harm. I am thought trashy and a little mad. I have been reckless and arrogant. I have been silly. I must recapture my reputation. I must be cautious and more serious. I must not try to do so much, and must endeavour to do what I do with greater depth and application. I must avoid the superficial.

Yet in spite of all this – what fun life is!

Rome, 5 January 1932. Tom talks to me about his impressions. He feels that one of our disadvantages as compared with these people is actual costs. In Italy you can run even a daily paper at a little loss. Our own compositors' union is so exacting that we can never compete with the great combines. He believes therefore in the future of our clubs. He feels that we should have two categories: one the Nupa [Youth Movement] clubs, and the other Young England clubs. The latter would be wholly unpolitical. The former would correspond to the S.S. or *Schutzstaffel* organization of the Nazis. Christopher [Hobhouse, the author] insists that the movement should be working class. I insist that it should be constitutional and that Tom should enter Parliament. He thinks he could do so with the backing of Winston and the Harmsworth press.

Berlin, 27 January. There was a moment when Hitler stood at the crest of national emotion. He could then have made either a *coup d'état* or forced a coalition with Brüning. He has missed that moment. The intelligent people feel that the economic situation is so complicated that only experts should be allowed to deal with it. The unintelligent people are beginning to feel that Brüning and not Hitler represents the soul of Germany. In Prussia it is true Hitler is gaining ground. But he is losing it in Bavaria and Würtenberg which are comparatively prosperous. Hitlerism, as a doctrine, is a doctrine of despair. I have the impression that the whole Nazi movement has been a catastrophe for this country. It has mobilized and coordinated the discontented into an expectant group: Hitlerism can never satisfy these expectations: the opinion they have mobilized may in the end swing suddenly over to communism. And if that be a disaster (as to which I am still not certain), then Hitler is responsible. The Ambassador [Sir Horace Rumbold] feels that anything may happen and that the only certain thing is uncertainty.

31 January. Plant wistaria upon dead apple trees. Feeling depressed. Why? Is it merely that after the debauchery of Berlin I have a liver reaction? Or is it that while at Berlin I have been able to push from myself the realization of my own practical difficulties and these have swung back upon me with sudden vigour?

There is a dead and drowned mouse in the lily-pond. I feel like that mouse – static, obese and decaying. Viti is calm, comforting and considerate. And yet (for have I not been reading a batch of insulting press-cuttings?) life is a drab and dreary thing. I had a great chance. I have missed it. I have made a fool of myself in every respect . . .

4 August 1933. Wystan Auden reads us some of his new poem in the evening. It is in alliterative prose and divided into Cantos. The idea is Gerald Heard as Virgil guiding him through modern life. It is not so much a defence of communism as an attack upon all the ideas of comfort and complacency which will make communism difficult to achieve in this country. It interests me particularly as showing, at last, that I belong to an older generation. I follow Auden in his derision of patriotism, class distinctions, comfort, and all the ineptitudes of the middle classes. But when he also derides the other soft little harmless things which make my life comfortable I feel a chill autumn wind. I feel that were I a communist, the type of person I should most wish to attack would not be the millionaire or the imperialist, but the soft, reasonable, tolerant, secure, self-satisfied intellectual like Vita and myself. A man like Auden with his fierce repudiation of half-way houses and his gentle integrity makes one feel terribly discontented with one's own smug successfulness. I go to bed feeling terribly Edwardian and back-number, and yet, thank God, delighted that people like Wystan Auden should actually exist.

26 August. After luncheon at Lympne [Sir Philip Sassoon's house] Colonel T. E. Lawrence, the uncrowned king of Arabia, arrives. He is dressed in an Air Force uniform which is very hot. Unlike other privates in the Air Force he wears his heavy uniform when he goes out to tea. He has become stockier and squarer. The sliding, lurcher effect, is gone. A bull terrier in place of a saluki.

11 October. Go to see Tom Mosley at Ebury Street. He has had a bad back and is lying down. One of his fascist lieutenants is there but leaves us. He says he is making great progress in town and country alike. He gets very little money from the capitalists but relies on canteens and subscriptions. His aim is to build up from below gradually, and not to impose construction from above as we did in New Party days. Whenever anything happens to remind him of Cimmie [who died five months earlier aged 34], a spasm of pain twitches across his face. He looked ill and pasty. He has become an excellent father and plays with the children. Cimmie's body is still at Cliveden in the chapel, and he visits it once a week . . .

9 April 1939. In the afternoon Viti and I plant annuals. We sow them in the cottage garden and then in the border and then in the orchard. We rake the soil smooth. And as we rake we are both thinking, 'What will have happened to the world when these seeds germinate?' It is warm and still. We should have been so happy were it not for the thought which aches at our hearts as if some very dear person was dying in the upstairs room. We discuss whether we might be defeated if war comes. And if defeated, surely surrender in advance would be better? We ourselves don't think of money or privilege or pleasure. We are thinking only of that vast wastage of suffering which must surely come. All because of the insane ambitions of one fanatic, and of the vicious theory which he has imposed on his people.

JAMES LEES-MILNE
(b. 1908)

It is not unusual, thank goodness, for a diarist to have to go in search of a date or some other fact among the long-discarded manuscripts in his attic, only to find an earlier and quite undiscardable self. This is what happened to James Lees-Milne. As the most youthful and most active employee of the National Trust during its expansionist years, which included the troubled Forties, it had fallen to him to vet and collect historic houses, thus also to have met and interviewed their somewhat extraordinary owners. So, it was suggested, why not make a record of these encounters? Old diaries confirmed more than dates and appointments. Here, forgotten, were the fullest and liveliest records possible, plus the recklessly exposed young man who had kept them. He, his ageing self decided, had better remain partly hidden, but this discretion apart the succession of Lees-Milne diaries which have come to light since 1975 possess the quality of a happy, rueful tale which one doesn't want to end.

Lees-Milne is keen that we shouldn't tidy up our younger selves. For him a diary isn't a work of art but a chronicle of inconsistencies and a reflection of shifting tastes and loyalties. Once calculation comes into it, it ceases to be a true diary: '. . . the candid diarist does not know himself. Nor is he to be known by his diaries, for he is an irrational being, a weathercock, a piece of chaff drifting on every wind of circumstance. And if anyone needs proof of this assertion, he has only to look beneath the mask into his own soul.'

The diaries with their Coleridgean titles, *Ancestral Voices, Prophesying Peace* and *Caves of Ice,* are elegant, patrician, and also homely in their unaffectedness and simplicity. They show a grand facet of British society which has been thrown into confusion and muddle by the war and by the modest revolution which followed it. The diarist goes traipsing through the land, saving its architectural glories (marvellous descriptions of their current seediness and cranky owners), on foot, on his bike, in dreadful buses and darkened trains, returning when he can to his circle in London. Hard labour and frivolity. Between the serious work and the fun there emerges an original and certainly unintended 'war book'. This is connoisseur's diary-reading.

Meeting George Bernard Shaw

Wednesday, 9 February 1944. A young member of the Trust called for me at the office and at 11.30 we set off in the car for Hitchin. He is a nice, earnest black-coated worker, called Teagle, madly keen on archaeological remains, birds and nature. He hikes every weekend in the summer in the Home Counties with his wife, and stays in youth hostels. I took him to a British restaurant in Hitchin where we had a tolerable meal of thick soup, roast mutton and baked potatoes. This was quickly over and we went to an area of land which he has found and wants us to save. We got out and walked for an hour. A small river valley bounded by a straight stretch of the Icknield Way. In this sunswept, windswept landscape our noses ran. He wiped his nose with the back of his hand. I had one handkerchief and debated with myself whether to share it. Decided against. I motored him as far as Ayot St Lawrence where we looked at the old ruined church and the new. At the gate of Bernard Shaw's house I parted with him.

Shaw's Corner is a very ugly, dark red-brick villa, built in 1902. I rang the bell and a small maid in uniform led me across the hall to a drawing-room, with open views on to the garden and the country beyond, for the house is at the end of the village. There was a fire burning in the pinched little grate. Walls distempered, the distemper flaking badly in patches. The quality of the contents of the room was on a par with that of the villa. Indifferent water colours of the Roman Campagna, trout pools, etc. in cheap gilt frames. One rather good veneered Queen Anne bureau (for which G.B.S. said he had given £80) and one fake lacquer bureau. In the window a statuette of himself by Paul Troubetskoy. On the mantelpiece a late Staffordshire figure of Shakespeare (for which he paid 10/-), a china house, the lid of which forms a box. Only a few conventionally bound classics, plus Osbert Sitwell's latest publication prominently displayed on a table. Two stiff armchairs before the fire and brass fender. A shoddy three-ply screen attached to the fireplace to shelter from draughts anyone sitting between the fire and doorway.

I waited five minutes and looked around, at a chronometer and the serried row of Shakespeare plays in soft leather bindings. Presently the door opened and in came the great man. I was instantly struck by the snow-white head and beard, the blue eyes and the blue nose, with a small ripe spot over the left nostril. He was not so tall as I imagined, for he stoops slightly. He was dressed in a pepper-and-salt knickerbocker suit. A loose, yellow tie from a pink collar over a thick woollen vest rather than shirt. Several waistcoats. Mittens over blue hands. He evidently feels the cold for there were electric fires in every room and the passage. He shook hands and I forget what he first said. Nothing special anyway. Asked me to sit down, and put questions to me straight off, such as, could he make over the property now and retain a right of user.

His friend, Lord Astor (Arstor), had done so. I had not expected the strong Irish brogue. This peasant origin makes him all the more impressive. It put me in mind of Thomas Carlyle, of whom, curiously enough, he spoke. I said I preferred Mrs to Mr Carlyle. He said Carlyle was out of fashion because of the prevailing anti-German prejudice; that there had been worse husbands than he. G.B.S. said he wished to impose no conditions on the hand-over, but he did not wish the house to become a dead museum. Hoped it would be a living shrine. He wanted to settle matters now, for since his wife's death he was bound to re-make his will, and in three years' time he might be quite dotty, if he was alive at all. He is 88, and very agile. He showed me his statuette, which he likes, and bust (copy) by Rodin which he does not care for. Took me into his study where he works at an untidy writing table. In this room is another Queen Anne bureau. The wall facing it is covered with reference books, and all the bound proofs of his own books, corrected by him. These, I said, ought to remain here. There are no pictures or photographs of his wife to be seen. The dining-room is far from beautiful. It contains some fumed oak furniture and a portrait of him done in 1913. He ran upstairs, pointing admiringly to the enlarged bird etchings on the stair wall. He showed me his wife's room and his bedroom, and the one spare room. He has lived in this house since 1908.

When he smiles his face softens and becomes engaging. He is not at all deaf, but comes close up to one to talk, breathing into one's face. His breath is remarkably sweet for an old man's. Having looked upstairs we descended. He tripped going down, and I was afraid he was going to fall headlong. He then said, 'We will go out and have a look at the curtilage' – rolling the 'r' of this unusual word. It was fearfully cold by now, and raining heavily. He put on a long, snow-white mackintosh and chose a stick. From the hall hat-rack, hung with a variety of curious headgear, he took an archaic rough felt hat, of a buff colour, high in crown and wide of brim. In this garb he resembled Carlyle, and was the very picture of the sage, striding forth, a little wobbly and bent perhaps, pointing out the extent of the 'curtilage' and the line of the hedge which he had de-rooted with his own hands so as to lengthen the garden. The boundary trees of spruce were planted by him. 'Trees grow like mushrooms in these parts,' he said. We came to a little asbestos-roofed summer house that revolves on its own axis. Here he also writes and works. There is a little table covered with writing material, and a couch. The summer house was padlocked. I said, 'Do you sit out here in the winter then?' 'I have an electric stove,' and he pointed to a thick cable attached to the summer house from an iron pylon behind it. 'This will be an attraction to the *birthplace,* if it survives,' he said. We passed piles of logs, which he told me he had chopped himself. He showed me his and his wife's initials carved on the coach-house door and engraved on a glass pane of the greenhouse. Took me into the coach-house where there are three cars under dust sheets, one a Rolls-Royce. 'When I want to use this,' he said, 'I become very decrepit, and the authorities allow me coupons.' We continued down the road.

A collie puppy dog met us in the road and jumped up at the old man who paid it much attention. He led me to Revett's curious church. He explained at length that the reigning squire began demolishing the old church because he considered it 'an aesthetic disgrace' and 'barbarous Gothic'. The Bishop stopped it entirely disappearing, but not the erection of Revett's church in the 'fashionable Palladian'. G.B.S. walked up the steps and with reverence took off his hat. We walked inside. The interior is certainly cold and unspiritual. 'But it has good proportions,' Shaw allowed. The worst mistake is the ugly coloured glass in the windows. Classical churches are always spoilt by coloured glass. The organ case is contemporary. When we left he tapped with his stick a scrolled tombstone and made me read the inscription. It was to some woman who had died in the 1890s, aged 76, and below were inscribed the words, 'Cut off ere her prime', or words to such effect. 'That,' G.B.S. said, 'is what persuaded me to come and live in the parish thirty-six years ago, for I assumed I stood some chance of at least reaching my ninetieth year.' We continued past the house and across the field, to the old church. He explained that although he never worshipped in the church he had spent £100 on its preservation. He remarked that the font had been overturned at some time. Took me outside to see the grave of Queen Victoria's tallest army officer, and admire the tracery moulding on a doorway, now blocked, at the west end. He wishes to buy the little corner cottage in order to destroy it, because it hides a view of the church from his own house. By the time we got back to the house I was wet through.

Tea was brought on a tray to the drawing-room. A glass of milk only for him; but tea and cakes for me. I was given a mug to drink out of. We talked of Esher's letter to *The Times*, of which he heartily approved. Decried the madness of the times, and the war. He said wars cease to be wars when chivalry is altogether excluded, as now, and become mass murder. That we had yet to witness the day when conscientious objection would be organized on such a universal scale that wars just could not happen. Up to now conscientious objection had failed, but one day it would succeed. It would be interesting to see how it would work if ever this country declared war on Soviet Russia. The present war was due, not to man's wickedness, but to his ignorance. In the last war he wrote a letter to *The Times* urging that air-raid shelters be provided for children. *The Times* refused to publish it because the editor was shocked by the implied suggestion that the enemy could, or would bomb schoolchildren. The *News Chronicle* refused likewise. I asked, 'What would you do if you were given Winston Churchill's powers and position today?' He said wisely enough, 'All action depends upon actual circumstance, but I would endeavour to bring fighting to an instant conclusion.' I said, 'I doubt whether the Germans would follow suit.' He condemned the folly of insisting upon unconditional surrender. There can be no such thing. The Government ought to tell the Germans what conditions we would accept and what terms we should impose. He mocked at the press's pretence that Winston Churchill and Stalin were in agreement. Their aims were becoming more widely divergent. He was nauseated by the lies disseminated by the press. At the same time he laughed at the Left Wing for supposing that today they could achieve their aims by general strikes, for 'You do not do well to starve on the enemy's doorstep.'

We talked about Hardy's Max Gate. 'Pull it down,' he said. He advised the National Trust to hold his house alienably, so that, supposing in twenty years' time we found that his name was forgotten, we could reap the benefit of selling it. He liked the idea of our holding T. E. Lawrence's Cloud's Hill, for 'it is good for nothing else'. Talked a lot about Lawrence. Said people would not grasp that T.E.L. was physically under-developed and never grew up, scarcely shaved, and also was mentally adolescent. He used to tell Lawrence that he knew no one who kept his anonymity so much in the limelight. He and his wife corrected the proofs of *The Seven Pillars*. The published version was scarcely recognizable. The Shaws cut out so much that was sheer guilt complex. Lawrence was tormented by the recollection of the lives he had personally 'terminated'. Lawrence's great discovery had been that the surest way of directing affairs of any department was by enlisting at the bottom and remaining there. His was the lowest rank of aircraftsman and he had to pretend to be illiterate in order to avoid promotion. Shaw tried to persuade Baldwin, 'that pure humbug', to give T.E.L. a pension. Lawrence refused to consider one although he confessed to Shaw that sometimes to get a square meal he would hang around the Duke of York's steps until a friend took him off to luncheon.

At 5.15 G.B.S. jumped up, saying it was getting dark and he had kept me a quarter of an hour too long. Thanked me for coming. I said I had enjoyed the afternoon immensely. He said he had too. Before I left however he talked about his will again; said he would not leave any money to his relations for he did not wish them to grow up in idleness and luxury. He wanted to leave his money for the sole purpose of inaugurating a new alphabet of something like 140 letters instead of the 26. He had calculated that the saving of expense in print and paper within one generation would be enough to finance three more world wars. And if that didn't appeal to this government, what would? He came on to the road without hat or coat and stood until I drove off. In the mirror I watched him still standing on the road.

2. THE DIARIST IN LOVE

JONATHAN SWIFT
(1667–1745)

Swift's strange and intimate journal-letters to Stella were written between 1710 and 1714 when he had left Ireland for London in a vain attempt to obtain for himself a bishopric in the Church of England. 'Stella' was Esther Johnson, niece of Sir William Temple of Moor Park. Swift had spent ten youthful years at Moor Park as tutor to Stella and also as chaplain to her uncle. There was already a precedence of what might be called a high literary correspondence at Moor Park, for Sir William's wife was Dorothy Osborne, whose courtship letters are perhaps the most exquisite private writings of the seventeenth century. Sir William himself had a prose style which delighted Swift. It was Sir William who had negotiated the marriage of William of Orange and Mary. When Sir William died in 1699, Swift arranged for Stella and her friend Miss Dingley to live near him in Dublin.

The *Journal to Stella* was a first thing in the morning, last thing at night task for the Dean of St Patrick's Cathedral, and through it can be seen the tumbling, kaleidoscopic intelligence as it began and ended each extraordinary day. It is actually addressed to Miss Dingley as well as Esther Johnson and is quite uninhibited. The tone is playful and this only emphasizes the seriousness of its content. The journal has left most of its readers considerably in the dark about what was going on between the Dean and the ladies half his age. Sexual innuendo, power politics, code, male exhibitionism, baby-talk – and genius – rub along together in the diary in a fashion which makes little sense to us. But then it was not for our eyes. One reader, foxed as all readers have been, said, 'They doubtless had an earnest intensity of meaning for this strange grim middle-aged lover and his mistress, but for us they are dumb, and like shrivelled petals found between the leaves of some old romance; we can only dimly wonder what was the message they carried to the eyes which brightened as they saw them.' Swift calls himself 'Presto' in the *Journal*.

Naughty girls

22 November 1710. I dined with Secretary St John; and Lord Dartmouth, who is 'tother Secretary, dined with us, and Lord Orrery and Prior, &c. Harley called, but could not dine with us, and would have had me away while I was at dinner; but I did not like the company he was to have. We stayed till eight, and I called at the coffee-house, and looked where the letters lie; but no letter directed for Mr Presto: at last I saw a letter to Mr Addison, and it looked like a rogue's hand, so I made the fellow give it me, and opened it before him, and saw three letters all for myself: so, truly, I put them in my pocket, and came home to my lodging. Well, and so you shall hear: well, and so I found one of them in Dingley's hand, and 'tother in Stella's, and the third in Domville's. Well, so you shall hear: so, said I to myself, What now, two letters from MD together? But I thought there was something in the wind; so I opened one, and I opened 'tother; and so you shall hear, one was from Walls. Well, but 'tother was from our own dear MD; yes it was. O faith, have you received my seventh, young woman, already? then I must send this to-morrow, else there will be odd doings at our house, faith. – Well, I won't answer your letter in this: no faith, catch me at that, and I never saw the like. Well, but as to Walls, tell him, (with service to him and wife, &c.) that I have no imagination of Mr Pratt's losing his place: and while Pratt continues, Clements is in no danger; and I have already engaged Lord Hyde he speaks of, for Pratt and twenty others; but if such a thing should happen, I will do what I can. I have about ten businesses of other people's now on my hands, and, I believe, shall miscarry in half. It is your sixth I now have received. I writ last post to the Bishop of Clogher again. Shall I send this to-morrow? Well, I will, to oblige MD. Which would you rather, a short letter every week, or a long one every fortnight? A long one; well, it shall be done, and so good night. Well, but this is a long one? No, I warrant you: too long for náughty girls.

23 November. I only ask, have you got both the ten pounds, or only the first; I hope you mean both. Pray be good housewives, and I beg you to walk when you can for health. Have you the horse in town? and do you ever ride him? how often? Confess. Ahhh, sirrah, have I caught you? Can you contrive to let Mrs Fenton know, that the request she has made me in her letter, I will use what credit I have to bring about, although I hear it is very difficult, and I doubt I shall not succeed. Cox is not to be your Chancellor: all joined against him. I have been supping with Lord Peterborow, at his house, with Prior, Lewis, and Dr Freind. 'Tis the ramblingest lying rogue on earth. Dr Raymond is come to town: 'tis late, and so I bid you good night.

24 November. I tell you pretty management: Ned Southwell told me the other day, he had a letter from the bishops of Ireland, with an address to the Duke of Ormond, to intercede with the Queen, to take off the First-Fruits. I dined with him today, and saw it, with another letter to him from the Bishop of Kildare, to call upon me for the papers, &c. and I had last post one from the Archbishop of Dublin ... Your mother sent me last night a parcel of wax candles, and a bandbox full of small plumcakes. I thought it had been something for you; and without opening them, sent answer by the maid that brought them, that I would take care to send the things, &c. but I will write her thanks. Is this a long letter, sirrahs? Now, are you satisfied? I have had no fit since the first: I drink brandy every morning, and take pills every night. Never fear, I an't vexed at this puppy business of the bishops, although I was a little at first.

16 January 1711. O faith, young women, I have sent my letter N.13, without one crumb of an answer to any of MD's; there's for you now; and yet Presto ben't angry faith, not a bit, only he will begin to be in pain next Irish post, except he see MD's little hand-writing in the glass frame at the bar of St James's Coffeehouse, where Presto would never go but for that purpose. Presto's at home, God help him, every night from six till bed time, and has as little enjoyment or pleasure in life at present as any body in the world, although in full favour with all the ministry. As hope saved, nothing gives Presto any sort of dream of happiness, but a letter now and then from his own dearest MD. I love the expectation of it, and when it does not come, I comfort myself, that I have it yet to be happy with. Yes, faith, and when I write to MD, I am happy too; it is just as if methinks you were here, and I prating to you, and telling you where I have been.

LADY ELEANOR BUTLER
(1745–1829)

Lady Eleanor, sister of the 17th Earl of Ormonde, and Miss Sarah Ponsonby, cousin of the Earl of Bessborough, shocked their great families by eloping together one spring night in 1783. They were captured and brought home but soon escaped for good to Llangollen, where, as 'the Ladies of the Vale', they lived for over fifty years in a state of exquisite retreat, and where they gained a reputation for an intellectual version of the simple life which spread to France and Germany. Their house, Plas Newydd, became an essential port of call to anyone with cultural ambitions and they lived in a climate of celebrity tinged with notoriety. They wore male clothes, or rather a masculine version of women's attire, and were passionately devoted to each other. From the day they arrived at Plas Newydd Lady Eleanor began to keep a journal of their happiness. For long after their deaths this journal was reputed to contain much sensational and scandalous material, but recent access to its complete pages reveals only a picture of sapphic dignity and bliss, if an occasionally comic one. The domestic detail and social information are fascinating.
Elizabeth Mavor, the Ladies' witty apologist, wrote:

The truth is that the Ladies' lives were not so much a linear progression from point to point as a kind of dignified *eddying*. For though connected not a little slyly by gossip to the foibles of the fashionable world outside, their lives were in fact securely yoked, as were the lives of the Llangollen villagers themselves, to the seasons ... Their life, accordingly, was repetitive, but it was a repetition which they loved and savoured year after year like connoisseurs, never taking it for granted, and always finding in its simplest manifestations a delight and beauty quite 'unknown', as Eleanor would insist, 'to Vulgar minds'.

Tuesday, 20 January 1789. Freezing hard. Windy. Cold, but very Comfortable in the Dressing Room – an Excellent fire. Shutters Closed. Curtain let down. Candles lighted – our Pens and Ink. Spent the evening very pleasantly reading *Tristram Shandy* aloud – adjourned to the library. Worked – laughed. From Home Since the First of January 1789, Not once Thank Heaven.

Monday, 6 April. Fine evening. Reading. Drawing. My Beloved and I walked for an hour admiring the beauty of the Evening, the heavenly light and Shadow Wandering about the Mountains, the Plough close beside us, Sheep and Lambs in the field. A Woman riding up the road which undulates through it, the Miller driving his horse laden with Sacks of Corn, Children returning from School, an old man bent double with years and leaning on short crutches.

Saturday, 11 April. A crowd of people, the attendants of a wedding from Wrexham, with the Bride and Bridegroom, entreated permission to see the shrubbery. Could not refuse them on this, most probably, happiest day of their lives. Looked at them as they walked. Very well dressed in a plain clean way befitting their station in life.

Sunday, 19 April. Our good landlord came with a letter to us from that Price who was condemned for sheep stealing. His sentence was reserved and the judge promised to recommend him as an object of mercy and that he should be Transported. He writes to us, to entreat we will get him off from Transportation. Threw his letter in the fire as we cannot consider a noted Sheep Stealer entitled to much lenity even had we interest to get him off.

Wednesday, 22 April. Visited our painter and whitewasher. Staid with them some time, Then came to our Apartment which I admire more every time I see it. I am sure it is like Madame Sevigné's Cabinet ... A little dwarvish smiling man all in Tatters came to offer his service as a Portrait Painter.

Saturday, 25 April. The Parlour and Library windows painted a beautiful rich white – the Doors varnished. Skirting board chocolate colour. Kitchen Window white. Seat and settle chocolate colour and linen press Door Varnished. Hall and Door going to the cellar and Larder varnished – Stairs and Skirting board Bannisters painted – the ceilings of the Library – Parlour – Hall – Kitchen whitened ... This vile Mrs Vent* counteracts all the Salutary effects which Madame Pluie's† presence would have done our Trees ... My beloved and I walked in *l'infini*.

[*Undated – 1789*] List of Roses in the Garden '... taken when the pales were new painted ...'

Provence; Maiden Blush; Frankfort; Childing; Blush Belgie; Rose Unique; Moss Provence; Double Marbled; White Damask; Thornless; Virgin Damask; Double Red; Red Austrian; Double Velvet; Red Belgie; Great Royal; Monthly; Double Musk; Rosa Mundi; Double Yellow; Miss Horts; Yellow Austrian; Singleton's hundred leaved; Double Apple bearing; Blush hundred leaved; Rose d'amour; Blush Provence; Dwarf Burgundy; Stepney; Pomponne; Double Burnet leaved; Scarlet Sweet Briar; Double Sweet Briar; Red Scotch; Evergreen Musk; Painted Lady; Tall Burgundy; Wright's; Blush Cluster; American double blush; Double Scarlet Sweet Briar; Small Pompadour; Large Sweet Crimson.

Tuesday, 9 June. Discharged Moses Jones from our service for repeated and outrageous Drunkenness. He had lived fourteen months with us in the capacity of gardener. For the last seven months he has been drunk three days in the Week. This morning he began to mow. He cut three Swards of Grass, laid Down his Scythe, ran to the Ale House. Returned, began to Mow. Then went again. But

* The wind.
† The rain.

when he returned the third time, my Beloved and I met him, took the keys of the garden from him, paid him one-and-twenty pence, which was all that was due to him for one day's work, as every Saturday from the time we Hired him we paid him Ten Shillings.

1 January 1790. My beloved and I woke at seven. Found by our bed side Petticoats and Pockets, a new year's gift from our *truest Friends* [each other].

ELIZABETH BARRETT BROWNING
(1806–61)

Elizabeth Barrett was three when her rich father bought and pulled down a seventeenth-century country house near Malvern and erected on the site an architectural fantasy which might have come straight out of Tom Moore's poem *Lalla Rookh*. She and her many brothers and sisters were to grow up in a neo-Turkish palace set in some 600 acres of parkland, and surrounded by beautiful gardens designed by the famous J. C. Loudon. There were minarets, peacocks and, for Elizabeth herself, a floral man planted out on the lawn.

But in the summer of 1831, when she was twenty-five, there came the reckoning, and the prophetically named Hope End had to be sold. Her father had run out of money and 'a fat gentleman with rings' descended on them. It was a disaster for Elizabeth, for not only had she at that time become enslaved to Hope End, but also to a neighbour, the blind scholar Hugh Boyd.

It was then that she turned to diary-writing as an outlet for her double loss. She kept the diary from June 1831 to April 1832, and it was to be the only one she ever wrote. In it can be traced all the elements of her future life: her subservience to her widowed father, the passion which Robert Browning would re-awaken when she was nearly forty, and her literary power. Many years later she was to tell Richard Horne, 'Once indeed, for one year, I kept a diary in detail and largely, at the end of the twelve months, was in such a crisis of self-disgust that there was nothing for me but to leave off the diary. Did you ever try the effect of a diary upon your own mind? It is curious, especially where elastic spirits and fancies work upon a fixity of character and situation . . .'

This diary was the account of a plight of which not even her dearest sister had any full understanding. She had fallen in love with the blind – and married – man to whom she read the Greek classics, and who lived at Ruby Cottage, just down the road. Describing this horrified her: 'I wonder if I shall burn this sheet of paper like most others I have begun in the same way . . . Adam made fig leaves necessary for the mind, as well as for the body. And such *a* mind as I have . . . so very very often *wrong*! Well! But I will write: I must write . . .'

Friday, 10 June 1831. I can take breath again. The people are gone. Their message thro' Lane to Papa was, that they were sent by Mr Reid to see the house. Papa's message to them was – that nobody belonging to Mr Reid was here to show them the house. So they went away. I hear that their name is Brydges, & that they have come from Canonfrome (how is the word spelt?) – & that their servant spoke to ours of having seen Hope End advertised to be sold this month. How is it to be? Are we really to go? I am sick at heart about it; but will hope on still. Something may be doing, still. Papa in bad spirits at dinner. Bro said something of my note to Mr Boyd, which made Papa exclaim 'What! you were there yesterday – & did you write today – ?' So then I explained how he had wished me to go to see him during Mrs Boyd's absence; & how I had first agreed to go on Monday, & afterwards put it off. No objections made. Papa is *not* in good spirits today. If *they* dont go to Malvern on Monday, *I* must & will do so by myself.

Saturday, 11 June. Sam told me that Hope End is advertised in the Sun newspaper, to be sold in August – no name, but a full description. He & Bro heard it yesterday from Henry Trant! I begged him to tell nobody, & to let me tell Bummy. Ran down stairs & found Bummy in the drawing room by herself. Told her. She shed tears – we both shed tears! When will tears cease to be shed? She seems to fear the worst . . .

Monday, 4 July. I took courage & begged [Mr Boyd] to employ me, & assured him of my liking & wishing for the employment. 'Ah! I am well aware that *you* would do it for me sooner than any body else would. But I should not like you to drudge for me. And suppose you should be ill –' 'Ill! I am not going to anticipate being ill. Do let me manage it for you. I should like it so very much!' 'But we must see first whether you leave Hope End or not.' I said that whether I left Hope End or not, the sheets might be sent to me – & I said more – & he said more – & I think it will end by my doing what I wish to do.

My dear friend Mr Boyd! – If he knew how much it gratifies me to assist him in any way (I wish . . . I cd. do so in *every* way) all his *'drudgeries'* wd. . . . devolve upon me. It pleased me to hear him acknowledge that I would do more for him than other people would! And is not that true? I think so.

I left Malvern somewhere between 7 & 8, & got home to the relics of tea . . .

The auction of the *crops,* at the farm today. I am glad it is over. Oh if there is no chance of our staying here altogether; & I believe there is little chance: and if Mr Boyd were not at Malvern, I would yearn to be away from the sight & hearing of all that we see & hear every day. But it is God's will! – And I have in spite of everything, felt happy several times today! –

Mrs Boyd called me Miss Barrett. She used to call me Ba. Quære *why*? Another Quære – *Why should I care?* Certainly I don't care very much for Mrs Boyd.

Tuesday, 19 July. . . . Mrs Boyd was going to walk home with Mr Spowers. Therefore I decided in walking with her. There was a little remonstrance on the side of my party – about the possibility of my being tired; but nothing vehement. I walked & was tired – what with the walk & what with the wind. Mrs Boyd placed me on the sofa, & would have bolstered & pillowed me if I had been passive. She is a good natured woman. After five or ten minutes, I began more to fidget, & wonder why Mr Boyd did not send for me. After a quarter of an hour or half an hour, I could have cried – in thinking that I had exposed myself to all this fatigue willingly, & that he seemed to have no will or wish to fatigue himself by talking to me until the carriage came. I could have cried! – At last Mrs Boyd who was reading the newspaper close to me, (just as if I had gone there to see her read it), observed 'Are you not going to Mr Boyd?' 'Why he is not ready: is he?' 'Yes to be sure he is! & waiting for you.' And so he was. A mistake had kept *me* down stairs, & him in an expectation for half an hour or more. How provoked I was. He did not shake hands with me when I went first into his room . . .

After a little talking . . . Obliged to go. Was not with him a quarter of an hour, – & tired to death for it. Oh *so* tired. Got home, – but could scarcely get thro' dinner – & then to oblige Bummy, off to Mrs Martin's. There I sate in the armchair more dead than alive, – certainly more disagreable than agreable – until tea-time. The tea was a collation for the cricketers & sinecure visitors; & it was hardly over, before I fainted fairly away. They dragged me out of the room, & packed me up on the sofa.

Saturday, 28 August. Miss Gibbons [a guest of the Boyds] inclined to returning to Hope End [after chapel] . . . She glued herself to me all day, & we talked eternally . . .

She asked me when I was going again to Malvern. 'Whenever I can,' I said, 'for my Malvern days are my happy days – they are my holidays . . . But I must not go too often.' 'You *cannot* go too often. Mr Boyd does so thoroughly enjoy the days which you spend with him! they are *his* holidays!' 'I did not exactly mean that – I meant that I must not leave home & occupy the carriage too often. I like to dream that Mr Boyd has pleasure in seeing me, tho' I know that whatever pleasure his is, mine must double it.' 'Indeed! I don't think it does! and how can you know this?' 'By certain inward oracles.' 'But tho' you understand your own oracles, you cant understand Mr Boyd's.'

I am half sorry that this conversation shd. have passed: but passed it has.

ARTHUR MUNBY
(1828–1910)

The diary as a receptacle for fantasies is obvious. But to succeed beyond just building up imagined pleasures day by day the fantasy has to be a written confession of the diarist's hidden emotional drives, however strange, reprehensible or absurd. Also, the diary must not be the record of such longings and actions only, but an account of their place in the context of the diarist's ordinary activities. To say that his passion for tough, work-marked labouring women was the chief drive in Arthur Munby's life would be to miss the point. What made him tick were the thrills of subversion. By the greatest good fortune which a sexual and social fantasist can come by he had found in his maid-of-all-work Hannah the perfect participant in his game, and their secret marriage was to provide endless satisfactions for the pair of them. Outsiders may stare, will moralize, could laugh, and should, perhaps, be angry or disgusted, but when they get to the end of Munby's diary (deposited in Trinity College, Cambridge, and marked 'Not to be opened until 1950') they will have to admit that few Victorians could have so bent the class system to their own ends.

Apart from being obsessed by muscular, toil-stained women who were low and illiterate, Munby was a poet, a political progressive and the friend of Browning, the Dilkes, Rossetti and Ruskin, a fighter for women's liberation, and a Mayhew. His diary begins in 1859 and one of the first entries sets his own strange scene:

> Back through Upper Poppleton: and behind one of the farms in the village, pumping water in the yard, appeared a creature worth seeing. A farm servant girl really worthy of the name: tall & strong as a man – short thick neck and square massive shoulders – square broad back, straight from the shoulder to the hip with no waist to weaken it – stout, solid legs, & arms as thick as legs, bare and muscular throughout . . .
>
> Altogether a noble creature, refreshing to behold: simple

and unconscious – thinking only, if she thought at all, that she was very dirty . . .

From then on Munby's descriptions of his cultured, upper-middle-class existence are regularly punctuated with portraits (written and photographic) of menials, collier-girls, women deformed by cease-less toil, females barely distinguishable from strong men. His editor, Derek Hudson, sees in Munby a deep passivity and a nature which was probably homosexual but which, in the work-degraded women of the London basements, the fields and mines, many of the latter wearing trousers and carrying huge loads, found a heterosexual outlet for his feelings. When he met his ideal, a young kitchen-maid named Hannah Cullwick, he dressed her in a man's shirt, cut off her hair himself and required her to love him when 'in her dirt'. She found in him her perfect mate and could not be said to be 'deceived'. She called him 'Massa' and cleaned his boots on her knees before him. After eighteen years of such role-playing they were secretly married.

The useful by-product of his forays into sculleries, sweatshops, collieries, parks, farms, etc. is an amazing sociological documenta-tion of the conditions of female labour in the late nineteenth century. Munby's diary is, amongst so much else, a revelation of English class pathology.

Wednesday, 29 February 1860. Came a note from Hannah, asking me to go and see her, her mistress being out and she all alone. I went up . . . and sat with her till after nine in her kitchen, she on her stool at my feet. I found her dirty and unkempt, as she had been all day, she said; and the poor child evidently thought I liked to see her so. I made her wash herself at the sink – her only toilette place! – and stood by, among an entourage of foul pots and pans, which it is her work to clean. Most sad, to see her wearing out her youth in such sordid drudgery, her only haunts the kitchen the scullery the coal-cellar! She unconsciously increased this sadness in me, by bringing out a portrait of herself, taken five years ago, and looking all tenderness & refinement. Then, if I had had the means, she might have passed into a drawing room at once: now, it is too late. I looked at the portrait and then at her, and seemed for the first time to see the change that five years of exposure and menial work have made in her: five years of scrubbing & cleaning, of sun & wind out of doors and kitchen fires within. And she was pleased with the change – *pleased* that she is now 'so much rougher and coarser'.

Tuesday, 21 August. ... by train to the Crystal Palace, to see something of 'the Foresters' Day' ... Last year at this time there were 63,000 present, and now it was thought there were still more. This Foresters' anniversary, to which thousands come up from the country, is of all others the scene and the time to see the English working classes ... Here I would bring a foreigner, to show him whatever of picturesque or of mirthful is left among us.

... I passed a tallish young woman, evidently a servant, who was noticeable for the size of her gloveless hands. She seemed to be alone in the crowd, and (with a view to her hands) I asked her if she meant to dance? No, she couldn't dance at all – only liked to look on: for which I was not sorry. So after a little chat we walked away, and I (still with a view to my hobby) proposed to rest on the bank near, under the trees. She gave me her hand to help her up – and, oh ye ballroom partners, what a breadth of massive flesh it was to grasp! She sat down by me, ready to talk, after the blunt fashion of such maidens, but not forward ... She was a maid of all work at Chelsea, it seemed ... I looked at her hands, and spoke my opinion of them. 'How can you like them?' she says, like Margaret in the garden; 'they are so large and red, I'm ashamed of them.' 'They are just the hands for a servant,' say I: 'they show you are hardworking, and you ought to be proud of them. You wouldn't wish them to be like a lady's?' 'Yes I should!' said she, bitterly: 'and I should like to be a lady, and I wish my hands were like yours!' And she looked enviously at my hand, which was quite white and small by the side of hers. I could not then understand her vehemence: but remembering the difference between my fist and those small taper ladyhands one sees in drawing rooms, it did seem pathetic that this poor wench should envy my hands, and fancy that if her own were like them, she would have reached a ladylike pitch of refinement. Her right hand lay, a large red lump, upon her light-coloured frock: it was very broad and square & thick – as large and strong & coarse as the hand of a sixfoot bricklayer . . . the skin was rough to the touch, and hard & leathery in the palm: there was nothing feminine about it in form or texture . . . and yet she was only nineteen . . . I lifted it too – it was quite a weight, heavy and inert . . . My companion's name, it appeared, was Sarah Goodacre, & she was born at Grantham: father and mother died before she was a year old. Did she know what her father was? 'Yes,' she only said, looking down, and seemingly strangely confused . . . hesitating long, at last she said, looking another way – 'He was *Curate to the Vicar of Grantham*.'

I turned to her in amazement: there was nothing suspicious in her stolid face – 'Impossible!' I said: 'your father a *clergyman*! You do not know what you are saying.' 'Yes I do,' she answered quietly . . .

Saturday, 1 September. Met Hannah in Oxford Street and had several photographs taken of her in working dress and attitudes. With what meakness she submitted to be posed, and handled, and discussed to her face; the coarseness of her hands examined and the best mode of showing them displayed! She came home with me, for the first time to *stay*: a dangerous experiment, which I had much considered, & almost feared. For on Tuesday, in her innocence, she begged me to stay with *her*; 'for then she could get my breakfast and clean my boots in the morning'! and it took some self-control to refuse. And now, when after a quiet evening together, she melted into the full tenderness of artless endearment, I learnt somewhat of physical temptation and of resistance. But *she* never knew what I was learning – I had not miscalculated myself. And when she had gone to rest, under my roof, in a bed that was not mine, I went in & kissed her rosy face as it lay on the white pillow and smiled; and thought, as well one might, that 'God do so to me and more also, if I harm her anywise.' And so, I left her to her virgin sleep.

Saturday, 18 January 1861. I walk past the South Kensington Museum and along the Cromwell Road to see the Exhibition building. When I was here last, some three or four years ago, all this country was a tract of market gardens, with bridleroads between & footpaths, where sweethearts walked for privacy, between

Brompton & Kensington. Now, broad streets of lofty houses; and further on, roadways terraced on arches in all directions; the wretched grass of the old fields still visible below, with here & there a doomed tree, where the houses have not yet been begun. Crowds of welldrest people hanging about, looking at the Exhibition: a vast building – hideous enough, of course, but having a certain massiveness, as of good masonry . . .

Sunday, 16 February. [Munby returns from spending a night at Gillingham with Cuyler Anderson] I changed at the Crystal Palace, and reached London Bridge at 5.30.

I found Hannah waiting for me at the station, by appointment. I had meant to take her to church, but it was too early, so I told her we would go home. She would not take my arm – for it was still daylight & many people were about – but walked apart, till we got down into the empty streets about the Borough Market – for I led her that way to avoid observation; and even then she hung back, and whispered, 'You know I have no gloves on'! Gloves, indeed! I took the poor child's bare hand and laid it on my sleeve; and so we walked arm in arm in the dusk along Bankside and over Blackfriars Bridge. 'And how would you like, dear, to be servant at one of these old houses by the waterside, where the coal agents and foremen of timberyards live?' Oh, she would like it very well: and it 'ud be near me, too!

I left her for a few moments to call in Chatham Place and inquire after Rossetti, whose invalid wife, I was shocked to hear, died on Monday, through an overdose of Laudanum. He is in a sad state of grief; Ruskin says so, who has seen him.

I rejoined Hannah and we went on to the Temple together. She unpinned her coarse shawl and took off her simple bonnet, and rolled up the sleeves of her Sunday frock – a black stuff one, old, and rent in places – as usual: but her manner was sad & spiritless, and she looked weary & workworn. It was bitter to see her bonny tender face all roughened and red, and her hair, that was once so soft and beautiful, all foul with dust & overheat, that she cannot get it clean. 'Oh, it's dreadful!' she said: 'they can see it for all my cap, and every one stares at me so! And Sarah says she shouldn't wonder if my face was to break out all in blotches, in the Spring, with overheat!' Presently she broke away from me, and hid her face, and began a long low cry that ended in sobs and tears.

I drew her down toward me, wondering and anxious; and she lay and cried softly against my knee, while I tried to soothe her and learn what was the matter. At last it all came out. 'Everybody hates me!' she sobbed; 'I'm so dirty and shabby! The missis did look so upon me this morning when I waited at breakfast – and I know it was because I was dirty. And Neal . . . sent me a nasty Valentine, of a cookmaid scrubbing . . .'

Munby taught Hannah to keep a diary and this is from her 'Account of the Year 1864':

When this year began i was general servant to Mr Foster the beer merchant, at 22 Carlton Villas. i was kitchen-servant like, & did all the dirty work down stairs, besides the dining room & hall & steps & back stairs. There were 12 steps to the front door, & it took me ½ an hour to clean 'em crawling backwards, & often ladies & that come in while i was a doing 'em & their feet close to where my hands was on the steps. i liked that, & made foot-marks wi my wet hands on the steps like they did wi their wet feet. it made me think o the contrast. i clean'd all the boots & knives & some o the windows & the grates belonging to the dining room, kitchen & the room down stairs what the children play'd in & the nurse sat in to work & that – i had 3 or 4 pair o boots of a day & about 2 dozen knives & six forks – & i clean'd the watercloset & privy & the passage & all the rough places down stairs & my wages was 15 lbs a year. All that is my sort o work what i *love*, but i had to wait at breakfast, what i couldn't do well, cause there was no set time & i couldn't keep myself clean enough to go up any-time i the morning – to go before my betters – be star'd at, & the Missis told me once or twice of it. But i *couldnt* be clean, & besides i'd liefer be dirty, & no grand folks to stare at me. at last i got warning. the Missis said to me when i was clearing away the things 'Hannah, your Master & me think you'd better leave & get a place where you've no waiting to do' – i look'd surprised, & she says 'you're a good hard-working servant she says, & we like you, but that strap on your wrist your Master cant bear to see it nor yet your arms all naked & black'd some-times & you so dirty'. i felt a bit hurt to be told i was too dirty, when my dirt was all got wi making things clean for *them*, & as for the leather strap i couldn't leave *that* off, when it's the sign that i'm a drudge & belong to Massa. But after all, i was glad i was to be sent away for been dirty, for then Massa may know i *am* dirty. and i thought of what May the housemaid said to me, as i wasn't fit to be a gentleman's servant. Still, i *am* a gentleman's servant, & one that wont turn me away, however low i may be. i left in February & Misser's Foster give me a very good character – i was there 3 years come March – & i went to Massa, but i was very down about it all, so sudden, & got to go & earn my living again among strangers as a servant. And I lay on the hearth rug & cried a bit – but Master sat down by me & kissed & comforted me, & said how gladly he would keep me there always if he could, & told me how my home is with him wherever i go – & so i got better . . .

3. THE DIARIST AND THE DIFFICULT MARRIAGE

LADY ANNE CLIFFORD
(1590–1676)

Lady Anne Clifford was the only daughter of the romantically handsome Earl of Cumberland, one of Elizabeth I's sea-brigands and a great North Country magnate. Her parents were wed in the presence of the Queen when they were teenagers. Cumberland neglected his wife almost from the start and the marriage soon foundered. 'When my mother and he did meet their countenance did show their dislike they had of one another,' wrote their formidable child.

When Lord Cumberland died, a clause in his will was eventually to involve James I, Anne of Denmark and many members of their courts. This clause forms the central dramatic theme of Lady Anne's diary. Essentially, what occurred was that her first husband Lord Dorset, the extravagant owner of Knole, took it for granted that she would sell off her Westmorland properties, which he thought of as mere heathland. But neither he nor her second husband Lord Pembroke, nor even the King himself, was able to persuade her to dispose of a single acre of what she thought of as her own ancestral kingdom. In 1643 she came into full inheritance of all the vast Clifford lands in the north and also entered into her full matriarchal personality.

Her tenacity is described in what she called 'my Day-by-Day book', which is one of the earliest and best diaries. In it, piety and selfishness go hand in hand. Lady Anne trundles from palace to castle with a retinue of hundreds, reads Spenser and Montaigne, plays games, and – without ceasing – consolidates her position and possessions.

May 1616. The 12th at night *Grosvenor** came hither and told me how my Lord had won £200 at the Cocking Match and that my Lord of *Essex* and Lord *Willoughby* who was on my Lord's side won a great deal and how there was some unkind words between my Lord and his side and Sir *William Herbert* and his side. This day my Lady *Grantham* sent me a letter about these businesses between my Uncle *Cumberland* and me and returned me an answer.

All this time my Lord was in *London* where he had all and infinite great resort coming to him. He went much abroad to Cocking, to Bowling Alleys, to Plays and Horse Races, and commended by all the world. I stayed in the country having many times a sorrowful and heavy heart, and being condemned by most folks because I would not consent to the agreements, so as I may truly say, I am like an owl in the desert.

Upon the 13th being Monday, my Lady's footman *Thomas Petty* brought me letters out of *Westmoreland,* by which I perceived how very sick and full of grievous pains my dear Mother was, so as she was not able to write herself to me and most of her people about her feared she would hardly recover this sickness, at night I went out and pray'd to GOD my only helper that she might not die in this pitiful case. The 14th *Richard Jones* came from *London* to me and brought a letter with him from *Matthew* the effect whereof was to persuade me to yield to my Lord's desire in this business at this time, or else I was undone for ever . . .

November. Upon the 12th I made an end of my cushion of Irish stitch which my Coz. *C. Neville* began when she went with me to the *Bath,* it being my chief help to pass away the time at work.

Upon the 19th *William Punn* came down from *London* with letters from my Lord whereby I perceived there had passed a challenge between him and my Coz. *Clifford* which my Lord sent him by my Coz. *Cheymy,* the Lords of the Council sent for them both and the King made them friends giving my Lord marvellous good words and willed him to send for me because he meant to make an agreement himself between us.

* *Mr Grosvenor, Gentleman Usher.*

This going up to *London* of mine at this time I little expected. By him I also heard that my Sister *Sackville* was dead.

Upon the 20th I spent most of the day in playing at Tables. All this time since my Lord went away I wore my black taffety night gown and a yellow taffety waistcoat and used to rise betimes in the morning and walk upon the leads and afterwards to hear reading.

Upon the 23rd I did string the pearls and diamonds left me by my Mother into a necklace.

Upon the 23rd I went to Mr *Blentre*'s house in *Cumberland* where I stayed an hour or two and heard music and saw all the house and gardens.

Upon the 26th *Thomas Hilton* came hither and told me of some quarrels that would be between some gentlemen that took my Lord's part and my Coz. *Clifford*'s which did much trouble me.

Upon the 29th I bought of Mr *Clebom* who came to see me a clock [?cloak] and a saveguard of cloth laced with black lace to keep me warm on my journey.

December. This night Mrs *Matthews* lay with me. About this time died Mr *Marshall*, my Lord's auditor and surveyor, and left me a purse of 10 angels as a remembrance of his love.

Upon the 18th I alighted at *Islington* where my Lord who came in my Lady *Witby Pole*'s coach which he borrowed, my Lady *Effingham* the widow, my Sister *Beauchamp*, and a great many more came to meet me so that we were in all 10 or 11 coaches and so I came to *Dorset House* where the Child met me in the Gallery. The house was well dressed up against I came.

Upon the 23rd my Lady *Manners* came in the morning to dress my head. I had a new black wrought taffety gown which my Lady *St John*'s tailor made. She used often to come to me and I to her and was very kind one to another. About 5 o'clock in the evening my Lord and I and the Child went in the great coach to *Northampton House** where my Lord Treasurer† and all the company commended her and she went down into my Lady *Walden*'s chamber

---

* Now Northumberland House.

† *Mr Marsh, attendant on my Lady.*

where my Coz. *Clifford* saw her and kissed her but I stayed with my Lady *Suffolk*.

All this time of my being at *London* I was much sent to, and visited by many, being unexpected that ever matters should have gone so well with me and my Lord, everybody persuading me to hear and make an end. Since the King had taken the matter in hand so as now.

Upon the 27th I dined at my Lady *Elizabeth Gray*'s lodgings at *Somerset House* where I met my Lady *Compton* and Lady *Fielding* and spoke to them about my coming to the King. Presently after dinner came my Lord thither and we went together to my Lady *Arundel*'s where I saw all the pictures and statues in the lower rooms.

Upon the 28th I dined above in my chamber and wore my nightgown because I was not very well, which day and yesterday I forgot that it was fish day and ate flesh at both dinners. In the afternoon I play'd at Glecko with my Lady *Gray* and lost £27 and odd money.

January 1617. Upon the 10th my Lord went up to *London* upon the sudden, we not knowing it till the afternoon.

Upon the 16th I received a letter from my Lord that I should come up to *London* the next day because I was to go before the King on Monday next.

Upon the 17th when I came up, my Lord told me I must resolve to go to the King the next day. Upon the 18th being Saturday I went presently after dinner to the Queen to the Drawing Chamber where my Lady *Derby* told the Queen how my business stood and that I was to go to the King so she promised me she would do all the good in it she could. When I had stay'd but a little while there I was sent for out, my Lord and I going through my Lord *Buckingham*'s chamber who brought us into the King, being in the Drawing Chamber. He put out all that were there and my Lord and I kneeled by his chair sides when he persuaded us both to peace and to put the whole matter wholly into his hands, which my Lord consented to, but I beseech'd His Majesty to pardon me for that I would never part from *Westmoreland* while I lived upon any condition whatsoever. Sometimes he used fair means and persuasions and sometimes foul means but I was resolved before so as nothing would move me. From the King we went to the Queen's side. I brought my Lady *St John* to her lodgings and so we went home. At this time I was much bound to my Lord for he was far kinder to me in all these businesses than I expected and was very unwilling that the King should do me any public disgrace.

Upon the 19th my Lord and I went to the Court in the morning thinking the Queen would have gone to the Chapel but she did not, so my Lady *Ruthven* and I and many others stood in the Closet to hear the sermon. I dined with my Lady *Ruthven*. Presently after dinner she and I went up to the Drawing Chamber where my Lady D., my Lady *Montgomery*, my Lord *Burleigh*, persuaded me to refer these businesses to the King. About 6 o'clock my Lord came for me so he and I and Lady *St John* went home in her coach. This night the Masque was danced at the Court but I would not stay to see it because I had seen it already.

The 2-3-4-5th I sat up and had many ladies come to see me, and much other company, and so I passed the time.

My Lord went often to the Court abroad and on Twelfth Eve lost 400 pieces playing with the King.

The 6th the Prince had the Masque at night in the Banqueting House. The King was there but the Queen was so ill she could not remove from *Hampton Court* all this Xmas, and it was generally thought she would have died.

The 11th my Lord went to *Knole*.

The 12th the Banqueting House at *Whitehall* was burnt to the ground and the writings in the signet office were all burnt. The 16th came my Lord of *Arundel* and his Lady. The same day I sent my Coz. *Hall* of *Gletford* a letter and my picture with it which *Sarkinge* drew this summer at *Knole*.

SAMUEL JOHNSON
(1709–84)

Johnson's diary evokes compassion. Here, simply exposed, is the pathology of a virtuous and brilliant man. His Dictionary says that a diary has to be 'an account of the transactions, accidents, and observations of every day' – which suggests something less profound than what he attempted. Yet no one heeded more the advice he gave to his friends when he urged them to keep diaries in which 'the great thing to be recorded is the state of your mind'. His own diary is above all the troubled record of a greatly troubled mind. 'A man loves to review his own mind,' he liked to say. But did he review his? Could he? He kept a diary to learn from his own shortcomings and to be reconciled to the disparity between his discoveries and his hopes. He wrote it in full view of the eye of God and the result is awesome, and yet at the same time sweetly intimate, like a William Cowper hymn.

He can never accept what he is. He can never say, 'I am the sort of man who cannot get up in the morning and who likes drink, women, etc.' These are trifling faults compared with his natural goodness. Year after year he makes resolutions which are beyond his capacity to keep, 'to rise early', 'to lose no time', and so on. Yet we know by many confessions of the type of 'I do not remember that since I left Oxford I ever rose early by mere choice . . .' that he failed and we shake our heads at his inability to take himself as he is – a late riser and a man who works in tough, irregular bouts. His guilt is terrible. 'I have now spent fifty years in resolving, having from the earliest times almost that I can remember been forming schemes for a better life, I have done nothing . . .'

Not true, of course. Johnson's diary, although only scrappily known to us, is as well as much else a powerful meditation on the progress of the orthodox Anglican spirit. Morbidity alternates with notes on work in progress. Eventually, with a horror unequalled by anything to be found in other diaries, he moves from his habitual hypochondria into a plain medical account of his cumbersome journey to the grave, writing now in august Latin, and not baulking all that is implied by his now being 'under dread of death'. His Christianity only intensifies his fears, yet however great the terror nothing unsettles the majestic sanity of his mind. The reader's heart goes out to him.

The diary is also a declaration of his love for his 'dear poor Tetty', the middle-aged widow whom he had married when he was twenty-seven and whom, in spite of her addition to drink and drugs and tedious women friends, he loved most tenderly until her death in 1752. The entries about her are heavy with remorse, about what might have been, and should have been. Johnson's love for Tetty was frankly unbelievable to most of his circle, and we have Garrick's unsparing picture of her as 'very fat, with a bosom of more than ordinary protuberance, with swelled cheeks of a florid red, pro-duced by thick painting, and increased by the liberal use of cordials; flaring and fantastic in her dress, and affected both in her speech and her general behaviour'. Yet Johnson came to treat her grave as a shrine and the fact that she died about Easter caused him to entwine her memory with concepts of religious renewal. Thirty years after he had buried her in Bromley churchyard he wrote, 'On what we did amiss, and our faults were great, I have thought of late with more regret than at any further time . . .'

The judgement of posterity has always been that the Doctor was far too hard on himself. His practical kindness, ceaselessly recorded by his friends, was not of the cheques and petitions sort, but one which would lead him to go to the utmost personal inconvenience to help a fellow creature.

Some of Johnson's diaries were used by James Boswell for his *Life,* two large quartos of them were burnt by the Doctor just before his death, and others came only to light among the vast haul of papers discovered at Malahide Castle just before the last war. While visiting Johnson in May 1776, Boswell managed to copy some of the large diary which Johnson was later to destroy. Except for the travel diaries, what is left is terse and full of gaps. In 1783 he had the stroke which led to his death and in July that year started his solemn 'Sick Man's Journal', writing it until a month of his death on 13 December 1784. This diary is a mixture of savage self-doctoring and heroism in the face of physical misery, and it reminds one how heartfelt were those old prayers for an 'easy end' before the age of trustworthy sedatives and pain-killers.

28 March 1753. I kept this day as the anniversary of my Tetty's death with prayer & tears in the morning. In the evening i prayed for her conditionally if it were lawful.

3 April. I began the 2ᵈ vol of my Dictionary, room being left in the first for Preface, Grammar & History none of them yet begun.

O God who has hitherto supported me enable me to proceed in this labour & in the Whole task of my present state that when I shall render up at the last day an account of the talent committed to me I may receive pardon for the sake of Jesus Christ. Amen.

22 April. As I purpose to try on Monday to seek a new wife without any derogation from dear Tetty's memory I purpose at sacrament in the morning to take my leave of Tetty in a solemn commendation of her soul to God.

23 April, Easter Monday. Yesterday as I purposed I went to Bromley where dear Tetty lies buried & received the sacrament, first praying before I went to the altar according to the prayer precomposed for Tetty and a prayer which I made against unchastity, idleness, & neglect of publick worship. I made it during sermon which I could not perfectly hear. I repeated mentally the commendation of her with the utmost fervour larme à l'oeil before the reception of each element at the altar. I repeated it again in the pew, in the garden before dinner, in the garden before departure, at home at night. I hope I did not sin. Fluunt lacrymae. I likewise ardently applied to her the prayer for the Church militant where the dead are mentioned and commended her again to Eternal Mercy, as in coming out I approached her grave. During the whole service I was never once distracted by any thoughts of any other woman or with my design of a new wife which freedom of mind I remembered with gladness in the Garden. God guide me.

18 September 1760. Resolved D. j. (with God's aid)
To combat notions of obligation.
To apply to Study.
To reclaim imagination.
To consult the resolves on Tetty's coffin.
To rise early.
To study Religion.

To go to Church.
To drink less strong liquours.
To keep Journal.
To oppose laziness, by doing what is to be done.
To morrow
  Rise as early as I can.
  Send for books for Hist. of war.
  Put books in order.
  Scheme life.

21 April 1764. −3−M. My indolence, since my last reception of the Sacrament, has sunk into grosser sluggishness, and my dissipation spread into wilder negligence. My thoughts have been clouded with sensuality, and, except that from the beginning of this year I have in some measure forborn excess of Strong Drink my appetites have predominated over my reason. A kind of strange oblivion has overspread me, so that I know not what has become of the last year, and perceive that incidents and intelligence pass over me without leaving any impression.

This is not the life to which Heaven is promised . . .

28 March 1777. This day is Good Friday. It is likewise the day on which my poor Tetty was taken from me.

My thoughts were disturbed in bed. I remembered that it was my Wife's dying day, and begged pardon for all our sins, and commended her; but resolved to mix little of my own sorrows or cares with the great solemnity. Having taken only tea without milk, I went to church, had time before service to commend my Wife, and wished to join quietly in the service, but I did not hear well, and my mind grew unsettled and perplexed. Having rested ill in the night, I slumbered at the sermon, which, I think, I could not as I sat, perfectly hear.

I returned home but could not settle my mind. At last I read a Chapter. Then went down about six or seven and eat two cross buns, and drank tea. Fasting for some time has been uneasy and I have taken but little.

At night I had some ease. L.D.* I had prayed for pardon and peace. I slept in the afternoon.

* Laus Deo = praise God.

4. THE DIARIST IN THE VILLAGE

THE REV. JAMES WOODFORDE
(1740–1803)

It was shortly after the First World War that a Hertfordshire doctor showed his neighbour, John Beresford, a diary which had been kept by an ancestor who had been the rector of a parish near Norwich during the years 1776–1802. The diary actually began in the summer of 1759 when its owner, James Woodforde, heard the news that New College, Oxford, had accepted him as a scholar, thus at that moment (although he could not have known it) decreeing his entire future. Beresford read the sixty-eight exquisitely written journals and was enthralled, as every reader of Parson Woodforde has been to this day, and in 1924 began to publish his five volumes of edited extracts from them. These have established our view of Woodforde for good or ill.

Beresford wants us to see the rector as 'that very rare and beautiful bird – a typical Englishman ... a man who loved his father and his family and his home with a completely contented love, and who loved good food, good drink and sport, specially coursing hares and fishing, country life and established institutions'. Reading this diary, says Beresford, whose editing of it has so powerfully shaped our concept of its author, 'is like embarking on a long voyage down a very tranquil stream. There is no grand or exciting scenery; there are no rapids, nor is there any ultimate expectation of the sea.' He is correct where this last is concerned, and spiritually and emotionally it can be said to add a pathetic element which frequently denies Woodforde the 'peace' in which his editor has so firmly set him. But when it came to publication what was the latter, or any diary editor faced with half a century's

71

daily outpourings, to do except present what honestly appeared to him as a fair revelation of his subject? We are, however, obliged to remember the extent to which Beresford had a hand in making Parson Woodforde as celebrated a clerical character as any from Sterne or Trollope, and that a further half-dozen volumes drawn from the unpublished material could not but disestablish the popular view of him. But thus it would be for all substantial diarists in the learned though practical grasp of their editors, and thus it was for the great Samuel Pepys until recently, when Robert Latham was allowed to bring the entire magnificent literary achievement into our possession.

Woodforde's popularity is now only equalled by another and quite different parish voice, that of Francis Kilvert, published a few years later. Woodforde writes from the spiritually comatose Anglican base which existed before the Wesleys and the sacramentalists of the Oxford Movement disturbed it. He is a country gentleman occupying a living and doing his duty. He is a sociable bachelor who is cared for by his attractive niece Nancy (who is also a diarist) and five servants. He is neither eccentric nor passionate, he is not clever, saintly, scandalous or, in the usual sense of the word, interesting. Yet he fascinates. How unimaginable it would have been for him to know that he would do this. In his diary he never puffs or censors himself but just allows his ordinariness to run on from page to page in handsome handwriting. He reveres small happenings – always the hallmark of a first-rate diarist – and never disdains the domestic odds and ends of existence. 'This I thought deserving of notice, even in so trifling a book as this,' he enters on 27 November 1789, as he describes a cure for the cramp. In his autobiographical *Finding the Gate,* V. S. Naipaul remarks, 'as diarists and letter-writers repeatedly prove, any attempt at narration can give value to an experience which might otherwise evaporate away.' The world can only guess at James Woodforde's motive for not letting his stolid life vanish into thin air, although it certainly wasn't vanity.

He was the son of the vicar of Ansford, Somerset, and came of a line of literary priests who had been friends of writers such as Thomas Ken, George Herbert and Izaak Walton. James Woodforde was ordained when he was twenty-three, but it was not until ten years later, on Guy Fawkes Day 1774, that he heard of the vacancy at Weston Longeville, Norfolk, one of the many livings which were in the gift of his college. He arrived to take up his duties a year and a half after being appointed, accompanied by his good-looking nephew Bill, whose effect on the servants was to make him 'uneasy'. There followed a memorable line of male servants, including the Shakespearianly-named Brettingham Scurl and Barnabas Woodcock. The Parson always refers to his servants as 'our folk'. They and he, and everybody in the village, observe rank and have an ease with each other which would be incomprehensible to the Victorians. Pregnancies among the maids are more of an economic than a moral disaster, willing lads all too soon mature into 'saucy' young men who have to be sacked, and it is in his dealings with these boisterous youngsters that we come closest to the 'inner' Woodforde. The more one reads his diary, the more each member of the little household takes on the mystery of one of those figures in a novel who make a lasting impact by the gradualness with which they are revealed.

The diary unfolds in the immediate pre-Industrial Revolution, pre-Enclosure Acts countryside, during the 'golden age of English agriculture', as the historian Lord Ernle called it. Woodforde and niece Nancy themselves 'rotate', as they describe their regular pattern of dinners, cards, backgammon and dances, among half a dozen of what Jane Austen calls the 'first families' of the neighbourhood. Woodforde reports little dialogue but an enormous amount of activity. His observations are masculine and lack nuance, insight or even inquisitiveness. He ties in human behaviour to the season's weather, food, and, somewhat perfunctorily, to the Church calendar. The diary is one of the most English books ever written.

And here we must say something about what Woodforde mentions so often: food. Meals. The emphasis on eating is so disproportionate to that placed on anything else that he has acquired a reputation for gluttony, when he meant no more than to prove that his days were convivial – a much sought-after state at that time. Such tucking-in must have had something to do with the Parson's (and Nancy's) ill-health, which, with the putting down of his complete expenditure, his minimal churchmanship and strong, unprying portraits of his many friends, creates at times a quite overwhelming feeling of robust life fighting mortality. There are many funerals and Woodforde is an authority on how we used to die. He watches executions, once at Norwich of five young men together. He regularly buys smuggled goods. He is discreet and never a gossip. He is a freemason and a pillar of the establishment. He is the purveyor of accurate, unadorned information and not a storyteller, but as a diarist he is vastly readable because of the way in which he can get down on the page such a direct daily image of himself.

24 August 1776. Gave Michael Andrew's Harvest Men that were cutting wheat at the end of my garden a largess of   .   .   0.1.0
     They gave me three cheers for the same . . .

14 September. Very busy all day with my Barley, did not dine till near 5 in the afternoon, my Harvest Men dined here to-day, gave them some Beef and some plumb Pudding and as much liquor as they would drink. This evening finished my Harvest and all carried into the Barn – 8 acres. I had Mrs Dunnell's Cart and Horses, and 2 men, yesterday and to-day. The men were her son Thomas and Robin Buck . . .

20 January 1777. Mr du Quesne, Mr Howes and Mr Donne dined and spent the afternoon with us being my Clubb day. I gave them for dinner a couple of Rabbits smothered with onions, a Neck of Mutton boiled and a Goose rosted with a Currant Pudding and a plain one. They drank Tea in the afternoon, played a pool of Quadrille after, drank a glass or two of Punch, and went away about 8 o'clock. No Supper is a Rule. And no vails [tips] to servants, however Mr Donne gave 0.1.0 to my servant Will. The other two gave nothing. Mr Frost called on me in the afternoon, and I paid him a Bill for deals etc. 9.11.0
Gave Mrs Dunnell's Man Robin 0. 1.0
At Quadrille this evening, lost 0. 0.3

6 February. Had $\frac{1}{2}$ an Anchor of Rum brought me this evening about 10 o'clock by one Richard Andrews (the smuggler) paid him for it 1.15.0
He brought me also $\frac{1}{2}$ an Anchor of Geneva, for that paid   1. 5.0

9 February. I buried one John Greaves of East Tuddenham this afternoon at Weston – recd for burying him as he was a stranger the sum of 0.6.8 and which I gave back to his widow as she is poor and has many children . . .

14 February. To 36 children being Valentine's day and what is customary for them to go about in these parts this day gave 0.3.0 being one penny apiece to each of them.

18 March. My Servants Will and Suky went to a Puppet Show this evening at Morton and kept me up till after 1 o'clock.

23 March. I read Prayers and preached this morning at Weston. I gave notice this morning at Church that there would be Prayers on Friday night being Good Friday – there used to be none that day, which I think was very wrong.

25 March. My great Pond full of large toads, I never saw such a quantity in my life and so large, was most of the morning in killing of them, I daresay I killed one hundred, which made no shew of being missed, in the evening more again than there were, I suppose there are thousands of them there, and no froggs . . .

27 March. We took half a large basket of toads this morning out of the great Pond, put them into a kettle and poured some boiling water upon them, which killed them instantaneously. I daresay we killed 200. Harry Dunnell and my boy Jack Warton took them up in their hands alive and put them into the basket . . .

28 March. I read Prayers this morning at Weston Church at 11 o'clock. No Sermon. I had a tolerable good congregation. I did not dine to-day being Good Friday till 5 in the afternoon, and then eat only a few apple fritters and some bread and cheese.

29 March. Andrews the Smuggler brought me this night about 11 o'clock a bagg of Hyson Tea 6 Pd weight. He frightened us a little by whistling under the Parlour Window just as we were going to bed. I gave him some Geneva and paid him for the tea at 10/6 per Pd 3.3.0

21 May 1778. We all breakfasted, dined and slept again at Weston. I walked up to the White Hart with Mr Lewis and Bill to see a famous Woman in Men's Cloaths, by name Hannah

Snell,* who was 21 years as a common soldier in the Army, and not discovered by any as a woman. Cousin Lewis has mounted guard with her abroad. She went in the Army by the name of John Gray. She has a Pension from the Crown now of 18.5.0 per annum and the liberty of wearing Men's Cloaths and also a Cockade in her Hat, which she still wears. She has laid in a room with 70 Soldiers and not discovered by any of them. The forefinger of her right hand was cut off by a Sword at the taking of Pondicherry. She is now about 60 yrs of age and talks very sensibly and well, and travels the country with a Basket at her back, selling Buttons, Garters, laces etc. I took 4 Pr of 4d Buttons and gave her 0.2.6. At 10 o'clock we all went down to the River with our Nets a-fishing . . . At Lenswade Bridge we caught a Prodigious fine Pike which weighed 8 Pound and half and it had in his Belly another Pike, of above a Pound. We caught also there the finest Trout I ever saw which weighed 3 Pound and two ounces. Good Pike and Trout we also caught besides.

24 May. About 10 o'clock this evening my servant Will: came home rather intoxicated and was exceedingly impudent and saucy towards me. Said he would leave me at Midsummer or to Morrow morning etc. Will's behaviour made me very uneasy, I gave him notice that now he should go away at Midsummer . . .

13 October 1780. Mr Cary's daughter (the Widow Pratt) is we hear with child by her Servant that lived with her last year, but she pretends to say that she was ravished one night coming from her Father's by a man whom she does not know.

15 October. Will came home drunk this evening after Supper from Barnard Dunnell's at Morton and he and my head Maid had words and got to fighting. Will behaved very saucy and impudent and very bold in his talk to me. Shall give it to him to-morrow for the same . . .

---

* Hannah Snell (1723–92) had enlisted in 1745, after being deserted by her husband, a Dutch seaman. It was not till 1750 that she revealed her military adventures, a book of them being published under the title *The Female Soldier: The Surprising Adventures of Hannah Snell,* which the author of the notice of her in the D.N.B. considers much embroidered. She married a second and third time. An account of her extraordinary career will also be found in Fortescue's monumental *History of the British Army.*

16 October. I gave Will a Lecture this morning concerning last night's work.

24 October. My Squire Mr Custance called on me this morning and spent the best part of an hour with me. He talked with me about his new Tenants, Galland and Howlett, concerning Tithe, but spoke very open and ingenuous about it, and left it entirely to me respecting the same. Mrs Davie came to us this morning and dined and spent the afternoon with us ... Mrs Davie slipped off the Horse as she was getting up to go home; she did not hurt herself – I laughed much.

20 March 1781. About 12 o'clock I took a ride to Dereham and Will went with me. Got there about 2 o'clock, put up my Horses at the King's Arms kept by one Girling and there I supped and slept, had a very good Bed. Soon after I got to Dereham I walked to Mr Hall's Rooms, he lodges at a Barbers by name Field, and there I dined and spent the afternoon with him by appointment. We had for dinner a fine Lobster hot and some Mutton Stakes, had from the King's Arms. Before dinner Mr Hall and myself took a Walk about Dereham, went and saw a whimsical Building called Quebec. We dined at 3 o'clock and after we had smoked a Pipe etc., we took a ride to the House of Industry about 2 miles West of Dereham, and a very large building at present tho' there wants another Wing. About 380 Poor in it now, but they don't look either healthy or cheerful, a great Number die there, 27 have died since Christmas last. We returned from thence to the King's Arms and then we supped and spent the evening together. To Mr Hall's Clerk of Garvaston who came to give him notice of a Burial on Friday, being very poor, gave, 0.1.0.

20 August 1784. Mr and Mrs Bodham and Mrs Davy breakfasted, dined and spent the Afternoon with us till 7 in the Evening and then they went in Lenewade Bridge Chaise for Mattishall directly after Tea. We had for Dinner to-day some Beef Stakes, a large Piece of boiled Beef, a Couple of rost Chicken, Tarts &c. It rained incessantly all the Day long and very heavy. Mr Bodham and self got to Back-Gammon this Morn' about 11 o'clock and played till Dinner Time. I lost at Back-Gammon to Mr Bodham 0.0.6. I sent a Letter to Mr Francis this Evening by Cary respecting the Servants Tax.

23 August. This Morning one Sally Barber (Servant Maid at present to Mr Hewitt of Mattishall) came here to offer as a Servant in Betty's Place who is going to be married at Michaelmas – After some Conversation and being so well recommended by Mrs Hewitt, I agreed to take her and give her five Guineas Per Annum but no Tea at all – She demurred a little about the smallness of the Wages, but at last agreed, and took the Earnest Money of me, being usual here, of 0.1.0. Mr Custance sent me a Note and begged that I would dine with him on Friday next on a fine Haunch of Venison – which I promised – It is very kind in him.

27 August. Nunn Davy came here about 1 o'clock with a Note from his Mother to my Niece – Nunn stayed and dined with Nancy on beef stakes and a rost Fowl. Between 2 and 3 o'clock I walked by myself up to Weston House and there dined and spent the Afternoon with Mr Custance, Lady Bacon, a Miss Hickman and an old Maid but immensely rich, a little Boy, a Nephew of hers by name Baker – Mr Du Quesne, Mr Priest of Reepham, and a Mr Eaton a young Man and is Rector of Elsing – A neat and agreeable Man. We had for dinner some Pike, a Couple of Fowls boiled and Piggs Face, green Peas Soup and a prodigious fine and fat Haunch of Venison given by Sr John Wodehouse to Mr Custance – The second Course was a Fricasse, a Couple of Ducks rosted, green Peas, plumb Pudding, Maccaroni &c. We broke up about eight in the Evening. I was at home by nine – I walked home as I went by myself.

1 September. Mr Hardy and Boy fastened up 3 Windows with Brick for me, and having finished by Noon I sent them both into my Wheat Field to sheer Wheat with my three Men. – And they dined, &c. here. A very fine Day, than[k] God, for the Harvest. Mr Custance sent us a brace of Partridges which was very kind of him as it is the Day of Shooting.

4 September. I sent Mr Custance about 3 doz: more of Apricots, and he sent me back another large Piece of fine Parmesan Cheese – It was very kind in him. Nancy had a Letter from her Brother Sam, nothing in it. I finished carrying Wheat this morning.

26 December 1786. We breakfasted, dined, &c. &c. again at home.

To the Weston Ringgers, the annual Gift of   .   .   . 0.2.6
To my Malsters Man a Christmas Gift gave   .   .   . 0.1.0
To my Blacksmiths Son a Christmas Gift   .   .   . 0.0.6
Mr Girling, Mr Custances Steward, called here this Afternoon and paid me Mr Custances Composition for Land in hand, for Tithe the Sum of 13.12.6. Very sharp Frost indeed last Night and this Morning it froze the Water in my Bason this Morning that I wash in, quite over, in half an Hour after it had been brought up Stairs.

29 December. Had another Tub of Gin and another of the best Coniac Brandy brought me this Evening ab^t 9. We heard a thump at the front Door about that time, but did not know what it was, till I went out and found the 2 Tubs – but nobody there.*

CORNELIUS STOVIN
(1830–1921)

Farm logs and account-books are comparatively plentiful but a farmer's diary which goes far beyond the agricultural round and into the farmer's entire personal experience is a rarity. Cornelius Stovin's diary, published in 1982 by his granddaughter, has an added attraction for the rural historian because it was kept during the early 1870s, just when British agriculture was sliding into the terrible depression from which there would be no lasting recovery until Second World War subsidies and inventions brought about the 1970s boom. As well as farming over 600 acres in the Lincolnshire wolds, Stovin was a Methodist lay-reader, a family man, bookworm and philosopher. His diaries are not only illuminating on farming, but on marriage, the class system and on the special learnedness of the self-taught.

Stovin farmed Binbrook Hall, near Louth, for many years. His diary-keeping began, as with so many people of his time, with a

---

* From his friend the smuggler.

journey. There were visits to Dublin and Oxford, and they were carefully entered, every detail, in his 'Principal Teacher's Log Book'. The diary is a spasmodic one, as he made up his mind to 'unfold in a literary drama' his 'private, personal, domestic, social and public [i.e. chapel] life'. When he was old he wrote, 'There is something that makes my life and character and history of vast importance. The fact of having lived through six decades of the world's most progressive career.' He had an eye and an ear for everything, from the new town halls, which filled him with admiration, to the furnishings of rooms, the wearing of 'rational' clothes, the education of children, the sickliness of women, the drama of his chapel, the distance between himself and his men on the one hand and his landlord on the other, but most of all for the farm's work cycle, the many descriptions of which could have come out of Hardy. Stovin's thankful lyricism is counterbalanced by a hard-headed attention to farming practice and economics, and his diaries are invaluable as an authoritative source for the cruel facts of what farmers called their 'coming-down time'.

Thursday, 7 September 1871. Hands are so scarce that we have made very slow progress with harvest operations. I have still sixty acres of barley down unbound. It is in a very critical condition. The early part of yesterday was very bright and breezy and by noon they had finished binding the wheat. By the time the barley was fairly dry the clouds had gathered and the rain began to fall. I am afraid a second drenching such as continued through the night will spoil the sample. The prospect is a very anxious and dark one. The extreme luxuriance of the clover may possibly prove fatal to the corn. We need a drying apparatus this morning to save our barley crop from deterioration if not destruction. Perhaps the Almighty may send us one. He has abundance in His stores. He can change the winds and disperse the clouds and dry up the moisture as well as send it. How delightfully welcome the streaks of blue sky which I beheld this morning in looking out from my bedroom window. The barley was no sooner dry than it became saturated a second time. Would it be presumption if I urge my case before the Lord?

Saturday, 9 September. Rose this morning about 5 o'clock. I thought I heard the pattering of the rain upon my garden groves. In drawing aside the blind to my utter dismay the water was standing in a pool on the carriage drive, which indicated a heavy fall of rain for several hours. This is the third drenching for my barley. It is a mercy that it had become tolerably dry yesterday, for under the hedgerows it has already begun to sprout. This is a morning of disappointment to us farmers. Yesterday we were vigorously retrieving matters, carrying in the morning and tying in the afternoon, and the foreman and I were planning for managing most of the binding today. But all our schemes are upset by Divine Providence for some wise end. Perhaps to drive us to prayer to more humble dependence upon His Almighty power and wisdom and love. He makes us behold His severity as well as goodness. How dark and gloomy the prospect! How thick and hazy the air! How leaden the skies! Yesterday I was pulling ketlocks out of the turnips, also neadles, redrobbin and scarlet poppies. It is a proverb that weeds grow apace. Experience brings home the truth. There is not a weed now growing in my turnip fields but will come to maturity and yield its thousandfold increase many months before the turnip itself. It forms part of the curse still lingering in the ground. What a tenacious hold they have upon our soil. If we cease our vigilance they soon become predominant. A skilful and persevering hand is required to maintain empire over this department of natural laws and forces.

Thursday, 22 February 1872. The panic among the labourers is somewhat waning; though a small riot took place in Horncastle last Saturday. It originated in the pulling down of a stump orator by the police. His intention was to incite the labourers to strike. It was an indiscretion to interfere with him. The mob made use of every loose brick for the purpose of destruction. The fray ended in broken windows, etc.

I am now enclosing the gardens for Smith and Coney. My Lizzie will feel it a relief to have a little more privacy in her garden. It has always been distasteful to her seeing labourers' wives entering upon the seclusion. I am reading Froud's [Froude's] 'Short Studies'. They are studies of no mean order. He has spent his life in the study of the Elizabethan period. Some of the studies are worth half a dozen readings. There is great force and beauty in some of his paragraphs though very unripe in his opinions. He assisted me much in the thought of my address at Market Rasen last Monday night. I occupied the chair at their Missionary Meeting. The thought came with great force while I was speaking, viz. the material framework which our glorious constitution had formed for itself, this being one amongst the crowd of material transformations which the Gospel has effected and is still effecting in this beautiful land.

My Lizzie is ill in bed. She took a violent cold in returning home from Matlock last Thursday. What a life of protracted suffering to experience!

This evening I sold Mr Sawyer 7 Porket pigs, half-bred Berkshire, for £27.

Wednesday, 4 September. My shearling rams are in a fearfully crippled condition. It is painful to witness the amount of suffering the poor animals have to endure, and all on account of man's sin. No man can look sympathetically over his crambling flocks and herds writhing in the anguish of physical pain, with tongues like pieces of raw flesh and feet a mass of fevered corruption without feeling regret and remorse concerning his sins which have produced such a train of diseases through the ranks of animal life.

Friday, 6 September. The acknowledged immoral condition of the servants and the broken and disorganized relationships existing between them and masters and mistresses. Authority, human and Divine, appears to be clean set at nought. Obedience, whether to God or man, is well nigh repudiated. Both morality and religion are trampled underfoot. No kind or degree of good treatment produces corresponding industry or decent behaviour. Shrinking from work except for self is fast becoming the order of servant life. Every advantage is taken in this house of my dear wife's affliction. In her absence all manner of misconduct, extravagance, waste of time and substance, light and rude and immoral conversation, false representation of the authorities, slipping of work, uncleanness. What a rampant spirit of murmuring discontent pervades the culinary department of the house! Last night in the yard the two waggoners were lewedly singing an obscene song. I felt it my duty to hush them.

Better wages and better living and more kind treatment does not in the least change their moral dispositions. The intensity of moral corruption only luxuriates and fattens and becomes more gross in proportion to the increase of material prosperity. Luxuries are only a richer soil for sin and iniquity to grow in unless the carnal nature is destroyed by supernatural power. It is only the grace of God which can transmute our life's surroundings into subservience to purity and godliness. The salt of grace alone can stop the progress of decay. Oh, for a larger measure of this seasoning power! I would want and plead for it. Glory be to God it may be obtained in overflowing abundance!

Saturday, 8 September, 8.20 a.m. We carried the first sheaf of barley home yesterday. One or two slight showers fell during the afternoon but not to stop our proceedings.

I asked the shepherd about the rams. He thought they had the foot and mouth disease but now improving. I told him about half a dozen receipts recommended for lameness.

This morning does not indicate much influence exercised by the so-called dry change of the moon. There is no importation of corn into the rickyard at present as more rain has fallen.

Tipler's hock is so far recovered as to admit once more of the collar. Old Jack has enjoyed about a month's run but is not yet quite sound; he plants the foot of his lame hind leg more firmly. A few weeks ago it appeared well nigh useless to him. Perhaps he has done more continuous hard service than any horse upon the farm.

Memorable Wednesday, 11 September, 5.30 p.m. My dear Lizzie was confined this morning about 12.20. While I was at Louth market she gave birth to a manchild. This presentation of another son creates a new era in our domestic history. God has given him a splendid physical organization. He has laid the foundation of a grand physical manhood. He has a face wide open already, a broad back, an expanded chest, and other limbs well formed and elegantly knitted together. He is an admirable piece of Divine workmanship. I found the new immortal in a widely different place from where I left him. He was born some time before Dr Higgins arrived. The nurse said he just peeped in and felt the mother's pulse and pronounced matters all right as far as can be seen at present. It must be favourable to have a good pulse under such circumstances.

We have been kept in suspense some weeks. He has received a kindly welcome from his parents, brother and sister, and general pleasure seems to prevail upon the first introduction. His visit into this world will constitute the present year the most memorable since Denison and Mabel were born.

THOMAS HARDY
(1840–1928)

In 1917 Hardy and his second wife Florence began the extraordinary literary deception of producing between them a 'biography' which would silence for ever what he believed was an excessive interest in his origins and personal life. Called *The Early Life of Thomas Hardy, 1840–1891,* the title-page declared that it was 'compiled from contemporary notes, letters, diaries, and biographical memoranda, as well as from oral information in conversations extending over many years by Florence Emily Hardy'. It was in fact written by Hardy himself in the third person, each page being typed by his wife as it was handed from his table to hers; then both his manuscript and the diaries, letters, etc., used to produce it were destroyed. Thus he hoped to both block the avalanche of biographical inquiry which would descend after his death and leave behind him a suitably dignified background for one of the country's greatest novelists and poets. For today's reader such a deception will seem not so much immoral as pathetic and bewildering. But today isn't yesterday. Only Hardy's stories can convey the full pain and implacability of class in nineteenth-century village England. It must also be remembered that Hardy was making the most of his possible ancestors at a time when completely bogus family trees were being run up for the rich manufacturers and tradesmen whose names increasingly appeared in the Honours List. Hardy had also to deal with his slight formal education, not to mention the wounds inflicted on him by his first wife Emma when their marriage went wrong in the 1890s. She was a lady and she increasingly harped on his not being a gentleman. It was vulgar and cruel, and her diary, found and read by him on the day after her death, was so full of violence towards him on this score that he at once burnt it.

The strangest thing to us is Hardy's inability or refusal to recognize that his autobiography was already in full existence in his work. But he is not alone in dreading and hating biography. Amidst all the stuffy subterfuge his diary fragments – his true first-person statements made long before – sparkle like rain on leaves.

28 June 1877. Being Coronation Day there are games and dancing on the green at Sturminster Newton. The stewards with white rosettes. One is very anxious, fearing that while he is attending to the runners the leg of mutton on the pole will go wrong; hence he walks hither and thither with a compressed countenance and eyes far ahead.

The pretty girls, just before a dance, stand in inviting positions on the grass. As the couples in each figure pass near where their immediate friends loiter, each girl-partner gives a laughing glance at such friends, and whirls on.

29 June. Have just passed through a painful night and morning. Our servant, whom we liked very much, was given a holiday yesterday to go to Bournemouth with her young man. Came home last night at ten, seeming oppressed. At about half-past twelve, when we were supposed to be asleep, she crept downstairs, went out, and on looking from the back window of our bedroom I saw her come home from the outhouse with a man. She appeared to have only her night-gown on and something round her shoulders. Beside her slight white figure in the moonlight his form looked dark and gigantic. She preceded him to the door. Before I had thought what to do E. had run downstairs, and met her, and ordered her to bed. The man disappeared. Found that the bolts of the back-door had been oiled. He had evidently often stayed in the house.

She remained quiet till between four and five, when she got out of the dining-room window and vanished.

30 June. About one o'clock went to her father's cottage in the village, where we thought she had gone. Found them poorer than I expected (for they are said to be an old county family). Her father was in the field haymaking, and a little girl fetched him from the haymakers. He came across to me amid the windrows of hay, and seemed to read bad news in my face. She had not been home. I remembered that she had dressed up in her best clothes, and she probably has gone to Stalbridge to her lover.

4 July. Went to Stalbridge. Mrs— is a charming woman. When we were looking over the church she recommended me to try a curious seat, adding, though we were only talking about the church itself, 'That's where I sat when Jamie was christened, and I could see him very well.' Another seat she pointed out with assumed casualness as being the one where she sat when she was churched; as if it were rather interesting that she did sit in those places, in spite of her not being a romantic person. When we arrived at her house she told us that Jamie really could not be seen – he was in a dreadful state – covered with hay; half laughing and catching our eyes while she spoke, as if we should know at once how intensely humorous he must appear under those circumstances. Jamie was evidently her life, and flesh, and raiment ... Her husband is what we call a 'yopping, or yapping man'. He strains his countenance hard in smiling, and keeps it so for a distinct length of time, so that you may on no account whatever miss his smile and the point of the words that gave rise to it. Picks up pictures and china for eighteen-pence worth ever so much more. Gives cottagers a new set of tea-cups with handles for old ones without handles – an exchange which they are delighted to make.

Country life at Sturminster. Vegetables pass from growing to boiling, fruit from the bushes to the pudding, without a moment's halt, and the gooseberries that were ripening on the twigs at noon are in the tart an hour later.

13 July. The sudden disappointment of a hope leaves a scar which the ultimate fulfilment of that hope never entirely removes.

27 July. James Bushrod of Broadmayne saw the two German soldiers [of the York Hussars] shot [for desertion] on Bincombe Down in 1801. It was in the path across the Down, or near it. James Selby of the same village thinks there is a mark. [The tragedy was used in *The Melancholy Hussar,* the real names of the deserters being given.]

13 August. We hear that Jane, our late servant, is soon to have a baby. Yet never a sign of one is there for us.

25 September. Went to Shroton Fair. In a twopenny show saw a woman beheaded. In another a man whose hair grew on one side of his face. Coming back across Hambledon Hill (where the Club-Men assembled, temp. Cromwell) a fog came on. I nearly got lost in the dark inside the earthworks, the old hump-backed man I had parted from on the other side of the hill, who was going somewhere else before coming across the earthworks in my direction, being at the bottom as soon as I. A man might go round and round all night in such a place.

28 September. An object or mark raised or made by man on a scene is worth ten times any such formed by unconscious Nature. Hence clouds, mists, and mountains are unimportant beside the wear on a threshold, or the print of a hand.

7 February 1878. Father says that when there was a hanging at Dorchester in his boyhood it was carried out at one o'clock, it being the custom to wait till the mailcoach came in from London in case of a reprieve.

He says that at Puddletown Church, at the time of the old west-gallery violin, oboe, and clarinet players, Tom Sherren (one of them) used to copy tunes during the sermon. So did my grandfather at Stinsford Church. Old Squibb the parish-clerk used also to stay up late at night helping my grandfather in his 'prick-noting', (as he called it).

He says that William, son of Mr S— the Rector of W—, became a miller at O— Mill, and married a German woman whom he met at Puddletown Fair playing her tambourine. When her husband was gone to market she used to call in John Porter, who could play the fiddle, and lived near, and give him some gin, when she would beat the tambourine to his playing. She was a good-natured woman with blue eyes, brown hair, and a round face; rather slovenly. Her husband was a hot, hasty fellow, though you could hear by his speech that he was a better educated man than ordinary millers.

G.R.— (who is a humorist) showed me his fowl-house, which was built of old church-materials bought at Wellspring the builder's sale. R.'s chickens roost under the gilt-lettered Lord's Prayer and Creed, and the cock crows and flaps his wings against the Ten Commandments. It reminded me that I had seen these same Ten Commandments, Lord's Prayer, and Creed, before, forming the sides of the stone-mason's shed in that same builder's yard, and that he had remarked casually that they did not prevent the workmen 'cussing and damning' the same as ever. It also reminded me of seeing the old font of — Church, Dorchester, in a garden, used as a flower-vase, the initials of ancient godparents and Churchwardens still legible upon it. A comic business – church restoration.

A villager says of the parson, who has been asked to pray for a sick person: 'His prayers wouldn't save a mouse.'

12 February. Sketched the English Channel from Mayne Down.

I am told that when Jack Ketch had done whipping by the Town Pump [Dorchester] the prisoners' coats were thrown over their bleeding backs, and, guarded by the town constables with their long staves, they were conducted back to prison. Close at their heels came J.K., the cats held erect – there was one cat to each man – the lashes were of knotted whipcord.

Also that in a village near Yeovil about 100 years ago, there lived a dumb woman, well known to my informant's mother. One day the woman suddenly spoke and said:

> 'A cold winter, a forward spring,
> A bloody summer, a dead King';

She then dropped dead. The French Revolution followed immediately after.

8 July. A service at St Mary Abbots, Kensington. The red plumes and ribbon in two stylish girls' hats in the foreground match the red robes of the persons round Christ on the Cross in the east window. The pale crucified figure rises up from a parterre of London bonnets and artificial hair-coils, as viewed from the back where I am. The sky over Jerusalem seems to have some connection with the corn-flowers in a fashionable hat that bobs about in front of the city of David ... When the congregation rises there is a rustling of silks like that of the Devils' wings in Paradise Lost. Every woman then, even if she had forgotten it before, has a single thought to the folds of her clothes. They pray in the litany as if under enchantment. Their real life is spinning on beneath this apparent one of calm, like the District Railway-trains underground just by – throbbing, rushing, hot, concerned with next week, last week ... Could these true scenes in which this congregation is living be brought into church bodily with the personages, there would be a churchful of jostling phantasmagorias crowded like a heap of soap bubbles, infinitely intersecting, but each seeing only his own. That bald-headed man is surrounded by the interior of the Stock Exchange; that girl by the jeweller's shop in which she purchased yesterday. Through this bizarre world of thought circulates the recitative of the parson – a thin solitary note without cadence or change of intensity – and getting lost like a bee in the clerestory.

THE REV. FRANCIS KILVERT
(1840–79)

Born in the same year as Thomas Hardy, the son of a Wiltshire rector, Francis Kilvert takes us into the world of rural Anglicanism, with all its fulfilment and complexity, as does no other writer. His career took him to the Welsh border, to St Harmon, Bredwardine and Clyro, the villages of Radnorshire and Herefordshire which he immortalized. His life was brief but rich and heavy with a kind of sensuous innocence, like a rose. He was a bachelor until he was thirty-nine, when he married a girl from near Woodstock. Death from peritonitis followed within a month. Elizabeth Kilvert found the diaries, saw the account of their relationship (it is presumed), and the destruction began. But many years were to pass before an aged niece inherited twenty-two volumes of the diaries, read (presumably) about the girls, and burnt most of them. Three notebooks survive, and these – perfectly edited by the poet and novelist William Plomer – were published in succession from 1938 to 1940, to become one of the most loved and understood of diaries.

Photographs reveal Kilvert as a tall, strong-looking, glossy-haired young man who was far from the popular notion of the Victorian curate as guyed in *Punch* or depicted in fiction. 'Why do I keep this voluminous journal?' he asked himself. 'I can hardly tell. Partly because life appears to me such a curious and wonderful thing that it almost seems a pity that even such a humble and uneventful life as mine should pass altogether away without some such record as this, and partly because I think the record may amuse and interest some who come after me.' So there was nothing furtive about the way he wrote of girls and desire, nothing he minded posterity knowing. Like many Victorians of his class, he had had virtually no experience of sexual innocence. His father had run the prep school attended by Augustus Hare, whose astounding account of what happened in it is to be found in *The Story of My Life*. The beatings by Mr Kilvert, Hare's rape by the boys on his first night ('At nine years old, I was compelled to eat Eve's apple quite up – indeed, the Tree of Knowledge of Good and Evil was stripped absolutely bare; there was no fruit left to gather') and what Francis Kilvert himself witnessed there throw a disconcerting light on the exquisite Christian background of the diary itself. William Plomer believed that 'certain peculiarities' of his character derived from what he had seen at Hardenhuish rectory school.

Yet a balance is struck. Kilvert and girls become a natural part of Kilvert and the poor, of provincial society with its dances and dinners, of local church functions, of the ministry, of Kilvert and the local landscape. The only writer who can equal him on the realities of the countryside is Hardy himself. Kilvert is not a puritan. He is a young man without a lover living in a world socially divided between the 'gentle' and the 'simple', with all its ancient rites and customs still intact, and his beautiful diary admits the reader to the languorous, dutiful, mid-Victorian afternoon. It was written as a gesture against oblivion and as an outlet for his emotions. It was begun in 1870 and ended abruptly in March 1879, the same month in which he published a poem on the Clyro shepherd's little son whom he had buried the previous Christmas

Day. In the poem Kilvert makes the boy request Clyro Water – the village stream – to be his remembrancer. The diarist himself is one of rural England's purest remembrancers.

Saturday, 22 July 1871. Within the cottage sat old Richard Clark and the pretty girl lately Edward Morgan's concubine, now happily his wife. I had thought Edward Morgan had a comfortless, miserable home. I was never more mistaken or surprised. The cottage was exquisitely clean and neat, with a bright blue cheerful paper and almost prettily furnished. A vase of bright fresh flowers stood upon each table and I could have eaten my dinner off every stone of the floor. The girl said no one ever came near the house to see it, and she kept it as clean and neat and pretty as she could for her own satisfaction. The oven door was screened from view by a little curtain and everything was made the most and best of. I don't wonder Edward Morgan married the girl. It was not her fault that they were not married before. She begged and prayed her lover to marry her before he seduced her and afterwards. She was very staunch and faithful to him when she was his mistress and I believe she will make him a good wife. She was ironing when I came in and when I began to read to old Clark she took her work and sat down quietly to sew. When I had done reading she had me into the garden and shewed me her flowers with which she had taken some pains for she was very fond of them. No one ever came to see her garden or her flowers she said. The only people she ever saw passing were the people from the farm (the Upper Bettws where her husband works). They come on Market days along the footpath through the field before the house. The girl spoke quietly and rather mournfully and there was a shade of gentle melancholy in her voice and manner. I was deeply touched by all that I saw and heard. With a kind carefulness she put me into the footpath to the Upper Bettws farm, which passes by the solitary barn and over the lofty bridge across the brook and deep dingle. Miss Allen was at home and kindly brought me some cider. Sitting in the window seat she told me of the almost sudden death after three days' illness of the daughter of Mrs Davies of the Pentre aged 17 – inflammation of the bowels. I went on up to Pentwyn Forge and had a long chat

The Penguin Book of Diaries

with Mrs Nott the blacksmith's wife. She told me her next door neighbour Mrs Williams was 'a wicked woman' and prostituted herself to her lodgers, while her husband as bad as herself took the money and asked no questions.

Mrs Nott told me that Louie of the Cloggau was staying in Presteign with her aunt Miss Sylvester, the woman frog. This extraordinary being is partly a woman and partly a frog. Her head and face, her eyes and mouth are those of a frog, and she has a frog's legs and feet. She cannot walk but she hops. She wears very long dresses to cover and conceal her feet which are shod with something like a cow's hoof. She never goes out except to the Primitive Methodist Chapel. Mrs Nott said she had seen this person's frog feet and had seen her in Presteign hopping to and from the Chapel exactly like a frog. She had never seen her hands. She is a very good person. The story about this unfortunate being is as follows. Shortly before she was born a woman came begging to her mother's door with two or three little children. Her mother was angry and ordered the woman away. 'Get away with your young frogs,' she said. And the child she was expecting was born partly in the form of a frog, as a punishment and a curse upon her.

Sunday, 23 July. This morning Mr Bevan went up to the Volunteer Camp above Talgarth, on the high common under the Black Mountain. He is Chaplain to the Forces and attended to hold an open air service and preach a sermon to the Volunteers. When the Chaplain arrived on the Common, the Builth Volunteers were already well drunk. They were dismissed from the ranks but they fought about the common during the whole service. The officers and the other corps were bitterly ashamed and scandalized.

Thursday, 27 July. In the afternoon I took the old soldier the first instalment of his pension, £8 0 4 for half a year. Mr Venables has got the pension for him at last after a long correspondence with the War Office. The old soldier told me some of his reminiscences. In the Battle of Vittoria as they were rushing into action his front rank man, a big burly fellow, was swearing that 'There wasn't a bloody Frenchman who had seen the bullet yet which should strike him'.

Monday, 17 June 1872. Went to Bockleton Vicarage.

Wednesday, 19 June. Left Bockleton Vicarage for Liverpool. At

92

Wrexham two merry saucy Irish hawking girls got into our carriage. The younger had a handsome saucy daring face showing splendid white teeth when she laughed and beautiful Irish eyes of dark grey which looked sometimes black and sometimes blue, with long silky black lashes and finely pencilled black eyebrows. The girl kept her companion and the whole carriage laughing from Wrexham to Chester with her merriment, laughter and songs and her antics with a doll dressed like a boy, which she made dance in the air by pulling a string. She had a magnificent voice and sung to a comic popular air while the doll danced wildly,

> 'A-dressed in his Dolly Varden,
> A-dressed in his Dolly Varden,
> He looks so neat
> And he smells so sweet,
> A-dressed in his Dolly Varden.'

Then breaking down into merry laughter she hid her face and glanced roguishly at me from behind the doll. Suddenly she became quiet and pensive and her face grew grave and sad as she sang a love song.

The two girls left the carriage at Chester and as she passed the younger put out her hand and shook hands with me. They stood by the carriage door on the platform for a few moments and Irish Mary, the younger girl, asked me to buy some nuts. I gave her sixpence and took a dozen nuts out of a full measure she was going to pour into my hands. She seemed surprised and looked up with a smile. 'You'll come and see me,' she said coaxingly. 'You are not Welsh, are you?' 'No, we are a mixture of Irish and English.' 'Born in Ireland?' 'No, I was born at Huddersfield in Yorkshire.' 'You look Irish – you have the Irish eye.' She laughed and blushed and hid her face. 'What do you think I am?' asked the elder girl, 'do you think I am Spanish?' 'No,' interrupted the other laughing, 'you have too much Irish between your eyes.' 'My eyes are blue,' said the elder girl, 'your eyes are grey, the gentleman's eyes are black.' 'Where did you get in?' I asked Irish Mary. 'At Wrexham,' she said. 'We were caught in the rain, walked a long way in it and got wet through,' said the poor girl pointing to a bundle of wet clothes they were carrying and which they had changed for dry ones. 'What do you do?' 'We go out hawking,' said the girl in a low voice. 'You have a beautiful voice.' 'Hasn't she?' interrupted the elder girl eagerly and delightedly. 'Where did you learn to sing?' She smiled and blushed and hid her face. A porter and some other people were looking wonderingly on, so I thought it best to end the conversation. But there was an attractive power about this poor Irish girl that fascinated me strangely. I felt irresistibly drawn to her. The singular beauty of her eyes, a beauty of deep sadness, a wistful sorrowful imploring look, her swift rich humour, her sudden gravity and sadnesses, her brilliant laughter, a certain intensity and power and richness of life and the extraordinary sweetness, softness and beauty of her voice in singing and talking gave her a power over me which I could not understand nor describe, but the power of a stronger over a weaker will and nature. She lingered about the carriage door. Her look grew more wistful, beautiful, imploring. Our eyes met again and again. Her eyes grew more and more beautiful. My eyes were fixed and riveted on hers. A few minutes more and I know not what might have happened. A wild reckless feeling came over me. Shall I leave all and follow her? No – Yes – No. At that moment the train moved on. She was left behind. Goodbye, sweet Irish Mary. So we parted. Shall we meet again? Yes – No – Yes.

Monday, 14 October. Last night I had a strange and horrible dream. It was one of those curious things, a dream within a dream, like a picture within a picture. I dreamt that I dreamt that Mr and Mrs Venables tried to murder me. We were all together in a small room and they were both trying to poison me, but I was aware of their intention and baffled them repeatedly. At length, Mr Venables put me off my guard, came round fondling me, and suddenly clapping his hand on my neck behind said, 'It's of no use, Mr Kilvert. You're done for.' I felt the poison beginning to work and burn in my neck. I knew it was all over and started up in fury and despair. I flew at him savagely. The scene suddenly changed to the organ loft in Hardenhuish Church. Mr Venables, seeing me coming at him, burst out the door. Close outside the door was standing the Holy Ghost. He knocked him from the top to the bottom of the stairs, rolling over head over heels, rushed downstairs himself, mounted his horse and fled away, I after him.

This dream within a dream excited me to such a state of fury, that in the outer dream I determined to murder Mr Venables. Accordingly I lay in wait for him with a pickaxe on the Vicarage lawn at Clyro, hewed an immense and hideous hole through his head, and kicked his face till it was so horribly mutilated, crushed and disfigured as to be past recognition. Then the spirit of the dream changed. Mrs Venables became her old natural self again. 'Wasn't it enough,' she said, looking at me reproachfully, 'that you should have hewed that hole through his head, but you must go and kick his face so that I don't know him again?' At this moment, Mr Bevan, the Vicar of Hay, came in, 'Well,' he said to me, 'you *have* done it now. You have made a pretty mess of it.'

All this time I was going about visiting the sick at Clyro and preaching in Clyro Church. But I saw that people were beginning to look shy at me and suspect me of the murder which had just been discovered. I became so wretched and conscience-stricken that I could bear my remorse no longer in secret and I went to give myself up to a policeman, who immediately took me to prison where I was kept in chains. Then the full misery of my position burst upon me and the ruin and disgrace I had brought on my family. 'It will kill my father,' I cried in an agony of remorse and despair.

I knew it was no dream. This at last was a reality from which I should never awake. I had awaked from many evil dreams and horrors and found them unreal, but this was a reality and horror from which I should never awake. It was all true at last. I had committed a murder. I calculated the time. I knew the Autumn Assizes were over and I could not be tried till the Spring. 'The Assizes,' I said, 'will come on in March and I shall be hung early in April.' And at the words I saw Mrs Venables give a shudder of horror.

When I woke I was so persuaded of the reality of what I had seen and felt and done in my dreams that I felt for the handcuffs on my wrists and could not believe I was in bed at home till I heard the old clock on the stairs warn and then strike five.

Wednesday, 16 July 1873. As I walked along the field path I stopped to listen to the rustle and solemn night whisper of the wheat, so different to its voice by day. The corn seemed to be praising God and whispering its evening prayer. Across the great level meads near Chippenham came the martial music of a drum and fife band, and laughing voices of unseen girls were wafted from farms and hayfields out of the wide dusk.

Monday, 21 July. A splendid summer's day, burning hot, sitting under the linden reading *Memorials of a Quiet Life,* Augustus Hare's book. As I sat there my mind went through a fierce struggle. Right or wrong? The right conquered, the sin was repented and put away and the rustle of the wind and the melodious murmurs of innumerable bees in the hives overhead suddenly seemed to me to take the sound of distant music, organs. And I thought I heard the harps of the angels rejoicing in heaven over a sinner that had repented. Then I thought I saw an angel in an azure robe coming towards me across the lawn, but it was only the blue sky through the feathering branches of the lime.

Tuesday, 22 July. To-day the heat was excessive and as I sat reading under the lime I pitied the poor haymakers toiling in the burning Common where it seemed to be raining fire.

Wednesday, 23 July. Came to Hawkchurch for three days. A pleasant and lovely journey with the air cleared and cooled by the storm. Uncle Will met me at Axminster Station with Polly and the dog cart.

After tea Dora and I went up the high field in front of the cottage to look for mushrooms and glow worms in the dusk.

Thursday, 24 July. This morning Uncle Will, Dora and I drove to Seaton with Polly and the dog cart. It was a lovely morning. At Seaton while Dora was sitting on the beach I had a bathe. A boy brought me to the machine door two towels as I thought, but when I came out of the water and began to use them I found that one of the rags he had given me was a pair of very short red and white striped drawers to cover my nakedness. Unaccustomed to such things and customs I had in my ignorance bathed naked and set at nought the conventionalities of the place and scandalized the beach. However some little boys who were looking on at the rude naked man appeared to be much interested in the spectacle, and the young ladies who were strolling near seemed to have no objection.

5. THE DIARIST AS NATURALIST

Few diarists are not to some degree naturalists if we allow for the inescapable mentions of climate, views, creatures and seasons. Liturgies, household-books and country calendars by such writers as Edmund Spenser, John Clare, Thomas Tusser and Flora Thompson, games, food, clothes and human habits generally, all reveal the close impacting of thought and action with the natural cycle of the year. Whatever the diarist's occupation – farming, travelling, running the parish or the state, or authorship itself – and whether the diarist is a rake or a saint, a clever woman or a simple soldier, the environment has to get some kind of mention, if it is only 'Wet day'. Daily weather readings feature large in British diaries, flatly stated though most of them are. It is as though the writer's movements or moods can only be fairly assessed when seen in the context of storm, sun or ice. A devotion to weather is *de rigueur* in this country and its ceaseless variants have to be recorded. Until recently it was thought proper for all such 'community diaries' as the service register in the church and the school log to carry a running meteorological report, and as far as the individual diary is concerned there are still few more effective ways of breaking down a time barrier than by the simple words which suddenly bring the May sunshine of 1662 flooding across the page, or which stun the reader with the leadenness of a February afternoon in 1904.

Some diarists who did not regard themselves as naturalists 'painted' in language what they observed and felt in order to preserve the intensity of the particular moment when they and nature shared the earth and were one with it. Gerard Manley

Hopkins would write single-word entries like 'Fine', 'Beautiful,' 'Dull', etc., for days, then suddenly plunge into whatever was closest to hand. Here he is at Finchley in the summer of 1866.

11 July. Dull and shallow sunlight. Saw an olive-coloured snake on hedge of Finchley wood and just before its slough in the road – or at all events a slough. Oats: hoary blue-green sheaths and stalks, prettily shadow-stroked spikes of pale green grain. Oaks: the organization of this tree is difficult. Speaking generally no doubt the determining planes are concentric, a system of brief contiguous and continuous tangents, whereas those of the cedar would roughly be called horizontals and those of the beech radiating but modified by droop and by a screw-set towards jutting points. But beyond this since the growth of the normal boughs is radiating and the leaves grow some way in there is of course a system of spoke-wise clubs of green – sleeve-pieces. And since the end shoots curl and carry young and scanty leaf-stars these clubs are tapered, and I have seen also the pieces in profile with chiselled outlines, the blocks thus made detached and lessening towards the end. However the star knot is the thing: it is whorled, worked round, a little and this is what keeps up the illusion of the tree: the leaves are rounded inwards and figure out ball-knots. Oaks differ much, and much turns on the broadness of the leaf, the narrower giving the crisped and starry and Catherine-wheel forms, the broader the flat-pieced mailed or shard-covered ones, in which it is possible to see composition in dips, etc. on wider bases than the single knot or cluster. But I shall study them further. See the 19th. [Where 'I have now found the law of the oak leaves.']

Then there are those diarists who regard themselves as naturalists but whose journals penetrate their own souls, young men like Barbellion and Richard Jefferies whose knowledge of the plants and fields painfully emphasizes the brevity of their beloved association with them. It made Barbellion bitter and Jefferies mystical. The latter filled up notebooks as he wandered through Sussex and Wiltshire, often adding small pencil drawings, and it was from these walk-diaries that he constructed both the philosophical and scientific backgrounds to his essays and stories. The following is taken from his out-of-doors notebook for the summer of 1879:

31st July. Some rain early morning. Hot fine evening. Sedge in pond.

1st August. Rain in night: some early morning; fine hot day. Burdock in flower (thistle-like). Thistles in flower in barley so thick as to give it a purple tint over two or three acres.

2nd August. Fine morning. Afternoon cloudy, N.E. wind strong and cool. Night at eleven lightning, continuous came up from N.W. Moonlight brilliant – violet lightning – hailstones, a little larger than a shilling – see roses in the garden and the water glancing in the flashes – thunder louder after storm passed as if blown back by N.E. wind. Lightning long flashes quivering several seconds.

3rd August. Morning dull, hot. Thrushes and blackbirds do not sing: but did up to within a day or two. Willow wren singing zit-zit – yellow hammer very much – greenfinch too.

4th August. Rain early morning: hot fine day.

5th August. Cloudy: evening heavy rain. A little while since plantain flowered in wet ditch.

6th August. Fine morning; showers later. Lightning, heavy thunder. At 4 exceedingly heavy rain. Fog came on early afternoon – rooks stopped in copse instead of going home to wood – not done it for fifty years – could not find way.

7th. Cloudy morning: afternoon light showers. Bunch of sod apple in bloom . . . Rooks fond of maize, Rooks nest in tall Scotch firs: also spruce very high. Bramble still in flower very much: plane trees leaves already brown leathery in spots – wood pigeons calling? spring and autumn not summer: sparrows in oats, scores, on stalk below grain still green, out for grain.

8th August. Small rain morning: afterwards dry. Barley – thistles rise from roots, not seed: a spindle root. Yesterday saw a small dragonfly: either first or else rare. Swifts still here and screaming.

11th August. Cloudy misty morning: Farmer market morning waiting at stile till another came along with trap, for ride. A large green dragonfly: it is their season then. Last full moon was very high in the sky: near zenith.

There is nowhere where you can put £100 and be certain of getting it back again – no deposit (consuls pay 90 and receive 94) – nothing like the earth after all.

12th August. Fine hot N.E. wind. Grasshoppers singing in grass.
15th August. Hot cloudy morning – fine despite clouds. Drovers come in, ask for hard biscuits, and toast at the fire: then take tallow candle from table and drop grease from it on biscuit till it would not suck up any more – and eat it as very good: as special relish after 2 days' drinking.

In *The Story of My Heart*, the spiritual autobiography which Jefferies began to formulate when he was only eighteen, his usual diary notes were to prove a handicap. But a few lines written while he was visiting Pevensey Castle helped him to start his 'real record – unsparing to myself as to all things – absolutely and unflinchingly true'.

Henry David Thoreau opens his immense journal of over two million words with questions from his early mentor, Ralph Emerson: 'What are you doing now? Do you keep a journal?' Under which Thoreau writes, 'So I make my first entry today.' The year was 1837. Gradually, right up until his death at the age of forty-five, the journal kept pace with the American naturalist's spiritual development and eventually became, as its editor Robert Sattelmeyer says, 'the major document of his imaginative life'. Thoreau's journal is not merely a source-book for *Walden* and *A Week on the Concord and Merrimack Rivers*, but a third masterpiece. Thoreau was a happy, witty hermit – 'Some circumstantial evidence is very strong, as when you find a trout in the milk.' His journal is timely stuff for the late twentieth century and its preoccupations. It brings our materialism up close to the wilds to prove how much better they are for us. 'Our life is frittered away by detail . . . Simplify, simplify,' he wrote in *Where I Lived, and What I Lived For*.

Naturalist journals of all kinds were to proliferate throughout the nineteenth century and were to include Sir Charles Bunbury's *Botanical Diaries, 1834–1885*, Sir Charles Lyell's mainly geological journals, and T. H. Huxley's *Diary of the Voyage of H.M.S. Rattlesnake* during the four cruises he made in the South Pacific and in the waters round Australia. Such published diaries influenced world travellers or simply Home Counties explorers to record plants, minerals, climate, etc. with scientific accuracy. Gilbert

White's *Journals* and Charles Darwin's *Journal of Researches into the Geology and Natural History of the Countries Visited by H.M.S. Beagle* are the classics of this genre.

THE REV. GILBERT WHITE
(1720–93)

White began his journal-keeping when he was fifteen but it wasn't until he was thirty that he began to create the first of his formal journals, *The Garden Kalendar*. This was by no means confined to gardening, for into it crept, ran and flew all the living things of Selborne, including most of its human population. Everything is noted with that odd mixture of artistry, taste and scientific precision which makes him unique among naturalist-diarists. In 1767 a friend of his brother Benjamin, the Fleet Street bookseller, sent White a beautiful diary which was set out in divisions for recording rainfall, temperature, etc. There was a page for each week and a wide right-hand column for 'Miscellaneous Observations and Memorandums'. This journal was the invention of the Hon. Daines Barrington, who gave it to White, having heard of his strict recording habits. But soon White found the ruling of this diary far too inhibiting and his writing burst from its limits into additional pages, borders and end-papers; before long he was writing across the prim spacings in his need to say far more than they somewhat mechanically required. Many other naturalists were filling up such forms at the time, and producing useful records, but great diarists and daily form-fillers are opposites, and one of the delights of White for the reader is to see him inevitably spreading himself, to observe him bursting the banks.

His biographer Richard Mabey says of the enigmatic and perennially agreeable White that

    ... it is possible to read the journals as a simple historical record of natural events, and spanning forty years without a break ... yet it is the lucidity and resonance of the best of the entries that are his most important legacy. Stripping away pastoral allusions, adjectival excess, self-examination, searches for meaning, he distilled a form of spare, literary miniature which had an immediacy not seen in this kind of English prose before ... Yet it is doubtful if White saw his journals as 'writing' in any literary sense. For him, I think, they were his intellectual ledger, where he took stock of his understanding of the physical world. They always have this probing, investigative sense about them that lifts them beyond merely passive records: 'Thatched roofs smoke in the sun; when this appearance happens rain seldom ensues that day. This morning they sent up vast volumes of reek' (14 November 1777). The tone and structure of this note aren't really those of a casual diary entry. The details are too carefully selected and ordered, as if they were part of the answer to a larger, half-formed question.

Seeded in the journal is much of *The Natural History of Selborne*. The journal itself lay dormant until 1931, when it was edited and published by Walter Johnson.

21 June 1783. The late ten dripping days have done infinite service to the grass, & spring-corn.

22 June. Corn-flags, fraxinella, martagons, pinks, & dark-leaved orange-lilies begin to blow. Bees swarm. Cherries look finely, but are not yet highly ripened.

23 June. Vast honey-dew; hot & hazey; misty. The blades of wheat in several fields are turned yellow, & look as if scorched with the frost. Wheat comes into ear. Red even: thro' the haze. Sheep are shorn.

24 June. Vast dew, sun, sultry, misty & hot. This is the weather that men think is injurious to hops ... The sun 'shorn of his beams' appears thro' the haze like the full moon.

25th June. Turned the swarths, but did not ted [scatter for drying] the hay. Much honey-dew on the honey-suckles, laurels, great oak.

26 June. Tedded the hay, & put it in small cock. Sun looks all day like the moon, & sheds a rusty light. M^r & Mrs Brown, & niece Anne Barker came from the county of Rutland.

27 June. Nose-flies, & stouts [either gad-flies or gnats] make the horses very troublesome.

28 June. Ricked the hay of the great meadow in lovely order: six jobbs. The little meadow is hardly made. The country people look with a kind of superstitious awe at the red louring aspect of the sun thro' the fog . . . 'Cum caput obscurā nitidum ferrugine texit.' *

29 June. My garden is in high beauty, glowing with a variety of solstitial flowers. A person lately found a young cuckow in a small nest built in a beechen shrub at the upper end of the bostal. By watching in a morning, he soon saw the young bird fed by a pair of hedge-sparrows. The cuckow is but half-fledge; yet the nest will hardly contain him: for his wings hang out, & his tail & body are much compressed, & streightened. When looked at he opens a very red, wide mouth, & heaves himself up, using contorsions with his neck by way of menace, & picking at a person's finger, if he advances it towards him.

1 July. Thatched the hay-rick. M^r & Mrs Brown & Niece Anne Barker left me.

1 & 2 July. Tremendous thunder-storms in Oxford-shire & Cambridge-shire!

2–3 July. [Bramshot place]. The foliage on most trees this year is bad. Vast damage this day by lightening in many counties!! Great thunder-shower at Lymington, & in the New forest, & in Wilts, & Dorset, & at Birmingham, & Edinburg.

3 July. Mr Richardson's garden abounds with fruit, which ripens a fortnight before mine. His kitchen-crops are good, tho' the soil is so light & sandy. Sandy soil much better for garden-crops than chalky.

11 July. The heat overcomes the grass-mowers & makes them sick.

---

* '. . . when he covered his shining head with dusky gloom'. (Virgil, *Georgics*, I).

There was not rain enough in the village to lay the dust. The water in my well rises! tho' we draw so much daily! watered much. No dew, sun, & hase, rusty sunshine! The tempest on friday night did much damage at West-meon, & burnt down three houses & a barn. The tempests round on thursday & friday nights were very aweful! There was vast hail on friday night in several places. Some of the standard-honey-suckles, which a month ago were so sweet & lovely, are now loathsome objects, being covered with aphides, & viscous honey-dews. Gardens sadly burnt.

13 July. Five great white sea-gulls flew over the village toward the forest.

14 July. When the owl comes-out of an evening the swifts pursue her, but not with any vehemence.

15 July. No rain since June 20th at this place; tho' vast showers have fallen round us, & near us.

17 July. The jasmine, now covered with bloom, is very beautiful. The jasmine is so sweet that I am obliged to quit my chamber.

19 July. Men talk that some fields of wheat are blighted: in general the crop looks well. Barley looks finely, & oats & pease are very well: Hops grow worse, & worse.

21 July. Lapwings flock. Lark-spur figures . . .

31 July. The after-grass in the great meadow burns. The sheep-down burns & is rusty. Much water in the pond on the hill! This morning Will Tanner shot, off the tall meris-trees in the great mead, 17 young black-birds. The cherries of these trees amuse the birds & save the garden-fruit.

1 August. Much smut in some fields of wheat. Goody Hampton left the garden to go gleaning. Barley cut about the forest-side. We shot in all about 30 black-birds. Vast shooting star from E. to N. My nephew Sam: Barker came from Rutland thro' London by the coaches.

2 August. Burning sun. Workmen complain of the heat.

3 August. My white pippins come-in for kitchen uses. The aphides, of various species, that make many trees & plants appear loathsome, have served their generation, & are gone, no more to be seen this year: perhaps all are dead. Thistle-down flies . . .

18 August. The *Colchicum*, or autumnal crocus blows. On the evening of this day, at about a quarter after nine o' the clock, a luminous meteor of extraordinary bulk, & shape was seen traversing the sky from N.W. to S.E. It was observed at Edinburg, & several other E^{rn} parts of this Island. No accounts of it, that I have seen, have been published from any of the western counties. It was also taken notice of at Ostend. This meteor, I find since, was seen at Coventry, & Chester. 4 swifts at Guildford; 1 swift at Meroe [Merrow]; 1 swift at Dorking.

16 October 1784. Mr Blanchard passed by us in full sight at about a quarter before three P: M: in an air-balloon!!! He mounted at Chelsea about noon; but came down at Sunbury to permit Mr Sheldon to get out; his weight over-loading the machine. At a little before four P: M: M^r Bl: landed at the town of Romsey in the county of Hants. [Newspaper cutting pasted on inserted leaf.] Extract of a Letter from a Gentleman [G. White] in a village fifty miles S.W. of London, dated Oct. 21. 'From the fineness of the weather, and the steadiness of the wind to the N.E. I began to be possessed with a notion last Friday that we should see Mr Blanchard [in his balloon] the day following, and therefore I called upon many of my neighbours in the street, and told them my suspicions. The next day proving also bright and the wind continuing as before, I became more sanguine than ever; and issuing forth, exhorted all those who had any curiosity to look sharp from about one to three o'clock [towards London] as they would stand a good chance of being entertained with a very extraordinary sight. That day I was not content to call at the houses, but I went out to the plow-men and labourers in the fields, and advised them to keep an eye at times to the N. and N.E. But about one o'clock there came up such a haze that I could not see the hill; however, not long after the mist cleared away in some degree, and people began to mount the hill. I was busy in and out till a quarter after two and observed a cloud of *London smoke*, hanging to the N. and N.N.E. This appearance increased my expectation. At twenty minutes before three there was a cry that the balloon was come. We ran into the orchard, where we found twenty or thirty neighbours assembled, and from the green bank at the end of my house, saw a dark blue speck at a most prodigious height dropping as it were out of the sky, and hanging amidst the regions of the air, between the weather-cock of the Tower and the Maypole: at first, it did not seem to make any way, but we soon discovered that its velocity was very considerable, for in a few minutes it was over the Maypole; and then over my chimney; and in ten minutes more behind the wallnut tree. The machine looked mostly of a dark blue colour, but some times reflected the rays of the sun. With a telescope I could discern the boat and the ropes that supported it. To my eye the balloon appeared no bigger than a large tea-urn. When we saw it first, it was north of Farnham over Farnham heath; and never came on this (east) side the Farnham road; but continued to pass on the N.W. side of Bentley, Froil, Alton, &c. and so for Medstead, Lord Northington's at the Grange, and to the right of Alresford and Winchester. I was wonderfully struck with the phaenomenon, and, like Milton's "Belated Peasant", felt my heart rebound with joy and fear at the same time. After a while I surveyed the machine with more composure, without that concern for two of my fellow creatures; for two we then supposed there were embarked in that aerial voyage. At last seeing how securely they moved, I considered them as a group of cranes or storks intent on the business of emigration, who had

> '. . . Set forth
> Their airy caravan, high over seas
> Flying, and over lands, with mutual wing
> Easing their flight . . .'

> [*Paradise Lost*, VII, 11]

THOMAS BLAIKIE
(1750–1838)

There are but the most fleeting contemporary references to the young Scot who when still only in his twenties arrived in France to advise the aristocracy on the art of English gardens. Another Scot, the great gardener J. C. Loudon from Lanarkshire, mentions him briefly in his *Encyclopedia of Gardening* (1822):

> Blaikie, Thomas Esq., of Beechwood near Edinburgh, C.M.H.S., a gentleman settled in France since 1775. [Blaikie was then seventy-two.] He first travelled there as a collector and sent home most of the plants mentioned in the *Hortus Kewensis* as introduced by Drs Fothergill and Pitcairn. He afterwards modelled the Duke of Orleans' gardens at Mousseau [Monceaux], near Paris, and from that time has followed the profession of landscape gardener in France. At the commencement of the revolution he furnished the potatoes with which the Thuilleries were planted and for which he was never paid, but was offered the title or office of Inspector of Gardens for the department of the Seine and Ouse [Oise], which he declined. He now resides at St Germans, and has lately given some extensive designs for the Prince of Salm Dyck in the Netherlands.

This has a vague interest but barely touches on Blaikie's astonishing career as a visiting botanist-gardener witness to the French Revolution. His diary, published in 1931, is as remarkable for its oddly elegant Scottish-Gallic style as for its historic contents. France is aflame, the Terror approaches, but to Blaikie it is all wickedness and folly, and garden-making continues.

He was born on Corstorphine Hill, Edinburgh, at a climactic moment in horticulture and botany. William Aiton was creating Kew, Linnaeus and Jussieu were transforming the world of plants with their systems, Sir Joseph Banks was about to become President of the Royal Society, and throughout Britain and Europe there was an intellectual and aesthetic response to plant-hunting and garden-

107

making. Blaikie probably made his way to the centre of French gardening via an apprenticeship at Dr Fothergill's celebrated botanical garden at Upton, near Stratford, and employment by the eccentric Comte de Lauraguais, a revolutionary who nonetheless was rewarded with a dukedom at the Restoration. But Blaikie's grandest garden schemes were devised for the anglophile Duc de Chartres, later Duc d'Orléans ('Philippe Egalité'). Blaikie moved in these exalted circles with a panache and splendour all his own.

18 April 1781. Sowed a great many seeds in the nursury that Archibald had brought from England. Received a large quantitie from Sir Joseph Banks of those brought home by the Descovery Ships which went out with Captain Cook the 10th Feby 1776 and likewise some Seeds from Mr Morison with a great many other ever green tree seeds; made a compleat Nursury; the only thing wanted was a Hottehouse for several sorts of seeds from the friendly Islands and Ottahiette [Otahiti].

April 10 went to St Leu and began the Park of Taverny to lay it down with grass; the concierge Mr Barry told the Duke that it had been tryed and that it would not produce grass but however I began giving it a good deep ploughing which I doubt not will bring it to bear good grass; at the same time began a Bassoon by the Pavilion at Taverny and Made a Modelle for a rock and the beginning of the River at St Leu in a more natural way; dined with Mr Lebrun and Sequin the Dukes tresorer where they exclamed much against Ettinghaussen.

March 1783. Mr Scott Gardner at Monceau not agreeing with Mr Smith he left the place so that I was again aplyed to, to find a Gardner and undertake that place which I did, so that I had now the whole derection of the Gardins at Monceau as well as those at Bagatelle; those Gardens which had been done by Mr Carmontelle Architect to the Duke de Chartres at a very great Expence where there was Monuments of all sorts, Countrys and ages but placed in such a manner that from every part there was a confused Landskipe, for there was adjoining Chinesse & Gothick buildings, Egyptian Pyramides joined to Italian vineyards, the winter Garden adjoining to the Hotthouses, was more Beautifull than Elegant; the whole was a Small confusion of many things joined together without any great natural Plan, the walks Serpenting and turning without reason which is the fault of most of those gardens done without taste or reason; after I changed most of those Gardins and destroyed most of those walks which I thought unessary or unaturel, continued likewise the different changes of the Gardins of St Leu; those changes wrought a great effect upon those Gardins and upon the Mind of the Duke who began to See the difference from the changes I made in following the nature of the Ground and drawing perspectifs upon the different objects already placed that is in making the walks to pass at those places where the different objects and parts of the Gardins ar seen to the greatest advantage; in this I have succeeded at the first in this country and endeed that rulle is little observed in England where they think that Gardening or that part of pleasure ground is perfectioned.

1786. At this time received a letter from the Duchess of Rhohan Chabot who has a country house at St Mandé to go to speak with her relative to the Making a garden; went and met the Duchess at St Mandé, the place a narrow strip of garden with some lime trees to the left planted in little Salles and narrow walks and the right side a sorte of Kitchen garden running allong the wall; after examining the ground I asked the Duchess to make her nearly a small project of what I meant to do which with a Pencil was soon done and seemed to please her very much; she said that she had applied to Gabriel Thouin but he could give her no ideas of beauty or simplicity; however she wanted me to conduct the work and I asked one of her domisticks rather than the Gardner, so she adopted one Cleremont a very intiligent Man. The Duchess is a good friendly woman, she said she wished it done before the Duke should know anything of the changes as she wished to give him an agreeable surprize so that the work was began and ended very expeditiously in about three Months; so that she invited the Duke one day to dine and when he arrived he could hardly be made to beleive it was possible to have changed his place to what it then was; he loaded me with compliments and found every thing so fine; at this time the Duchess aplied to Me for a gardener but as she said

'Mr B. you know how my house is composed, I would desire something but perhaps you may laugh.' 'I ask you pardon' Said I 'dont think I would do such a thing.' She told me that she desired a good Gardener and a good Catholick at the same time. I told her I should examin. However I had at the same time a young man a German who was a Protestant whome I recomended and lived with them and pleased them well untill they left him at the Revolution; however the gardens in this country let them be ever so well done the keeping and fine grass in England is what is frequently more to be admired than the designe which is frequently little observed, allthough they might varie their gardens more than they do and frequently their Slopes badly executed. Every place if rightly understood may be rendered agreeable in observing the ground where nature has frequently made Beautys which is not observed by those that has the direction. About this time the Duchess of Rhohan desired me to go with her to see a garden belonging to one of her relations who was the Spanish Ambassador; this was a garden at his hottel rue de L'University the place tolerable large and planted in the Ancient manner with Straight walks of Limes; after several things proposed the Ambassador found pretty but what he said was so absurd that he wished to change the whole without changing any thing; such reasoning from the Ambassador made one laugh and the Duchess calling me aside said 'O le vilain homme!' so I told him not to think any more of the Changes as I found his garden well and I agreed not to change any thing, only that I wished him good day and so we parted and I returned with the Duchess to her hotel who exclaimed much against the absurdity of her relation; however as I said we must overlook these absurditys allthough they are rather provoking and loss of time which those people thinks little of. About this time the Queen brought over an English gardener who was to make the grass at Trianon as fine as in England but he soon was lost and returned in disgrace to England, as he was a Man of no Genius and as far as I could see knew very little, as he had a formidable rival in Richard who soon undermined him and as those gardens is allways under the direction of the Architect and as this man was not placed by Mr Micque, who was Architect and pretended to make and conduct the Gardens which was done with more expence than taste.

The arrest of Louis XVI and Marie Antoinette

June 1789. As the fermentation continued and the Assembly pretended they were not free at Versailles and the people emagining the falt of the government so they formed the resolution to go to Versailles and force the King and family with the Assembly to comme to Paris. As this was the project of the Jacobin club who Stuck at nothing all those revolutionary went of for Versailles to bring in the King and endeed such a rable was hardly ever seen; as they approached Versailles the gardes desired to defend the King but he ordered them to make no resistance although several of them was massacred and M. L'Heretier who was with the Paris gardes got into the appatements and saved the Queen who was in the greatest danger as the people hated the Queen as some people ensinuated that it was her that was the cause of the Scarcity of Bread &c which was all done by other intrigues. However she was conducted into the King's appartement and the whole brought to Paris but the Scene was most chocking to See the poissards mounted up on the Cannon some with one of the gards coats or hatts and the poor gardes obliged to be conducted along with them in this manner and the heads of their comerades that was killed at Versailles brought along with them. The King and Queen and Dauphin was likewise conducted in this humiliating condition; the Maire of Paris was at the Barriere des Bonnes hommes below Passy to receive them and as a form to present the Keys of the town to the King which might be looked upon rather as a Mockery than otherwise. The people was all roaring out 'Voila le Boulanger et la Boulangere et le Pitit Mitron' saying that now they should have Bread as they now had got the Baker and his wife and Boy. The Queen sat at the bottom of the Coach with the Dauphin on her Knees in this condition while some of the Blackguards in the rable was firing there guns over her head. As I stood by the coach one Man fired and loaded his gun four times and fired it over the Queens head. I told him to desiste but he said he would continue but when I told him I should try by force to stop him and not have people hurt by his imprudence some cryed it was right and so he Sluged of very quietelly and after the corte went on and they lodged the King and his familly in the thuilleries. So that every thing now began to change and the Jacobin club to triumph and the royale familly keept as prisoners.

CHARLES DARWIN
(1809–82)

Darwin was born in Shrewsbury. His grandfathers were Erasmus Darwin, the naturalist and poet, and Josiah Wedgwood, the celebrated potter. Destined for the Church, his real vocation was recognized by John Henslow, Professor of Botany at Cambridge. Henslow advised the unusual lad, who spent much of his time examining flora and insects in and around Cambridge, to study geology. So little did he apply himself to what he should have been learning that he came tenth in the pass or 'poll' examination for his B.A. degree. What brought him to intellectual life in the last year were two books: Humboldt's *Personal Narrative* and Sir John Herschel's *Introduction to the Study of Natural Philosophy*. Darwin wrote that they 'stirred up in me a burning zeal to add even the most humble contribution to the noble structure of the Natural Science'. The admirable Professor Henslow then immediately set him on this path by arranging for him to accompany Captain FitzRoy as an unpaid naturalist on board H.M.S. *Beagle*. The propitious voyage – for it was to change the direction of world science – lasted from 27 December 1831 to 2 October 1836. Darwin began his travels as a very seasick amateur and returned a highly experienced and professional geologist and naturalist.

His *Journal of Researches* was published in 1839 alongside Captain FitzRoy's *Voyages of the 'Adventure' and 'Beagle'*. Darwin said that 'the voyage of the *Beagle* has been by far the most important event of my life, and has determined my whole career'. With amazing restraint he allowed over twenty years to pass before gradually making public the evolutionary theory which his travels had promoted. There was a 35-page pencil sketch of them in 1842, and a longer statement in 1844, but it was not until 1859 that a shocked and excited Britain first read *On the Origin of Species*. He dedicated the *Journal* to another great naturalist-diarist, the geologist Charles Lyell.

The excursion from Rio de Janeiro to Cape Frio

13 April 1832. After three days' travelling we arrived at Socêgo, the estate of Senhôr Manuel Figuireda, a relation of one of our party. The house was simple, and, though like a barn in form, was well suited to the climate. In the sitting-room gilded chairs and sofas were oddly contrasted with the whitewashed walls, thatched roof, and windows without glass. The house, together with the granaries, the stables, and workshops for the blacks, who had been taught various trades, formed a rude kind of quadrangle; in the centre of which a large pile of coffee was drying. These buildings stand on a little hill, overlooking the cultivated ground, and surrounded on every side by a wall of dark green luxuriant forest. The chief produce of this part of the country is coffee. Each tree is supposed to yield annually, on an average, two pounds; but some give as much as eight. Mandioca or cassada is likewise cultivated in great quantity. Every part of this plant is useful: the leaves and stalks are eaten by the horses, and the roots are ground into a pulp, which, when pressed dry and baked, forms the farinha, the principal article of sustenance in the Brazils. It is a curious, though well-known fact, that the juice of this most nutritious plant is highly poisonous. A few years ago a cow died at this Fazênda, in consequence of having drunk some of it. Senhôr Figuireda told me that he had planted, the year before, one bag of feijao or beans, and three of rice; the former of which produced eighty, and the latter three hundred and twenty fold. The pasturage supports a fine stock of cattle, and the woods are so full of game that a deer had to be killed on each of the previous days. This profusion of food showed itself at dinner, there, if the tables did not groan, the guests surely did ... During the meals, it was the employment of a man to drive out of the room sundry old hounds, and dozens of little black children, which crawled in together at every opportunity. As long as the idea of slavery could be banished, there was something exceedingly fascinating in this simple and patriarchal style of living: it was such a perfect retirement and independence from the rest of the world.

18 April. In returning we spent two days at Socêgo, and I employed them in collecting insects in the forest. The greater number of trees, although so lofty, are not more than three or four feet in circumference. There are, of course, a few of much greater dimension. Senhôr Manuel was then making a canoe 70 feet in length from a solid trunk, which had originally been 110 feet long, and of great thickness. The contrast of palm trees, growing amidst the common branching kinds, never fails to give the scene an intertropical character. Here the woods were ornamented by the Cabbage Palm – one of the most beautiful of its family. With a stem so narrow that it might be clasped with the two hands, it waves its elegant head at the height of forty or fifty feet above the ground. The woody creepers, themselves covered by other creepers, were of great thickness: some which I measured were two feet in circumference. Many of the older trees presented a very curious appearance from the tresses of a liana hanging from their boughs, and resembling bundles of hay. If the eye was turned from the world of foliage above, to the ground beneath, it was attracted by the extreme elegance of the leaves of the ferns and mimosæ. The latter, in some parts, covered the surface with a brushwood only a few inches high. In walking across these thick beds of mimosæ, a broad track was marked by the change of shade, produced by the drooping of their sensitive petioles. It is easy to specify the individual objects of admiration in these grand scenes; but it is not possible to give an adequate idea of the higher feelings of wonder, astonishment, and devotion, which fill and elevate the mind.

19 April. Leaving Socêgo, during the two first days, we retraced our steps. It was very wearisome work, as the road generally ran across a glaring hot sandy plain, not far from the coast. I noticed that each time the horse put its foot on the fine siliceous sand, a gentle chirping noise was produced. On the third day we took a different line, and passed through the gay little village of Madre de Deôs. This is one of the principal lines of road in Brazil; yet it was in so bad a state that no wheel vehicle, excepting the clumsy bullock-waggon, could pass along. In our whole journey we did not cross a single bridge built of stone; and those made of logs of wood were frequently so much out of repair, that it was necessary to go on one side to avoid them. All distances are inaccurately known. The road is often marked by crosses, in the place of milestones, to signify where human blood has been spilled. On the evening of the 23rd we arrived at Rio, having finished our pleasant little excursion.

During the remainder of my stay at Rio, I resided in a cottage at Botofogo Bay. It was impossible to wish for anything more delightful than thus to spend some weeks in so magnificent a country. In England any person fond of natural history enjoys in his walks a great advantage, by always having something to attract his attention; but in these fertile climates, teeming with life, the attractions are so numerous, that he is scarcely able to walk at all.

The few observations which I was enabled to make were almost exclusively confined to the invertebrate animals. The existence of a division of the genus Planaria, which inhabits the dry land, interested me much. These animals are of so simple a structure, that Cuvier has arranged them with the intestinal worms, though never found within the bodies of other animals. Numerous species inhabit both salt and fresh water; but those to which I allude were found, even in the drier parts of the forest, beneath logs of rotten wood, on which I believe they feed. In general form they resemble little slugs, but are very much narrower in proportion, and several of the species are beautifully coloured with longitudinal stripes. Their structure is very simple: near the middle of the under or crawling surface there are two small transverse slits, from the anterior one of which a funnel-shaped and highly irritable mouth can be protruded. For some time after the rest of the animal was completely dead from the effects of salt water or any other cause, this organ still retained its vitality.

The excursion to the San Fernando Gold Mine

13 September 1834. From this place we rode to the town of San Fernando. Before arriving there, the last land-locked basin had expanded into a great plain, which extended so far to the south, that the snowy summits of the more distant Andes were seen as if above the horizon of the sea. San Fernando is forty leagues from Santiago; and it was my farthest point southward; for we here turned right angles towards the coast. We slept at the gold mines of Yaquil, which are worked by Mr Nixon, an American gentleman, to whose kindness I was much indebted during the four days I stayed at his house. The next morning we rode to the mines, which are situated at the distance of some leagues, near the summit of a lofty hill. On the way we had a glimpse of the lake Tagua-tagua, celebrated for its floating islands, which have been described by M. Gay. They are composed of the stalks of various dead plants, intertwined together, and on the surface of which other living ones take root. Their form is generally circular, and their thickness from four to six feet, of which the greater part is immersed in the water. As the wind blows, they pass from one side of the lake to the other, and often carry cattle and horses as passengers.

When we arrived at the mine, I was struck by the pale appearance of many of the men, and inquired from Mr Nixon respecting their condition. The mine is 450 feet deep, and each man brings up about 200 pounds weight of stone. With this load they have to climb up the alternate notches cut in the trunks of trees, placed in a zigzag line up the shaft. Even beardless young men, eighteen and twenty years old, with little muscular development of their bodies (they are quite naked excepting drawers), ascend with this great load from nearly the same depth. A strong man, who is not accustomed to this labour, perspires most profusely, with merely carrying up his own body. With this very severe labour, they live entirely on boiled beans and bread. They would prefer having bread alone; but their masters, finding that they cannot work so hard upon this, treat them like horses, and make them eat the beans. Their pay is here rather more than at the mines of Jajuel, being from twenty-four to twenty-eight shillings per month. They leave the mine only once in three weeks; when they stay with their families for two days. One of the rules in this mine sounds very harsh, but answers pretty well for the master. The only method for stealing gold is to secrete pieces of the ore, and take them out as occasion may offer. Whenever the major-domo finds a lump thus hidden, its full value is stopped out of the wages of all the men; who thus, without they all combine, are obliged to keep watch over each other.

When the ore is brought to the mill, it is ground into an impalpable powder; the process of washing removes all the lighter particles, and amalgamation finally secures the gold dust. The washing, when described, sounds a very simple process; but it is beautiful to see how the exact adaptation of the current of water to the specific gravity of the gold, so easily separated the powdered matrix from the metal. The mud which passes from the mills is collected into pools, where it subsides, and every now and then is cleared out, and thrown into a common heap. A great deal of chemical action then commences, salts of various kinds effloresce on the surface, and the mass becomes hard. After having been left for a year or two, and then rewashed, it yields gold; and this process may be repeated even six or seven times; but the gold each time becomes less in quantity, and the intervals required (as the inhabitants say, to generate the metal) are longer. There can be no doubt that the chemical action, already mentioned, each time liberates fresh gold from some combination. The discovery of a method to effect this before the first grinding, would without doubt raise the value of gold-ores many fold. It is curious to find how the minute particles of gold, being scattered about and not corroding, at last accumulate in some quantity. A short time since a few miners, being out of work, obtained permission to scrape the ground round the house and mill; they washed the earth thus got together, and so procured thirty dollars' worth of gold. This is an exact counterpart of what takes places in nature. Mountains suffer degradation and wear away, and with them the metallic veins which they contain. The hardest rock is worn into impalpable mud, the ordinary metals oxidate, and both are removed; but gold, platina, and a few others are nearly indestructible, and from their weight, sinking to the bottom, are left behind. After whole mountains have passed through this grinding-mill, and have been washed by the hand of nature, the residue becomes metalliferous, and man finds it worth his while to complete the task of separation.

6. THE SICK DIARIST

THE REV. RALPH JOSSELIN
(1616–83)

Ralph Josselin was born at Roxwell and was vicar of Earls Colne, Essex, from 1641 until his death, as well as acting as village schoolmaster during the Commonwealth. His diary was long in the possession of the Propert family of Colne Priory, the burial place of the Earls of Oxford. When it was first published in 1908, the 'trivial details of everyday life' were edited out as unimportant. They are now seen as vital by the seventeenth-century historian and ordinary diary-addict alike. Josselin married his sweetheart Jane Constable when he was twenty-three and she was nineteen. They had ten children and clearly enjoyed a very happy family life. The diary shows a close involvement by Josselin in the births of his children – something akin to today's shared birth experience by wives and husbands.

Josselin was a moderate Puritan of comfortable means who combined a little farming and the purchase of scattered parcels of land with being a dutiful clergyman. He disliked Laud, the Prayer Book and annoying sects such as the Quakers, but in spite of a certain cautiousness in his loyalty towards the revolution he had plenty of reasons for fearing that he might lose his living at the Restoration.

Alan Macfarlane quotes the diary of another Essex man to explain the popularity of journal-keeping in the seventeenth century: 'We have our State Diurnals, relating to National affairs,' writes John Beadle, the minister of Barnston, in *The Journal of a Thankful Christian* (1656):

Tradesmen keep their shop books. Merchants their Accompt books. Lawyers have their books of presidents [precedence].

Physitians their Experiments. Some wary husbands have kept a Diary of dayly disbursments. Travellers a Journal of all they have seen, and hath befallen in their way. A Christian that would be exact hath more need, and may reap much more good by such a Journal as this. We are all but Stewards, Factors here, and must give a strict account in that great day to the high Lord of all our wayes, and of his wayes towards us.

It has often been suggested that diaries such as Beadle's and Josselin's were an outlet for the kind of confessions once said to a priest, and also a discipline for getting rid of guilt. Certainly to eliminate either the religious or domestic element in these prolific seventeenth-century diaries is to misunderstand and finally to wreck them. They were, said another writer, David Reisman, 'a symptom of a new type of character' who recorded the 'evidence of the separation between the behaving and scrutinizing self'.

1 September 1644. On Monday it was related unto mee that Mr Pilgrim Minister of Wormingford fell downe dead in his pulpitt (he was an honest man but very weakly and sickly) ... Lord thou keepest mee, oh keepe me in a gratious and watchful frame that thou mayst find mee about my worke when you shall call mee ...

10 January 1645. The Archbishop [Laud] that grand enemy of the power of Godlines, that great stickler for all outward pompe in the service of God lost his head at Tower hill London, by ordinance of Parliament. This weeke the great snow melted gently, never were houses in many yeares so filled with snow and padled when it melted away ...

6–7–8 March. My Cousin Abraham Josselin came to us from New England, about by the Canaryes after a sad long jorny and one tedious fight with a King's pyratt: heard by him of the well-fare of the plantacion for which god be praised ... heard news of the routing of my Lord Fairfax his forces, which was reported as a very great losse, endangering much the North parts of England ...

18 June. This day was I ordered by the Committee as Constant

Chaplyn to attend upon Coll: Harlakenden regiment at musters and to receive 10s. per diem as salary for the same.

27 June. A day of thanksgiving for the great victory in Naseby fields over the King's army, by Sir Tho: Fairfax, the lord was pleased in some measure to raise up my heart in the worke, and helpe mee with many expressions and unstudyed meditacions, for which his name bee praised.

17 July 1646. My wife had taken pills and they wrought very kindly and carryed the winde sensibly out of her side, this the payne returnd and the toothake, which brought her as it were to deaths doore, before sun, shee tooke some tobacco, it gave her through mercy much ease, Mrs Mary rose so early to come over to her, at night my wife tooke tobacco found much ease in it, and slept very comfortably.

11 February 1647. On Friday morning, one houre and halfe before day my wife was delivered of her second sonne, the midwife not with her, onely foure women and Mrs Mary; her speed was great, and I thinke the easiest and speediest labour that ever shee had, and shee was under great feares, oh how is the lord to be noted and observed in his mercy. I was very ill, with a hott fever fitt, my freinds but especially Mrs Mary very carefull of mee.

17 February. My child was ill, full of phlegme, we sent for the physitian, he gave it syrrupe of roses: it wrought well, my wife persuaded herselfe that it would die it was a very sicke child indeed: I took my leave of it at night, not much expecting to see it alive, but god continued it to morning and it seemed to mee not hopeless: lord its thine, I leave it to thy disposing onely I pray thee give mee and my wife a submitting heart.

19 February. The day before and this my sonne was very still and quiet; in the last night very ill: at night I eat some oysters which I desired.

20 February. This night againe my sonne very ill, he did not cry so much as the night before, whether the cause was want of strength I knowe not: he has a little froth in his mouth continually ... he cheered up very sweetly at night: and in the night was very still, what god will doe I knowe not.

21 February. This day my deare babe Ralph, quietly fell asleepe ... the lord gave us time to bury it in our thoughts [to remember it], we lookt on it as a dying child ... it dyed quietly without shreekes, or sobs or sad groanes, it breathd out the soule with 9 gasps and dyed; it was the youngest, and our affections not so wonted unto it.

22 February. Thes 2 dayes were such as I never knewe before; the former for his death, and this for the buriel of my deare sonne whom I layed in the chancell on the North side of the great Tombe ... this little boy of 10 dayes old, when he dyed was buried with the teares and sorrow not onely of the parents and Mrs Mary Church, but with the teares and sorrowe of many of my neighbours.

31 January 1649. Heard K C [Charles I] was executed, but that was uncertaine, he was adjudged to dye Jan. 27. 1648. Bradshaw, the lord president pronounced sentence, this day was a frost a very cold day.

4 February. .... the death of the King talked much of, very many men of the weaker sort of christians in divers places passionate concerning it, but so ungroundedly, that it would make any bleed to observe it, the lord hath some great thing to do, feare and tremble at it oh England.

Monday it was debated about Kings and Peeres, on Tuesday the house of commons ordered to null the house of Lords as uselesse and on the next day to lay aside the government of Kings, and to sett up a councell of state.

26 November 1654. This night my wife dreamed, that towards a night shee saw 3 lights in the skie over Abbots fields which are North by West, and South a body as the Sun or Moone, the lights blazed and filled the skie with light often, and then the body in the South answered it with flames exceeding terrible ...

8 December. .... this morning my sonne Tom. told mee his wonderful dreame. Jesus Christ in a white robe, came into my pulpit while preaching and hugd mee, and I him. Then he came to him and put his inkhorn in his pocket, and carried him into the churchyard, and askt him, what hee would have, Tom. said. a blessing . . .

3 January 1655. Warme. dry. Calm christmas, grasse springing, herbes budding, birds singing plowes going; a little rain only in two dayes . . . cleare sun shining. Moon and starrs appearing by night. Most persons said never such a Christmas known in the memory of man.

DR JOHN RUTTY
(1698–1775)

Rutty was a most spartan Quaker whose *Spiritual Diary and Soliloquies*, published the year after his death, caused the literary world much amusement. Dr Johnson, reading quotes from it in a review, roared with laughter. And the diary continues to provoke a lot of fun at the expense of a good though humourless man. Johnson relegated him to the fourth class of egotists, in which he included 'journalists, temporal and spiritual: Elias Ashmole . . . John Wesley, and a thousand other old women and fanatic writers of memoirs and meditations'.

Rutty was in fact a dietitian in an age which ate and drank to excess. He gained his doctorate with a thesis entitled 'De Diarrhoea' and practised in Dublin. He sometimes ate nettles and was worried all his life because of the enjoyment he gained from eating. He never charged his poor patients, he analysed milk (the source of much disease) and wrote a book on drugs which still contains some useful information. He insisted on a strict regime for himself which had a certain similarity to that of the fasting medieval religious (he liked reading Thomas à Kempis) and he gave away what money he didn't need for his exceedingly simple life. However, all this undoubted virtue in no way alters the fact that he unintentionally kept a highly comic diary. Dr Johnson was sitting up late at night with Boswell when the pair of them read the following extracts from it in a review:

Tenth month, 1753, 23 Indulgence in bed an hour too long.

Twelfth month, 17 An hypochondriac obnubilation from wind and indigestion.

Ninth month, 28 An over-dose of whisky.

29. A dull, cross, choleric day.

First month, 1757, 22 A little swinish at dinner and repast. Dogged on provocation.

Second month, 5 Very dogged or snappish.

14 Snappish on fasting.

26 Cursed snappishness to those under me, on a bodily indisposition.

Third month, 11 On a provocation, exercised a dumb resentment for two days, instead of scolding . . .

Lord Ponsonby was to extract further hilarities:

I have sucked at the breasts of the world and am not satisfied.

Feasted again a little beyond the sacred medium.

Feasting beyond the holy bounds.

O that I may not abuse riches! Certain it is I often have, in guzzling.

I feasted pretty moderately, but with this notable difference in solitary and social eating, that in the last I eat more like a swine.

A little incubus last night on too much spinage.

A little of the beast in drinking.

Although I dined with saints I drank rather beyond bounds.

Piggish at meals.

Take care, take care of the fumes of cyder and whiskey, tremble at the mixture.

Gripes from excess.

Twice, unbridled choler.

A sudden irruption of ferocity.

Learn to repine less at small evils and flea bites, thou pitiful Jack Straw!

Lay a little too late for this day, rouse soul, death is at the door.

Spent my mattin in spiritual fox hunting.

Shortly before his death it was sex, not food, which bothered him:

12th Month, 1774, 3   Conscious that of late no fleshly indulgence hath taken place, beware that it creep not in now in the days of infirmity and sitting by the fire . . .

ALICE JAMES
(1848–92)

The sister of Henry, the novelist, and William, the psychologist, Alice James was an invalid spinster who spent the last eighteen years of her life in England, first in Leamington and then in London. She became a caustic commentator on the British scene and a courageous realist where her health was concerned. Like all her family, she was much travelled and casually educated. She was nearly always ill and had suicide ever at the back of her mind. Was it a sin? she asked Henry. He thought not. Should things prove unendurable she could, he said, kill herself, although she must 'do it in a perfectly gentle way in order not to distress [her] friends'. Although in great pain from breast cancer, she said 'naturally'. Her last diary words were: 'Oh the wonderful moment when I felt myself floated for the first time into the deep sea of divine *cessation*, and saw all the dear old mysteries and miracles vanish into vapour!'

Her diary is anything but deathly and is decidedly unmysterious. It developed out of a commonplace book in which she copied favourite extracts from literature and aphorisms, and was her own way of giving a stoic answer to the 'why?' of her existence. It was written in two fat scribblers and begun on 31 May 1889:

I think that if I get into the habit of writing a bit about what happens, or rather doesn't happen, I may lose a little of the sense of loneliness and desolation which abides with me. My circumstances allowing of nothing but the ejaculation of one-syllabled reflections, a written monologue by that most interesting being, *myself*, may have its yet to be discovered consolations. I shall at least have it all my own way and it may bring relief as an outlet to that geyser of emotions, sensations, speculations and reflections which ferments perpetually with my poor old carcass for its sins; so here goes, my first Journal!

Apart from many visits by her devoted brother Henry and occasional callers, Alice's diary years were constricted by her ill-health to the company of her great friend Katherine Loring, and to nurses and servants. She and Miss Loring had met in Massachusetts during their early thirties and were to remain together until the end. It was Katherine who had published four copies of the diary after Alice's death, sending one to each of her brothers. Neither had any idea that she kept a diary. Henry was horrified and destroyed his copy immediately; William received his in shocked silence. When Leon Edel edited the diary many years later, it was, he said, 'her way of conquering time, as Proust might say: it was also her way of asking for a hearing beyond the grave. Not her pages, but the spirit residing in them, gives the diary its unique place in literature and testifies to its continuing appeal.'

5 August 1889. They say there is little doubt that Mr Edmund Gurney* committed suicide. What a pity to hide it, every educated person who kills himself does something towards lessening the superstition. It's bad that it is so untidy, there is no denying that, for one bespatters one's friends morally as well as physically, taking them so much more into one's secret than they want to be taken. But how heroic to be able to suppress one's vanity to the extent of confessing that the game is too hard. The most comic and apparently the chief argument used against it, is that because you were born without being consulted, you would be very sinful should you

---

* The English psychologist and friend of William James.

cut short your blissful career! This had been said to me a dozen times, and they never see how they have turned things topsy-turvey.

12 August. William was most amusing about Ireland – he seems sound eno' on Home Rule, but how could a child of Father's be anything else!! He went to see the family of a little maid-servant they have, and such a welcome as he had! The refrain, 'The Lord be praised that Kerry should have seen this day!' was repeated every five min[ute]s during the two hours he was with 'em. He says that they are an absolutely foreign people, much more excessive than they are with us just like the stage Irishman. He was very funny about evictions, and says the horror of them entirely vanishes when you see the nature of the cabins, existence without being so much preferable to existence within. He says that it is the most extraordinary thing to see coming out from the midst of all this filth, misery and squalor, this jovial, sociable, witty, intelligent race, supported by, and living *entirely* upon an ideal, etc., etc.

Oh, the tragedy of it! when you think of the dauntless creatures flinging themselves and their ideal for seven centuries against the dense wall of British brutality, as incapable of an ideal inspiration or an imaginative movement as the beasts of the field . . .

July 1890. The things we remember have a *first-timeness* about them which suggests that that may be the reason of their survival. I must ask Wm. some day if there is any theory on the subject, or better, whether 'tis worth a theory. I remember so distinctly the first time I was conscious of a purely intellectual process. 'Twas the summer of '56 which we spent in Boulogne and the parents of the Mlle Marie Boningue our governess had a *campagne* on the outskirts and invited us to spend the day, perhaps Marie's fête-day. A large and shabby calèche came for us into which we were packed, save Wm.; all I can remember of the drive was a never-ending ribbon of dust stretching in front and the anguish greater even than usual of Wilky's and Bob's heels grinding into my shins. Marie told us that her father had a scar upon his face caused by a bad scald in his youth and we must be sure and not look at him as he was very sensitive. How I remember the painful conflict between sympathy and the desire to look and the fear that my baseness should be discovered by the good man as he sat at the head of the table in charge of a big frosted-cake sprinkled o'er with those pink and white worms in which lurk the caraway seed. How easy 'twould be to picture one's youth as a perpetual escape from that abhorred object! – I wonder if it is a blight upon children still? – But to arrive at the first flowering of my Intellect! We were turned into the garden to play, a sandy or rather dusty expanse with nothing in it, as I remember, but two or three scrubby apple-trees, from one of which hung a swing. As time went on Wilky and Bob disappeared, not to my grief, and the Boningues. Harry* was sitting in the swing and I came up and stood near by as the sun began to slant over the desolate expanse, as the deadly h[ou]rs, with that endlessness which they have for infancy, passed, when Harry suddenly exclaimed: 'This might certainly be called pleasure under difficulties!' The stir of my whole being in response to the substance and exquisite, *original* form of this remark almost makes my heart beat now with the sisterly pride which was then awakened and it came to me in a flash, the higher nature of this appeal to the mind, as compared to the rudimentary solicitations which usually produced my childish explosions of laughter; and I can also feel distinctly the sense of self-satisfaction in that I could not only perceive, but appreciate this subtlety, as if I had acquired a new sense, a sense whereby to measure intellectual things, wit as distinguished from giggling, for example.

18 July. How well one has to be, to be ill! These confidences reveal to you, dear Inconnu, so much mental debility that I don't want to rehearse herein my physical collapses in detail as well, altho' I am unable to escape a general tone of lamentation. But this last prostration was rather excessive and comic in its combination, consisting of one of my usual attacks of rheumatic gout in that dissipated organ known in the family as 'Alice's tum', in conjunction with an ulcerated tooth, and a very bad crick in my neck. By taking a very small dose of morphia, the first in three years, I was able to steady my nerves and *experience* the pain without distraction, for there is something very exhilarating in shivering whacks of crude pain which seem to lift you out of the present and its sophistications

---

* Henry James.

(great Men unable to have a tooth out without gas!) and ally you to
long gone generations rent and torn with tooth-ache such as we
can't dream of. I didn't succumb and send for my Primrose Knight,
having no faith in anything but that time-honoured nostrum
Patience, with its simple ingredients of refraining from muscular
contractions and vocal exclamations lest you find yourself in a
worse fix than you are already in!

KATHERINE MANSFIELD
(1888–1923)

Katherine Mansfield turned her back on New Zealand respectability
when she was twenty and sailed for England to become a writer.
Here and in Germany she met with the confusions and pleasures of
In a German Pension (1911) and her later stories. Her life was more
injudicious than wild, and through her lovers and a marriage which
lasted one night she got into great difficulties. In 1912 she met John
Middleton Murry, who was a year younger than herself, and lived
with him until they were free to marry. After her death at only
thirty-five it was very much to do with his remarkable editing of
her work, his biography of her, and most of all his publication of
her *Journal* in 1927 that she became widely accepted as being close
to Chekhov in her poetic use of reality.

In 1917 she developed tuberculosis and fought it in every way
possible, at one time becoming a disciple of Gurdjieff at Fontainebleau. It was during her illness and the many separations from
Murry which it entailed that she wrote most of her best stories –
Prelude (1918), *Bliss* (1920), *The Garden Party* (1922) and *The
Dove's Nest* (1923). Her *Journal* became one of the most influential
of all twentieth-century diaries for freedom-seeking women. She
interleaved it with a writer's notebook which she meant to publish,
though she did not intend the *Journal* itself to appear in print. The
latter is incomplete as she destroyed much of it, but what remains
is one of the most artistic of diaries, as well as a personal statement
which shocked its early readers.

2 January 1922. Little round birds in the fir-tree at the side window, scouring the tree for food. I crumbled a piece of bread, but though the crumbs fell in the branches only two found them. There was a strange remoteness in the air, the scene, the winter cheeping. In the evening, for the first time for — I felt rested. I sat up in bed and discovered I was singing within. Even the sound of the wind is different. It is joyful, not ominous. And black dark looks in at the window and is only black dark. In the afternoon it came on to pour with rain, long glancing rain, falling aslant.

I have not done the work I should have done. I shirk the lunch party [see *The Dove's Nest*]. This is very bad. In fact I am disgusted with myself. There must be a change from now on. What I chiefly admire in Jane Austen is that what she promises, she performs, i.e. if Sir T. is to arrive, we have his arrival at length, and it's excellent and excels our expectations. This is rare; it is also my very weakest point. Easy to see why . . .

6 January. The first quarter of the Moon. *Jour de fête*. The [Christmas] Tree is dismantled.

I had a very bad night and did not fall deeply asleep enough to dream.

In the morning, all white, all dim and cold, and snow still falling. While waiting in my room I watched the terrific efforts of a little bird to peck through the ice and get at the sweet food of the nut. He succeeded. But why must he so strive?

My heart is always bad to-day. It is the cold. It feels congested, and I am uneasy, or rather my body is. Vile feeling. I cough.

Read Shakespeare, read *Cosmic Anatomy,* read The Oxford Dictionary. Wrote. But nothing like enough.

In the afternoon W— came to tea. I suspect he is timid, fearful and deeply kind. Deep within that vast substance lurks the *seed*. That is not sentimental. He wished me sun as he left. I felt his wish had power and was a blessing. One can't be mistaken in such things. He *is* in his stockings – pea-green and red! J. came up after ski-ing, excessively handsome – a glorious object, no less. I never saw a more *splendid* figure.

I am wearing my ring on my middle finger as a reminder not to be so base. We shall see . . . No letters. Picture of Anna Wong. It asked for a story . . .

10 January. Dreamed I was back in New Zealand.

Got up to-day. It was fine. The sun shone and melted the last trace of snow from the trees. All the morning big drops fell from the trees, from the roof. The drops were not like rain-drops, but bigger, softer, more *exquisite*. They made one realize how one loves the fertile earth and hates this snow-bound cold substitute.

The men worked outside on the snowy road, trying to raise the telegraph pole. Before they began they had lunch out of a paper, sitting astride the pole. It is very beautiful to see people sharing food. Cutting bread and passing the loaf, especially cutting bread in that age-old way with a clasp-knife. Afterwards one got up in a tree and sat among the branches working from there, while the other lifted. The one in the tree turned into a kind of bird, as all people do in trees – chuckled, laughed out, peered from among the branches, careless. *At-tend! Ar-rêt! Al-lez!*

11 January. In bed again. Heard from Pinker *The Dial* has taken *The Doll's House*. Wrote and finished *A Cup of Tea*. It took about 4–5 hours. In the afternoon Elizabeth came. She looked fascinating in her black suit, something between a Bishop and a Fly. She spoke of my 'pretty little story" in the *Mercury*. All the while she was there I was conscious of a falsity. We said things we meant; we were sincere, but at the back there was nothing but falsity. It was very horrible. I do not want ever to see her or hear from her again. When she said she would not come, I wanted to cry *Finito!* No, she is not my friend.

There is no feeling to be compared with the joy of having written and finished a story. I did not go to sleep, but nothing mattered. There it was, *new* and complete.

Dreamed last night of a voyage to America . . .

12 January. I don't feel so sinful this day as I did, because I have written something and the tide is still high. The ancient landmarks are covered. Ah! but to write better! Let me write better, more deeply, more *largely*.

Baleful icicles hang in a fringe outside our window panes.

29 January. H. came. He says my right lung is practically all right.

Can one believe such words? The other is a great deal better. *He* thinks my heart will give me far less trouble at a lower level. Can this be true? He was so hopeful to-day that T.B. seemed no longer a scourge. It seemed that one recovered more often than not. Is this fantastic?

Tidied all my papers. Tore up and ruthlessly destroyed much. This is always a great satisfaction. Whenever I prepare for a journey I prepare as though for death. Should I never return, all is in order. This is what life has taught me.

In the evening I wrote to Orage about his book. It has taken me a week to write the letter. J. and I seem to have played cribbage off and on all day. I feel there is much love between us. Tender love. *Let it not change!*

30 January. There was a tremendous fall of snow on Sunday night. Monday was the first *real* perfect day of the winter. It seemed that the happiness of Bogey and of me reached its zenith on that day. We could not have been happier; that was the feeling. Sitting one moment on the balcony of the bed-room, for instance, or driving in the sleigh through masses of heaped-up snow. He looked so beautiful, too – hatless, strolling about with his hands in his pockets. He weighed himself. 10 stone. There was a harmonium in the waiting-room. Then I went away, after a quick but not hurried kiss . . .

It was very beautiful on the way to Sierre. Then I kept wondering if I was seeing it all for the last time – the snowy bushes, the leafless trees. 'I miss the buns.'

Pinker told me *The Westminster* had taken *The Garden Party*.

31 January. Travelling is terrible. All is so sordid, and the train shatters one. Tunnels are *hell*. I am frightened of travelling.

We arrived in Paris late, but it was very beautiful – all emerging from water. In the night I looked out and saw *the men with lanterns*. The hotel all sordid again, – fruit peelings, waste-paper, boots, grime, ill-temper. In the evening I saw Manoukhin. But on the way there, nay, even before, I realized my heart was not in it. I feel divided in myself and angry and without virtue. Then. L.M. and I had one of our famous quarrels, and I went to the wrong house. Don't forget, as I rang the bell, the scampering and laughter inside. M. had a lame girl there as interpreter. He said through her he could cure me completely. But I did not believe it. It all seemed suddenly unimportant and ugly. But the flat was nice – the red curtains, marble clock, and pictures of ladies with powdered hair.

1 February. At 5.30 I went to the *clinique* and saw the other man, Donat. I asked him to explain the treatment and so on. He did so. But first: as I approached the door it opened and the hall, very light, showed, with the maid smiling, wearing a little shawl, holding back the door. Through the hall a man slipped quickly carrying what I thought was a *cross* of green leaves. Suddenly the arms of the little cross waved feebly, and I saw it was a small child strapped to a wooden tray. While I waited, voices came from another room – very loud voices, M.'s over and above them: *Da! Da!* and then an interrogatory: *Da?* I have the feeling that M. is a really good man. I have also a sneaking feeling (I use the word 'sneaking' advisedly) that he is a kind of unscrupulous impostor. Another proof of my divided nature. All is disunited. Half boos, half cheers.

Yes, that's it. To do anything, to be anything, one must gather oneself together and 'one's faith make stronger'. Nothing of any worth can come for a disunited being . . .

W. N. P. BARBELLION
(1889–1919)

Born Bruce Frederick Cummings in Barnstaple, the son of the editor of the local newspaper, the *Devon and Exeter Gazette,* Barbellion began keeping a journal when still a child. His longing to be a professional naturalist was frustrated from the start by ill-health. In 1912, although now ominously aware that something very serious was wrong with him (it was the onset of multiple sclerosis), he got a job in the Entomology Department of the Natural History Museum, South Kensington. In 1915 he married his cousin Eleanor Benger, a young fashion designer, both of them fully aware that he must soon die; a daughter was born a year later.

In 1917 he had to resign from the Museum. Throughout his short life Barbellion struggled not only against sickness but also against poverty and his inadequate education for the work he was vocationally so well qualified to do. His *Journal of a Disappointed Man* was a bitter apologia for his fate, but it was too a triumphant statement of the glories he had managed to extract from life. Pain and frequent disgust with his body rarely took away his greedy appetite for talk, music, plants and insects, the seasons and the bright world. This lanky, dark young man, eager for girls and a good career, had no option but to watch himself rot. As with Denton Welch in the Second World War, the maiming and killing of countless males of his own generation appeared to lessen his own tragedy. Brief life was the order of the day; who was he to make a fuss? He at least was perishing 'naturally'; he was not being mown down on the Western Front.

The Journal of a Disappointed Man caused a great sensation when it was published a few months after the Armistice, but a second volume put together by Barbellion's brothers from what remained of the writer's papers, and called *A Last Diary*, brought accusations that both books were fakes, and probably written by H. G. Wells. They are in fact genuine, and among the most moving diaries ever created. Cummings made up his pseudonym from W(ilhelm) N(ero) P(ilate), in his estimation three human failures, and 'Barbellion' from the name above a sweetshop in Bond Street. He said that his literary lineage was through Sir Thomas Browne and Marie Bashkirtseff – the latter had many close diary-writing descendants at that period.

A 'brilliant career'

14 July 1912. My old head master once prophesied for me 'a brilliant career'. That was when I was in the Third Form. Now I have more than a suspicion that I am one of those who, as he once pointed out, grow sometimes out of a brilliant boyhood into very commonplace men. This continuous ill-health is having a very obvious effect on my work and activities. With what courage I possess I have to face the fact that to-day I am unable to think or express myself as well as when I was a boy in my teens – witness this Journal!

I intend to go on however. I have decided that my death shall be disputed all the way.

Oh! it is so humiliating to die! I writhe to think of being overcome by so unfair an enemy before I have demonstrated myself to maiden aunts who mistrust me, to colleagues who scorn me, and even to brothers and sisters who believe in me.

As an Egotist I hate death because I should cease to be I.

Most folk, when sick unto death, gain a little consolation over the notoriety gained by the fact of their decease. Criminals enjoy the pomp and circumstance of their execution. Voltaire said of Rousseau that he wouldn't mind being hanged if they'd stick his name on the gibbet. But my own death would be so mean and insignificant. Guy de Maupassant died in a grand manner – a man of intellect and splendid physique who became insane. Tusitala's death in the South Seas reads like a romance. Heine, after a life of sorrow, died with a sparkling witticism on his lips; Vespasian with a jest.

But I cannot for the life of me rake up any excitement over my own immediate decease – an unobtrusive passing away of a rancorous, disappointed, morbid, and self-assertive entomologist in a West Kensington Boarding House – what a mean little tragedy! It is hard not to be somebody even in death.

22 January 1913. This Diary reads for all the world as if I were not living in mighty London. The truth is I live in a bigger, dirtier city – ill-health. Ill-health, when chronic, is like a permanent ligature around one's life. What a fine fellow I'd be if I were perfectly well. My energy for one thing would lift the roof off . . .

We conversed around the text: 'To travel hopefully is better than to arrive and true success is to labour.' She is – well, so graceful. My God! I love her, I love her, I love her!!!

25 June 1915. If sometimes you saw me in my room by myself, you would say I was a ridiculous coxcomb. For I walk about, look out of the window then at the mirror – turning my head sideways perhaps so as to see it in profile. Or I gaze down into my eyes – my eyes always impress me – and wonder what effect I produce on others. This, I believe, is not so much vanity as curiosity. I know I am not prepossessing in appearance – my nose is crooked and my skin is blotched. Yet my physique – because it is mine – interests me. I like to see myself walking and talking. I should like to hold myself in my hand in front of me like a Punchinello and carefully examine myself at my leisure.

28 June. Saw my brother A— off at Waterloo en route for Armageddon. Darling fellow. He shook hands with P—and H—, and P— wished him 'Goodbye, and good luck.' Then he held my hand a moment, said 'Goodbye, old man,' and for a second gave me a queer little nervous look. I could only say 'Goodbye,' but we understand each other perfectly ... It is horrible. I love him tenderly.

1 August. Am getting married at — Register Office on September 15th. It is impossible to set down here all the labyrinthine ambages of my will and feelings in regard to this event. Such incredible vacillations, doubts, fears. I have been living at a great rate below surface recently. 'If you enjoy only twelve months' happiness,' the Doctor said to me, 'it is worth while.' But he makes a recommendation ... At his suggestion E— went to see him and from his own mouth learnt all the truth about the state of my health, to prevent possible mutual recriminations in the future. To marry an introspective dyspeptic – what a prospect for her! ... I exercise my microscopic analysis on her now as well as on myself ... This power in me is growing daily more automatic and more repugnant. It is a nasty morbid unhealthy growth that I want to hide if I cannot destroy. It amounts to being able at will to switch myself in and out of all my most cherished emotions; it is like the case in Sir Michael Foster's *Physiology* of a man who, by pressing a tumour in his neck could stop or at any rate control the action of his heart.

6 August. The most intimate and extensive journal can only give each day a relatively small sifting of the almost infinite number of things that flow thro' the consciousness. However vigilant and artful a diarist may be, plenty of things escape him and in any event recollection is not re-creation ...

To keep a journal is to have a secret liaison of a very sentimental kind. A *journal intime* is a super-confidante to whom everything is told and confessed. For an engaged or married man to have a secret super-confidante who knows things which are concealed from his lady seems to me to be deliberate infidelity. I am as it were engaged to two women and one of them is being deceived. The word 'Deceit' comes up against me in this double life I lead, and insists I shall name a plain thing bluntly. There is something very like sheer moral obliquity in these entries behind her back . . . Is this journal habit slowly corrupting my character? Can an engaged or married man conscientiously continue to write his *journal intime*?

This question of giving up my faithful friend after September I must consider.

Of course most men have something to conceal from someone. Most married men are furtive creatures, and married women too. But I have a Gregers Werle-like passion for life to be lived on a foundation of truth in every intercourse. I would have my wife know all about me and if I cannot be loved for what I surely am, I do not want to be loved for what I am not. If I continue to write therefore she shall read what I have written . . .

My Journal keeps open house to every kind of happening in my soul. Provided it is a veritable autochthon – I don't care how much of a tatterdemalion or how ugly or repulsive – I take him in and – I fear sponge him down with excuses to make him more creditable in other's eyes. You may say why trouble whether you do or whether you don't tell us all the beastly little subterranean atrocities that go on in your mind. Any eminently 'right-minded' *Times* or *Spectator* reader will ask: 'Who in Faith's name is interested in your introspective muck-rakings – in fact, who the Devil are you?' To myself, a person of vast importance and vast interest, I reply, – as are other men if I could but understand them as well . . .

3 September 1916. I smile with sardonic amusement when I reflect how the War has changed my status. Before the War I was an interesting invalid. Now I am a lucky dog. Then, I was a star turn in tragedy; now I am drowned and ignored in an overcrowded chorus. No valetudinarian was ever more unpleasantly jostled out of his self-compassion. It is difficult to accustom myself to the new role all at once: I had begun to lose the faculty for sympathizing in others' griefs. It is hard to have to realize that in all this slaughter, my own superfluous life has become negligible and scarcely anyone's concern but my own. In this colossal *sauve qui peut* which is developing, who can stay to consider a useless mouth? Am I not a comfortable parasite? And, God forgive me, an Egotist to boot?

The War is searching out everyone, concentrating a beam of inquisitive light upon everyone's mind and character and publishing it for all the world to see. And the consequence to many honest folk has been a keen personal disappointment. We ignoble persons had thought we were better than we really are. We scarcely anticipated that the War was going to discover for us our emotions so despicably small by comparison, or our hearts so riddled with selfish motives. In the wild race for security during these dangerous times, men and women have all been sailing so closehauled to the wind that their eyes have been glued to their own forepeaks with never a thought for others: fathers have vied with one another in procuring safe jobs for their sons, wives have been bitter and recriminating at the security of other wives' husbands. The men themselves plot constantly for staff appointments, and everyone is pulling strings who can. Bereavement has brought bitterness and immunity indifference.

And how pathetically some of us cling still to fragments of the old regime that has already passed – like ship-wrecked mariners to floating wreckage, to the manner of the conservatoire amid the thunder of all Europe being broken up; to our newspaper gossip and parish teas, to our cherished aims – wealth, fame, success – in spite of all, *ruat coelum!* Mr A. C. Benson and his trickling, comfortable Essays, Mr Shaw and his Scintillations – they are all there as before, revolving like haggard windmills in a devastated landscape! . . .

3 November. I must have some music or I shall hear the paralysis creeping. That is why I lie in bed and whistle.

'My dear Brown, what am I to do?'* (I like to dramatize myself like that – it is an anodyne.)

---

* This is from a letter written by the dying Keats in Naples to his friend Brown.

I feel as if I were living alone on Ascension Island with the tide coming up continuously, and up and up.

6 November. She has known *all* from the beginning! M— warned her *not* to marry me. How brave and loyal of her! What an ass I have been. I am overwhelmed with feelings of shame and self-contempt and sorrow for her. She is quite cheerful and an enormous help.

Boxing Day 1918. James Joyce is my man (in the *Portrait of the Artist as a Young Man*). Here is a writer who tells the truth about himself. It is almost impossible to tell the truth. In this journal I have tried, but I have not succeeded. I have *set down* a good deal, but I cannot *tell* it. Truth of self has to be left by the psychology-miner at the bottom of his boring. Perhaps fifty or a hundred years hence Posterity may be told, but Contemporary will never know. See how soldiers deliberately, from a mistaken sense of charity or decency, conceal the horrors of this war. Publishers and Government aid and abet them. Yet a good cinema film of all the worst and most filthy and disgusting side of the war – everyone squeamish and dainty-minded to attend under State compulsion to have their necks scroffed, the sensitive nose-tips pitched into it, and their rest on lawny couches disturbed for a month after – would do as much to prevent future wars as any League of Nations.

After those bright hopes of last autumn Justice will be done only when all power is vested in the people. Every liberal-minded man must feel the shame of it.

This is the end. I am not going to keep a diary any more.

1 June 1919. Rupert Brooke said the brightest thing in the world was a leaf with the sun shining on it. God pity his ignorance! The brightest thing in the world is a Ctenophor in a glass jar standing in the sun. This is a bit of a secret, for no one knows about it save only the naturalist. I had a new sponge the other day and it smelt of the sea till I had soaked it. But what a vista that smell opened up! – rock pools, gobies, blennies, anemones (crassicorn, dahlia – oh! I forget). And at the end of my little excursion into memory I came upon the morning when I put some sanded, opaque bits of jelly, lying on the rim of the sea into a glass collecting jar, and to my amazement and delight they turned into Ctenophors – alive, swimming, and iridescent! You must imagine a tiny soap bubble about the size of a filbert with four series of plates or combs arranged regularly on the soap bubble from its north to its south pole, and flashing spasmodically in unison as they beat the water.

3 June. To-morrow I go to another nursing home.

The rest is silence.

7. THE DIARIST IN THE SHOP

THOMAS TURNER
Shopkeeper (1729–93)

Turner has suffered more than most diarists by having certain sensational incidents picked from his life; he has often been made to sound like a Georgian booby. One of these incidents, much anthologized, is certainly among the funniest to be found in any diary – or in any novel, if it comes to that. But Turner's character was until recently more distorted than that of any major diarist by being seen only when in his cups. David Vaisey changed all this when he published a third of the very full diary which Turner kept from 1754 to 1765. He revealed how previous editors from the 1850s onwards made such a travesty of what it contained in order to amuse the public that in 1925 J. B. Priestley could write, 'What his Diary lacks in length, fullness and historical importance, it makes up for in richness, quaintness and comical-pathetic naïveté.' Turner was, said Priestley, 'a little figure from the past' and 'an eighteenth-century nonentity'. On the contrary, Thomas Turner was in fact a most remarkable man whose daily life, put down in a third of a million words, allows the reader to take one of the most direct steps which literature supplies into the Georgian countryside. One can smell it, hear it, taste it. All the values, figures, etc., are to hand too with which to measure its economy. The diarist himself emerges as the reliable being who, in a village or small town, eventually has to shoulder most of its official tasks. Above all, Turner infuses his pages with the boisterousness of his times in a way which one usually only associates with Sterne and Fielding. His is the wild, half anarchic, half ponderously formal England on which the Industrial Revolution was soon to clamp down. He was twenty-five when he began to keep his diary and to record the powerful ordinariness of his existence. He was the kind of shop-keeper who would found London's great stores – Whiteley's, Fortnum & Mason, and so on. David Vaisey says that Turner kept a diary to ensure that his actions were rightly remembered and his books were straight.

The Inquest

Tuesday, 13 July 1756. This day died Eliz. Elless, and immediately after she was dead, Mr Adams told me Mr French and I would be fined on account of her death. The reason was because we carried her before a justice and asked her to swear the father.*

Wednesday, 14 July. At home all the forenoon. Paid Jos. Fuller for a bullock's heart 1½d. We dined on the heart baked in the oven and stuffed and a pudding under it. About 4 o'clock Mr Porter came to me and told me he thought it was the parish's duty to examine into the death of this poor creature who died yesterday, and have her opened. For there was, according to all circumstances, room to suspect she or some other person had administered something to deprive herself or child of life. For they had agreed with a nurse to come a-Monday, which she accordingly did, and was agreed with for only a week, and a person an entire stranger. Now this creature was very well all the day a-Monday and baked. And after she had taken the bread out of the oven, she took a walk and returned about 8 o'clock. And about 10 o'clock, or between 9 and 10, she was taken with a violent vomiting and purging and continued so all night until Tuesday, 5 o'clock, at which time she expired. And the latter part of her time she was convulsed, and if asked where in pain, she would answer 'All over.' Now what was very remarkable,

* Had Turner and French taken Elizabeth Elless before a magistrate on 3 July, as they had originally intended, and had her questioned as to her pregnancy, they would have been breaking the law. The statute 6 George II, c. 31 forbade such action until one month after an illegitimate child was born. However, Adam's threat was an empty one, since Turner and French had eventually decided that there was little point in getting her to swear the father.

she had not above 2 or 3 days more but her time as to child-bearing was expired. And during all the time of her sickness she never had any pangs or throes like labour, not no external symptoms whatever, and complained of great heat, and was afflicted with an uncommon drought. And what more increased our suspicion was as Mr John Vine's two men and apprentice was a-coming home from work a-Monday night, they saw Peter Adams's horse stand tied up at a pair of bars which lead into a very remote and obscure place in a wood, and upon which they immediately concluded to see whether he was alone and accordingly placed the boy at or near the bars whilst they went into the wood. Before they had went far, they saw Mr Adams, who made directly for the bars where the boy see him get on his horse and ride off. And as the men also knew him, they went forward, but not far, before they found where two people had stood and also two places where people had lain down. They then agreed to separate and endeavour to find out his partner, and one of them had walked but a little way before he see this unhappy creature, with whom he shook hands and talked to. And afterwards they all three see her together. This the men offer to swear before any magistrate. And as the affair has occasioned much talk, it led Mr Vine the elder to see if there was anything in what they said as to there being a place as if people had lain down, where he found two as they described and also found a horse had been tied up at the bars. They were also seen on Saturday night by another person, conversing over a pair of bars, he on horseback, leaning over his horse's neck, and she a-leaning over the bars. And during the whole time of her illness they never sent for any midwife or apothecary, nor did not call in any neighbours till near noon on Tuesday, and then only 2 or 3 simple creatures. And he, Peter Adams, were with her a great part of the day on Tuesday until she became speechless, and then shook hands with her and parted. And for a great while past they have been as conversant and familiar as if they were lovers though he was a married man. To do him justice he has had one child before by another woman, and his wife, poor woman, is now big with child. Upon this suspicion we went down to Mr Jer. French's to consult him, whom we found of the same opinion. From there we went to Mr Coates to consult him where we found him already very strong in the same opinion. And we all agreed to have her opened in order if possible to discover whether she or any one else had administered anything to deprive her or the child of life. We stayed and drank a mug of beer and all came away together, Mr French going home and Mr Porter and I came up the street, it being then about 6 o'clock. Mr Porter lent me a horse upon which I immediately set out for Luke Spence's Esq., to ask his advice and which way to proceed, but he not being at home, I went forward to John Bridger Esq. and very luckily met him a-walking in his garden near Offham. He told me he thought it was our duty and also very proper to have her opened, and as she was an inhabitant of the parish, her friends nor no other person could prevent our doing it. I then went to Lewes to get Dr Snelling to perform the operation, and whom I found at T. Scrase's. But he told me if there should be anything found in the midwifery, he could not report it; so it would be proper to have a man midwife to assist him, and on that account I did not agree with him to come until such time as I had again consulted the parish. I saw Mr Tucker at T. Scrase's, who informed me that at Windsor Fair wool sold for no more than 6*d.* per lb, which he said was about of equal goodness with our common wool, but not so clear from filth; and lamb wool was from 5½*d.* to 6*d.*; and farther added that Mr Tho. Friend's orders out of Yorkshire were all stopped. I stayed at Mr Scrase's while my horse was a-baiting and drank one mug of mild ale between Mr Tucker and Scrase and myself. I came home just at 10 o'clock. It lightened very much all the way I came home at times. I went directly to Mr Porter's to consult him again in the affair. He seemed to blame me a little for not getting Dr Davy, or some other man midwife; but however, we agreed that I should set out early tomorrow morning in order to get Snelling and Davy both to come along with me as early as possible. I then went to Joseph Fuller's and borrowed a horse to go upon tomorrow (who I found all in bed, and who I called, and they accordingly promised me I should have one). I came to my own house about 11 o'clock . . .

Thursday, 15 July. About 4 o'clock in the morn I rose and went down to Jos. Fuller's and called up Jo., T., and R. Fuller and got their horse and set out about 5 o'clock and called at Whyly to inform Mr French of our intentions (whom I found abed) but called him up; and as Mrs French was just going to breakfast, I stayed and breakfasted with them. I got to Lewes about 6.20 where I called up Mr Davy as also Mr Snelling. I borrowed of Mr Snelling in cash £7 4s. 0d. I also left with Mr Tho. Scrase, who I called up, £6 15s. 0d. which he was to pay to Mr Geo. Kemp, and take up a bill which he had of the same value, drawn on me by Mr Richd. Waite, which bill he was to send me by the post. Mr Snelling, Mr Davy and myself came to Mr Porter's about 10 o'clock, where we went in and stayed just the time of eating a bit of bread and drinking a glass of wine. We came up to my house where we provided ourselves with all things necessary for the operation, to wit, a bottle of wine and another of brandy and aprons and napkins, together with a quantity of fragrant herbs such as mint, savory, marjoram, balm, pennyroyal, roses etc., and threaded all the needles. We then proceeded to the house when we duly examined the nurse, who confirmed all we had heard before, with the addition that it was such a case as she never saw before and that she was fearful all was not right. The doctors then proceeded to the operation after they had dressed themselves and opened their instruments. They first made a cut from the bottom of the thorax to the os pubis and then two more across the top of the abdomen as:

The operation was performed in mine and the nurse's presence. They also opened the uterus where they found a perfect fine female child, which lay in the right position and would, as they imagined, have been born in about 48 hours. And as the membranes were all entirely whole, and the womb full of the water common on such occasions, there was convincing proof she never were in travail. The ilea were all very much inflamed, as was also the duodenum, but they both declared they could see no room to suspect poison. But if anything else had been administered, it had been carried off by her violent vomiting and purging (though they said circumstances looked very dark and all corroborated together to give room for suspicion). We came back to my house about 1 o'clock and Mr Snelling and Mr Davy went to Mr Porter's. The doctors both allowed this poor unhappy creature's death to proceed from a bilious colic (so far as they could judge). After dinner they both came up to our house when I paid Dr Snelling the £7 4s. 0d. I borrowed of him in the morn and also gave each of the gentlemen one guinea for their trouble . . .

Saturday, 17 July. In the morn after breakfast went down to Mr French's to get him to bring me from Lewes ½oz. cauliflower seed, and when I came there, I found Mr French, his servants, and Tho. Fuller a-catching of rats; so I stayed and assisted them about 3 hours, and we caught near 20. The method of catching them was by pouring of water into their burrows, which occasioned them immediately to come out, when either the dogs took them or [we] killed them with our sticks. Just as we had done, Mr John Vine came in. We stayed about ½ an hour and came all away together, Mr Vine and T. Fuller coming round by our house and only for the sake of a dram. What a surprising thing it is that a man of Mr Vine's sense and capacity should so much give way to the unruly dictates of a sensual appetite.

Tuesday, 7 March 1758. In the morn about 5 o'clock my brother and I set out on our intended journey. We arrived at Seaford about 8.20 where, after viewing the goods (which consisted of about 26 quarters of peas, 18 quarters groats, 5230 lbs of Smyrna raisins, and 20 bags of hops – all very much damaged with sea-water) in company with Mr Geo. Beard, we then walked down to the seaside. The sale begun about 11.20 when the peas was sold from 15s. to 22s. per quarter, and the groats nearly the same, the raisins from about 14s. to 18s. per cwt. But they having lost much of their goodness, neither Mr Beard or myself bought any. The sale ended about 1 o'clock . . . After I came home, my wife and I went down to Jos. Fuller's where we drank tea. We stayed and played at brag with the company hereafter mentioned. My wife and I won 18d. We stayed and supped there on two boiled chickens, a roasted shoulder of mutton, part of a cold ham, cold tongue, a cold veal pasty, tarts etc. in company with Mr and Mrs Porter, Mr Coates, Mr and Mrs French, Mr Calverley, Tho. Fuller and his wife, Dame Durrant, Master Fuller's family and Mrs Atkins. After supper my wife being very ill, she went home, as would I very gladly, making several vigorous attempts, but was still opposed by Mr Porter, so that at last I was obliged to sit myself down contentedly and make myself a beast for fashion sake, or else be stigmatized with the name of bad company. There we continued drinking like horses (as the vulgar phrase is) and singing till many of us was very drunk, and then we went to dancing and pulling off wigs, caps and hats. And there we continued in this frantic manner (behaving more like mad people than they that profess the name of Christians) till 9 o'clock when I deserted them and was twice pursued, but at last got clear off with first being well-rolled in the dirt. I came home far from being sober, though I must charge all this upon our reverend clergyman, whose behaviour I am sorry to see, for I shall always think it is contrary as well to the Christian religion as my own conscience. They then continued their perambulation from house to house till 12 o'clock when they got home and with imprudence and impudence declared themselves neither sick nor sorry. Now whether this is consistent to the wise saying of Solomon, let anyone judge: 'Wine is a mocker, strong drink is raging: and he that is deceived thereby is not wise.' Gave Molly Fuller 12*d*.

Wednesday, 8 March. Abed all day . . .

Thursday, 9 March. At home all day. Very uneasy for yesterday morn's frolic, though I am still of the same mind that it was contrary to my mind and that it was quite by force.

Friday, 10 March. About 3.50 my wife went down to Mr Porter's previous to an invitation given us yesterday by Mr Porter and about 7.20 I went down. We played at brag the 1st part of the even; my wife and self won 4*s*. 4½*d*. We stayed and supped at Mr Porter's on a shoulder [of] mutton roasted, a cold veal pasty, some fried veal, a cold ham, tarts, etc. in company with Mr Gibbs and his wife, Mr Piper and his wife, Tho. Fuller and his wife and Mrs Virgoe.

Saturday, 11 March. At home all day very piteous . . .

GEORGE STURT
Wheelwright (1863–1927)

Sturt was born at Farnham, Surrey, as was William Cobbett, and like the great rural apologist he questions the gains of 'progress'. Sturt, who wrote under the name of 'Bourne' in case the customers at his wheelwright's shop should think that he was not giving his full attention to business, and also, no doubt, to help to disguise the fact that his excellent books were full of close studies of his neighbours, began writing his journals when he was twenty-seven. They are exceptionally complex in that they display the double life of a man who ran the family workshop while dedicated to literature. The entries move from the ordinary events of each country day into essays, characterizations and episodes which could find a place in fiction or social history. The poverty, limitations and stifling class-consciousness of the pre-1914 village existence, on the one hand, and the 'release' of books, nature, and culture generally, on the other, pervade Sturt's often sombre pages. E. D. Mackerness, his editor, sees him linking the thought of Ruskin and William Morris to that of D. H. Lawrence. The journals provided Sturt with material for his masterpiece *The Wheelwright's Shop,* and for all his other works.

When young, Sturt had – like many literary beginners – made the acquaintance of similar hopefuls. One of these was Arnold Bennett. In 1906, when Sturt was beginning to realize that he was not a novelist and would have to be a very different kind of writer from his now iridescent friend, he confessed:

> Some ten years ago Arnold Bennett, taking me into his confidence not so much to obtain my advice as to offer me his own, informed me that he had begun to keep a journal. As yet he had published no books . . . as he viewed it, the keeping of a journal was a most valuable part of the apprenticeship to that career.

Sturt's *Journals*, 'the best book I shall ever write', are the annals of the old traditional, hard, yet rich village world, plus an expression of the isolation in which such a man would find himself in a small rural community.

Sunday, 22 October 1899. At the Duttons': Mr Wren and his luckless marriage: connections between matrimony and 'fortune' . . .

I had not realized until quite lately how life in England is permeated by suspicion, like the Frensham Vicar's, of social intercourse between girls and young men. Our own vicar protested solemnly, a few weeks ago, against the opening of evening classes in the schools, for girls: his reason being that in gathering the girls together, we very practically advertised to the village youths where and at what time of night they might be found.

I think that the vicar's suspicion is tacitly endorsed by society in general. When one considers, it is a somewhat rare thing to see men and maidens together, 'courting': and the sight is viewed with a grudging tolerance at best. House-mistresses, of course, object to 'followers': and the maids know it. But there is a wide-spread feeling that for a man and girl to be seen together is not quite right. Hence the interviews are furtive: they take place in bye-lanes, or are postponed till dark. A girl who should neglect such precautions would certainly be regarded as a wanton, and would suffer for it.

8 March 1900. Lizzie Binfield has left school to go to 'service'. I saw her cleaning a step, yesterday.

Of the little girls whose presence made it feel a privilege to visit the Board School, I think Lizzie was the most wonderful. A tall girl, of graceful growth and delicate clearness of skin. Not tidily dressed. Her dress gaped at the throat, showing a fine whiteness: her hair very soft and fine, broke loose over her brow on one side, waving prettily. The charm of her, above all, was in her eyes, soft rich brown eyes that seemed to judge you, searching whether you had any friendship, and ready to light up gratefully – though always retiringly – if you were found worthy. A soft reserved smile dimpled her cheeks. Not a 'clever' girl. She was through the fifth standard and I had thought she would be long at school. But I suppose her age exempted her: and, with her tall well-fashioned body – full of grace and beauty – she was thought 'big enough to work': and some idle utilitarian house mistress perceived in her 'strength' – as one perceives it in a horse that he buys.

And so the cream of the sweet flesh and blood of our parish was being used yesterday morning to put white stuff on a piece of stone. It seemed to me a waste. I hardly knew the girl in her print dress – made too voluminous for her slenderness: but there was the rebellious wave of hair, the beautiful soft skin, and the rich eyes. And the child's brain left in fifth standard ignorance: a whitened piece of stone the advantage purchased by this loss.

25 January 1906. Numerous tales are coming out, of attempts to coerce the labourers into voting conservative. The Brewery men were all told how to vote, by the chiefs. A district visitor (Miss Crump, I think) visiting her own tenants, told them that if they supported the Liberal candidate, they could not be allowed to stay in their cottages. Bide affirmed that he was going to bring his 100 men to vote for Brodrick. It is said that Charrington of Frensham Hill is so overcome as to threaten that if he finds any man of his to have voted for Cowan, that man will be immediately dismissed: further, he will deal no more in Farnham: we are not to 'get the big loaf out of *him*'! At Waverley Abbey, all the men had to wear the Tory colours and were taken to the poll. But amongst themselves they said, of Brodrick, 'he's the feller as wants to interfere with our grub'; and they voted against him. They didn't talk so, though, when their master was by. (This is the tale of the wife of one of the men, who had spoken so to Miss Ketchell, Aunt Ann's lodger, in her shop.)

24 May. Much talk of the old days again, at Aunt Ann's this afternoon, Uncle Jack being there. It began by an observation *à propos* of Miss Ketchell's passion for amusements: a passion which there would have been no means of gratifying, in the old craftsmen, when they lingered lovingly over their work, putting tiles on their roofs in pretty patterns, taking pains to lay their bricks corner-wise (like a simple mosaic), paving their cottage courtyards in decorous design of pebble-work, clipping their yew hedges, and so on. This will be, when the land is put to its right use once more: when once more we have got back to the gregarious [and] away from the predatory ideal (that bad dream of civilization by competition); and in this aspect, Socialism looks like a sort of New Feudalism: a Feudalism in which the Nation is King and the Town Council is the Lord of the Manor, and under which a well-to-do population may resume the sanity of the Folk temper, and its almost forgotten joy in living.

Viewed so, civilization (with Progress and Liberalism) looks like a digression: as though the Nation had walked into a cul de sac.

Yet oddly enough, to reach the new Folk life, it is absolutely necessary to get out of all the old folk habits. Not prejudices, traditions, conventions, can help us: but Free Taste and Free Thought. The effect of civilization so far has been to leave people their prejudices but destroy their pleasure.

11 October. I happen to know this pain of unquiet; but I think others feel it, not recognizing what it is. I think in general a living is not only harder to get as time goes on, but is less worth getting from year to year. And, observing tendencies, I grow more and more pessimistic.

Once it seemed to me that our Empire – great overgrown absurdity that it is – would prove a sort of husk in which some intensely beautified mode of living would slowly ripen. I thought that the English, with their democracy, might survive the climacteric so deadly to oligarchies when they mature, and go on afterwards to a richer existence. But I begin to doubt.

The race appears to be to the hustler: to the millionaire trust. (And I am glad therefore if it is true that people of the hustling ranks are ceasing to breed.) There seems no escape. For why do we hurry so? And why is it that men of better tastes have to wear themselves to death against their will? It is the pressure of the developing hustler. Into the quiet sleepy old town, there comes first some unscrupulous tradesman, greedy and possessing the business instinct. At once the old-fashioned have to toe the line with him, or be left out of the running. So it goes on, stage after stage; at last comes the syndicate with the big capital and the dead conscience. All but all hate it; yet must compete with it in its own vices. It is the victorious type.

Artists, and quiet souls, are powerless to resist this advance.

8. THE DIARIST AT WAR

Wars have always been great diary-keeping times, even when, as in the First World War, they were forbidden on security grounds. The involvement of individuals in what was often the most sensational activity of their life drove many men who would not otherwise have kept journals to record what they saw, felt and did. Commanders of armies and fleets, or of a single ship or garrison, often placed their experiences within the context of martial skills, victories, and so forth. But the ordinary fighting man tended to isolate himself from crews and regiments in his diary. There is a deeper justice than was intended when, in the days of Elizabeth I, the lowest-ranked fighting man was dubbed 'private', for only through diaries and letters can the corporate mass of vivid feelings which comprise a battlefield be examined. The soldiers', sailors' and airmen's diaries make up a rational language which has been severed from the roar of battle, and represent a different truth from that mentioned in dispatches.

Some of the war diaries are very early. Anonymous fighting men kept them during the expedition against Calais (1544) and the defence of Bergen-op-Zoom (1588). Two admirals, Sir Richard Grenville and Lord Wimbledon, wrote journals during the naval actions off the Spanish coast during the 1620s. Seamen accustomed to keeping ships' logs turned naturally to personal daily records. But it was the Civil War which stimulated military diarists as never before. The seventeenth century was England's time of profound introspection; Puritan and Royalist alike, though chiefly the former, searched himself on the page, as it were, as he fought. Many Civil

151

War diaries are about marches. There is a stern restlessness and much claiming of divine leadership. Whether Parliamentarians or followers of the King, these brother-versus-brother diarists are deadly serious and often describe their factional lives with a strong sense of history being made. Several diaries record the siege of Colchester in 1648 – the last time such a classic military operation took place in England – and there are a number of journals covering Cromwell's grim military expedition to Ireland. These seventeenth-century diaries display very anxious warring men who are busy justifying their military activities to God. Similar attitudes fill the many diaries written by soldiers during the Battle of the Boyne and the rest of the cruel fighting in Ireland during the 1680s and 1690s. On the whole, these diaries tend to be under some 'military control' where their authors' emotions are concerned. A typical Jacobite soldier's diary is that written by Captain John Stevens from 1689 to 1691. Stevens was not only a fighting man but also an archaeologist. His journal is a counterbalance to the predominantly Protestant diarizings of a war which was to have lethal consequences for many generations to come.

The arrival of Prince Charles Edward Stuart in the Hebrides, his abortive march south and defeat at Culloden, initiated a spate of military diaries. The diary kept by Sir John Moore from 1793 to 1808, which reveals both the excellent general and the private man, is among the finest of all soldierly writings. Lord Hastings' *A Journal Kept in the British Army* also shows the diarist moving away from mere campaign reporting to personal note-taking about himself and his attitudes during service in the regiment. Nelson kept a sea diary, and Wellington's career is copiously documented in the many diaries written by his officers. Lieutenant Swabey's diary of the Peninsular War is dashing and odd, and the youthful Lieutenant Woodberry of the 18th Hussars fills his diary with matters which fascinate him a great deal more than drill and fighting, as does Colonel Montgomery Maxwell, whose military diary during the Peninsular campaign shows him having a ball as much as a war.

By the mid nineteenth century, war diaries began to change. For one thing, women like Mrs Henry Duberly (*Journal Kept during the Russian War* – the Crimea) began to write them and soldiers such as Captain Vincent Wing described the actual miseries suffered by their men. Doctors (for instance, George Buchanan, who worked alongside Florence Nightingale and her nurses) made diary notes for books with titles like *Camp Life Seen by a Civilian* which, to the irritation of the generals, cast a critical eye over what the latter would have preferred to remain a hidden area. Naturally, appalling things happened during battles but they were the affair of the army alone. But now journalists began to publish objective reports; Sir William Russell's *My Diary During the Last Great War* (the Franco-Prussian War) described the fighting as he witnessed it from the Prussian H.Q., and Felix Whitehurst contributed his sensational *My Private Diary of the Siege of Paris*.

The First World War could claim to be the most diarized event in history. William Matthews in his *Annotated Bibliography of British Diaries* lists over fifty for the years 1914 to 1918, and there have been many further discoveries since he published his indispensable catalogue more than forty years ago. Soldiers and nurses kept them at Gallipoli and on the Western Front; sailors kept them at sea. Many were fragmented by the writer's death. Those written by conscripts – a very different intelligence in the trenches from that of the traditional soldier – are full of questionings and confessions which, on the whole, would not have been made by a regular. Mrs Constance Miles kept a 'home front' diary for her children, and many wives exchanged diarized letters with their husbands. Although there was strict censorship and a conventional reticence – not to mention the *de rigueur* 'cheerfulness' of the times – reality could not be denied for long. One has only to read what John Masefield, a medical orderly in France, wrote to his wife to realize how the horrors of war refused to be kept off the page. The two World Wars were fought by battalions and squadrons of enlisted farmers, poets, priests, teenage labourers, sharp townees, clerks, actors, and great numbers of women, who, there being no help for it, so to speak, went public via that most private document, the diary. Writing down each day's happenings brought hard thinking, if not judgement, to bear on them. The self under stress, or simply under strange orders, was taken an honest look at whenever there was a pause. All kinds of 'books of the Self' took shape, and were to be a considerable impediment to military annals as such.

The professional soldiers in their tents and spartan bedrooms frequently used diaries in order to retreat from their official image, and to reveal complicated personalities in which simple values vied with far from simple emotions, or were entangled with them. General Gordon's Khartoum journals and Chinese diaries are classics of this kind. Towards the end of the 317-day siege which was to bring his death, he wrote:

> During the blockade we have often discussed the question of being frightened which, in the world's view, a man should never be. For my part I am always frightened and very much so. I fear the future of all engagements. It is not the fear of death, that is past, thank God, but I fear defeat and its consequences. I do not believe a bit in the calm unmoved man. I think it is only he does not show it outwardly. Thence I conclude no commander of forces ought to live closely in relationship with his subordinates who watch him like lynxes, for there is no contagion equal to that of fear . . .

On 14 December 1883 he wrote up his journal for the last time. On his way to the Sudan he had hugged himself with delight at escaping the lionizing social whirl of England:

> I dwell on the joy of never seeing Great Britain again with its horrid wearisome dinner parties and miseries. How we can put up with such things passes my imagination . . . we are all in masks saying what we do not believe, eating and drinking things we do not want and then abusing one another. I would sooner live like a Dervish with the Mahdi than go out to dinner every night in London.

Now he knew that his country was about to let its hero down:

> Arabs fired two shells at the Palace this morning: 566 ardebs dhoora [forage] in store; also 83,525 okes of biscuit! 10.30 a.m. The steamers are down at Omdurman engaging the Arabs consequently I am on tenterhooks! 11.30. steamers returned; the *Bordeen* was struck by a shell in her battery; we had only one man wounded. We are going to send down the *Bordeen* tomorrow with this journal. If I was in command of the two

hundred men of the Expeditionary Force which are all that are necessary for the movement I should stop just below Halfeyeh and attack the Arabs at that place before I came on here to Kartoum [*sic*]. I should then communicate with the North Fort and act according to circumstances. Now *mark this* if the Expeditionary Force, and I ask for no more than two hundred men, does not come in ten days, *the town may fall*; and I have done my best for the honour of my country. Good bye. C. G. Gordon.

Khartoum fell on 26 January 1885, Gordon was slaughtered and his severed head carried to the Mahdi. Sir Charles Wilson's relief arrived two days later. When Gordon's journals appeared in print that same year they were received as a humiliating indictment of Britain's unwillingness to exert her full powers to rescue the good and the brave. It was his published diaries rather than what others wrote of him which made Charles Gordon an Empire saint. Prints of his martyrdom on the Palace steps would hang in classrooms for many years to come, along with the last sentence from his diary, and would be remembered later in Flanders. Gordon was a diarist who was involved in, though he did not deliberately create it, his own myth and symbolism.

EDMUND WHEATLEY

With so many to choose from, it is not easy to select any single 'most representative' early military diary, but that kept by the 21-year-old Edmund Wheatley during the Peninsular War and the Waterloo campaign is certainly one of the most wonderfully written. Wheatley was an artist from Hammersmith who had joined up as an ensign in the 5th Line Battalion of the King's German Legion in 1812 after the customary confusions that beset the young. 'Not an individual related to you approves of me,' he wrote sadly to his girl, Eliza Brookes. And who could be surprised, for already he had fought a duel, run riot at Brighton and done everything possible to make any respectable girl's parents take against him. So in November 1812, with the whole country war-mad, he went to Bexhill and became a soldier 'without purchase'. His regiment had been in existence for nine years and was officered almost entirely by Hanoverians who had escaped to England when Napoleon overran their land in 1803. In his battalion Ensign Wheatley made a friend of Llewellyn and an enemy in Captain Nötting. These figures haunt his diary, which he wrote for Eliza and illustrated with beautiful water-colour drawings. It contains passages which might have come out of a great novel. Here is the diarist at Waterloo.

June 1815. On the opposite ascent stand hundreds of young men like myself whose feelings are probably more acute, whose principles are more upright, whose acquaintance would delight and conversation improve me, yet with all my soul I wished them dead as the earth they tramped on and anticipated their total annihilation. 'Tis inconceptible how one's ideas should be so diametrically reversed from what is equitable and correct. When I looked at my own comrades I could not conceive why my animosity was diverted from them in preference to the French who are, by far, more commendable characters than these heavy, selfish Germans.

Here stood a swelled-faced, ignorant booby, raw from England, staring with a haggard and pallid cheek on the swarms of foes over against him. One could perceive the torture of his feelings by the hectic quivering of his muscles, as if fear and cold were contending for the natural color of the cheek. And this man is one of the mighty warriors shortly to deal out thunder and confusion to the opposers of the British constitution.

Close behind him stalked a dark, swarthy weather-beaten man, whose arm had aided in expelling the opposite nation from the Tagus to the Garonne. Frequent flashes from the pan had dyed his brows with a never-failing black. The horrid preparations before him gave no surprise to his soul. The scene afforded no novelty to his eye. Yet a side glance on turning at his walk's end bespoke the uppermost thoughts in his mind, [for] the oldest veteran must have been struck with the solemnity of the scene.

About ten o'clock, the order came to clean out the muskets and fresh load them. Half an allowance of rum was then issued, and we descended into the plain, and took our position in solid Squares. When this was arranged as per order, we were ordered to remain in our position but, if we like, to lay down, which the battalion did [as well as] the officers in the rere.

I took this opportunity of surveying our situation. It was singular to perceive the shoals of Cavalry and artillery suddenly in our rere all arranged in excellent order as if by a magic wand. The whole of the horse Guards stood behind us. For my part I thought they were at Knightsbridge barracks or prancing on St James's Street.

A Ball whizzed in the air. Up we started simultaneously. I looked at my watch. It was just eleven o'clock, Sunday (Eliza just in Church at Wallingford or at Abingdon) morning. In five minutes a stunning noise took place and a shocking havock commenced.

One could almost feel the undulation of the air from the multitude of cannon shot. The first man who fell was five files on my left. With the utmost distortion of feature he lay on his side and shrivelling up every muscle of the body he twirled his elbow round and round in acute agony, then dropped lifeless, dying as it's called a death of glory, heaving his last breath on the field of fame. *Dieu m'engarde!*

A black consolidated body was soon seen approaching and we distinguished by sudden flashes of light from the sun's rays, the iron-cased cavalry of the enemy. Shouts of 'Stand firm!' 'Stand fast!' were heard from the little squares around and very quickly these gigantic fellows were upon us.

No words can convey the sensation we felt on seeing these heavy-armed bodies advancing at full gallop against us, flourishing their sabres in the air, striking their armour with the handles, the sun gleaming on the steel. The long horse hair, dishevelled by the wind, bore an appearance confounding the senses to an astonishing disorder. But we dashed them back as cooly as the sturdy rock repels the ocean's foam. The sharp-toothed bayonet bit many an adventurous fool, and on all sides we presented our bristly points like the peevish porcupines assailed by clamorous dogs.

The horse Guards then came up and drove them back; and although the sight is shocking 'tis beautiful to see the skirmish of Cavalry.

The French made repeated attacks of this kind. But we stood firm as the ground we stood on, and two long hours were employed in these successive attacks.

About two o'clock the cavalry ceased annoying and the warfare took a new turn. In order to destroy our squares, the enemy filled the air with shells, howitzers and bombs, so that every five or six minutes, the whole Battalion lay on its face then sprang up again when [the danger] was over.

The Prince of Orange gallop'd by, screaming out like a new born infant, 'Form into line! Form into line!' And we obeyed.

About this time the battle grew faint and a mutual cannonade with musketry amused us for one and a half hours, during which time I walked up and down chatting and joking with the young officers who had not [until] then smelt powder.

An ammunition cart blew up near us, smashing men and horses. I took a calm survey of the field around and felt shocked at the sight of broken armour, lifeless bodies, murdered horses, shattered wheels, caps, helmets, swords, muskets, pistols, still and silent. Here and there a frightened horse would rush across the plain trampling on the dying and the dead. Three or four poor wounded animals standing on three legs, the other dangling before [them]. We killed several of these unfortunate beasts and it would have been an equal Charity to have perform'd the same operation on the wriggling, feverish, mortally lacerated soldiers as they rolled on the ground.

About four o'clock the battle was renewed with uncommon ardour. We still stood in line. The carnage was frightful. The balls which missed us mowed down the Dutch behind us, and swept away many of the closely embattled Cavalry behind them.

I saw a cannon ball take away a Colonel of the Nassau Regiment so cleanly that the horse never moved from under him. While [I was] buisy in keeping the men firm in their ranks, closing up the vacuities as the balls swept off the men, inspecting the fallen to detect deception [or] subterfuge, a regiment of Cuirassiers darted like a thunderbolt among us. At the instant a squadron of horse Guards dashed up to our rescue. In the confusion of the moment I made [for] the Colors to defend them. And we succeeded with infinite difficulty in rallying the men again.

I parried with great good fortune a back stroke from a horseman as he flew by me and Captain Sander had a deep slice from the same fellow on the head the instant after.

The battalion once more formed into a solid square, in which we remained the [whole] afternoon.

I felt the ardor of the fight increase very much within me, from the uncommon fury of the engagement.

Just then I fired a slain soldier's musket until my shoulder was nearly jellied and my mouth was begrimed with gunpowder to such a degree that I champed the gritty composition unknowingly.

Nothing could equal the splendor and terror of the scene. Charge after charge succeeded in constant succession. The clashing of swords, the clattering of musketry, the hissing of balls, and shouts and clamours produced a sound, jarring and confounding the senses, as if hell and the Devil were in evil contention.

About this time I saw the Duke of Wellington running from a charge of Cavalry towards the Horse-Guards, waving his hat to beckon them to the encounter.

All our artillery in front fell into the french power, the bombardiers skulking under the carriages. But five minutes put them again into our hands and the men creeping out applied the match and sent confusion and dismay into the retreating enemy.

Several times were these charges renewed and as often defeated. Charge met charge and all was pellmell. The rays of the sun glittered on the clashing swords as the two opposing bodies closed in fearful combat and our balls clattered on the shining breastplates like a hail shower.

As I stood in the square I looked down, I recollect, to take a pinch of snuff and thought of the old ballad, which I had seen somewhere, of the aged Nurse who describes the glorious battles of Marlborough to the child. After each relation of valor and victory, the infant [says]

> 'Ten thousand slain you say and more?
> What did they kill each other for?'
> 'Indeed I cannot tell,' said she,
> 'But 'twas a famous victory.' *

* The diarist is faultily recollecting 'The Battle of Blenheim' by Robert Southey.

The field was now thickened with heaps of bodies and shattered instruments. Carcases of men and beasts lay promiscuously entwined. Aid-de-Camps scoured across with inconceivable velocity. All was hurry and indefatigable exertion. The small squares on our right kept up incessant firings and the fight was as obstinate as at the commencement.

The Duke of Wellington passed us twice, slowly and cooly.

No advantage as yet was discernible on either side. The French Cavalry were less annoying. Their brave, repeated assaults had cost them very dear.

About six o'clock a passe-parole ran down the line – not to be disheartened, as the Prussians were coming up to our left, which news we received with loud cheers. And on looking [to] the left I perceived at some distance a dark swarm moving out of a thick wood. In twenty minutes a fresh cannonading began as if in rere of the French and the battle raged with increased vehemence.

A French Regiment of Infantry before us opposite the Farm house called the holy hedge (La Haye Sainte) advanced considerably just then and poured a destructive fire into our Battalion.

Colonel Ompteda ordered us instantly into line to charge, with a strong injunction to 'walk' forward, until he gave the word. When within sixty yards he cried 'Charge', we ran forward huzzaing. The trumpet sounded and no one but a soldier can describe the thrill one instantly feels in such an awful moment. At the bugle sound the French stood until we just reached them. I ran by Colonel Ompteda who cried out, 'That's right, Wheatley!'

I found myself in contact with a French officer but ere we could decide, he fell by an unknown hand. I then ran at a drummer, but he leaped over a ditch through a hedge in which he stuck fast. I heard a cry of, 'The Cavalry! The Cavalry!' But so eager was I that I did not mind it at the moment, and when on the eve of dragging the Frenchman back (his iron-bound hat having saved him from a Cut) I recollect no more. On recovering my senses, I look'd up and found myself, bareheaded, in a clay ditch with a violent head-ache. Close by me lay Colonel Ompteda on his back, his head stretched back with his mouth open, and a hole in his throat. A frenchman's arm across my leg.

So confused was I that I did not remember I was on the field of

Battle at the moment. Lifting up a little, I look'd over the edge of the ditch and saw the backs of a french Regiment and all the day's employment instantly suggested itself to my mind. Suddenly I distinguished some voices and heard one say '*En voici! En voici!*'

I lay down as dead, retaining my breath, and fancied I was shot in the back of my head. Presently a fellow cries, '*Voici un autre b.*' And a tug at my epaulette bespoke his commission. A thought struck me – he would turn me round to rifle my pockets. So starting up, I leaped up the ditch; but a swimming seized me and I was half on the ground when the fellow thrust his hand in my collar, grinning, '*Ou va's tu, chien?*' I begged of him to let me pick up my cap and he dragged me into the house.

The inside of La Haye Sainte I found completely destroyed, nothing but the rafters and props remaining. The floor, covered with mortar bricks and straw, was strewed with bodies of the German Infantry and French Tirailleurs. A Major in Green lay by the door. The carnage had been very great in this place.

I was taken over these bodies out of a door on the right, through a garden to the back of the house where I found several Officers and men standing. [They] instantly crowded round me. One of my wings was on and the other half off. My oil skin haversac [was] across my shoulder, and my cap fastened to my waist, by running my sash through the internal lining.

A multitude of questions was put to me by the men and Officers while I fastened on my Cap: '*Vous êtes Chef de Battalion, Monsieur?*' . . .

Wheatley was cruelly dealt with after his capture but managed to escape after some days of shocking treatment behind the French lines.

THE REV. ANDREW CLARK
(1856–1922)

Clark's diary for 1914 to 1919, which he carefully called *Echoes of the Great War,* is one of the most important 'home front' documents of the period. It was discovered in the Bodleian Library during the early 1970s by James Munson while he was researching material for an Oxford doctorate, and first became widely known and admired through a series of BBC Radio 4 programmes based on it by Alan Haydock. The diarist was the Rector of Great Leighs, Essex, from 1894 till his death, and no ordinary country parson. He was an Oxford don who had held the livings of St Michael's-at-the North-Gate and, later, All Saints, a lecturer in logic, a fine historian, and chaplain of Lincoln College. He was born at Dollarfield, Clackmannanshire, the son of a farm labourer. Nearby Dollar Academy swiftly sent him on his way to St Andrews University and then to Oxford, where he took a double first in Greats. It was there that his interest in diaries as historic source-books began to preoccupy him, especially those of the seventeenth century.

Exactly why he left Oxford, which he loved and where a distinguished career obviously awaited him, remains conjectural. Some members of his family thought that his wife wasn't happy there. At any rate, he accepted his college's living at Great Leighs and remained there for four years. He tried unsuccessfully to obtain the professorship of Humanity at St Andrews in 1899, attempted soon after this to get back to Oxford, then settled down in Essex as the Boer War showed him what limitless matters there were to discover and write about in an average rural parish. His moment came in August 1914; all the rest had been an apprenticeship for it. He would keep a diary, not about himself but about his adopted village at what he knew to be its greatest time of change. The diary would be circumscribed and only those things which came to his knowledge in the parish – and these could include gossip, newspapers, and letters and chat from the Front – would be entered in it. He wrote it in ninety-two exercise books which he deposited in batches in the Bodleian Library every few months for the duration of the war. Along with the diary, Clark kept a huge record of the way in which the language was affected by the crisis, which he called *English Words in War-Time*, plus a vast scrapbook of official notices and other documents. Only a fraction of this parish record-extraordinary has been published, but already the Rector of Great Leighs is regarded as a fitting companion for Kilvert and others on the 'first-rate diarists' shelf.

Saturday, 29 August 1914. Letter received by afternoon post, 2 p.m.:

> 28, August 1914
> Dear Dr Clark,
>   Now that the harvest is over I am arranging to summon a meeting of the men and women of Great and Little Leighs in the barn here on Sunday afternoon, Sept. 6, in order to make clear to them the causes and the justice of the war and the Nation's need for soldiers; and further to make an appeal to the young men to offer themselves. It is especially necessary to get the women, otherwise I would have suggested a joint parish meeting. It will be at 3 o'clock and I trust will have your approval and if possible, your presence.
>
> > Yours truly,
> > J. H. Tritton.

It is reported that after a special meeting at Great Waltham under Col. W. Nevill Tufnell, to beat up recruits, only one recruit joined. The Colonel is *the* territorial magnate of this part of the country, but is at present not in highest favour in his own parish.

Sunday, 30 August. Reports from Braintree: twenty-eight men of Courtauld's Braintree crape-works, after a recruiting meeting, volunteered for service. The government is said to allow – per week – to each man 8s. 9d., to his wife 7s. 7d. and 1s. 2d. for each child. The hospital of the Red Cross at Braintree was very much out of pillow cases. Mrs Lave of Gosfield Hall, a very wealthy but most eccentric widow-lady, had lent four, all carefully marked with her name and stringent orders that they should be returned when no longer needed.

On my way to Church for a Christening at 6 p.m., Miss Lucy Tritton, elder daughter of H. L. M. Tritton of the Hole Farm, Great Leighs, met me, jumped off her bicycle and told me that her father had heard from someone in the 'Home' office (she said) that a large Russian force from Archangel had landed in Scotland and was being speeded south by rail to take its place in the theatre of war in Belgium. I mentioned the report of Saturday's evening paper, that a train-load of 200 Russians escaped from Germany into Switzerland and France, had reached England. But Miss Tritton was positive that her information was authentic and correct.

My elder daughter, Mary Alice, attended the evening service at Fairstead, one of the ring of parish churches which lie round Great Leighs. The Rector, Thomas Sadgrove, preached a horrifying sermon, on the horrible scenes of the battlefield and exhorted all the young men to join the army. He had a big Union Jack hung in front of the pulpit, instead of the pulpit-hanging.

Tuesday, 1 September. Village lads are not very pleased at pressure put by the Squire to compel his two footmen to enlist. To use the phrase of one of the lads, the 'idle sons' of the house ought to have set the example of going, though married, with children and something over the age.

Village gossip makes fun of the projected savings of Lyons Hall (Village opinion is always spiteful and disparaging and ungrateful.):

(a) either butter or jam, not both.

(b) no cake at tea – but only one seed-cake (for show) which no one cares for and is not cut.

(c) meat at only one meal a day.

(d) only fruit from Lyons Hall gardens.

(e) no cream; all cream to be made into butter which now sells at a high price.

Wednesday, 2 September. Dr H. G. K. Young of Braintree told Miss Mildred Clark that on Su. 30 Aug., the Russian troops were fed in Colchester; that the Gurkhas were in highest feather at coming to European War. King George was the greatest and wisest of Kings. He first had gone to India to be crowned there and he first had perceived that they were worthy to stand shoulder to shoulder with the British troops in the greatest of wars.

Mrs Albert Taylor, wife of Albert Taylor, postman, son of Henry Taylor, wheelwright, and Sub-Postmaster of Great Leighs – an exceptionally kindly natured, gentle-spoken woman, said (14 Sept. 1914) 'Well, it may be very wrong; but I don't mind saying it, that I should be very glad if the Kaiser were shot.'

At 5 p.m. an aeroplane passed over the Rectory grounds, but very high up. (Aeroplanes have been seen crossing over this parish on several days, but these occurrences have not been noted as I had no definite hours given me.)

At 5.45 p.m. James Turner, farm labourer at Lyons Hall, came for a 'harvest-home'. This is a traditional tip contributed by the parson to each farm towards the jollification which the men hold on their own account on completion of harvest.

Sunday, 6 September. Another day of intense heat – deep blue sky – only the faintest white clouds; pastures and gardens burnt up by the long drought. Apples, pears and acorns falling prematurely. Mr T. Stoddart, Rector's Churchwarden, tells me that although it is a time of stress and sorrow of war, it is the wish of the parish that the Harvest Festival shall be held next Sunday just as usual in thankfulness for the extraordinary bounty of this year's harvest and unbroken harvest weather.

Wednesday, 25 August 1915. Mrs Tritton had a number of wounded soldiers to tea. I counted sixty-one men. I had a talk with some: [One man] is in the Westminsters (16th London). He went through all the Boer War. This war is a much bigger thing, but it is much better organized. There is no fear of disease over there – now. Burial arrangements are almost perfect. The Germans don't bury their dead. They pile them up as a screen in front of their trenches. At night our lads creep out and bury as many Germans as they can. It is a risky business because if the Germans hear, or fancy they hear a movement, they turn their flash-lights on and fire. The water supply in all cases is good. The hospital arrangements are almost perfect. The grumbles among the men are all about small matters.

I was surprised at the extreme lowness in which men spoke to each other as well as to myself. I asked the retired medical man in charge, whether this was a subdued tone they had got into owing to having been long in hospital. He said possibly it was part cause, but the main cause was the trenches, in which any voice louder than a whisper brought a hail of shrapnel on them.

There was some talk about the German army. All agreed that they were splendid fighters, especially the Prussians. Many of the men had picked up a good deal of French. So far as simple sentences went they could understand French spoken and could speak French themselves. All were loud in praise of the extreme kindness they received from the French peasantry everywhere.

Several of them were very sore about recruiting not being brisker. A common suggestion was that now our forces had gone some way ahead, and left behind them battlefields and towns and villages over which the tide of war has flowed and ebbed, this country should run cheap railway and motor excursions for some weeks. If our men at home could only see what has happened in France and Flanders there would be recruits galore.

PRIVATE HORACE BRUCKSHAW
(1891–1917)

Horace Bruckshaw may have been the kind of person who saves diary-writing for special occasions, holidays, military service and foreign travel. His social background is a little reminiscent of Wilfred Owen's, with the family sliding from 'county' to lower-middle-class circumstances during the late nineteenth century. Bruckshaw was the youngest of seven children of a commercial traveller who worked for a celebrated firm of railway and turret clock-makers. He was apprenticed as a draughtsman in the hope that he might eventually become an architect. But when his father died he left home and began to train as a manager at a cotton-mill near Manchester. Here he met the girl who was to become his wife and later his widow of half a century. She received his modest diary and treasured it until she died, when it was sold at auction, discovered and published.

Bruckshaw had volunteered in August 1914, one of the half-million young men swept off their feet by patriotism and the chance to abandon dull lives. He belonged to the local Territorials and the only surprising thing about his going to war was that he enlisted in the Royal Marines and not in one of Kitchener's 'Pals' battalions. The choice was to be an auspicious one. As a member of the Royal Naval Division, Bruckshaw was in at the very beginning of Churchill's ill-fated attempt to force the Dardanelles. His Gallipoli diary begins at Tavistock in January 1915 and records the days leading up to the historic embarkation. On Sunday, 25 April, he waded ashore on a beach lying between Cape Hellas and Gaba Tepe, advancing under very heavy fire. Many of his comrades were killed and the following day he and the other survivors dragged themselves back to the ships. Soon a bridgehead was established, and Bruckshaw's sharp and unadorned account of what happened tells the rest. This is among the best 'ordinary soldier' accounts of Gallipoli extant. The diarist, like so many youngsters of his generation, is physically unfit and easily exhausted, but brave and enduring. After Gallipoli he was sent to the Western Front, where he was killed during the battle of Arleux, a battle which the Royal Marines still call the capture of Gavrelle Windmill. His body was never found. He had left his diaries with his wife during his last leave.

Sunday, 9 May 1915. Spent a rotten night of it. This is a terrible place simply infested with snipers. Nine of us went out with Capt. Andrews hunting them during the morning. Could find nothing however although we were sniped at every step we took. Luckily we all got safely back to our trench. Chapman wounded in chest this morning just as he got up to go to the assistance of another wounded man. It made us a wee bit nervous as he was sitting against me. After dark we went over the back of the trench to a point about a mile back to fetch rations up. We had just returned when the Turks greeted us with a fusillade of rapid fire. This they kept up all night.

Monday, 10 May. Things went quieter by breakfast time but the snipers kept very busy. We laid pretty low all day. We have lost nearly all our officers with these blessed snipers. Captain Tetley is the latest victim having been hit in both legs while leading a party sniper hunting. Very few of them got back again. Heavy firing commenced at dusk and continued all night.

Tuesday, 11 May. Getting our full share of casualties. Poor Capt. Andrews killed by a sniper just after dinner. We have lost our best friend. We have only about five officers left. We are to be relieved today sometime. Left the trenches after dark and made our way back to some open ground about a mile and a half back. We had to doss down in the open. To make things worse it started raining.

Wednesday, 12 May. It poured with rain all night but we were tired out and slept through it all. We got some breakfast and then made ourselves as comfortable as we could in some vacated trenches waiting for further orders. We buried Captain Andrews this morning together with Lieut. Barnes. The Colonel read the service and was very much cut up. The poor Captain's men felt it very much, most of us turning away before the service was finished. A mound, a small wooden cross and a few pebbles alone mark the last resting place of as brave a gentleman as ever walked. In the afternoon we moved further back and dug rest trenches for ourselves. Sir Ian Hamilton paid us a visit and complimented Col. Matthews on the work he and his men had done.

Thursday, 13 May. Enjoyed a good, long nights sleep for we were very tired. Our artillery has been bombarding since yesterday afternoon. We dug a hole in the ground first thing and put a waterproof sheet in it, which we filled with water. Stripping ourselves we then enjoyed a much needed bath. Soon after we had completed our rough and ready toilet a big shell dropped right in amongst us knocking out seven or eight. Pollard and Madden were two victims out of our section. Duckworth, the man who did such good work in the landing was blown to atoms. It gave us a terrible shaking up. We got shelled all the afternoon so were obliged to remain in the trenches. It went quieter towards evening however. The Turks very rarely fire the big guns after dark, thank goodness, so that we can get a bit of peace at night.

Friday, 14 May. Got shells for breakfast and got the meal crouching down in the trench. Some of the shells, which were for the most part shrapnel, did not burst, but buried themselves. Went trench digging elsewhere in the afternoon. At tea time the enemy started putting some big shells into us. We were bobbing in and out of the trench all tea time. In the evening they shifted their range to the aeroplane base at the back of us. It was a lively evening but we were consoled with a quiet night.

Saturday, 15 May. Turks seem to be attacking this morning. Very heavy firing is going on. We are getting our fair share of shells in our camp. We spent the morning cleaning our ammunition. Went to W. Beach in the afternoon gathering big stones for road making etc. In the evening heavy firing recommenced and the artillery started on both sides. Our chaplain arranged an open air concert to take place after dark. It was the most weird concert I have ever attended. It went very dark and lightning was playing in the sky. The artillery were roaring a solo with a chorus of rifle fire, stray bullets even reaching the spot where we were. Every now and then Veras Lights were shot up from the French and our own lines, bursting into a shower of stars when in the air. All the while our fellows were in turn singing comic, secular and sacred songs. The limit however was reached when Gilbert Wilson, a chum of mine, and who is a professional sang Will o' th' Wisp. He sang it splendidly but the effect was almost unearthly. We piped down about 10 p.m. to dream of Turks, Germans, goblins and goodness knows what.

Sunday, 16 May. We are commencing the week well with the usual shelling. They kept it up nearly all the morning. We had an early dinner today and spent the afternoon making a new road. The rough and ready way of making a new road employed here is to dig a trench having sloping sides on either boundary. These trenches are about three feet wide and eighteen inches deep. All the earth is taken from these trenches and utilized to make a camber on the roadway. We got back for tea about 5 p.m. and were quite ready for it.

Seeing that it is Sunday and that I have now had time to look round I cannot do better than give a few of my impressions of the peninsula of Gallipoli.

The ideas I had formed of the peninsula were altogether wrong in most respects. I had always imagined a rocky, barren land, but instead I found it quite fertile, cultivated, in many parts with orchards, vineyards and fields sprouting up with good crops of barley. There is plenty of good sandy soil. The uncultivated portions are covered with heather and wild sage for the most part, the latter giving off an odour which reminds one of last Christmas dinner.

The place lends itself naturally to defensive purposes. On all sides there are very steep cliffs right from the edge of the sea. From the southern end of the peninsula to Achi Baba is a stretch of plain or plateau extending four or five miles. Achi Baba rises here, not to a very great height, but extends itself across the peninsula in such a way that it effectively bars the way to an intruder. It has barred it to us anyway. The ground is broken up by deep ravines and gullies most of them having a stream running in the bed. These gullies abound with frogs which make the nights lively indeed with their continual and loud croaking. Lizards of the common variety are to be plentifully found. I have seen snakes as big as four feet in length and as thick as my wrist. I am no naturalist but should take them to be the ordinary grass snake.

The only two towns on this, the southern side of Achi Baba, are Sedd-el-Bahr and Krithia. Sedd-el-Bahr is on the mouth of the Straits and was the Turkish fortress. Our ships soon laid that base. Krithia is a small town on the slopes of Achi Baba and looks very quaint and picturesque from our front line of trenches. I have not yet had the privilege of seeing it from a nearer point owing to the strenuous resistance of the Turks.

Tuesday, 13 July. We spent the remainder of the night in our old spot on the gully after aimlessly wandering about half the night as usual. At dawn we moved from here, which now were the supports and went into the new fire position which was taken from the Turks yesterday. We just had to go into a Turkish communication trench which now formed part of our supports. This was in a terrible state, simply full of dead bodies and filth of all kinds. Up to dinner time all our time was taken in burying the dead and cleaning up. Where some of the dead had already been half buried was a sight awful to witness and the stench was terrific. Heads, arms and legs were sticking up from the ground and out of the parapets. It was terrible and a sight I can never forget. In addition to cleaning all this mess up we had to make this trench possible for a fire trench should it be necessary.

LADY CYNTHIA ASQUITH
(1887–1960)

Lady Cynthia Asquith, daughter of Lord Wemyss, married Herbert Asquith, the son of the Prime Minister, in 1910. In 1915 she and Duff Cooper, a young Foreign Official soon to be fighting in Flanders, swore that they would begin a diary on the same day and that each would make sure that the other did not abandon the task. Duff Cooper gave her a book which was so beautiful that at first it 'paralysed' her when it came to filling it. But once started, she needed no urging to go on, although she was always to suspect that it could never give the world an accurate picture of herself: 'I wonder if all diaries are as representative of their writers as this is of me?' Her friend L. P. Hartley thought that she took herself very lightly – as a figure of fun in a mirror. A form of trained modesty, once required in women of her position, certainly inhibited her diary-writing in some ways, although as it proceeds we see the war destroying such restraints.

Lady Cynthia's *Diaries 1915–18* are remarkable for their closely observed accounts of the deaths of the 'golden generation' which perished on the Dardanelles and in France, and for the slow realization by the 'home front' of the true meaning of modern war. We see her own growing suffering as her young friends were killed – Patrick Shaw-Stewart, Raymond Asquith, Julian Grenfell, Edward Horner, Bimbo Tennant and her beloved brother Lord Elcho. Myth-making valedictions were to be heaped upon these and others, the expectations of whose very privileged lives carried with them so much political hope. She was there when the telegrams arrived, so to speak, and her diary is the record – among much else – of a patrician crisis.

During the latter part of the war she became secretary to J. M. Barrie as a preliminary to her own literary career. Unlike the soldier poets and novelists, she never quite repudiates the war – she is too close to its administration to admit its madness – but her last entry, just before the Armistice and when she was on the brink of a nervous illness brought on by seeing so much suffering, is penetratingly critical: 'One will have to look at long vistas again, instead of short ones, and one will at last finally recognize that the dead are not only dead for the duration of the war.'

Saturday, 1 July 1916. I don't know how to write about this awful day. I didn't expect Beb till 2.20, so had arranged to lunch with my grandmother. Was back soon after two, ran into room in high spirits. Beb said, 'I'm afraid there's bad news', and gave me an opened letter from Papa. 'The worst is true about Ego. The officer prisoners of Angora certify that he was killed at Katia ... I have wired to Guy Wyndham at Clouds. I don't know how Letty will be told. It is very cruel and we must all help each other to bear it.'

Oh God – Oh God, my beautiful brother that I have loved so since I was a baby – so beautiful *through* and *through*! Can it be true that he'll never come back? At first I could only think of Letty, just the blank horror of that gripped me. Mamma's away at Clouds – that's unthinkable, too! Letty will occupy her for the first days, but afterwards I'm so frightened for her.

Papa telephoned to me and I went round to Cadogan Square. Poor, poor Papa! He really proudly loved those two perfect sons. He said he had been round to Kakoo – she expected John back in the afternoon and they thought he had better tell Letty. Her mother was not coming back till nine and Diana was away. We walked round to Eaton Square together and found Kakoo in. No John, and we discussed what had better be done. Came to conclusion that if John had not arrived by five, Papa and I would go round to Letty. We telephoned and found out she would be in between five and six. I went home to Beb and waited – no message came, so after five I went to Cadogan Square and picked up poor Papa. The poignancy of what followed was so inconceivably beyond anything in my experience that I don't feel as if I could ever be unhaunted by it for a minute.

Letty was alone with the children playing the piano to them. Papa went up – I waited downstairs. The music stopped and I heard a gay 'Hulloa', then silence. I rushed up and found Letty clinging to Papa. It's indescribable – it was just like somebody in a fearful, unimaginable, physical pain. Streams of beautiful, eloquent words were torn from her heart. The children were scared. 'What has happened to you, Mummie? What is the matter with you? Will you be better in the morning?' I ran up to Sparks – she came and fetched them, and brought sal volatile and was wonderfully nice and good with Letty. We tried to make Letty go upstairs, but she wanted to stay down a little.

Papa was wonderfully sweet, and she seemed to cling to him: 'Oh Papa, it can't be true! How could God be so cruel? There was no one else in the world in the least like him – no one – I have been so wonderfully happy. His beautiful face, his smile . . . my Ego, come back to me. Oh God! Oh God! It's no use calling to God – nothing is any use – nothing in all the world can help him. I'm only twenty-eight – I'm so strong – I shan't die!'

Marjorie came in, perfectly self-controlled and bracing – spoke to Letty as you would to a housemaid being vaccinated. 'Now, now Letty – come, come.' At last we got her to go upstairs and carried her to her room. Then she saw his photographs and the bed. She sent for the children – his lovely little boys, and tried to make them understand. 'David, I want you to understand Poppa's – you remember what he looked like – Poppa's never coming back to us.' David said at once, 'But, I want him to . . .' but he didn't understand and said, 'I must go now, or I shall be late for bed.' She was afraid that they would never remember him and the children – the one platitude one clung to for her – became one of the most poignant stabs.

Papa went away and I stayed alone with her. She got quieter. John came after six and took the line that there *was* hope with her, clinging to the fact that it was not 'official'. I have *none*. Is it cruel or kind to give it to her? I think one ought to give her the evidence, but not colour it with subjective optimism at all – she is so open to suggestion. Nothing could be crueller than the way it has come.

EDWARD THOMAS
(1878–1917)

The diary which Edward Thomas kept from New Year's Day to 8 April 1917, the final entry written only a few hours before he was killed during the opening barrage of the Battle of Arras, is among the most moving private statements of the First World War. It was written in a little two-shilling pigskin pocket-book published by Walker, which still bears its own Arras scars in the form of creased and crushed pages. It was discovered among the papers of Thomas's son Merfyn, who died in 1965. It contains the first draft of Thomas's last poem, a photograph of his wife Helen, an army pass for the rail journey from Loughton to Lydd and the addresses of his friends.

Almost forty years old, the poet was an efficient and inspiring officer to the much younger men of 244 Battery. War had in some strange sense unified and strengthened him. He was quiet, controlled and impressive. In the diary, preparations for yet more human slaughter on the grand scale are calmly described but are interwoven with matter-of-fact domestic detail, nature notes and sharp reportage of the shelling, trench-digging, burnings and pain. Family names and those of writers – Frost, de la Mare, Hudson, Bottomley – break into the confusion. Thomas is laconic but not cynical. The diary of his last weeks on earth is a kind of savouring of what is appalling and what is precious. The seasons themselves, winter running into spring, are the great reality, not the by now crazy fighting.

1 March 1917. Sunny and breezy. Wrote to Helen, Mother, Eleanor and Ellis. Indoors all morning doing nothing. Mostly a quiet morning. Out with Berrington round the marsh towards 244 who were doing their 1st shoot. Enemy planes over. 2 rounds across 244 position on to Doullens Road. Great deal of anti-aircraft shells singing by. Sat down on hill above 244 and watched German lines. At Beaurains ghastly trees and ruins above Achicourt church tower. A bullet passes. Quite warm to sit down for quarter hour. Evening in mess. Colonel talks of the General (Poole) who was all for 'Fire, fire, fire! Loose her off! Deliver the goods! Annoy the Hun.' With artillery shelling heavy from about 5 a.m. I only dressed because I thought it would be better to have my clothes on. In any case I had to be up at 6 to go to Achicourt. A very misty still morning: could see nothing from bedroom except the trees and the stone dog – our artillery really made most of the noise, and I being just wakened and also inexperienced mistook it.

2 March. Up at 5.30 and went out to Achicourt Chateau to see 141's gun into its forward position. A misty frosty morning luckily and no plane could observe. Afternoon to Faubourg Ranville, its whistling deserted ruined streets, deserted roadway, pavement with single files of men. Cellars as dugouts, trenches behind and across road. Dead dry calf in stable. Rubble, rubbish, filth and old plush chair. Perfect view of No Man's Land winding level at foot of Hun slope, and Beaurains above to one side and woods just behind crest on other side (M.B.110). With Horton and Lushington to see 3 O.P.s there: – Letters from Helen, Mother, Eleanor and J. Freeman.

3 March.* No post. Morning dull spent in office. But afternoon with Colonel to Achicourt to see O.P.s and then to new battery positions. A chilly day not good for observing. Court of Inquiry on a man burnt with petrol – Lushington presiding and afterwards I went back with him to 244's new billet and saw my new quarters to be. Wrote to Mother and Helen.

4 March. Cold but bright clear and breezy. Nothing to do all morning but trace a map and its contours. Colonel and I went down to 244 before lunch to see the shell holes of last night and this morning. Hun planes over. More shells came in the afternoon. The fire is warm but the room cold. Tea with Lushington and Thorburn. Shelling at 5.30 – I don't like it. I wonder where I shall be hit as in bed I wonder if it is better to be on the window or outer side of room or on the chimney or inner side, whether better to be upstairs where you may fall or on the ground floor where you may be worse crushed. Birthday parcels from home.

* E.T.'s thirty-ninth birthday.

5 March. Out early to see a raid by VI Corps, but snow hid most but singing of Field shells and snuffling of 6″ – Ronville's desolate streets. To 244's orchard which has had numerous 4.2 shells over, meant for the road. Wrote to Helen, Mervyn and Bronwen. After-noon indoors paying etc. After tea to 244 to dine, not very happy with Lushington, Horton and Smith. They have the wind up because of the shells (which may have been meant for the road behind). Letters from de la Mare, Helen, Bronwen and de la Mare. A beautiful clear moonlit night after a beautiful high blue day with combed white clouds.

6 March. Bright and clear early and all day and warm at 1. Walked over to 244's position with Colonel and then up to 234 beyond Dainville station, and listened to larks and watched aeroplane fights. 2 planes down, one in flames, a Hun. Sometimes 10 of our planes together very high. Shells into Arras in afternoon.

7 March. A cold raw dull day with nothing to do except walk round to 244 to get a pair of socks. The wind made a noise in the house and trees and a dozen black crumpled sycamore leaves dance round and round on terrace. Wrote to Pearce and Irene. Rather cold and depressed and solitary.

8 March. Snow blizzard – fine snow and fierce wind – to Achicourt O.P. but suddenly a blue sky and soft white cloud through the last of the snow – with Colonel and Berrington. Returned to hear that the Group has to leave this billet. I liked the walk. Indoors afternoon fitting together aeroplane trench photographs. Letters from Helen, Eleanor, Oscar and Frost (saying he had got an American publisher for my verses). A still quiet night up to 11 with just one round fired to show we have not left Arras. Up till 1 for a despatch from Corps. Colonel snotted interpreter.

9 March. Snow and very cold indoors doing nothing but look at a sandbag O.P. My last day at the Group. Weir of 2/1 Lowland takes my place. I return to 244 – Lushington, Horton and Rubin. I am fed up with sitting on my arse doing nothing that anybody couldn't do better. Wrote to de la Mare, Frost and Eleanor.

10 March. Up at 5.15 for a raid, but nothing doing. A misty mild morning clearing slightly to a white sky. 10 rounds gunfire C-B. Snowdrops at foot of peartrees by Decanville Railway, R.F.C. wireless man reading 'Hiawatha'. 3 shoots of 10 rounds gunfire suddenly at N.F. targets unobserved. Men mending a caved-in dugout in the dark. Parcel from Janet Hooton.

11 March. Out at 8.30 to Ronville O.P. and studied the ground from Beaurains N. Larks singing over No Man's Land – trench mortars. We were bombarding their front line: they were shooting at Arras. R.F.A. officer with me who was quite concerned till he spotted a certain familiar Hun sentry in front line. A clear, cloudy day, mild and breezy. 8th shell carrying into Arras. Later Ronville heavily shelled and we retired to dugout. At 6.15 all quiet and heard blackbirds chinking. Scene peaceful, desolate like Dunwich moors except sprinkling of white chalk on the rough brown ground. Lines broken and linesmen out from 2.30 to 7 p.m. A little rain in the night; . . .

12 March. . . . then a beautiful moist clear limpid early morning till the Raid at 7 and the retaliation on Ronville at 7.30–8.45 with 77 cm. 25 to the minute. Then back through 6 ins. of chalk mud in trenches along battered Ronville Street. Rooks in tall trees on N. side of Arras – they and their nests and the trees black against the soft clouded sky. W. wind and mild but no rain yet (11 a.m.). Letters, mess accounts, maps. Afternoon at maps and with Horton at battery. Evening of partridges calling and pipsqueaks coming over behind.

13 March. Blackbird trying to sing early in dull marsh. A dull cold day. One N.F. shoot at nightfall. I was in position all day. Letters from Eleanor, Mother and Ellis: wrote to Bronwen, Mother and Eleanor.

14 March. Ronville O.P. Looking out towards No Man's Land what I thought first was a piece of burnt paper or something turned out to be a bat shaken at last by shells from one of the last sheds in Ronville. A dull cold morning, with some shelling of Arras and St Sauveur and just 3 for us. Talking to Birt and Randall about Glostershire and Wiltshire, particularly Painswick and Marlborough. A still evening – blackbirds singing far-off – a spatter of our machine guns – the spit of one enemy bullet – a little rain – no wind – only far-off artillery.

8 April. [The last entry]. A bright warm Easter day but Achicourt shelled at 2.15 so that we all retired to cellar. I had to go over to battery at 3 for a practice barrage, skirting the danger zone, but we were twice interrupted. A 5.9 fell 2 yards from me as I stood by the f/C post. One burst down the back of the office and a piece of dust scratched my neck. No firing from 2–4. Rubin left for a course.

> *The light of the new moon and every star*
> *And no more singing for the bird*

SIEGFRIED SASSOON
(1886–1967)

Sassoon came from a rich Anglo-Jewish background from which he was able to draw his enthusiasm both for conventional country sports and for poetry. He enlisted at the beginning of the First World War, with an acceptance – shared by so many youngsters like him – of what it was officially said to be all about. But again as with great numbers of his contemporaries on the Western Front, the massacres of 1917 onwards opened his eyes to the war's foolishness and evil. After being wounded twice and winning the M.C., Sassoon caused consternation by publicly coming out against the whole business. The embarrassed authorities sent him to Craiglockhart War Hospital, near Edinburgh, where he met Wilfred Owen.

Sassoon kept a diary of some kind from his teens until 1956 and, like Henry Williamson, was to mine it for his partly novelized autobiographies, *Memoirs of a Fox-Hunting Man* (1928), *Memoirs of an Infantry Officer* (1930), *Sherston's Progress* (1936) and *Siegfried's Journey* (1945). Sassoon wanted his diary to be published as a possible help for those who shared his complex make-up of sportsman-poet, ascetic and solitary. The years 1914 to 1918 haunted him; he could be said to be a First World War poet who continued to write as such until the day he died. The following passages are from his *Diaries, 1920–1922*, written at a time when he was trying *not* to be his old self and when he was endeavouring to be a full literary man, a lover, and a welcomer of the post-war world.

A visit to Thomas Hardy

21 February 1921. As on my two previous visits (November 1918 and November 1919) to Max Gate, I have to pinch myself and ask 'Are you awake, and have you really been talking to the real Thomas Hardy?' Arrived at 4.30; I am in my bedroom at 11.15. Have been conversing with T.H. continuously, except for ten minutes before dinner. Well over six hours, talking to a man who will be eighty-one in June. But, as I've felt before, he is *no* age at all. A nimble wizard. Sometimes he seems, for a moment, incredibly agèd with the rural antiquity of an old tree or house, but most of the time he is merely T. Hardy – eager and interested like a young man – and yet so wise, for all his simplicity.

In the last six hours he has repeated several things which I remember him saying before – that is the only sign of age (i.e. about 'people in London seeming so clever when first one goes there: and then one finds that they are all repeating the same ideas, like squirrels in a cage'). Alert and active is T.H. He never sits in the comfortable chair or on the sofa, but perches himself on a straight-backed chair, and leans his head lightly on his hand, in an easy attitude, dignified and self-possessed and calm.

In the afternoon light he looked rather white and wizened, but by lamplight, when the wrinkles were hidden and the glow gave colour, and he had drunk a glass of Sauterne, his face was the face of a hale man of sixty, and at times he wore a strangely delicate and spiritual expression.

He showed me a 'new old' poem, 'On Stinsford Hill at Midnight', and told me how he saw a girl singing alone one night as he returned home (a Salvationist girl who died soon after). She had a tambourine (he called it 'a timbrel' in the poem). The poem leaves the reader to decide whether it was a live woman or a ghost.

Some day this evening will be a miraculous memory, as if I'd spent six hours with Ben Jonson or John Milton. Now I ask myself again, 'Was it the author of *The Dynasts* who went up the dark stairs in front of you carrying a silver candlestick, and showed you, with a touch of pride, the new bathroom which has superseded the previous hip-bath brought into the bedroom before breakfast?'

He told me over again his little story of acquiring his first edition of Hobbes's *Leviathan*. For sixpence, bicycling from Bristol to Bath, and muddy from a tumble, he saw it among some old books, in a basin in some shop-window of old rubbish. 'How much?' 'Will sixpence hurt you?' asked the shabby woman who kept the shop, eyeing his mud-stained clothes.

The dog Wessex is a dominant character in this quiet household. The large white rough-haired dog, who barks and jumps about when the roast mutton is carried out of the dining-room before he has had his share.

How much of all this is worth remembering or noting down with conscientious pen for future inquisitive eyes? The whirring clock jangles twelve on the stair-top. The house is silent.

Outside the frosty moonlight is white on the brick-and-stone porch with its two urns, and the peaks of the stone-pines around the house are misty-dark, and I hear the bleat of sheep, a dog barking, and an owl hooting – all at a distance. Hardy's house. Turning I see myself sitting in a chair with a straight-burning candle – reflected in the tall mirror of the wardrobe in the best bedroom at Max Gate.

22 February. After breakfast I left about 10.30 on T.H.'s bicycle and went about eleven miles, stopping at Cerne Abbas, and finally reached the fine view across Blackmore Vale toward Sherborne. Back in a hurry, and reached Max Gate about 2. Huge lunch; T.H. very gay. At 4 walked across the field-path toward Winterbourne Cave, with him. He walked slowly; not so well as last time, but the path was uneven. I tried to draw him out about eye (visual) and ear (non-visual) music; but he seemed a bit hazy, and thought I meant rhyme-endings done by spelling instead of sound (lion and carrion idea). People confuse 'poetry' with 'verse', he said (re polyphonists and imagists etc.).

Mentioned *'The Last Signal',** pointing out William Barnes's rectory among the trees.

Writing to order. He was asked to do *Titanic*† and Armistice Day (1920) poems:‡ but did not feel that he was forced to, and wrote them with feeling of spontaneity.

30 June. I've given up thinking about the War. I am clear of it all, steadily settling down into a new state of mind, craving only for development in the technique of expression in verse and prose; trying to analyse love; learning more and more to appreciate and understand music; stimulated by my talks with Turner.

But the War comes back to me occasionally. To-night I feel that I'd like to remind myself of it. A poem called 'Anniversaries' perhaps.

I watched Oxford batting at Lord's this afternoon; and then dined alone at the Reform, and went on to a piano-recital, quite a good one. Strolling back, along Oxford Street, the town seemed so tranquil, almost beautiful.

As I sit here, with some Elgar music in my head, I pull out my war-notebooks, and turn up June 30th 1916. Five years ago. It was the night before the Somme attack started. 'Last night' I was 'out cutting our wire from 12 till 3.30. Driven in once by shelling. Gibson's face in the first grey of dawn when he found me alone at wire-cutting.' (Gibson was killed seventeen days later.)

The diary makes me realize that I shall never partake of another war. It makes me wonder whether five years ago was *real*. 'Gibson's face in the first grey of dawn . . .' Gibson is a ghost, but he is more real to-night than the pianist who played Scriabine with such delicate adroitness. I wish I could 'find a moral equivalent for war'. To-night I feel as if I were only half-alive. Part of me died with all the Gibsons I used to know.

24 August. Went to Renishaw.** Gabriel there. Blighted skies and

---

* Hardy's poem about the funeral of the Dorset poet William Barnes in 1886 (published in *Moments of Vision*, 1917).

† 'The Convergence of the Twain' (1912).

‡ 'And there was a great calm', published in *The Times* on 11 November 1920, the day of the burial of the Unknown Soldier.

** The Sitwell family home in Derbyshire.

blasted trees and blackened landscapes. Atmosphere of nerve-twitching exhaustion. Women in a gloomy room. What time is the next meal? Look at this! Look at that! Ancestor-worship in oil-paintings. Who will die first? Disgruntled offspring of distrusted parents. Rich food: the house a stronghold; decayed and morose dignities fronting the encroachments of industry. An oasis of landscape-gardening and terraced formality, girdled by iron and tunnelled by coal-mines.

Conflicting influences, against the seven weeks past.

Blake and Whitman, superseded by Beardsley and Strindberg.

Only common factor is stone statues.

Harassed and skulking servants; furtive gardeners.

Undoubtedly wicked influences. Crazy behaviour late at night.

Reconsidering the past. Impulse toward secrecy. Broken down.

26 August. The sun comes out. Beyond the gently swaying bee-visited hollyhocks the male and female statues have their heads averted from where I sit; they seem to have seen something coming from the direction of the iron-works. Silver-grey with leaden-blue shadows are the statues' tones. Half-gracious and half-hateful is everything here. The big dog Sem is the only calm element. Visitors are interlopers, half-overhearing hysterical wranglings, admitted to the subsequent discussions and Ginger* fantasies. Is it eating too much good food that makes me increasingly hostile? Crescendo last evening.

Still, sweet champagne, twenty-five years old perhaps, only made me worse. Osbert listens to everything one says until one has got half-way through the explanation or whatever it may be; but he cannot sustain his interest until the end. Last night at dinner he asserted that I am the worst judge of character he knows. That may be so, but he said it because he thinks I misjudge his own character. The Sitwells are parasitic on their possessions (like most old families). They fasten on an old house with its charming pictures etc., like lice in a cavalier costume. What a delightful comparison to use about one's hosts! Wasps in wall-fruit also applies.

There *must* be something wrong with them or me; otherwise I'd

* The Sitwells' nickname for their father Sir George.

not feel so malicious. But all this incessant wrangling about money, Osbert trying to snatch money from Ginger, etc. Why does O. let himself be under G's thumb? A complete break away would be more dignified, surely? But O. is too fond of luxuries and prestige to sacrifice a single square meal. So they go on with their skirmishings about 'pay and allowances', and wait for someone to die off.

Like his dad, Osbert is, above all, 'a man of taste' – distinguished *taste*. His 'Parade' poem (in the *Spectator* to-day) proves it; a very accomplished affair, derived from his appreciation of an eighteenth-century French painting, 'Poem by a Person of Quality'.

The baronet walks on his own squat shadow, crosses the green carpet of his lawns among the green-black pyramids of clipped yews, stops to stare at stocks and sweet peas in box-edged beds. Starlings and crows watch him from muffled tree-tops shaken by west-wind breathings; I too observe him from the roof; I am among the chimneys; I can see the top of his round gray hat-crown. Everything belongs to the baronet – everything except me.

On the roof at Renishaw. A possible poem. Birdseye view of a baronet pacing, strolling between his festooned flower-beds. This place is his fortress. He accumulates encrustations of 'family history' of Reresbys, Sacheverells, Sitwells and so on, ancestor-worship, consolidation of funds; snail-like he puts out cautious horns; or is he a porcupine, plucking quills from his own back and writing records of his great-great-grandfather's butcher's bill?

The lake is large, ornamental, and too shallow for an effective suicide . . .

16 June 1922. I left here early on Monday morning, and reached Clare station about 12.30. From Liverpool Street to Mark's Tey (where I changed trains) I sat next to a moderately attractive young man whose proximity worried me greatly. These speechless animal attractions are an unmitigated nuisance. Luckily for me they never go any further.

It was a sunshiny day, and there was little Blunden* waiting for me in his shabby blue suit. He had just picked up a first edition of *Atalanta in Calydon* for a shilling, in a little shop in Clare. And

* Edmund Blunden.

outside the station sat Mary B. in a smart blue cloak, in a tiny ramshackle wagonette drawn by a small white pony. (A conveyance hired from a farmer and driven by his juvenile daughter.) Slowly we traversed the four miles to Stansfield, up and down little hills among acres of beans and wheat. Arrived at Belle Vue, a stone-faced slate-roofed box of a house by the roadside. And for three days B. and I talked about county cricket and the war and English poetry and our own poetry and East Anglia and our contemporaries. While Mary B. (on her best behaviour) produced beef, mutton and pork and several sorts of vegetables for our nourishment. And B. wrote reviews for *The Times* and the *Nation* and the *Daily News*; and I read Clare and Bloomfield and Blunden. And the weather became chilly and it rained on Tuesday and Wednesday; and we drank port by a small fire after dinner. And B. hopped about the house in his bird-like way; and we both received a letter from 'old Hardy' by the same post. And we admired the old man's calligraphy. And we bicycled to Sudbury and lost our road home and had to push the machines across three wheat-fields ...

FRANCES PARTRIDGE
(b. 1900)

Conscientious objectors had a bad time in both wars, though particularly in the First World War. Frances Partridge's husband Ralph was an archetypal hero-figure of 1914–1918, a tall, handsome major with Military Cross and Bar, who became a pacifist during 1939–45. The Western Front had disillusioned him and he no longer believed that war was the way to solve matters. He appeared before a Tribunal and spent these latter years in the awkward limbo in which society casts such people. Frances Partridge's diary, *A Pacifist's War*, is not by any means the general picture of such a fate as its conscientious objection is powerfully defended by Bloomsbury and its ideals, but it does vividly convey the odd sense of a family under a kind of house arrest for the duration. The diary is suffused with the melancholy of life on the sidelines, as it were, of waiting and inaction. It is exceptionally well written.

8 October 1941. A foundation of melancholy underlies these days – Russia, Gerald, the sadness of autumn. In me it takes the form of subhuman apathy, in R. of irritability and saying: 'I don't like my fellow-men', the implication behind which is usually that one doesn't like oneself.

Italian prisoners are now working in the potato fields in Ham; Burgo and I walked to see them and listen to their soaring, trilling voices singing in Italian against a background of English mud and a grey sky. Three soldiers were guarding them. They had nothing against the prisoners except that they got more cigarettes than they did themselves.

To tea with some Inkpen ladies, whose snobbish county smugness and unimaginative self-confidence depressed me. They appear to question nothing, neither the war and the way it is conducted, nor the inferiority of everyone else to themselves, and of course of all Germans to all English people. The thought of these women and their beastly form of patriotism and their stupidity and the brave way they tackle their hens and jam and the servant shortage is somehow profoundly indigestible. I am alarmed by the insidious way we are getting drawn into their company. We *must* get out of it all.

Listened to the wireless all evening, well aware that the war is passing through one of the most acute crises it has yet produced. During the News I gradually became aware of a faint voice, speaking in far-off sepulchral tones like Hamlet's ghost: 'Tell us the TRUTH!' Then 'ROT!' it boomed out, and quite a lot more about the Jews and the Americans having 'sold us down the river'. When the news ended, the Voice made quite a long speech beginning rather mysteriously: 'Winston Churchill will never be Duke of Marlborough.' The English announcer then said primly: 'If you have been hearing interruptions, it is the enemy.' The 'enemy' – how fantastic it sounds! But the Voice gave us a great deal of pleasure, so strange a manifestation was it.

14 October. To combat the anxiety produced by the Russian situation I forced myself to do mechanical tasks, like painting beehives and sweeping the verandah.

In to Hungerford, but there was no food to buy except salted cod, no offal. As we drove home talking about our cupboard of reserve tins, R. said: 'We'd better keep them for the invasion. I firmly believe there will be one', in such a matter-of-fact voice that the Hungerford–Ham road with its familiar ranks of telegraph poles looked all at once menacing and unreal. But I suppose I don't, at this moment anyway, believe in invasion.

Started reading Pepys this evening. Bad news on the wireless – 'A deterioration in the position of the Russian front.' This is the beginning of the end, I thought, and visualized us pathetic human beings like crabs trying to crawl out of the pot of boiling water that is about to finish them off. And then came the Voice again, distantly booming: 'Kick Churchill *out*! We want Revolution! Churchill must go-o-o!' And last of all: 'Britain is *doo*med! Britain is DOOMed! God save our King – from the Jews!' This last word came out in a protracted hiss, and we were quite cheered up by realizing that the Germans could be so imbecile as to imagine that such remarks could have any effect.

11 July 1942. Today women born in 1900 had to register for National Service. Took B. with me and went into Hungerford to do so. Other forty-twos seemed to be mountainously large or weakly nervous and uncontrollably talkative. ('Are you married?' 'Married? I should say I am, very much so', etc., etc.) I was asked the same, any children under fourteen and how many I 'catered' for. I was sent away with a slip of paper, saying that if I was called for an interview I should be legally obliged to take the work I was directed to. People, people. Kitty [West] and her baby have come to stay for a week's rest cure. Roger Fulford over from Oxford to lunch. I know he admires R. but am far from sure he approves of me. He doesn't like 'the sex', as he likes to call women, to be at all free in their conversation. Then I ask myself how he can reconcile his theoretical belief in God and the Royal Family with his practical interest in smut and scallywags. Also I felt he had no right to rub his hands over Burgo's atheistical remarks if he really sets store by

Christianity. In *theory* he disapproves of malicious characters like Maurice Bowra, and 'all dons' wives who flirt with the under-graduates and permit loose talk particularly about unnatural vice in the greatest possible physical detail'.

The other day we ran into Julia in Hungerford and walked with her to the 'British Restaurant' where cheap meals are served to all and sundry. As it wasn't open we sat on a bench outside, surrounded by villas with gardens full of Dorothy Perkins. Inside a large spacious polished hall we had coffee, while the music of Haydn and a poster of Churchill's confident boozy face embraced us in a democratic aura. I gave way to the spell. It is the temple of Universality; individuality has to be disinfected out like a germ.

10 May 1945. I feel happier and more conscious of peace even than I expected. I am very much aware this morning of something that has just gone: – a background to our daily existence as solid as one of the scenes in Burgo's toy theatre – a background coloured by the obscenity of violence, and my own disgust at it. The fields, Downs and woods *look* peaceful now, seen with eyes that know the murder and destruction have stopped. If my pleasure in our being at peace is a more or less steady quality, R.'s is growing gradually, as though it was something he hardly dared trust to, and it makes me very happy to see signs on his face that the load is lifting. This morning he was radiating good humour, which was no doubt why the girl cashier in the Bank leant over the counter and confided all her marriage plans to him; when he's in a benign mood no-one I've ever known attracts more confidences than he does.

I have been reading Flaubert's *Letters*, and have just reached the Franco-Prussian war. How his reactions remind me of ours! First, horror at the bestiality of human beings. As the Germans invade he develops a more conventional desire to defend his country, followed by the most frightful agitation and despair, such as only a literary man can indulge in. *No-one*, he feels sure, can hate the war so much as he does; he resigns from the Home Guard, returns to his views about the beastliness of human beings, is physically sick every day from sheer disgust, and dislikes his fellow-Frenchmen almost as much as the Prussians. As for 'evacuees' they are the worst feature of the whole war.

News of V.E. Day in London: Janetta writes: 'I've found the crowds very depressing indeed, and the flags and decorations pathetic although often very pretty. Some bonfires were wonderful, bringing back the old ecstasies of staring into a fire, but also having that appalling smell of burning debris, too terrifyingly nostalgic of blitzes. And I so loathe the look of masses of boiling people with scarlet dripping faces, wearing tiny paper hats with "Ike's Babe" or "Victory" written on them.'

Julia: 'We walked to Buckingham Palace, and there found a spectacular scene – all the fountains, balustrades, not to mention trees, were crowded with these little pink penguins in their droves, all facing the Palace, which was brilliantly illuminated with beautiful golden light, and draped with red velvet over the balcony. It was charmingly pretty. Everyone was fainting by the roadside, or rather sitting down holding their stockinged feet in their hands and groaning. A few faint upper-class cries of "Taxi – taxi!" came wailing through the air from voices right down on the pavement; whilst cockney tones, slightly more robust, could be heard saying, "I'm fucking well all in now."' Of her own reaction to peace she goes on: 'It's something to do with the war having gone on just *too* long, one was at last crushed, and personally I no longer feel human any more; I mean the dynamic principal has given way and one feels like a sheet of old newspaper or pressed dried grass.'

At Hungerford Station we ran into Dora Romilly, who had news of the celebration of peace at Charleston. Quentin made a lifesize image of Hitler to burn on Firle Beacon, Duncan defended Hitler in a comic mock trial, and the 'Baroness' (Lydia Keynes) had 'thudded away in an abandoned Russian drinking song'.

This evening we drove to Shalbourne to give Olive a present of bacon. I remembered how after the First War some pacifists had been turned on by the merry-making crowds, for instance how Cambridge undergraduates had pushed down Harry Norton's garden wall; and wondered if our village neighbours, and 'old retainers' like Olive, might say to themselves, 'Well, *they* did nothing to help. *They*'ve no cause to rejoice.' But the warm way Olive and her family welcomed us and exchanged handshakes and kisses did nothing to confirm my fears.

After all, surely it's only logical that pacifists – of all people – should rejoice in the return to Peace?

KEITH VAUGHAN
(1912–77)

For the artist Keith Vaughan, writing a journal was 'therapeutic and consolatory'. Few diarists admit as much. It was in 1939, and he was twenty-seven. Two years later, when he was serving in the army, he sent an entry from it to *Penguin New Writing*. It described the unloading of ambulance trains from Dunkirk, and was published. Few further pages were sent to the magazine but because John Lehmann, the editor, gave confidence to the young artist-soldier Vaughan began to write a very considerable journal, illustrating it with drawings, and he kept it until the mid 1960s. It is a journal of the inner life, serious, sensuous, and predominantly 'visual'.

Vaughan first served in the Pioneer Corps and his journal ponders ceaselessly on a type of helplessly dull and exploited man he saw in the barrack-room. From 1941 to 1946 he was employed as an interpreter in a German prisoner-of-war camp in Yorkshire, where he continued to draw and write. It was in these places that he first conceived what he called his 'assemblies' of human figures which were to become a major subject of his paintings. The nearest thing to Vaughan's illustrated journal is, perhaps, Ronald Searle's eloquent Japanese prison sketch-book.

Prisoners

11 October 1944. The night they arrived was also the night of the gale. We heard it said afterwards that in the opinion of many it was the worst gale around these parts within living memory, but there was nothing to suggest its approach when the blurred ranks of field grey appeared at the entrance about five o'clock on a mild autumn afternoon. In the watery yellow light the only immediate difference between the straggling rows of men and the rows of kit that were stood alongside them was that the former could move of their own accord.

For weeks we had been sufficiently occupied with the details of administration to have no time to speculate on any personal aspects, but when the first words of German rang out on the still air a spell seemed to fall over the camp. One had the feeling of something sinister and dangerous being near. For a short moment when the guarded eyes of the British met the glazed stare of the lines of Germans, the well-rehearsed course of probability seemed to hesitate, and one felt it conceivable that anything could happen. Then organization took control and everything went as planned.

They were herded through the barbed wire and divided and sub-divided into groups and parties, and the NCOs with fluttering white papers went in and out of the slowing, shaping mass like sheepdogs. All was orderly and quiet. One was conscious of white faces and enormous staring eyes which followed one's every movement.

There was the search and documentation and medical inspection and allocation of huts and bedding. The search was first and took longest.

Three tables had been set up in the biggest hut with an officer or NCO at each and the prisoners formed up in three lines. Each in his turn emptied his kit bag on the floor and the contents of his pockets on to the table. We took their name and rank and regiment and age and religion and profession and gave in return a number of many figures. All this took time because of difficulties with the spelling and the fact that the interpreters had not yet arrived. A few knew some English and some of us a little German, the formal, excessively polite idioms of the phrase books, so the whole thing was conducted with the utmost decorum.

When they had first appeared all together it had seemed impossible ever to distinguish one from the other, but now that they came up singly to the tables quite important differences became apparent.

Some were hardly able to stand or speak, either from exhaustion or because they were hollowed right out with fear. They fumbled and dropped things, or they just stood trembling and inert. Some came up smiling and smothered the table instantly with worthless rubbish, shaking out their inverted pockets to convince us of their innocence, eager to supply a short history of each article and to disclose the identities of photographs. Some smiled cynically, saluted smartly, and were deliberately slow and casual. Others, a few older ones, cried quietly the whole time, letting the tears cut white channels down their grimed cheeks. They brought out their belongings like disgraced schoolboys showing their copybooks to the headmaster. Mostly, they were young. Some were just children.

Some had nothing but a few crumpled letters, a photograph, and a crust of bread rolled up in what might once have been a pair of socks. Others had many and various possessions. There was one who was short and fat with a bald head and thick glasses. He happened to be in my group and I had noticed him when he was still some way down the line because he was incessantly fidgeting and fussing and keeping a check on his things which he carried in two cases and two sacks. Everyone was amused at him because he was so like a flustered tourist who cannot find a porter. When his turn came he was sweating with anxiety and his hands trembled as he laid on the table one after another leather cases of shaving tackle, writing materials, books, fountain pens, a watch, a travelling ink bottle, and a long silver pencil. I felt his breath beating on the top of my head as I bent over and ran my hands quickly over his pockets. I picked up the silver pencil. It was the sort that is made to hold a short length of cedar pencil, not the modern propelling type. It was beautifully wrought and embossed with vine leaves and laurel and engraved with initials, not his own.

'What a lovely pencil,' I said.

His face lit up with pleasure. 'You like it – Yes.' I asked him his profession and he said he was an architect from Wetzlar. I told him to put his things away while I filled up the forms. He packed everything away into the two cases and sacks and moved off quickly and left the pencil in the middle of the table.

'You've forgotten something,' I called, and pointed to the pencil.

He stopped and looked confused and said nothing. I held it out to him.

'Your pencil,' I said. He took it uncertainly, not knowing what to do with his embarrassment.

'Thank you,' I said, 'it's not allowed.'

'Not allowed – ah – verboten – verboten – entschuldigen.' And he went off bewildered, submissive, fat, middle-aged, unhappy.

It took nearly two hours to get through. With so many people

OFF

about it was the silence that was strangest. It was a positive silence like that of a cathedral, which made one want to lower one's voice. When the last man had left the air was rancid with the smell of dirt and sweat and exhaustion. A thick blanket of dust lay over everything – the soil of France. When we had finished and went outside it was dusk and the wind had started.

It began with a wild waving in the top branches of the elm trees beyond the compound. Doors banged suddenly and people walked as though they were climbing a steep gradient. Words were torn out of one's mouth before they could be uttered. As night closed in the wind bore down on the camp and fastened its million claws into every crevice. It tore screaming through the barbed wire and across the concrete and raced away howling into the dales. The two great marquees swayed and groaned like ships straining their moorings and searching for the rocks. The night was full of unidentifiable noises. Every inanimate thing found its own particular moan and note of protest until the darkness was crowded with furious torment. In the low howling huts the English lay and the Germans lay sleeping for the first time in safety. If anyone had called his words would not have been heard. All night the wind blew with fury, tearing at each standing thing, hollowing out all secret places, overturning the little tables of incomplete justice, impetuous, replenishing, cleansing.

EVELYN WAUGH
(1903–66)

Scarcely anyone knew that Waugh was a diarist, and a most prolific one at that, leaving at his death a manuscript of over a third of a million words. It dated back to when he was seven and ran on with hardly a break until the year before his death. Its last entry was made on Easter Day, 1965. He destroyed parts of it himself, such as the entries dealing with his homosexual phase at Oxford, his divorce from his first wife, and what he called his 'lunacy' during 1954, some of these destructions receiving artistic resurrection in works like *Brideshead Revisited* and *The Ordeal of Gilbert Pinfold*. Waugh had no intention of publishing any part of the diary, although he used it as a prompt for his books, nor could it be published posthumously in its original form, because of its libellous and offensive references. Eventually his widow, his son Auberon and his brother Alec agreed on an edited version. This was undertaken with consummate skill, considering Waugh's handwriting and the minefield of its contents, by Michael Davie and first published in 1976.

Waugh's celebrated mixture of genius, irascibility, success, Catholicism and social snobbery covered a sadness and vulnerability which only a diary could mention – could display to its often disgusted or accepting owner. Everything crashes against patrician aspiration; everything, that is, except his ability to write better and better as the hated decades pass. What he does and who he meets are imaginatively dovetailed into his stories. There never was such a constant meeting of fact and art. Such truthfulness, such pretentiousness, such unhappiness (in particular in the spheres where most of us look for pleasure), such nastiness and such honour. Waugh's is the most troubled of twentieth-century diaries and the most dreadfully entertaining.

Almost immediately after finishing *Brideshead Revisited* Waugh joined the military mission led by Randolph Churchill to Croatia, setting off on 4 July 1944. The war could scarcely have thrown two more incompatible men into gruesome propinquity. The adventure drew some of Waugh's deadliest comic fire in his diary.

Monday, 23 October 1944. Every evening last week Major Clissold has hoped for an aeroplane and has been disappointed, sometimes on the airfield itself. On Friday we took fifty-six Jews out in intense cold and sent them back to their straw after two hours' wait. There are also fifteen American aircrew, three of them injured in their jump, waiting to get away. Randolph sends petulant signals 'personal for Air Vice-Marshal' believing they will cause consternation at Bari.

On Friday Belgrade fell and there was a great discharge of rifles.

On Saturday the celebrations were more formal. A religious service by seven orthodox popes lately arrived from Dalmatia, a temporary altar in the frescoed tea-house, tattered vestments, incense, a few chants and then a purely political and patriotic sermon. The General there, all the Communist bosses and editors, Clissold and I by chance. Then the whole party, priests included, adjourned to the Catholic church. HQ troops formed up outside. Monsignore Rittig preached, introducing, Clissold told me, an element of religion, then a *te deum* in the church. None of the congregation seemed familiar with the usages of the place. The priests are said to be got together for a discussion. It seems to me conceivable that Broz [Tito] aims at a national secularized church.

Randolph got drunk in the early afternoon and had an endless argument with Mates, going round in ponderous circles, contradicting himself, heavily humorous, patronizing, appalling. Mates was even worse, showing a fiery and insane patriotism side by side with his Communism. He spoke of Istria in exactly the terms Hitler youths employed about the Sudeten Germans; he showed the same mystical interest in 'blood' both as a racial bond and as a sacrifice; he showed a more-than-German small-state sense of dignity (and vulgar esteem for physical toughness). And he is a likeable youth, typical of what is best in the Partisans. Later there were torchlight processions, more oratory, a Russian aeroplane, expected, which never came.

Yesterday we awoke to an air-raid – six or seven slow machines dropping small bombs and machine-gunning the village without opposition. Randolph became greatly overexcited. This, he said, was just how the Dvrar parachute attack had begun, and the raid of itself seemed so pointless that I gave some credence to this. However they flew away and Clissold and I went to look for damage and found little. There was a direct hit on the tea-house and the anti-Fascist fresco was untouched. In church at 11 o'clock there was an aeroplane buzzing round and several bursts of machine-gun fire. The congregation were a little apprehensive at first but the priest was admirably self-possessed and from the moment the canon of the Mass started no one looked from the altar. I half thought there might be a Ustashe attack and that we should come out to find the place in their hands or suddenly find the church invaded by bloodthirsty Croats. Freddy, whom I found alone and morose at the mission, believed a parachute attack was due at any moment. I packed my rucksack and haversack but we did not have to move. Heavy rain fell all the afternoon and evening; the light failed; Randolph and Freddy lay in bed; I strained my eyes re-reading *Quest for Corvo*. This morning I was awake early and dressed, not wanting to be caught in bed by air-raiders again, but there is a heavy mist everywhere so I am writing this instead in the sitting-room that reeks of *rakija*.

Randolph got up at 8 through restless fear of air attack, so that his conversation and telephoning and typing and clucking over the signals like an old hen began two hours earlier and I lost the part of the day I value. Clissold and I called on the HQ and got information about a Partisan attack on an oil refinery near Zagreb. Then to Glina in the jeep, taking cigarettes and old magazines to the American aircrews. The three injured men, particularly the former funny man who is hurt internally, were in low spirits and despair of getting taken out. It rained heavily all day and the airfield was pronounced unusable until it had had three days' clear weather.

At luncheon Randolph and Freddy became jocular. They do not make new jests or even repeat their own. Of conversation as I love it – a fantasy growing in the telling, apt repartee, argument based on accepted postulates, spontaneous reminiscences and quotation – they know nothing. All their noise and laughter is in the retelling of memorable sayings of their respective fathers or public figures; even with this vast repertoire they repeat themselves every day or two – sometimes within an hour. They also recite with great zest the more hackneyed passages of Macaulay, the poems of John Betjeman, Belloc, and other classics. I remarked how boring it was to be obliged to tell Randolph everything twice – once when he was drunk, once when he was sober. Two hours later, in a fuddled state, with a glass of *rakija* in his hand, he came to my room to expostulate with me for unkindness. Later he cooked kidneys for Zora making loud appreciative kisses and whistles when the dish appeared – these, his American slang, his coughing and farting make him a poor companion in wet weather. At least I have not to endure his snoring as Freddy must. Finished *Quest for Corvo*.

9. THE DIARIST AS ARTIST

WILLIAM BYRD
(1674–1744)

The remarkable and highly secret diaries of William Byrd, a Virginian aristocrat, first came to light in the Huntington Library, then in the University of North Carolina library and the Virginia Historical Society's library, during the last war. Written in a form of shorthand which Byrd had taught himself from a primer entitled *A Pen Pluck't from an Eagle's Wing* by William Mason, these are among the most fascinating and impressive of all early American diaries, albeit their author spent nearly half his life in England. But this in no way disbars them as American works, for they reveal with perfect accuracy the transitional stage of a grandee settler who imposes an English aristocratic culture on the huge estates he has inherited in the colonies.

Byrd was only eighteen when his father died and left him Westover and its neighbouring plantations in and around Richmond, Virginia, some 26,000 acres all told. He was to add to these 150,000 acres of country around the Dan, Irvine, Staunton and Meherrin Rivers, a territory he was to designate 'The Land of Eden' and which was to be the subject of an enthralling diary of his own. Although the diarist waxed lyrical over his purchased paradise, it was with the enthusiasm of a paradise-broker. Byrd's intention was in fact to open up this lovely North Carolina–Virginia border and sell it piecemeal to Swiss farmers, these being to him ideal immigrants and the reverse of those 'Goths and Vandals' the Scots. But the Swiss never came, and Scots it had to be. Byrd's journal of *A Journey to the Land of Eden*, and a later diary called *History of the Dividing Line*, describing how North Carolina was carved out of the vast land mass which until 1728 went under the general name of Virginia, are intimate and intriguing. He is the archetypal real-estate man.

But it is the accounts of Byrd's private life in London and Westover, which he hoped would be concealed for ever in his personal version of Mason's shorthand (easily transcribed by Mrs Tinling of the Huntington Library, who had made such tasks a hobby), that puts him in the Pepys class for lack of inhibition, if not for charm and genius. Byrd records, among much else, everything he could not otherwise mention concerning sex, food, religion and defecation – 'I danced my dance.' The food was almost too dull to talk about: quantities of boiled milk, sometimes from asses, potatoes, and – considering how rich he was – dishes whose only merit must have been to witness truthfully either to a lack of appetite or a 'plain fare' philosophy. The religion was as strict as that of any monk in its daily round of prayers, readings and invocations, but as it clearly exercised little or no effect upon Byrd's sexual behaviour, greed (he owned his own slave-ship), ambitions (he lusted for governorships, etc.) and worldliness generally, it must be regarded as the carefully maintained attribute essential to a gentleman. There is little guilt and no anguish when, after each sexual encounter, he closes his entry for the day with a routine 'God forgive me'. It could be said that where women were concerned Byrd was selfish to the last degree. He had them in bagnios, coaches, on the grass in St James's Park, in drawing-rooms and bedrooms, in lanes and, when in Virginia where pick-ups were hard to come by, in his own servants' quarters, especially Annie the maid who had accompanied him from England and in fact became his mistress. But this attempt at total sexual honesty is unlike that of James Boswell, say, for it omits everything – all love, all feeling – except climax. There is little pride and only a need for accuracy when he records reaching this twice and three times a night, and he is equally matter-of-fact when he fails to reach it.

Byrd's *London Diary* covering his four years in the city, begun when he was in early middle-age and separated for a while from his shrewish Virginian wife, is a strange book. Why should such a sophisticated and intelligent man feel compelled to tell himself, as it were, an almost daily formulary of having milk for breakfast, reading Hebrew and Greek, going to the lavatory, reaching sexual climax, praying, and so forth, and why, since he was intensely social, does he rarely record what was said when he went the London rounds? What he treasures as a diarist in England is the simple and domestically personal, and the routine of the flesh.

In Virginia it was another diarist altogether. Here Byrd is the unmysterious, able and stylish recorder of what he knows to be an important historic enterprise. It would have astonished him to know that we should moralize a great deal more over his slaving, grabbing, and seeking honours than over his somewhat mechanical whoring. He is certainly a brilliant writer on two levels. On one level he is looking at his physical self with the relentlessness Dürer exhibits in his naked portrait, while on the other he is looking out at the glorious prospect of his inherited American physical world. He was a colonial polymath, a Fellow of the Royal Society at twenty-two, a botanical scientist, a gifted if ruthless entrepreneur, a man capable of assessing his sexuality without fantasy, and above all a man determined to be an aristocrat. He adored Virginia and it permeates his diaries with the sweetness of Goshen. Curiously, although a journey of many weeks and hazards divided his two worlds, the diaries give little evidence of any division or preference in his feelings for England and America. There is no homesickness for either land. But the beautifully written *History of the Dividing Line* and *Journey to the Land of Eden*, the latter a classic land-agent's prospectus, reveal Byrd's subconscious patriotism for the new country which was coming into being. His biographer, Louis B. Wright, points out that his career is an example of 'the rise of that influential agrarian aristocracy that produced Washington, Jefferson, Madison, Marshall and a great galaxy of leaders'. William Byrd used Mason's shorthand to put on full view – quite unwittingly, for there was no intention to expose either himself or his society generally – the routine necessities which even those who hope or expect to end up as statues cannot avoid. Byrd isn't indiscreet; he is deliberate. Only *why*?

From The London Diary

13 June 1718. I rose about 8 o'clock and read a chapter in Hebrew and some Greek in Lucian. I said my prayers and had milk for breakfast. The weather was clear and warm, the wind west. Mr G-n-y was with me to let me know he could do nothing in my affair about the government of Virginia. About 11 o'clock I visited Mrs [Sands] and sat with them half an hour, and then went to my Lord Orrery's where I stayed about half an hour and then went to Ozinda's where I met Sir Wilfred Lawson and Mr B-r-t-n and went to dine with them at the Thatched House and ate some boiled chicken for dinner. Both these gentlemen told me they were clapped by Mrs W-l-m. After dinner I went with them to the surgeon and then I took leave of them and went home and received several letters from Virginia. About 6 o'clock I went to Will's Coffeehouse and read the news. Then I walked in the park and then drank a dish of chocolate at Ozinda's and went to the Spanish Ambassador's. About twelve I went home in a chair and said my prayers.

14 June. I rose about 7 o'clock and read a chapter in Hebrew and some Greek in Lucian. I said my prayers, and had milk for breakfast. The weather was clear and warm, the wind southwest. I wrote some English till 11 o'clock. I went to my Lord Bellenden's but he was from home; then to Mr O-r-d but he was from home; then to Mr B-r-t-n and sat with him about an hour and then I went to see the burning engine in the Privy Garden, and was well pleased with it. Then I went home and ate a roast rabbit. After dinner I took a nap till five and then went to Chelsea and at the College a gentlewoman came and told me she desired to speak with me, so I got out and walked with her in the college walk and she told me Mrs A-l-c had commerce with another man and showed me several of her letters. I thanked her and took leave and returned to London, and went to the park and afterwards to Mrs FitzHerbert's. From thence I took a walk and picked up a woman and carried her to the tavern and committed uncleanness and ate some roast fowl. About 1 o'clock I went home and neglected my prayers, for which God forgive me.

15 June. I rose about 8 o'clock and read a chapter in Hebrew and some Greek in Lucian. I said my prayers, and had milk for breakfast. The weather was clear and warm, the wind west. This day my new chariot came out and about 11 o'clock I went to Somerset Chapel and heard a pretty good sermon. After church I walked in the garden with Penny U-m-s and Mrs H-r-c-r and then dined with Mrs U-m-s and ate some roast beef. After dinner we drank tea till 5 o'clock and then I went to visit Mrs Southwell and drank tea again and would have carried Mr Southwell to the park but we discovered that my coachman was drunk so I set him down at White's Chocolate House and then went to Mrs [Sands'] where I stayed till 9 o'clock and then went to Ozinda's Chocolate House and from thence to the Spanish Ambassador's and walked home at twelve and neglected my prayers.

16 June. I rose about 8 o'clock and read a chapter in Hebrew and some Greek in Lucian. I said my prayers, and had milk for breakfast. The weather was cloudy and warm, the wind southwest. About 10 o'clock Colonel [Shutz] came to see me but did not stay because my chariot was come. About twelve I went to the Virginia Coffeehouse and saw Captain Randolph just come from Virginia. Then I went to Mr Perry's and dined with Mike and ate some fish. After dinner I wrote a letter and then went and sat with Mrs Cole, a milliner, and ate some cherries. Then I went to Chelsea and saw Mrs A-l-c for the last time because she had played the whore. However I drank tea with her and about 8 o'clock returned to London and went to Will's where I read the news and then went to the Union Tavern to meet a young woman who supped with me and I ate some roast chicken and then we went to the bagnio in Silver Street, where I lay all night with her and rogered her three times and found her very straight and unprecocious and very sweet and agreeable. I slept very little.

27 November 1719. I rose about 8 o'clock and read some Greek but no Hebrew. I said my prayers and had boiled milk for breakfast. The weather was cold and cloudy, the wind northwest. I danced my dance and about 9 o'clock the coach came for us and we took my cousin John Rand with us and we went to Dover but the weather did not favor us for it rained almost all the way. About 12 o'clock we got there and put up at the widow S-l-t-r, who was very handsome, and had tripe for dinner. We were very merry and stayed here till 2 o'clock and then went up to the castle that stands on the cliffs. About four we got home and had fish for supper. We sat and talked till ten and then retired and I kissed the maid and neglected my prayers.

28 November. I rose about 7 o'clock and read some Greek but no Hebrew. I said my prayers, and had boiled milk for breakfast. About 9 o'clock Daniel Horsmanden and Mr Carter took leave and went away in my coach, notwithstanding the coachman was very drunk. I danced my dance and wrote some English till dinner and then ate roast veal. After dinner my uncle and cousin Jack took a walk to Northbourne and made a visit to the parson but he was from home. However, his wife entertained us with some strong beer. Then we walked home and read the news which Mr D-d-s the parson brought us. I ate some boiled milk for supper and romped with Molly F-r-s-y and about 9 o'clock retired and kissed the maid so that I committed uncleanness, for which God forgive me.

29 November. I rose about 8 o'clock and read some Greek. I said my prayers, and had boiled milk for breakfast. The weather was cold and cloudy, and it rained a little. About 11 o'clock we went to church and Mr D-d-s gave us a good sermon and then came home to dine with us and I ate some roast mutton. After dinner it rained, that I could not walk so was content to romp with Molly F-r-s-y. In the evening we drank tea and then sat and talked till seven, when I ate some boiled milk for supper. After supper we sat and talked and romped a little. About ten I retired and kissed the maid and said my prayers.

30 November. I rose about 8 o'clock and I made the maid feel my roger. I said my prayers, and had boiled milk for breakfast. I read some Greek and settled several accounts. The weather was cold and cloudy, the wind west. I danced my dance and then read some English till dinner, when I ate some fish. After dinner we romped a little and the weather was so bad I could not walk out, so that I read more English till the evening, when Mr B-l-d and Mr D-d-s, two Northbourne ministers, came and stayed till 10 o'clock. I had milk for supper, and about 10 o'clock went to bed and neglected my prayers.

From The History of the Dividing Line

18 November 1728. All the nations round about, bearing in mind the havoc these Indians used formerly to make among their ancestors in the insolence of their power, did at length avenge it home upon them, and made them glad to apply to this government for protection. Colonel Spotswood, our then lieutenant governor, having a good opinion of their fidelity and courage, settled them at Christanna, ten miles north of Roanoke, upon the belief that they would be a good barrier on that side of the country against the incursion of all foreign Indians. And in earnest they would have served well enough for that purpose, if the white people in the neighborhood had not debauched their morals and ruined their health with rum, which was the cause of many disorders and ended at last in a barbarous murder committed by one of these Indians when he was drunk, for which the poor wretch was executed when he was sober ... The men rode more awkwardly than any Dutch sailor, and the ladies bestrode their palfreys a la mode de France, but were so bashful about it that there was no persuading them to mount till they were quite out of our sight. The French women used to ride a-straddle, not so much to make them sit firmer in the saddle, as from the hopes the same thing might peradventure befall them that once happened to the nun of Orleans, who, escaping out of a nunnery, took post en cavalier, and in ten miles' hard riding had the good fortune to have all the tokens of a man break out upon her. This piece of history ought to be the more credible, because it leans upon much the same degree of proof as the tale of Bishop Burnet's two Italian nuns, who, according to his lordship's account, underwent the same happy metamorphosis, probably by some other violent exercise.

19. From hence we despatched the cart with our baggage under a guard, and crossed the Meherrin river, which was not thirty yards wide in that place. By the help of fresh horses that had been sent us, we now began to mend our pace, which was also quickened by the strong inclinations we had to get home. In the distance of five miles we forded Meherrin Creek, which was very near as broad as the river. About eight miles farther we came to Sturgeon Creek, so

called from the dexterity an Occaneche Indian showed there in catching one of those royal fish . . .

25 April. Surely there is no place in the world where the inhabitants live with less labor than in North Carolina. It approaches nearer to the description of Lubberland than any other, by the great felicity of the climate, the easiness of raising provisions, and the slothfulness of the people. Indian corn is of so great increase that a little pains will subsist a very large family with bread, and then they may have meat without any pains at all, by the help of the low grounds and the great variety of mast that grows on the high land. The men, for their parts, just like the Indians, impose all the work upon the poor women. They make their wives rise out of their beds early in the morning, at the same time that they lie and snore till the sun has risen one-third of his course and dispersed all the unwholesome damps. Then, after stretching and yawning for half an hour, they light their pipes, and under the protection of a cloud of smoke venture out into the open air; though, if it happens to be never so little cold, they quickly return shivering into the chimney corner. When the weather is mild, they stand leaning with both their arms upon the cornfield fence, and gravely consider whether they had best go and take a small heat at the hoe: but generally find reasons to put it off till another time. Thus they loiter away their lives, like Solomon's sluggard, with their arms across, and at the winding up of the year scarcely have bread to eat. To speak the truth, 'tis a thorough aversion to labor that makes people file off to North Carolina, where plenty and a warm sun confirm them in their disposition to laziness for their whole lives.

27 April. Most of the houses in this part of the country are loghouses, covered with pine or cypress shingles three feet long and one broad. They are hung upon laths with pegs, and their doors, too, turn upon wooden hinges and have wooden locks to secure them, so that the building is finished without nails or other ironwork. They also set up their pales without any nails at all, and indeed more securely than those that are nailed. There are three rails mortised into the posts, the lowest of which serves as a sill with a groove in the middle big enough to receive the end of the pales: the middle part of the pale rests against the inside of the next rail, and the top of it is brought forward to the outside of the uppermost. Such wreathing of the pales in and out makes them stand firm, and much harder to unfix than when nailed in the ordinary way.

DOROTHY WORDSWORTH
(1771–1855)

In 1797–8 Samuel Coleridge and William Wordsworth and his sister Dorothy were living two or three miles apart in the Quantocks at a fertile moment which was to redirect the course of English poetry. Their manifesto, as it were, was *Lyrical Ballads*. Coleridge was to acknowledge Dorothy's hand in it when he called them 'three people but only one soul'. For him she was Wordsworth's 'exquisite sister'. The Wordsworths had moved into Alfoxden House to be within walking distance of Coleridge's cottage at Nether Stowey. Coleridge had recently married, and all four friends were in their mid-twenties. The industrious idyll, however, was almost immediately shattered; suspicion was aroused in the village by their walking about at all hours and by their radical talk. It was to force the Wordsworths to surrender the lease of Alfoxden after only a year. But what a year! It and the brief period following it which ended in her brother's marriage to Mary Hutchinson were to be the zenith of Dorothy's long life. She recorded them with perfect simplicity in her *Alfoxden Journal* and *Grasmere Journal*, two small diaries without compare. In them the reader is not only able to recognize her crucial role in the making of William's poems, but also her undisguisable love for both her brother and their mutual friend Coleridge. 'She gave me eyes, she gave me ears,' acknowledged Wordsworth; she 'Maintained for me a saving intercourse/With my true self . . .' But she gave Coleridge his first bitter realization that he had married someone who could not interest him. Dorothy Wordsworth's journals are not only remarkable for their beautiful descriptions of nature, but for the tender realism of their portraits of village toilers and wanderers.

From The Alfoxden Journal

3 February 1798. A mild morning, the windows open at breakfast, the redbreasts singing in the garden. Walked with Coleridge over the hills. The sea at first obscured by vapour; that vapour afterwards slid in one mighty mass along the sea-shore; the islands and one point of land clear beyond it. The distant country (which was purple in the clear dull air), overhung by straggling clouds that sailed over it, appeared like the darker clouds, which are often seen at a great distance apparently motionless, while the nearer ones pass quickly over them, driven by the lower winds. I never saw such a union of earth, sky, and sea. The clouds beneath our feet spread themselves to the water, and the clouds of the sky almost joined them. Gathered sticks in the wood; a perfect stillness. The redbreasts sang upon the leafless boughs. Of a great number of sheep in the field, only one standing. Returned to dinner at five o'clock. The moonlight still and warm as a summer's night at nine o'clock.

4 February. Walked a great part of the way to Stowey with Coleridge. The morning warm and sunny. The young lasses seen on the hilltops, in the villages and roads, in their summer holiday clothes – pink petticoats and blue. Mothers with their children in arms, and the little ones that could just walk, tottering by their side. Midges or small flies spinning in the sunshine; the songs of the lark and redbreast; daisies upon the turf; the hazels in blossom; honeysuckles budding. I saw one solitary strawberry flower under a hedge. The furze gay with blossom. The moss rubbed from the pailings by the sheep, that leave locks of wool, and the red marks with which they are spotted, upon the wood.

8 February. Went up the Park, and over the tops of the hills, till we came to a new and very delicious pathway, which conducted us to the Coombe. Sat a considerable time upon the heath. Its surface restless and glittering with the motion of the scattered piles of withered grass, and the waving of the spider's threads. On our return the mist still hanging over the sea, but the opposite coast clear, and the rocky cliffs distinguishable. In the deep Coombe, as we stood upon the sunless hill, we saw miles of grass, light and glittering, and the insects passing.

22 February. Coleridge came in the morning to dinner. Wm. and I walked after dinner to Woodlands; the moon and two planets; sharp and frosty. Met a razor-grinder with a soldier's jacket on, a knapsack upon his back, and a boy to drag his wheel. The sea very black, and making a loud noise as we came through the wood, loud as if disturbed, and the wind was silent.

23 February. William walked with Coleridge in the morning. I did not go out.

24 February. Went to the hill-top. Sat a considerable time overlooking the country towards the sea. The air blew pleasantly round us. The landscape mildly interesting. The Welsh hills capped by a huge range of tumultuous white clouds. The sea, spotted with white, of a bluish grey in general, and streaked with darker lines. The near shores clear; scattered farm houses, half-concealed by green mossy orchards, fresh straw lying at the doors; hay-stacks in the fields. Brown fallows, the springing wheat, like a shade of green over the brown earth, and the choice of meadow plots, full of sheep and lambs, of a soft and vivid green; a few wreaths of blue smoke, spreading along the ground; the oaks and beaches in the hedges retaining their yellow leaves . . .

From The Grasmere Journal

Wednesday, 14 May 1800. Wm. and John set off into Yorkshire after dinner at ½ past 2 o'clock, cold pork in their pockets. I left them at the turning of the Lowwood bay under the trees. My heart was so full that I could hardly speak to W. when I gave him a farewell kiss. I sate a long time upon a stone at the margin of the lake, and after a flood of tears my heart was easier. The lake looked to me, I knew not why, dull and melancholy, and the weltering on the shores seemed a heavy sound. I walked as long as I could amongst the stones of the shore. The wood rich in flowers; a beautiful yellow, palish yellow, flower, that looked thick, round, and double, and smelt very sweet – I supposed it was a ranunculus. Crowfoot, the grassy-leaved Rabbit-toothed white flower, strawberries, geranium, scentless violets, anemones two kinds, orchises, primroses. The heckberry was very beautiful, the crab coming out as a low shrub. Met a blind man, driving a very large beautiful Bull, and a cow – he walked with two sticks. Came home by Clappersgate. The valley very green; many sweet views up to Rydale head, when I could juggle away the fine houses; but they disturbed me, even more than when I have been happier; one beautiful view of the Bridge, without Sir Michael's. Sate down very often, though it was cold. I resolved to write a journal of the time till W. and J. return, and I set about keeping my resolve, because I will not quarrel with myself, and because I shall give Wm. pleasure by it when he comes home again. At Rydale, a woman of the village, stout and well dressed, begged a half-penny; she had never she said done it before, but these hard times! Arrived at home with a bad headach, set some slips of privett, the evening cold, had a fire, my face now flame-coloured. It is nine o'clock. I shall soon go to bed. A young woman begged at the door – she had come from Manchester on Sunday morn, with two shillings and a slip of paper which she supposed a Bank note – it was a cheat. She had buried her husband and three children within a year and a half – all in one grave – burying very dear – paupers all put in one place – 20 shillings paid for as much ground as will bury a man – a stone to be put over it or the right will be lost – 11/6 each time the ground is opened. Oh! that I had a letter from William!

1802. On Monday, 4th October 1802, my Brother William was married to Mary Hutchinson. I slept a good deal of the night, and rose fresh and well in the morning. At a little after 8 o'clock I saw them go down the avenue towards the church. William had parted from me upstairs. I gave him the wedding ring – with how deep a blessing! I took it from my forefinger where I had worn it the whole of the night before – he slipped it again onto my finger and blessed me fervently. When they were absent my dear little Sara prepared the breakfast. I kept myself as quiet as I could, but when I saw the two men running up the walk, coming to tell us it was over, I could stand it no longer, and threw myself on the bed, where I lay in stillness, neither hearing or seeing anything till Sara came upstairs to me, and said, 'They are coming.' This forced me from the bed where I lay, and I moved, I knew not how, straight forward, faster than my strength could carry me, till I met my beloved William, and fell upon his bosom. He and John Hutchinson led me to the house, and there I stayed to welcome my dear Mary. As soon as we had breakfasted, we departed. It rained when we set off. Poor Mary was much agitated, when she parted from her Brothers and Sisters, and her home. Nothing particular occurred till we reached Kirby. We had sunshine and showers, pleasant talk, love and chearfulness. We were obliged to stay two hours at K. while the horses were feeding. We wrote a few lines to Sara, and then walked out; the sun shone, and we went to the Churchyard after we had put a letter into the Post-office for the *York Herald*. We sauntered about, and read the Grave-stones.

WILLIAM ALLINGHAM
(1824–89)

Allingham's diary was first edited and published by his widow, the artist Helen Allingham, who illustrated Thomas Hardy's novels, and gained an unjust reputation as a record of cultural hob-nobbing. But John Julius Norwich has pointed out, 'A lion hunter he may have been, but his lions loved him.' Allingham's two major lions were Tennyson and Carlyle, both notorious for not suffering fools gladly or permitting themselves to be got at by celebrity-seekers. As each welcomed young Allingham – Tennyson in particular invited him to stay time and time again – it is clear that they were as pleased to be with him as he was to be with them.

Allingham was a minor poet from County Donegal who became a customs officer in Hampshire and who managed to free himself from this drudgery at the age of fifty-six. His considerable contemporary reputation rested upon the now unread epic poem *Laurence Bloomfield in Ireland*, which impressed Gladstone and Palmerston – and Turgenev! His Irish lyric verse was admired by many of the good poets of his day, and if Allingham's diary cascades with great names – Thackeray, Browning, the Pre-Raphaelites, Leslie Stephen –

it is because all these writers and painters saw him as a legitimate member of their fraternity. His diary is among the most genuinely intimate pictures of the Victorian cultural scene, and delightful to read. If he was shameless in giving priority to what his famous friends said or to how they looked, it was because, as Lord Norwich has remarked, he saw no reason to be ashamed. The diary is one of homage to the best-loved figures in the diarist's life. They welcomed him. He 'Boswellized' them, in miniature and often to perfection, and captured their genius in their varied domestic settings. Allingham is the *petit maître* of the Victorian literary interior, talk, fun, walks and all. There are signs that he wasn't above ingratiating himself for his diary's sake, but posterity can only thank him for that.

Saturday, 29 August 1863. Came to Freshwater and walked with Mrs Clough and Mrs Coltman on Afton Down; slept at the Albion Hotel, amid a noise of waves. The Landlady a big dreadful woman with fiery face. Next morning breakfasted at Mrs Clough's. They all went to Church. I was left at home with Clough's letters and American diary, which or a selection from them Mrs C. thinks of publishing. After an early dinner, we walked to Farringford and found that the family were expected in about ten days. Mr Tennyson was ill (the woman said), and coming to London from Harrogate. Mrs Clough being an intimate, we were admitted to the living rooms, and saw plenty of books on shelves and tables, including numerous presentation volumes of poetry, and the new magazines – among which I noted with some satisfaction *Fraser* with the new chapter of *Laurence Bloomfield* (so lately teasing me in MS).

Monday, 14 September. Note from Mrs Clough, from Bournemouth –'Mrs Cameron will be glad to see you at lunch, to meet Mr Henry Taylor.' Mrs Clough was returning to the island to-day, and I joined her with Mr and Mrs Coltman on the 3 o'clock steamer. The Tennysons on board. T. and I just spoke a few words, and then I went forward with Mrs Clough and kept out of his way. Returned to Lymington.

Wednesday, 16 September. Southampton: Heard Cardinal Wiseman lecture on 'Self-culture' at the Hartley Institute. An Irish priest, he, in general appearance; face like a shrewish old woman in spectacles; voice tuneless, accent a little mincing. The substance of the lecture commonplace, the style tawdry and paltry.

Saturday, 3 October. Cross by 3 o'clock Boat, invited to spend Sunday at Mrs Clough's. Rainy and roughish. The Coltmans are gone. Mrs Clough tells me I am invited to go to the Tennysons with her to-night. (Hurrah!) We drive to Farringford, picking up on the way Mr Pollock (afterwards Sir F.P.) and his son, a youth in spectacles. Drawing-room, tea, Mrs Tennyson in white, I can sometimes scarcely hear her low tones. Mrs Cameron, dark, short, sharp-eyed, one hears very distinctly. I wandered to the book-table, where Tennyson joined me. He praised Worsley's *Odyssey*. In a book of Latin versions from his own poetry he found some slips in Lord Lyttleton's Latin – 'Cytherea Venus', etc. 'Did I find Lymington very dull?' I told him that since coming here I had heard Cardinal Wiseman lecture (on 'Self-culture'), Spurgeon preach, and seen Tom Sayers spar. 'More than I have,' he remarked.

Farringford, Sunday, 27 December. A.T. comes in to breakfast without greeting, which is sometimes his way. I play football with the two Boys. (Hallam is about eleven, Lionel about nine.) Then walk with A.T., Palgrave, H. and L. along High Down to the Needles. Lionel talks to me; he is odd, shy, sweet, and, as his mother says, *daimonisch*. Hallam has something of a shrewd satirical turn, but with great good nature. To the cliff edge, then returning we creep up long slopes of down and rest at the Beacon. Thistles and other growths crouch into the sward from the fierce sea-winds. I quote 'a wrinkle of the monstrous hill'. We talk of 'Christabel'. Race down, I get first to the stile. After dinner more talk of 'Classic Metres'; in the drawing-room, T. standing on the hearth-rug repeated with emphasis (perhaps apropos of metres) the following lines, in the following way:

> Higgledy – piggledy, silver and gold,
> There's – (*it's nothing very dreadful!*)
> There's a louse on my back
> Seven years old.

> He inches, he pinches,
> In every part,
> And if I could catch him
> I'd *tearr* out his *hearrt*!

The last line he gave with tragic fury. Prose often runs into rhyme. T. imitated the waiter in some old-fashioned tavern calling down to the kitchen – 'Three gravies, two mocks, and a *pea*'! (soup understood). On 'pea' he raised the tone and prolonged it very comically.

Farringford, 28 December. A. T., Palgrave and I walk to Alum Bay and look at the coloured cliffs, smeary in effect, like something spilt. A. T. reproves P. for talking so fast and saying 'of – of – of – of,' etc. He also corrects me for my pronunciation (or so he asserts) of 'dew'. 'There's no *Jew* on the grass!' says he – 'there may be *dew*, but that's quite another thing.' He quotes Tom Moore's 'delicious night', etc. (four lines), with a little grunt of disapprobation at the end. Home at four. T. goes to have his hot bath. I revise *Laurence Bloomfield* (which Macmillan is printing) in the boys' room.

At dinner: Mr and Mrs Bradley of Marlborough, Mr and Mrs Butler of Harrow.

In the drawing-room A. T., P., and the two Bs. all on 'Classic Metres'. T. setting the schoolmasters right more than once, I noticed. I asked Mr Bradley afterwards, when he called on me at Lymington, did he think he could read one – any one – of Horace's Odes as it was intended to be read? He said he was sure he could *not*. He has brought into use at Marlborough the 'new' pronunciation (Italian vowel sounds K for C, etc.), which, he says, puzzles himself much more than the boys. I like him much, and wish he were not a Parson or that Parsonism were a different kind of thing. I had the ladies all to myself, and we discoursed profoundly on 'poets and practical people', 'benevolence true and false', 'the gulf between certain people and others', etc. Mrs T. confessed herself tired of hearing about 'Classic Metres'. The company gone, T., P. and I went to Palgrave's room, where the poet read to us the 'Vision of Sin', the 'Sea Fairies', and part of the 'Lotos Eaters' – a rich and solemn music, but not at all heavy. He will not admit that any one save himself can read aloud his poems properly. He suffered me to try a passage in the 'Lotos Eaters' and said 'You do it better than most people,' then read it himself and went on some way further. Thus I got from him *viva voce* part of a poem which has always seemed to be among his most characteristic works.

8 October 1864. Crossed to Yarmouth in the steamer. Mrs Cameron on board and Anthony Trollope and wife. I sat next Anthony outside the coach to Freshwater; he asked a great many practical questions about the houses and lands which we drove past – did not seem interested about Tennyson. Told me he had been in every *parish* in Ireland. He put up at Lambert's Hotel. I to Tennyson's, where a friendly reception. Macmillan here, also Mr and Mrs Pollock, the latter literary in the talk. Macmillan read aloud 'Boadicea', Tennyson at one point interjected, 'What a fine line!' (I forget what line it was). He also said, '"Maud" is wonderful!'

Monday, 10 October. Farringford. Cricket with the two boys. Mrs Tennyson's Alma Song: 'Frenchman, a hand in thine!' Poem: 'Dream of a Gate'.

October. Mrs Clough being at Bournemouth invited me to visit her there, and I went over on Friday the 28th.

Friday, 28 October. Up at 7 – fog. Drive to Christchurch, the sun breaking through fog. Enter the great Priory Church and look at the Shelley Monument. Call at the gate of Boscombe in passing and leave Lord Houghton's note of introduction with my card. After luncheon I walked out to Boscombe and found Lady Shelley at home – a small lively pleasant woman, who invited us to dinner for to-morrow. Dinner-tea at Mrs Clough's, and then I was left alone to examine Clough's letters, and MS. lectures on English Poetry. Mrs C. wants advice as to what to publish.

Saturday, 29 October. Boscombe. Sir Percy and Lady Shelley and *two sisters of Percy Bysshe Shelley*. I sat between them at dinner, having taken in Shelley's favourite sister, whose name is spelt 'Hellen'. She was lively and chatty, and I looked at and listened to her with great interest. She is tall, very slender, and must have been graceful and handsome in her youth. I saw, or fancied, a likeness to Shelley. She was sumptuous in light purple silk, which became her. She looked about fifty-six, but must be much more. Her sister, who seemed rather younger, was much less lively. Tennyson's name occurring in conversation, Miss Hellen Shelley let it plainly appear that neither he nor any modern poet was of the least interest in her eyes.

'After Shelley, Byron, and Scott, you know,' she said to me, 'one cannot care about other poets.'

GERARD MANLEY HOPKINS
(1844–89)

Hopkins was influenced by John Newman while at Balliol College, Oxford, and was converted to Roman Catholicism when he was twenty-two. Two years later he became a Jesuit and was ordained in 1877. In 1884 he was appointed Professor of Classics at University College, Dublin. He was a secret poet, afraid to publish because he believed his work would incur the anger of his Jesuit superiors, and was often pulled guiltily in opposing directions by the demands of his literary genius and his religion. Scarcely anyone knew that he was a poet during his short lifetime and he had to rely on the critical judgement of one or two close friends, who included Robert Bridges. The latter published Hopkins in 1918, almost thirty years after the great poet's death. The long delay probably did Hopkins a service, for the experimental nature of his work would almost certainly have caused it to be reviled and dismissed had it appeared in the 1880s. Hopkins had invented something he called 'sprung rhythm', a method of using language which moved in unison with what it described – a bird's flight, for example. He dealt with a sacred territory, that of nature and of Christ, which he termed 'inscape'.

Hopkins kept diaries and journals all his life, although as with his poetry he had similar anxieties where their spiritual rightness was concerned. His piety forced him to fight a strong and determined literary impulse and his own preoccupation with it. The diaries are evidence of the power of this impulse, of how for him everything had to be included in his writing: each architectural detail, every crevice in the bark of a tree, the 'pale shaven poles close on the railway leaning capriciously toward one another', the 'warped' sea, the analysis of his crying, his dreams, local crimes, lavishly written pictures of the unspoilt English countryside, his studies – every detail jewel-like, every sight and emotion set in his finest words. Occasionally he would destroy a diary, and he also had his sisters burn one marked 'Please do not open this'. But the remainder, like his poetry, crept out and into the general consciousness over many years. He kept two kinds of diary, which were sometimes parallel accounts of his ordinary and his spiritual life. But only Hopkins could have failed to realize that there was hardly a hair's-breadth to separate them.

23 January 1866. For Lent. No pudding on Sundays. No tea except if to keep me awake and then without sugar. Meat only once a day. No verses in Passion Week or on Fridays. No lunch or meat on Fridays. Not to sit in armchair except can work in no other way. Ash Wednesday and Good Friday bread and water.

Drops of rain hanging on rails etc seen with only the lower rim lighted like nails (of fingers). Screws of brooks and twines. Soft chalky look with more shadowy middles of the globes of cloud on a night with a moon faint or concealed. Mealy clouds with a not brilliant moon. Blunt buds of the ash. Pencil buds of the beech. Lobes of the trees. Cups of the eyes. Gathering back the lightly hinged eyelids. Bows of the eyelids. Pencil of eyelashes. Juices of the eyeball. Eyelids like leaves, petals, caps, tufted hats, handkerchiefs, sleeves, gloves. Also of the bones sleeved in flesh. Juices of the sunrise. Joins and veins of the same. Vermilion look of the hand held against a candle with the darker parts as the middles of the fingers and especially the knuckles covered with ash.

4 May. Fine. Alone in Powder Hill wood. Elms far off have that flaky look now but nearer the web of springing green with long curls moulds off the skeleton of the branches. Fields pinned with daisies. Buds of apple blossoms look like nails of blood. Some ashes are out. I reckon the spring is at least a fortnight later than last year for on Shakspere's birthday, April 23, it being the tercentenary, Ilbert crowned a bust of Shakspere with bluebells and put it in his window, and they are not plentiful yet. Beauty of hills in blue shadow seen through lacy leaf of willows.

At Skinner's Weir yesterday they were peeling osiers which gave out a sweet smell.

Valuation of my old rooms is £44. 3s. deducting 13s. for valuer.

5 May. Fine. Walk with Urquhart to Wood Eaton. Saw a gull flying. Fumitory graceful plant. Vetch growing richly. Some beeches fully out in pale silky fur when held against the light on the edge. Noble elms at the Manor House or other great house there.

A. has given himself a month's fast which will end on Friday next, that is of course Saturday, and is ill. That laughter on the 2nd was hysterical, as Urquhart says.

6 May. Grey. A little time ago on much such another day noticed Trinity gardens. Much distinctness, charm, and suggestiveness about the match of white grey sky, solid smooth lawn, firs and yews, dark trees, below, and chestnuts and other brighter-hued trees above, the young green having a fresh moist opaque look and there being in the whole picture an absence of projection, and apprehension of colour. On such a day also last Friday week boated with H. Dugmore to Godstow, but the warm greyness of the day, the river, the spring green, and the cuckoo wanted a canon by which to harmonize and round them in – e.g. one of feeling.

Liddon's 6th Bampton lecture. Walk with Addis: blue distance shading into nothing: boys idyllically playing cricket. Oxenham and F. Lockhart are up. A. and I dined with Wood.

Last Friday fortnight we were out above the Hinkseys on a charming day, sky pied with clouds, near the earth-line egg-blue, the longest graceful waved ribbons, also two columns of detached stacked clouds filing far away.

20 May. Whitsunday. As yesterday, hot yet fresh with wind. Dr Pusey preached. After Hall walk with Nettleship to Bablock Hythe, round by an untried way into the Appleton road up to Cumnor, and home by moonlight. Beautiful blackness and definition of elm tree branches in evening light (from behind). Cuckoos calling and answering to each other, and the calls being not equally timed they overlapped, making the triple *cuckoo*, and crossed.

21 May. As yesterday unless the wind was E. With Addis in meadows beyond Binsey. Stocks and Hall dined with me. Meadows yellow all over with buttercups. Strong dark shadows of trees through grass and buttercup stems chequering the effect. Heard corncrake.

ARNOLD BENNETT
(1867–1931)

Bennett began keeping a journal on a memorable day for any writer, that on which he writes the last page of his first novel. The date was Friday, 15 May 1896, and Bennett was twenty-nine. Journals were to follow until his death – eventually a million words, mostly on the business of turning out words. No author has so lavishly diarized the actual profession of authorship. The first entry contains the sentences, 'Yesterday, I sat down at 3 p.m. to write, and, with slight interruptions for meals, etc., kept at it till 1 a.m. this morning. The concluding chapter was written between 9 and 12 today.' Many years later and very close to the end of the diary itself, he confesses, 'Today I wrote three pages. 897 left to do! The thought is terrifying. Any serious novelist will agree with me as to the terrifyingness.'

Bennett was a solicitor's clerk from the Potteries, whose huge, uneven outpouring of fiction, plays, reviews and journalism was to bring him wealth, fame and much criticism. His best novels, *The Old Wives' Tale* (his masterpiece), *Clayhanger*, *Riceyman Steps*, and others, were never given their due by Bennett-mockers like Virginia Woolf, and he himself was never sufficiently self-critical of his need to write so much. Many of the attacks on him were false and he could say in all truthfulness, 'I don't care what anybody says, I am a nice man.' (He was looking at a painting of himself.)

He was also, in spite of being dubbed 'provincial' by sophisticates, a man of cosmopolitan taste and literary expression through his absorption of French culture, as well as being an unpretentious literary craftsman. His journals reflect his application to his craft with an almost crushing single-mindedness. 'Still unwell all week. Nevertheless I finished *The Great Adventure* this afternoon at 4.30 p.m., four days in advance of time. Actual dialogue 20,300 words. I shall doubtless cut it to less than 20,000.' And so on and so on. In between come descriptions of every type of magnificent and simple thing imaginable, a mainly Edwardian opulence alternating with a distinctly early-twentieth-century seediness, all wonderfully noted. Being so keen on his own, Bennett was naturally drawn to the work methods of any writer he met, and his journals are a monument to desk-industry.

Thursday, 23 May 1907. I am beginning to perceive, especially since M. has been here, that the habit of work, of being preoccupied with work, has got hold of me to an extent which is certainly excessive. On Tuesday I did far too much work, and I decided to do nothing yesterday. But I couldn't do nothing. I sketched out a poem in the morning, and wrote little odd things, such as this journal. After lunch I was bothered by ideas for another *Evening News* article, and to ease myself I sat down and wrote it at once, before tea; though my proper day for writing it was next Sunday. The fact is, I am always preoccupied by the thought of things I have to do, or ought to do; my novel, my articles, my journal, my letters, my accounts, my Italian, my physical exercises. And when one thing is done and cleared off I instantly begin to think of another thing; to create a new weight which I must lift away. So it goes on. I never have a free mind. And even when dallying with M., or eating, I am preoccupied. This ought to be curable. It is very annoying, especially when it is pointed out and the statement cannot be traversed.

After tea yesterday we went for an excursion. I had decided to abandon myself to an excursion, especially as I really had nothing of any urgency to do. The weather had brightened and cleared up; but was still unsettled. Lebert said it would not rain. But immediately we left the house it began to pour. We arrived at the station fifteen minutes before the Fontainebleau train, and before taking tickets we discussed whether it would clear up again. We both thought it might. But I had known precisely such afternoons when, under a continual promise of clearing-up the next minute it had rained, with constant unsteadiness for hours. However, we went to Fontainebleau. At Fontainebleau no rain had fallen at all. We took the electric car to the town.

Instantly we got out of the car in the Grande Rue it began to rain heavily. We reached my favourite Café des Postes and sat on the terrace, drinking sirop and absinthe, and watching the heavy rain, for an hour and a quarter. It is singular how calm a provincial town remains under heavy rain. In Paris people run in the streets, and feverishly seek shelter. But at Fontainebleau people strolled about with their umbrellas as calmly as I do myself. The electric cars kept passing every five minutes in the heavy rain.

Friday, 20 November 1914. On Wednesday afternoon I went to Burslem to see Mater, reported to be past hope. I saw her at 8 p.m. and remained alone with her for about half-an-hour. She looked very small, especially in the hollow of the pillows. The outlines of her face were sharp; hectic cheeks; breathed with her mouth open, and much rumour of breath in her body; her nose was more hooked, had in fact become hooked. Scanty hair. She had a very weak, self-pitying voice, but with sudden outbursts of strong voice, imperative, and flinging out of arms. She still had a great deal of strength. She forgot most times in the middle of a sentence, and it took her a long time to recall.

She was very glad to see me, and held my hand all the time under bedclothes. She spoke of the most trifling things as if tremendously important – as e.g. decisions as if they were momentous and dictated by profound sagacity. She was seldom fully conscious, and often dozed and woke up with a start. 'What do you say?' rather loud. She had no pain, but often muttered in anguish: 'What am I to do? What am I to do?' Amid tossed bedclothes you could see numbers on corners of blankets. On medicine table siphon, saucer, spoon, large soap-dish, brass flower-bowl (empty). The gas (very bad burner) screened by a contraption of Family Bible, some wooden thing, and a newspaper. It wasn't level. She had it altered.

She said it annoyed her terribly. Gas stove burning. Temp. barely 60. Damp chill, penetrating my legs. The clock had a very light delicate striking sound. Trams and buses did not disturb her, though sometimes they made talking difficult.

Round-topped panels of wardrobe. She wanted to be satisfied that her purse was on a particular tray of the wardrobe. The mater has arterial sclerosis, and patchy congestion of the lungs. Her condition was very distressing (though less so than the pater's), and it seemed strange that this should necessarily be the end of a life, that a life couldn't always end more easily.

Friday, 27 November. The mater died about 1 p.m. on Monday.

I learnt from Jennings that the 'last journey' had to be 'the longest', i.e. corpse must always go longest way to cemetery. I asked why. He sniggered: 'So as to prolong the agony, I suppose.' Real reason nowadays and for long past must be ostentation. We naturally altered this.

Funeral. Too soon. Orange light through blinds in front of room. Coffin in centre on 2 chairs. Covered with flowers. Bad reading, and stumbling of parson. Clichés and halting prayer. Small thin book out of which parson read. In dim light, cheap new carving on oak of coffin seemed like fine oak carving. Sham brass handles on coffin. Horrible lettering. Had to wait after service for hearse to arrive. Men hung their hats on spikes of hearse before coming in. No trouble in carrying coffin. I kept Uncle J.L.'s arm most of the time as he is nearly blind. He told me he still managed 700 accounts. Long walk from cemetery gates to region of chapel. By the way, the lodge at gates is rented as an ordinary house to a schoolteacher. John Ford's vault next to Longson, with records of his young wives ('The flower fadeth' etc.). This could be exaggerated into a fine story. No sign of any other coffins of course in Longson vault.

Curious jacket and apron of first gravedigger. Second stood apart. Both with hats off. Parson put on a skull-cap. On return, carriages trotted down slope from cemetery, but walked as we got to houses near Cobridge station.

Tuesday, 1 December. On Saturday ended the run of the first revival of *Milestones*. For nearly three years I had had a performance, and frequently two, every night without intermission in the West End of London.

Wednesday, 9 February 1927. Today I read in the *Continental Daily Mail* that George Sturt ['George Bourne'] was dead. This death produced no effect of sadness on me at all. George had been ill and half-paralysed for many years, and I don't think I had seen him at all for about sixteen years. When I did see him I drove down to Farnham, and he asked me to keep my car and chauffeur out of the way lest it should constrain or frighten or embarrass, or something, his household. And I had to eat at the inn. I understood all this perfectly well, however, and I had a couple of hours' fine time with him, chiefly in his garden. His later books, so far as I read them, were not as good as his earlier. I remember that when I started to keep a journal – it must be over thirty years ago – I made up and bound (in cardboard, etc.) the volumes myself. (I had them bound in calf later.) I showed the first volume, scarcely written in, to George. George said: 'If you'll bind me a volume like that, I'll keep a journal too.' So I did. Afterwards he kept on keeping a journal, but in large volumes. I think that he had made notes before, but he had never kept a journal. Of course all these notes and journals were the material of his books in a quite exceptional degree.

VIRGINIA WOOLF
(1882–1941)

Quentin Bell is emphatic on the status of Virginia Woolf's diary, calling it a masterpiece and one of the great diaries of the world, and the reader, not many pages through the five fat volumes of it, soon has little cause to disagree. Many diaries are peripheral to a writer's 'works': this one takes its rightful place alongside *The Waves, To the Lighthouse, Mrs Dalloway, The Common Reader*, etc., as an equal in artistry and meaning. Leonard Woolf offered a foretaste of its worth in a selection called *A Writer's Diary* in 1953, but even this did not convey the pleasures and power to be found in the diary *in toto*.

Virginia Stephen made several stabs at diary-writing between 1897 and 1915, when her diary proper began. She had then just become Mrs Woolf – and very ill. Her full journal-keeping genius, maintained with few breaks until her suicide in 1941, really took hold of her in the summer of 1917. Her method was to dash down the day's events and talk immediately after tea, purposely giving none of that attention to style and imagination which made the writing of her books and reviews so exhausting. 'There is a grave defect in the scheme of this book which decrees that it must be written after tea. When people come to tea I cant say to them, "Now wait a minute while I write an account of you." They go, & its too late to begin. And thus, at the very time I'm brewing thoughts & descriptions meant for this page I have the heartbreaking sensation that the page isn't there; they're spilt on the floor. Indeed its difficult to mop them up again' (18 April 1918).

All the same, the 'scheme' was to give her rest and enjoyment. Her day's toil was over, dinner and husband and friends lay ahead, she wasn't tired or dull, and she knew that this fast impressionism done from an armchair with a dip-pen possessed its own excellence. The diary flashes through the inter-war years, briefly and vividly lighting up faces, places, politics and attitudes. It is gossipy and profound, simple and complex. Quentin Bell makes the interesting point that it never seeks to entertain, which is something to remember when we read diaries, for it is why they are often so strange and inexplicable. Virginia Woolf felt compelled to comment on people, on streets or meadows, on other writers and manners, and tea-time was her 'flood of comment' time. It was for her the daily means of 'fulfilling . . . the function of healthy and enjoyable exercise', as Anne Olivier Bell remarked. It was too an outlet for the very necessary articulation of her nervous state, work anxieties and sense of tragedy.

The Webbs for the weekend

Wednesday, 18 September 1918. I have let the first freshness of the Webbs fade from my mirror; but let me bethink me of another metaphor which they imposed upon me, towards the end of Sunday. I was exalted above a waste of almost waveless sea, palish grey, & dented with darker shadows for the small irregularities, the little ripples which represented character & life love & genius & happiness. But 'I' was not exalted; 'I' was practically non-existent. This was the result of a talk with Mrs Webb. In truth though they deserve more careful handling. I wonder how I can recapture the curious discomfort of soul which Mrs Webb produces each time I see her again? In the intervals one forgets; in a second it comes over one again. There's something absolutely unadorned & impersonal about her. She makes one feel insignificant, & a little out of key. She represses warmth or personality. She has no welcome for one's individuality. She divines a little what one's natural proclivities are, & she irradiates them with her bright electric torch.

It was a pouring wet day, on Saturday; not a day for geniality. Webb however has some coat to shake; she is as bare as a bone. We sat down to tea, without George Young. They eat quickly & efficiently & leave me with hunks of cake on my hands. After tea we were soon disposing of our topics, & I began to feel nervous, lest our cupboards should be bare. Then G. Young appeared, having like all Youngs, rejoiced in his battle with distance & wet. Liked the walk, he said. While he changed Mrs Webb rapidly gave me her reasons for saying that she had never met a great man, or woman either. At most, she said, they possessed remarkable single qualities, but looked at as a whole there was no greatness in them. Shakespeare she did not appreciate, because a sister, who was a foolish woman, always quoted him wrong to her as a child. Goethe might conceivably have been a great man. Then, this having been dealt with, down came L. & G. Young & they all pounced together upon some spot of interest floating far out beyond my ken. I think it was to do with the General Election & the views of the private soldiers. Young came provided with facts, but I rather think these did not stand much investigation. He is a slow, stiff, kindly man, with all Hilton's romance, but less than Hilton's brain; & through following his ideals he has left the diplomatic service, & is now a marine officer at Portsmouth. After dinner Mrs Webb plunged from brisk argument to unconcealed snoring. Then Sidney had his turn. I thought he spoke a little quick to conceal the snores, but you have only to ask him a question & he can go on informing you till you can hold no more. He sketched his idea of a Supernational authority, & the future of Bills of Exchange. The work of Government will be enormously increased in the future. I asked whether I should ever have a finger in the pie? 'O yes; you will have some small office no doubt. My wife & I always say that a Railway Guard is the most enviable of men. He has authority, & he is responsible to a government. That should be the state of each one of us.'

And then we discussed L.'s plan of a state so contrived that each person has to do some work. Here there was a long argument upon the growing distance between men of different social grades & professions, Young affirming it, the Webbs denying it. I asked (in reporting conversations one's own sayings stand out like lighthouses) one of my most fruitful questions; viz: how easy is it for a man to change his social grade? This brought down a whole shower bath of information, but let us say that the Webbs' shower baths are made of soda water. They never sink one, or satiate. Webb told us how many scholarships were won in London in a given year, & also, reported upon the educational system of E. Sussex, which bad though it is, is slightly better than that of W. Sussex. 'I myself,' he said, 'came too early to profit by secondary education. My parents were lower middle class shopkeepers, possessed, like so many of their kind, with a blind determination to educate their sons somehow, but without a ghost of a notion how to set about it. They hit on the plan of sending me & my brother abroad to France & Germany; & so we learnt French & German at least. I can still read them, though I seldom do.' Our talk must have dealt fully with education, for I remember that Mrs Webb woke with a start & delivered herself of a statement upon the German 'wrong turning', & put Young right on some point about the division of character & intellect. He was simple enough to separate them & to prefer what he was quite unable to define. She thrust him through & through with her rapier, but he persisted.

Next day, which was said to begin for the W.'s at 5.30, when they begin tea-drinking in their bedrooms, I had to withdraw in order to do battle with a very obstinate review of Wells' 'Joan & Peter'. My ideas were struck stiff by the tap of Mrs W.'s foot, up &

down the terrace, & the sound of her rather high, a rather mocking voice, discoursing to L. while she waited either for W. to come or the rain to stop. They walked on the downs, till lunch. I must now skip a great deal of conversation & let us suppose that Sidney & Beatrice & I are sitting on the road side overlooking Telscombe, smoking cigarettes, in bright sunshine, while the Silver Queen slowly patrols above Newhaven. The downs were at their best; & set Mrs W. off upon landscape beauty, & recollections of India, which she turns to when lying awake at night, relishing the recollection more than the reality. Sidney, one perceives, has no organ of sight whatever, & pretends to none. Mrs W. has a compartment devoted to nature. So briskly narrating their travels & impressions, which were without respect for British rule, we set off home. I saw them from behind, a shabby homely, dowdy couple, marching with the uncertain step of strength just beginning to fail, she clutching his arm, & looking much older than he, in her angularity. They were like pictures in French papers of English tourists, only wanting spectacles & Ba[e]dekers to finish them. Their clothes looked ill dusted, & their eyes peering in front of them. My few private words came, as I knew they would come, when Mrs W. detached us two together, passing Southease Church. She asked me about my novel, & I supplied her with a carefully arranged plot. I wished, so at least I said, to discover what aims drive people on, & whether these are illusory or not. She promptly shot forth: 'Two aims have governed my life; one is the passion for investigation by scientific means; the other the passion for producing a certain good state of society by those investigations.' Somehow she proceeded to warn me against the dissipation of energy in emotional friendship. One should have only one great personal relationship in one's life, she said; or at most two – marriage & parenthood Marriage was necessary as a waste pipe for emotion, as security in old age when personal attractiveness fails, & as a help to work. We were entangled at the gates of the level crossing when she remarked, 'Yes, I daresay an old family servant would do as well.' On the way up the hill she stated her position that one should wish well to all the world, but discriminate no one. According to her the differences are not great; the defects invariable; one must cultivate impersonality above all things. In old age people become of little account, she said; one speculates chiefly upon the possibility, or the impossibility of a future life. This grey view depressed me more & more; partly I suppose from the egotistical sense of my own nothingness in her field of vision. And then we wound up with a light political gossip & chapter of reminiscences, in which Mr & Mrs Webb did their parts equally. & so to bed; & to my horror, in came Mrs W. early next morning to say Goodbye, & perched in all her long impersonality on the edge of my bed, looking past my stockings drawers & po.

BEATRICE WEBB
(1858–1943)

Lord Beveridge called Beatrice Webb's diaries 'a contribution of outstanding value to our power of understanding ourselves and our affairs. They show in their intimate frank detail how things get done, or do not get done; how men in public life behave to one another; and how they should and should not behave. They have two simple morals. The first moral is of how largely achievement in public affairs depends upon selflessness, on winning confidence of others by freedom from personal ambition. The second moral is of how much happiness depends on work in the right companionship.'

The marriage of the rich Miss Potter to the poor-ish and cockney-sounding Sidney Webb in 1892 was an incomprehensible union to their families and friends, but utterly logical to themselves. They had founded what Beatrice called 'the firm of Webb', whose business it was to lay the foundations of twentieth-century Britain. Industry, education, welfare, money – all would be different because of this 'partnership', as they preferred to call their seemingly disparate union. She was religious and a sparkling writer, he was a kind of flesh-and-blood computer, and the pair of them were totally committed to the enormous task before them. They were, said Beveridge, 'a ferment in society, bringing new ideas to men's minds, bringing new organizations and institutions to birth'. They achieved all this almost entirely outside the power centres of government and the establishment. Sidney was optimistic, Beatrice moody and emotional; their joint attitude towards what they had to do was one of 'aristocratic devotion to purpose'. They lived guiltily on a private income, but with monkish austerity.

Beatrice Webb's diaries were turned into two remarkable auto-biographies, *My Apprenticeship* (her life up to 1892) and *Our Partnership* (hers and Sidney's lives from 1892 to 1911), and both books have a literary value which is unique in what are really the annals of political economy. Beatrice loved her diaries and saw them as central to her private existence and her public work. 'The life I should enjoy, at present, would be a comfortable country house, noiseless, except for birds and the rustling of water and wind – with my diaries to type,' she wrote as the First World War raged. The following extracts are from the war and the immediate post-war diaries.

Partnership

10 May 1915. Last night I lay awake thinking over the absence of any recognized ethic of friendship. To most men friendship does not entail the continuance of the feeling of friendship when the intimacy has ceased to be a pleasure on both sides. Successive friendships seem, on this assumption, to have, each one, its natural life: to be born, to grow, to decay and finally to die. Some times the friendship will die a violent death, but among well-bred persons death by senile decay is preferred. 'We have ceased to be friends' is a no more tragic phrase than 'we have ceased to be neighbours'. There are even temperaments who would regard any more rigid view of friendship with distinct dislike and impatience. A friend is a book which you read and when you have satisfied your curiosity the thing is put on the shelf, in the waste-paper basket, or sold. This assumption of lack of permanence is, to me tragic – and the few troubles of my life have arisen from broken friendships. But if all friendships are to be permanent then it is unwise to enter into personal intimacy and mutual affection unless you are certain of your own and the other person's faithfulness. For there is no sense of decay or death when the relation has been one of impersonal friendliness to another human being, a friendliness which terminates because the occasion for it ends. Some of the pleasantest and most hopeful of human relations are discontinuous because they have never reached that degree of mutual affection which leads to their being carried on when the occasion for personal comradeship ceases. The test of a closer relation than mere friendliness is, I think, intimate written correspondence. One does not correspond for the joy of it with a friendly acquaintance, a colleague on a committee, a neighbour, or the most faithful of servants, unless you have permitted the relationship to become a friendship with some obligation of permanence. As one gets aged one is less inclined to take this step forward from human friendliness to personal friendship. There are, indeed, some persons – some of the holiest and most loving – who preserve this equable relationship of friendship with all their fellow beings; no more and no less intimacy with a person whom they judge to be admirable than with an unfortunate whom they know to be despicable. Towards all men they are pitiful, helpful and calmly and wisely sympathetic. They are never hurt or wounded by neglect because their love transcends any personal aspect. Such are the saints of the world, and it is they who are the most beneficent travellers through life. They measure their intimacy and their warmth of expression, the carefulness of their thought, not according to the attractiveness of the person concerned, but according to the person's need. Such one was our old nurse Dada, whose memory is the shining light of the childhood of the Potter girls. She had no friends because all who needed friendship were her friends, and she became unconscious of anyone who no longer desired her sympathy or help.

16 July 1921. Our personal life flows smoothly to its end with a settled conviction, on my part, that for me the end is not far off. Every night when I embrace my boy and give him my blessing before I retire to my room there is sadness in my heart at the thought that some day – and a day that cannot be far off it will be our last embrace and that one or other of us will have to live for days, months, possibly a decade of years, alone, bereft of our comrade in work, thought and happiness. But with this sadness there is always present a warmth of gratitude for our past and present happiness. For happy our life undoubtedly is, and that is exactly why I hate the thought of leaving it! In some ways Sidney and I have never been so happy in our personal lives. Welded by common work and experience into a complete harmony of thought and action, we are also in harmony with those with whom we work and have our being. Our servants and secretary are devoted to us: with our relatives we are on the best of terms. In our inconspicuous way we are successful: our books sell better than ever before, the London School of Economics (Sidney's favourite child) is brilliantly developing under the able direction of Beveridge, whom Sidney selected; *The New Statesman*, though still losing money, is not losing our money (!) and is daily gaining credit under Clifford Sharp's editorship and is now independent of our helping hand. And Sidney's work in the Labour Party, whether at Eccleston Square or in the constituency he is contesting, brings with it no personal friction and a good deal of pleasurable comradeship with men who respect and trust him. With Henderson, the officials at Eccleston Square, and with the leading Trade Union Secretaries, he is on the best of terms, and by rank and file he is respected more universally, I think, than any other intellectual. Witness his high place in the vote for the Labour Party Executive. Of course J.R.M.,* whilst outwardly friendly, is always trying to injure him. But then J.R.M. is equally bitterly malicious to the younger intellectuals of the Labour Movement, to Cole and Arnot and Tawney. So his malice is now universally discounted, and outside I.L.P. ex-Liberal circles he does not count.

For myself, I have not done badly these last nine months. I have carried out all the investigation into the Consumers' Co-operative Movement; I have planned the new sections of the book and helped Sidney with the actual composition of them. I have set going the Half-Circle Club; helped with Stephen Hobhouse's prison inquiry, and corrected the larger part of the MSS. of Stephen's chapters. And last and least, I have revised the diary of our first tour round the world and got the whole typewritten by Miss Schmidt. And though I suffer now and again from insomnia and indigestion and

* James Ramsay MacDonald.

aches and pains here and there and occasionally have a panic about a mortal complaint – usually cancer – which turns out to be wholly imaginary, I enjoy good health, if health be measured by capacity to walk eight or ten miles, to concentrate very rapidly on investigation of fresh subjects, and to do all the lecturing and entertaining that is required of me as Sidney's wife. So far, so good. What gives rise to fear is the thought of Sidney in Parliament, still more in a Government. He is young enough for such a change of life: I am not. However, the chances are that the political turnover will not come in my life time, and probably not in his working life. And if I were gone, the transformation of his activities might be wholly beneficial to his health of body and mind, might just save him from sinking into a dull and grey old age.

Charity

7 February 1922. A question of conscience has been agitating my mind these many days. I read those gruesome accounts of the Russian famine and wonder whether we are not brutes in failing to give all our available income, over and above the bare requirements for our own work, to the Russian Famine Fund? It is futile to salve one's conscience by giving a few guineas: *if it be right to give anything at all it would be right to make a big sacrifice.* Hitherto Sidney and I have refused to be moved: and for good or for evil I think we shall stand by this heartless decision. If we are to depart from our settled policy of expenditure, I would rather do so to save the family of a German professor or Austrian official from semi-starvation. Russia to me is not much better than China, and who ever suggested, outside the official British-China trading and financial firms, subscribing to save a Chinaman from death by famine? The always-present doubt whether, by saving a Chinese or Russian child from dying this year, you will prevent it from dying the next year, together with the larger question of whether those races are desirable inhabitants, compared to other races, paralyses the charitable impulse. Have we not English children dying from lack of milk? Obviously one would not spend one's available income in saving a Central African negro from starving or dying from disease;

I am not certain that I would deny myself to save a Frenchman! If I decided to reconsider our personal expenditure I should reconsider it in order to provide more scientific research for the world. Meanwhile we go on with our customary standard of life: I am comforted by the thought that our critics always abuse us as penurious and over-economical in our personal expenditure and our clothes and in our *way* of entertaining our friends. We keep open house: but the food and appointments are of the barest. Where I am extravagant is in resolutely refusing to use my scanty brains in *thinking out economies*: I either refuse to have the service or commodity or I afford it without wasting temper and thought on how to get it in the cheapest way. I might, of course, personally give up the daily stint of tobacco, the tea and coffee and the occasional whisky at the evening meal: I suppose I ought to do so *if I really followed the inner call of a scrupulous conscience*. But it would mean the perpetual friction of resisting constantly recurring temptation, and I am not certain that there would not be loss as well as gain.

IVY JACQUIER
(b. 1890)

Ivy Jacquier kept a diary for nineteen years and barely mentions the First World War and the other great events which occurred during the writing of it; her inner world takes precedence. She was one of the six children of an English Anglican mother and a French Catholic father, and the family home was at Saint-Germain-au-Mont-d'Or, near Lyon. The background was rich and cultured. Ivy went to school in Eastbourne and to art school in Dresden. Her diary is for all those – nearly everybody – who have forgotten first loves, first books, first beautiful clothes, and first impressions of first things. Hers is a nature which requires a sensuous and intellectual diet of art and companionship. She loves Gladys and Gretchen – and A., whom she marries. They live in 'ugly' Worcester. She records here enchantments, docketing pleasures, as it were. Yet she is not a seeker after diversion and amusement, sex, fashion or the colourful. Nor is she gentle. As a teenager she questions her desire for girls, her loss of faith and her hunger for literature and music. 'I have faith in the compassion of love and go my way childishly.' She is, however, always a grown-up child, delicately mature in every way. She became a book illustrator, and her diary was published by her friend Francis Meynell in 1960. It is a diary, he says, of something overheard rather than something proclaimed.

2 January 1911. We motor. The fields are flooded and have frozen and the skyline is darker than the country. A white bird flies before us frightened by the motor. 'Souvent on voit des mains qui sont faibles et lasses d'avoir voulu cueillir trop de roses ou d'âmes . . .' Whom do these lines, suggestive, suit? The beginning of the year finds me reading Bourget whose analysis fascinates, like a man-hunt. I would like to re-read all my books and then give them away. Possession spoils things, takes away much of their mystery and charm. Like Senhouse from 'Open Country', I would wish to simplify; Maurice Hewlett may not be a great writer, he loves life. He would scandalize Mother. But he is natural and spontaneous. Clary said a woman had shown him that life could replace religion when I asked him how he'd freed himself from catholicism. He lent me Lafcadio Hearn before I left, and I opened the book to find the first pages poetical. It is a glorious feeling, to plunge into a new personality – book after book. In this last year I have read Galsworthy and d'Annunzio; have met Clary, Antoine, Mrs Hardy, Dodo Holland and McNiel our massier, but paint, technically, little better. There has been Thibaud's rendering of the Beethoven concerto. It is sad, but absolutely sufficing and my prayer. I have become necessarily, independent, after parting with Gretchen. And I glory in this independence. I owe Romain Rolland much for 'Jean Christophe' and in Paris think often of this 'Vie de Beethoven': – 'nourrissons nous de la vaillance des grands hommes et, si nous sommes trop faibles, reposons un instant notre tête sur leurs genoux. Ils nous consoleront'.

8 September 1914. Old General d'Aubigny dines with us. He is aflame for France, but when it comes to 'jeunes filles' nursing he is scandalized. It means everything to me. Aunt upholds Doris and me. She understands. She is ill: she writes a diary now in her crabbed hand with the red-black ink. One has no doubt now which country one has to one's heart. Of the other one is proud, but France only makes one feel this. Patriotism is a live thing, tangible in one's body. At night the Zouave infantry march past with curious moaning music. Even in sleep one is aware of France and War ... I read Thackeray, Bourget ... L'attente ... Tony arrived from London to join up.

9 September. The government fly to Bordeaux. There is better news tonight. At 6 o'clock the town was blessed and the Vierge noire carried through the streets. People knelt down praying in the warm rain on the quays.

10 September. After the hospital I read 'Le Journal de Marie Bashkirtseff'. Antoine was in love with her. I am irritated and enchanted, and put her to a severe test, reading her now. I dislike her painting, but her diary is inestimably precious. I read her in the botanical garden where the sun is bringing out the heavy perfumes of the flowers, and two letters from Gladys who has not written to me for two years. She is fickle – but so pretty, with her thin body and blue eyes. Above all she is two years of my life. J'ai peur de n'être pas assez changée par cette guerre. Les autres reviendront changés. Serons-nous seulement éternellement les mêmes ... trop protégées – screened?

19 September. Tea with Gabrielle D. who, in her dark drawing-room with the bare floors, looks like a creole. She too, like me, is a Croix rouge nurse in order to grow, egotistically. The town is intense, waiting for news; the quays blue and swept by a cold wind. How dual one is; like the man in Merejkowsky's 'Mort des Dieux' who died trying to conciliate Christ and Apollo. Sometimes I feel my life a thing of nerves, sensation and colour. Sometimes a humble sincere thirst for intimacy with one or two occasionally, and as a second nature, a love of chic and hotels, soft cushions, electric broughams, snobbery!

23 September. The evenings smell of leaves and remind me of

Dresden and Gretchen. For many years Dresden is shut to me. I read – but put the books down. It is useless. I wonder if I shall regret reading so much ever. I have four friends: Gladys because she is the whole of my first conscious life and because she is beautiful. Mrs Hardy because she is so extremely intelligent and believes in me, and has cultivated me in brain as Gretchen did in art. Gretchen because I could not resist her if I tried; and Mabel because she is delicate and unprotected. I wish I had more. Two are in Germany. I can't write to them. With French girls there is no intimacy. I wish I were married. I want to have meals of my own choice, a garden of my own, do my hair as I like and love and be loved.

26 September. The winter mornings are sharp and lovely and the park reddens at the back of the hospital. At 9 we had a mass for the soldiers and one of them sang C. Franck's solo. The white infirmières kneeling . . . the men in bed.

7 October. The routine, the hard work, leaves one free. I read more entirely, with all my person engrossed, to escape the hospital. I read Bourget's boudoir novels, for their atmosphere of the Quartier St Germain, atmosphere of violets – of pink curtains – and the heavy intime scent of women's hands. The autumn makes one like this.

DENTON WELCH
(1915–48)

Welch wrote his diary in nineteen ordinary school exercise books, and in his classroom-like handwriting. He wrote quickly and without correction, following the example of André Gide – 'In Gide's Journal I have just read again how he does not wish to write his pages slowly as he would the pages of a novel . . . It is just what I have felt about this journal of mine. Don't ponder, don't grope . . .'

Welch was thirty-three and something of a celebrity when he died. There is a fretful, late-adolescent quality in his journals, the result of illness, pain, and a kind of sexual torture. Throughout their pages a thudding reality hammers home the likelihood of early death. Time had stopped for him on 7 June 1935, when a woman driver knocked him off his bicycle. His lower spine was fractured, with consequent bouts of bleeding, tuberculosis and partial impotence; he was often in agony. In his journals, he doesn't so much hark back to his days of physical strength and health as, by some inner power, drag all the poise of his early uninjured self into the present in order to lead an extraordinarily active emotional and creative – and social – life.

Then there was the war, and his odd position as a badly wounded young writer whose injuries had nothing to do with the fighting, and yet whose work became a correct part of the anti-heroic literature of the day. Everything about him focused an extreme attention and he became a cult figure. His autobiographical novel and stories, and his autobiography proper, carried a variety of courageous messages. His lifestyle formed a paradigm of what Mario Praz labelled 'the Romantic Agony' – the race of the artist against time. Cyril Connolly placed Welch with Katherine Mansfield and Barbellion.

At one time Welch thought of suicide and of destroying some of his diaries. Those that remain begin with a bounce: 'And then we all met at Penshurst; I and Maurice and Filthy Freddy, R.A.F. And first we had tea (I found them waiting for me with scone and butter on the table, when I came in from the rain) . . .' (Friday, 10 July). His remaining energy went into *A Voice Through A Cloud*. An abridged and expurgated edition of the *Journals* appeared four years after his death, to be followed by an edition by Michael De-la-Noy in 1984 which brings out Welch's particular genius and suffering.

20 August 1942. And as I walked by the river today all the corn had been cut, and there were no barges left where the soldiers would work like slaves to get them in and out of the water while the officer sat on the bank, not even watching, but paring his nails. The soldiers were dressed in flimsy football shirts and dirty singlets or nothing, but the officer had on his neat uniform and a white jersey which he must once have had for school sports.

Now those barges were not there. They and the men must have crossed the channel to take part in the great battle the day before yesterday. Each barge would hold a tank so snugly and the men would sweat and strain just as they did here, only now it would be to get the monsters on to a French beach, and overhead there would be bombers and gusts of machine-gun fire.

Then there is death and dying over there still and agony all night for some.

The five labourers forking the corn into the lorry see me by the river's brim and shout. I think one waves. It is so far away that I dare not answer for fear of a mistake or insults. I just watch the rhythm of the blue shirted and white shirted ones playing to each other with their movements like flute and oboe. I think that being still by the river with prunes and biscuits and coffee and precious chocolate is almost to be easy. To take your shirt off and lie back against the spiky satin grass! To feel the first heavy drops of rain on your skin and to know that no one will come near you. Yet how I loathe nature lovers! My thoughts are never on nature though I go out to roam for hours in the fields every day. My thoughts always go to history, to what has happened century after century on each spot of earth. To lovers lying on the banks, young men that are dead.

On a torn piece of note-paper that I found was an eagle coming out of a circle on which was written Per Ardua ad Astra, then in washed-away ink an address of some aircraftman. And I remembered how a month ago I had found the same piece of paper, only then I could read the address. Now I couldn't. What was the letter about?

7 April 1943. We were both drinking coffee out of my two mandarin cups in odd blue saucers, so pretty with bright paint and little figures – old, ancient, something to cherish. The handle was loose on the silver coffee pot with smug Victorian double B's and earl's coronet. (It's even got Breadalbane stamped on the bottom, so there could be no doubt about its owner.) I paid £5 for it in a shop in St James's and not all the 'B's' on the bottom or the side will ever take it back to that Victorian Lord Breadalbane's again.

As I say, I was pouring out more coffee, holding the pot close to the lid with my handkerchief because of the loose handle, when Lydia came in with the well-known exciting, thrilling, anti-climax yellow-orange envelope.

'It's pre-paid, twelve words,' she said.

I took it expectantly, but telling myself it was sure to be nothing but disappointment. I read it not quite grasping, because of queer writing and bad spelling.

> Will you lunch here 12.45 Monday Stiwell Sesame Club Grosvenor Street W1

In spite of 'Stiwell' I knew it was from Edith Sitwell, but because of my preconception that she would ask me to Osbert's Chelsea house I had the idea that I did not know where to send the answer.

I started to write Renishaw Hall, then I dismissed the waiting girl without a tip (which I am told is quite rococo nowadays) and rushed upstairs to ask everyone where I should send my answer to.

It was really so carefully worded, her telegram, with the name in front of the address so that I should know she was staying there, but I did not see this until Maurice pointed it out.

When he left I sent the wire and then went to a telephone box and waited nervously to get through to the Sesame Club.

The woman at the other end would insist on calling me Madam, while I gave her my message. I wanted to be quite sure that Edith was staying there.

'Yes, madam,' the woman said.

'Don't call her,' I shrieked. 'I only want to leave a message.'

'Is it Mr or Mrs Welch?' the woman asked right at the end, still definite in her own mind about my sex. I wanted to laugh.

'Mr,' I said, 'Mr Welch.'

Was my voice fluty and high through nervousness? I am not usually taken for a woman on the telephone.

19 April. Now it's happened, now I'm going up. It's rained in gusts. I've been reading *Street Songs* and eating breakfast with tickling contracting feeling in the centre of me. I think I will wear my blue suit. What will it be like?

20 April. Yesterday, up early in the morning – the washing, the dressing, the brushing; then to the station on my bicycle. Everything planned, everything done, the ticket bought, the clean gloves in the pocket.

How late the train was – waiting, waiting there. Then the bursting carriages and all the passage filled with soldiers – their tin hats, bottles, knapsacks hitting on the walls when they turned. I wondered how I could stand to Charing Cross. I looked into two lavatories, but they were too smelly to lock myself into. I tried to sit down in the loop of a strap, then on a fire extinguisher. Sore, painful, I felt desperate. How ill and tired I would be if I could not sit down.

I gazed at the fat suitcase for some time, then at last I dared to sit down on it. Pleasure, bliss, gazing out of the window, sitting down at last. The fields, the feathery trees, wonderful poison green, fresh as new lettuce. The large lonely young man carrying a huge implement across unending fields. Then the long, long tunnel with its whistle and the belching white smoke, not escaping, flowing over the train in a thick cape. Sparks flew and faded. The red demon glow on the white smoke belchings and the growing of it till I was really ready for some catastrophe. Can something be on fire? Will the engine burst and the driver be burnt to death in the steam, as I have read? Will I be groping in wreckage in the dark tunnel? All this through my mind and more. No change from early childhood.

Then the sooted wall seen faintly, the lamps of some workers, like miners' lamps or the lamps of gaolers in a dungeon. It is like the haunted house in the Luna Park at Margate. The green, luminous skeleton should descend, champing its terrible jaws, grinning. The concrete grime, then at last the air, on, on, quite happy now, almost peaceful. The very young petty officer in the carriage, cutting his nails with his mother's scissors:

'You should not cut them, you should file them,' said his red-haired sister.

'I've got better things to do than to waste my time filing my nails,' he said, in an extra manly voice, still puffing at a large, new, extremely smoking pipe. He wore glasses.

In London, walking up to the Leicester Gallery, then back again because I did not know whether to pay to go in, or take it as my right to enter free, as an exhibitor.

Then to the National [Gallery] for the pictures and, more

important still, for W.C.s and wash basin. Nice for Art and Nature to be thus allied.

Looking at the face, hoping it would do, no smuts, no dirt, no shiny sweaty bits at nose base or on forehead.

Off in the taxi to Grosvenor Street. Emptied out at the wrong door, so I walked and bought cigarettes and then went on feeling parched, so dry and yet about to be wet all over.

Into the rather drab hall of the Sesame Club, basket chairs, ugliness; in a fright that I might not recognize Edith Sitwell.

Sitting down, feeling embarrassed with the other old women there. So incurious on the surface; yet I felt watching.

'Miss Sitwell will be down in a moment, sir.'

The waiting, almost too much.

Then the tall figure dressed all in black, black trilby, Spanish witch's hat, black cloak, black satin dress to the ankles and two huge aquamarine rings. Wonderful rings on powder-white hands, and face so powder-pearly, nacreous white, almost not to be believed in, with the pinkened mouth, the thin, delicate, swordlike nose and tender-curling nostrils. No hair, I can remember no hair at first. The rings, the glistening satin, and the kid-white skin.

Down the long passage, this figure sweeping in front. Everything arranged for me.

'You will have Gin and French, or Bronx?'

ANAÏS NIN
(1903–77)

Anaïs Nin's is the most talked about and least read (the bulk of it is still unpublished) American twentieth-century diary. Verdicts on it have been very mixed. Nin's old friend Henry Miller said that it would take its place 'beside the revelations of St Augustine, Petronius, Abélard, Rousseau, Proust'. It will not, but it will certainly be consulted for its many vivid portraits of Bohemia between the wars, and for its tireless, limitless self-absorption. Nor has any modern diary been so exquisitely and astutely self-promoted. All the world was to know that Nin was all diarist. 'The period without the diary remains an ordeal. Every evening I want my diary as one wants opium. I wanted nothing else but the diary, to rest upon, to confide in ... During my struggle against the diary "opium habit" I had many misgivings. Should the diary disappear altogether? Was concerned with its value as a document, its usefulness to my work. Thought of the scenes I had extracted from the diary, the dreams and moods I used in the *House of Incest* [her prose poem, published in Paris, 1936]. Would it appear in a more objective form? I studied Da Vinci's notebooks. Rank [an analyst friend] has said that Da Vinci's notebooks were often more interesting than his actual work.'

Anaïs Nin was born in Neuilly, the daughter of the Spanish composer and concert pianist Joaquin Nin. Her parents separated and she was brought up by her Danish-born mother in New York. When she was eleven she began to write her diary in an attempt to recover her father, but it soon developed into a private landscape through which she could ceaselessly pursue and identify herself. It was 'an island, in which I could find refuge in an alien land, write French, think my thoughts, hold on to my soul, to myself'. Friends tried to push her out of the diary obsession into 'literature', and she wrote poems and stories, a study of D. H. Lawrence (her hero), and other slight works, many of them 'out of' the diary. It was, she said, 'my kief, hashish, and opium pipe. This is my drug and my vice. Instead of writing a novel, I lie back with this book and a pen, and dream ...'

A full assessment of Anaïs Nin's status as a diarist has still to be made. She made a career of journalizing, and the best diaries are usually those which are the daily asides on life and work proper. Time may make her seem less self-indulgent.

Life with Henry Miller

May 1932. Henry's responses to all things, his capacity for seeing so much in everybody, in everything. I had never looked at a street as Henry does: every doorway, every lamp, every window, every courtyard, every shop, every object in the shop, every café, every hidden-away bookshop, hidden-away antique shop, every news vendor, every lottery-ticket vendor, every blind man, every beggar, every clock, every church, every whore house, every wineshop, every shop where they sell erotica and transparent underwear, the circus, the nightclub singers, the strip tease, the girlie shows, the penny movies in the arcade, the bal musettes, the artist balls, the apache quarters, the flea market, the gypsy carts, the markets early in the morning.

When we come out of the café, it is raining. Rain does not bother him. Hunger or thirst only. Shabby rooms don't bother him. Poverty does not bother him. You drink a fiery Chartreuse at a zinc counter. In life he follows his impulses, always. The only thing which surprises me is that he has no desire to meet other writers, musicians, painters, his equals. When I talk about this, he shows no interest. Would you like to meet Julien Green? Hélène Boussinesq, the translator of Sherwood Anderson; Florent Schmitt, who lives near us in Louveciennes; Manuel de Falla, or others? 'No,' says Henry. 'What would they see in me?'

It all began with my reading of D. H. Lawrence. But Henry is no Lawrence. Lawrence was a romantic, and he sought to fuse body and soul. Henry asserts the primitive instincts. He leaves feeling out of his writing. No symbolism in Henry, no mythology. We do have a feeling at times of not being ordinary people. When we looked at photographs of D. H. Lawrence's house, Henry said he would someday show me his house in Brooklyn, where he lived out his childhood, and that he wanted to see 158 West Seventy-fifth, where I wrote the journal he is now reading.

November. Henry said: 'I have always thought a great deal, but there was a hub missing. And what was the missing hub? It was, as you said, an understanding of myself. It is your vision of me which keeps me powerfully together. You reject all the unimportant details. You never get confused as June does, and you give my acts and my experiences the correct proportion.'

When I saw him again, he was working on a synthesis, 'Form and Language', and I read the pages as he unwound them from the typewriter. We talked endlessly about his work, always in the same manner, Henry flowing, gushing, spilling, spreading, scattering, and I weaving together tenaciously. He ends by laughing at my tenacity. Until I reach a clear finality of some sort, I can't stop. I am always seeking the core, the hub, the center of all his chaotic and abundant ideas. I struggle to coordinate, to tie up loose ends.

Henry is a mold breaker. He obeys the rhythms, as Lawrence said, and all clear patterns can be damned.

At any moment he can begin to rant, rave, fume, drink, and the continuity of his thinking is broken by the fermentations of his body. And this is good. It gives a mobility to everything, the mobility of life itself. He accepts absurdities.

I walked through the streets which Henry taught me to love. Water is being thrown on the sidewalks and swept by an old man with a broom. Dirt is flowing down the gutter, windows are being opened, meat hung on hooks, vegetables poured in baskets for display, wheels are rolling, bread is baking, children are skipping rope, dogs are carrying the weight of downtrodden tails, cats are licking off bistro sawdust, wine bottles are being carried up from the cellar. I love the streets I did not know as a child. I always played in houses in Neuilly, Brussels, Germany, Cuba. Henry played in the streets. His world was filled with ordinary people, mine with artists.

Henry's recollections of the past, in contrast to Proust, are done while in movement. He may remember his first wife while making love to a whore, or he may remember his very first love while walking the streets, traveling to see a friend; and life does not stop while he remembers. Analysis in movement. No static vivisection. Henry's daily and continuous flow of life, his sexual activity, his talks with everyone, his café life, his conversations with people in the street, which I once considered an interruption to writing, I now believe to be a quality which distinguishes him from other writers. He never writes in cold blood: he is always writing in white heat.

It is what I do with the journal, carrying it everywhere, writing on café tables while waiting for a friend, on the train, on the bus, in waiting rooms at the station, while my hair is washed, at the Sorbonne when the lectures get tedious, on journeys, trips, almost while people are talking.

241

It is while cooking, gardening, walking, or love-making that I remember my childhood, and not while reading Freud's 'Preface to a Little Girl's Journal'.

Henry teases me about my memory for conversation. Every now and then he says: 'Put this down in your diary.' He never says, as others do: 'Do not put this down in your diary.'

Even his face is changing. I was looking at him in amazement while he explained Spengler. No trace of the gnome or the sensualist. A gravity. An intentness.

Talk about his work. I feel sometimes I have to hang on to the significance of it while he tosses about, fumbling, stumbling.

Fred criticizes Henry's reading, his efforts to think, attacks his knowledge of science, interest in movies, in theatre, in philosophy, criticism, biography. A big enough artist, I say, can eat anything, must eat everything and then alchemize it. Only the feeble writer is afraid of expansion. Henry is fulfilling a deep necessity: to situate himself, to adopt values, to seek a basis for what he is to build.

I laugh at my old fear of analysis. The possession of knowledge does not kill the sense of wonder and mystery. There is always more mystery.

I have no fear of clarity.

Henry is lost in a labyrinth of ideas, like an ostrich who has buried its head in a mountain of papers.

May 1933. My father came.

I expected the man of the photographs, a more transparent face. A face less furrowed, less carved, less masklike, and at the same time I liked the new face, the depth of the lines, the firmness of the jaw, the femininity and charm of the smile, all the more startling in contrast to the tanned, almost parchment-toned skin. A smile with a forceful dimple which was not a dimple but a scar from sliding down a stairway banister and piercing his cheek with an ornament when he was a child. The neatness and compactness of the figure, grace, vital gestures, ease, youthfulness. A gust of imponderable charm. A supreme, open egotism. Webs of talk, defenses against unuttered accusations, justifying his life, his love of the sun, of the south of France, of luxury, preoccupation with the opinion of others, fear of criticism, susceptibility, continuous play-acting, wit and articulateness, violence of images, the lusty and vivid imagery of the Spanish language transposed into French.

He had come to France, had studied with Vincent d'Indy, had been made the youngest professor at the Schola Cantorum, when I was born. A childlike, disarming smile. Always charm. The predominance of charm. Undercurrents of puerility, unreality. A man who had pampered himself (or been pampered by women?), cottoned himself against the deep pains of living by luxury, by salon life, by aesthetics, yet preoccupied with the fear of destructiveness, compelled to expand, obeying his quest of sensuality, of pleasure, having found no other way to obtain his desires but by deception. A passion for aesthetics and for creation. Concerts, composition, books, articles.

10. DIARIES AND ROYALTY

KING EDWARD VI
(1537–53)

The boy King Edward's diary, or 'Chronicle', as he called it, is one of the most fascinating of all royal literary creations. He kept it from the age of thirteen until within a few months of his death at sixteen. He wrote it on folio paper on a desk 'covered with black velvet, garnished with plates of copper and gilte' and which had 'ij litle boxes of silver gilte for duste [sand] and ynke'. It is believed that the King's tutor, Sir John Cheke, advised him on the value of diary-keeping. Sir John said: '. . . a dark and imperfect reflection upon affairs, floating in the memory, is like words dispersed and insignificant; whereas a complete view of them in a book is like the same words pointed in a period, and made significant'.

Like Queen Victoria, King Edward was a natural author and in his brief lifetime filled ten volumes with his excellent letters, a poem on the Eucharist, classroom compositions, state papers and his diary. He wrote with ease in Greek, Latin, French and English, played the lute and, had he lived, would have shown similar intellectual qualities to those of his half-sister Elizabeth. 'Among all the remains of the last age . . . none pleased me better . . . than the Journal of King Edward's reign, written all with his own hand,' declared Bishop Burnet. One of the King's teachers, the great Roger Ascham, observed that 'the nobility of England was never more devoted to literature than at present. Our most illustrious King Edward, alike in ability, in industry, perseverance, and acquirements, far exceeds what is usually expected from his years.'

The death of this brilliant youth threw the Reformers into confusion (his diary chillingly records the greed and opportunism of some of these 'new men'). He became very ill in the spring of 1553 and in June willed the crown to 'Jane of Suffolk' (Lady Jane Grey), by-passing both his half-sisters on the advice of the leading Protestant families. His last words were to his doctor:

EDWARD: Are ye so nigh? I thought ye had been further off.
DOCTOR: We heard you speak to yourself, but what you said we know not.
EDWARD: I was praying to God.

26 April 1550. Certein wer taken that went about to have an insurrection in Kent upon May-day following, and the priest who was the cheaf worker ran away into Essex, wher he was laid for.

30 April. Dunglas was deliverid, as the treaty did require.

2 May. Jhon [Joan] Bocher, otherwis Jhon [Joan] of Kent, was burnt for holding that Christ was not incarnat of the Virgin Mary, being condemned the yere befor, but kept in hope of conversion; and the 30 of April the bishop of London and the bishop of Elie were to perswad her. But she withstode them, and reviled the preacher that preached at her death.

4 May. The lord Clinton, befor captain of Bolein,* come to the courte, where, after thankes, he was mad Admirall of England, upon the surrendre of th'erle's of Warwic patent. He was also taken into the previe counsel, and promised farther reward. The capitaines also and officers of the town wer promised rewardes. Mons. de Brisay also passed by the court to Scoteland, where at Grenwich he cam to the King, telling him that the French king wold see that if he laked any commodite that he had, he wold give it him, and likewis wold the constable of Fraunce, who then bar al the swinge.

5 May. The marquis du Means departid into Scoteland with mons. de Brisay, to comfort the quen of the death of the duc of Guise.

---

* Boulogne.

Secondly, to Newmanbrig* to make a hie bulwerk in the middest, with flankers to beat throw al the straight, and also four sluses to make Cales† haven better. Afterward he was bid to goe to Guisnes, where first he shuld take away the iiij-cornered bulwerk, to mak the outward wall of the kepe, and to fill the space betwen the keep and the said outward wall with the foresaid bulwerk, and to raise the old kepe that it might [beat?] the town. Also he was bide to make Purton's bulwark wher it is now round without flankers both pointed, and also with 6 flankers to bete hard to the kepe.

Atwood and Lambert were sent to take view of Aldernay, Syllay, Jernsey, Gernsei, and th'il of Gitto.

The duke of Somerset, with 5 other of the counsel, went to the bishop of Winchester, to whom he made this answere: 'I, having deliberatly seen the book of common praier, although I wold not have made it so my self, yet I find such thinges in it as satisfieth my conscience, and therefor both I wil execut it myself, and also see other my parishoners‡ to doe it.' This was subscribed by the foresaid counsailours, that they herd him saing thies wordes.

4 June. Sir Robert Dudeley, third sonne to th'erle of Warwic, maried sir Jon Robsartes daughter,** after wich mariage ther were certain gentlemen that did strive who shuld first take away a gose's heade, wich was hanged alive on tow crose postes.

5 June. Ther was tilt and tornay on foot with as great staves as the[y] run withal on horsbake.

19 June. I went to Detford, being bidden to supper by the lord Clinton, where before souper I saw certain stand upon th' end of a bote without hold of any thing, and rane one at another till one was cast into the water. At supper mons. vicedam and Henadoy supped with me. After supper was ther a fort made upon a great lighter on the Temps, wich had three walles and a watch towre in the middes, of wich mr. Winter was captain, with forty or fifty other souldiours in yelow and blake. To the fort also apperteined a

---

* Nieullet, a fort out of Calais.
† Calais.
‡ Those in his diocese.
** Amy Robsart.

galey of yelow colour, with men and munition in it, for defence of the castel. Wherefor ther cam 4 pinessis with their men in wight ansomely dressed, wich entending to geve assault to the castel, first drove away the yelow piness, and after with cloddes, scuibes, canes of fire, dartes made for the nonce, and bombardes, assaulted the castel; and at lenght came with their pices, and burst the utter walles of the castill, beating them of the castil into the second ward, who after issued out and drove away the pinessis, sinking one of them, out of wich al the men in it, being more than twenty, leaped out, and swamme in the Temps. Then came th' admiral of the navy with three other pinessis and wanne the castil by assault, and burst the tope of it downe, and toke the captain and under-captain. Then the admiral went forth to take the yelow ship, and at lenght clasped with her, toke her, and assautid also her toppe, and wane it by composicion, and so returned home.

JOHN DEE
(1527–1608)

Dee, mathematician and astrologer, kept his dangerous diary from 1577 to 1600. He was most probably the son of a gentleman server at the court of Henry VIII, although he claimed grand Welsh roots. He was educated at St John's College, Cambridge, and eventually became a founder-Fellow of the King's new Trinity College. It was the youthful Dee's artful stage effects for the performance of an Aristophanes comedy at Trinity which initiated his fame as a magician – disreputable fame, as it happened. When he was twenty he brought back a quantity of astronomical instruments from Holland, further creating for himself the kind of interest which any wise person at that time would be careful to avoid. He was a dazzling lecturer in mathematics, and in Paris his classes were so crowded that scores of students had to stand outside the hall and listen through the windows. Edward VI gave him an allowance, but when Mary came to the throne he was thought to be more enchanter than scientist, and imprisoned for four years. It was through his influence that at least some of the treasures of the pillaged monastic libraries were saved from the destroyers and looters, and made to form the nucleus of a national library.

Throughout his life Dee bridged the divide between the new science (much suspect) and the old mysticism, pragmatic scholarship and the occult. Queen Elizabeth liked him and asked him to cast a felicitous day for her coronation by means of a horoscope. And when a wax image of herself, stuck through with pins, was found in Lincoln's Inn Fields, she consulted him in a hurry. Soon she was to ask his opinion on all kinds of matters, from toothache to her title to the sovereignty of the New World lands being discovered by her mariners. Dr Dee's fee for these consultations was the usual one of ecclesiastical preferment, plus cash, but of course no deanery and very little money came his way.

His diary indicts the Queen's celebrated stinginess:

> The Quene's Majestie called for me at my dore circa 3½ meridie as she passed by and I met at Estschene [East Sheen] Gate when she graciously, putting down her mask, did say with merry chere 'I thank thee Dee there was never promise made but it was broken or kept.' I understood her Majesty to mean of the hundred angels she promised to send me this day.

Mostly all the Queen gave to Dr Dee was 'her right hand to kiss'. Sometimes 'she sayd she wold send me something to kepe Christmas with' but she usually forgot. However, he did benefit from the security which her friendship gave him and his diary is partly a Tudor social register of the great but superstitious who came to him for help.

> The Erle of Lecester, Mr Phillip Sydney, Mr Dyer came to my house. The Countess of Kent and the Countess of Cumberland visited me in the afternoon. The Lord Willoughby dyned with me.
>
> The Lady Walsingham [what a particular risk!] cam suddenly into my house very freely.
>
> The Erle of Derby with Lady Gerard, Sir — Molyneux and his lady daughter to the Lady Gerard, Master Hawghton and

others cam suddenly uppon me after three of the clok. I made them a skoler's collation and it was taken in good part.

In 1583 we find the Queen, on her way to a dinner party and passing Dr Dee's house, unable to resist coming to seek his advice on the absurd matter of herself and the Duc d'Anjou, who had come to England to propose marriage to her. 'The Quene lying at Richmond went to Mr Secretary Walsingham to dynner; she coming by my dore gratiously called me to her and so I went to her horse side . . . Her Majesty asked me obscurely of Monsieur's state *dixi biothanatos erit . . .*'

In 1594, 'Between 6 and 7 after none the Quene sent for me to [come to] her in the privy garden at Grenwich when I delivered in writing the hevonly admonition and her Majesty tok it thankfully. Onely the Lady Warwyk and Sir Robert Cecil and his lady were in the garden with Her Majesty.'

From the 1580s on Dr Dee became obsessed with alchemy and its wild-goose chase of the philosopher's stone. He also installed a crystal ball in his study, only to have the mortification of never being able to see into it. A friend, Barnabas Saul, had to become the 'see-er' (seer). Dr Dee also became involved with a personable young rogue named Edward Kelly and the pair of them set off for Glastonbury to discover the elixir of life. Kelly claimed he could transmute base metals into gold; he sent the Queen a warming-pan with a hole in it, together with a gold piece which exactly fitted the hole, as proof of his necromancy. On one occasion he and Dr Dee went to Mortlake and summoned up the angel Uriel.

While the Court might countenance such goings-on, the local Thames-side inhabitants could not, and one day when Dr Dee was abroad they destroyed both his library and his laboratory.

As a magician-cum-scientist Dr Dee was a discreet diarist. John Aubrey says that he possessed a Merlin-like beauty, being 'of a fair clean sanguine complexion, with a long beard white as milk, a very handsome man tall and slendour' who 'wore a gown like an artist's gown with hanging sleeves and slitt'.

Most of Dr Dee's diary is about the weather, his domestic life, want of money, etc., but dreams and the occult constantly break into these humdrum affairs. Where Edward Kelly is concerned, the

Doctor is clearly in thrall. 'My terrible dream that Mr Kelly would by force bereave me of my bokes, toward day break.' Loss of his books haunted him. 'Saturday night I dreamed that I was deade and afterwards my bowels wer taken out I walked and talked with the Lord Treasurer who was cam to my house to burn my books when I was dead thought he loked sourly at me.'

Dr Dee wrote his diary on the margins of old almanacks. When he was an adviser on the abortive 1584–5 attempt to introduce the Gregorian calendar, the old almanacks which filled the house came in very useful. The diary was published by the Camden Society in 1842, along with the Doctor's own catalogue of his library.

Astrology was a suspect business in his day and he could have been prosecuted under the 1563 Witchcraft Act. There was even an Act forbidding the calculation of the Queen's 'nativity' – the making of a birthday horoscope. The diary is both cautious and give-away, and it allows us to see into the mind of a man who was both ancient and modern, Ptolemaic, medieval – and early-Newtonian. A strange sight.

JOHN MANNINGHAM
Barrister (d. 1622)

The death of Queen Elizabeth I

23 March 1602–3. I dyned with Dr Parry in the Privy Chamber and understood by him, the Bishop of Chichester, the Deane of Windsor etc. that hir Majestie hath bin by fitts troubled with melancholy some three or four monthes but for this fortnight extreme oppressed with it, in soe much that shee refused to eate anie thing to receive anie phisike or admit anie rest in bedd till within these two or three dayes. She hath bin in a manner speechless for two dayes, very pensive and silent, since Shrovetide sitting sometimes with hir eye fixed upon one object many howres togither, yet shee always had hir perfect senses and memory and yesterday signified by the lifting up of hir hand and eyes to heaven a syne which Dr Parry entreated of hir, that she believed that fayth which she had caused to be professed and looked faythfully to be saved by Christe's merits and mercy only and noe other means. She took great delight in hearing prayers, would often at the name of Jesus lift up hir hands and eyes to heaven. She would not heare the Archbishop speake of her longer lyfe, but when he prayed or spake of Heaven and these joyes, she would hug his hand. It seems she might have lived yf she would have used meanes, but she would not be persuaded and princes must not be forced. Hir physicians said shee had a body of a firme and perfect constitution likely to have lived many yeares. A royall Majestie is noe priviledge against death.

24 March. This morning about three o'clock hir Majestie departed this lyfe, mildly like a lamb, easily like a ripe apple from the tree, *cum leve quadam febre absque gemitu.* Dr Parry told me that he was present and sent his prayers before hir soule, and I doubt not that shee is amongst the royall saints in Heaven in Eternal joyes.

DR EDWARD LAKE
Chaplain to Princess Mary (1641–1704)

The marriage of Princess Mary to the Prince of Orange, 4 November 1677

21 October 1677. The Duke of York [the bride's father] dined at Whitehall, after dinner return'd to Saint James', took Lady Mary into her closet and told her of the marriage designed between her and the Prince of Orange, whereupon her highness wept all that afternoon and the following day.

4 November. At nine o'clock at night the marriage was solemnized in her highness's bedchamber. The King [Charles II] who gave her away was very pleasant all the while, for he desir'd that the Bishop of London would make haste less his sister bee delivered of a son and so the marriage be disappointed, and when the prince endowed her with all his worldly goods, hee willed to put all up in her pockett, for 'twas clear gains. At eleven o'clock they went to bed, and his majesty came and drew the curtains and said to the prince, 'Now nephew to your worke! Hey! St George for England!'

9 November. I went to her highnesse to take leave of the princesse who departed for Holland with her husband the Friday after. I perceived her eyes full of tears, herself very disconsolate ... Her highnesse gave mee thanks for all my kindnesses and assured mee shee would do all shee could for mee but was able to say no more because of weeping and so turned back and went into her closet.

16 November. The wind being easterly their highnesses were still detain'd at St James's. This day the court began to whisper the prince's sullenness or clownishnesse, that he took no notice of his princesse at the playe and balle nor came to see her at St James' the day preceding this design'd for their departure.

19 November. This morning about 9 o'clock their highnesses accompani'd with his majesty and royal highnesse and took barges at Whitehall with several other persons of quality. The princesse wept grievously all the morning ... The Queen observing her highnesse to weep as she took leave of her Majesty would have comforted her with the consideration of her own condition when shee came to England and had never till then seen the King, to whom her highnesse presently replied 'But madam you came into England, but I am going out of England.'

FANNY BURNEY (MADAME D'ARBLAY)
(1752–1840)

In her will Fanny Burney left to her niece Charlotte Barrett 'the whole of my own immense Mass of Manuscripts, collected from my 15th year, consisting of Letters, Diaries, Journals, Dramas, composition in prose and rhyme'. Her niece began to edit this material immediately, confident that 'the very names will sell the book' – a reason for the publication of many diaries. In Fanny Burney's case these names are fully integrated with her own experiences. She is not one of those people who are on sightseeing terms with the world, but an insider who reports from an unusually varied set of interiors: the cultural, the Court, the rural and the metropolitan – even the battlefield. A not altogether happy series of circumstances had thrust her into some highly interesting but wearing situations. Famous at twenty-five, popularly placed among the clever women of her day, Madame de Staël, Mrs Montagu and Mrs Siddons, she had no option but to conduct herself as a celebrity.

She was born in King's Lynn, the third child of a church organist who was soon to come to London and make his name as a musicologist. Her maternal grandmother was French, two of her sisters were educated in Paris, and Fanny herself was to marry a refugee from the Revolution, the Chevalier D'Arblay, a friend of Lafayette, and live with him at Passy for ten years. This considerable Frenchness in her life, often overlooked by those who have seen her as the proto-English lady novelist, can be felt in the diary. She began it when she was fifteen and feeling that it 'ought to be addressed to somebody – I must imagine myself to be talking', she thinks first of a sister but opts for Nobody. 'To Nobody, then, will I write my Journal! – since to Nobody can I be wholly unreserved, to Nobody can I reveal every thought, every wish of my heart, with the most unlimited confidence, the most unremitting sincerity, to the end of my life! ... From Nobody I have nothing to fear.' Nobody did very well until, quite soon, his confidante became the authoress of *Evelina* and *Cecilia*, when sister Susan took his place, and occasionally Fanny's friend Mr Crisp of Chessington. When she heard that *Evelina* was a best-seller and the talk of the town, Fanny ran out into the garden and did a dance round the mulberry tree.

Its success took her straight into the Thrale–Johnson circle at Streatham. She, who had had no education whatever beyond her own random reading, had invented the domestic novel. Her admirer Jane Austen took the words 'Pride and Prejudice' from a future Burney tale and used them for the title of her novel. Another fan, Mrs Delany, an old lady living in a grace-and-favour house at Windsor, was to compliment her by bringing her into contact with the Royal Family.

Fanny Burney, the young literary celebrity, could never have wanted to be at Court, and certainly never have wished to be Queen Charlotte's Second Keeper of the Robes (or glorified lady's maid) under the thumb of the appalling Mrs Schwellenberg. The journal of the uncomfortable five years spent at Court is dutiful and uncomplaining on the whole, but bright with comic amazement. Her appointment coincided with George III's mental illness, now thought to have been porphyria but then simply treated as madness, and the journal contains a dreadful Kafka-esque account of what occurred. The palaces were icy cold and her rooms were menial. A severe Germanic etiquette was never for one second relaxed. It was uncomfortable, but it was also rare meat for a diarist. When she is writing her diary, Fanny Burney is primarily a storyteller with an expert control of the narrative process. Her chief difficulty lay in keeping her two selves separate – the famous writer and the high-grade domestic who was virtually the Queen's prisoner.

In the following episode Fanny Burney is embarrassed by herself being courted by a distinguished literary visitor, Madame de la Roche, a German novelist married to a Frenchman, whose daughter was to become the 'Mlle B.' of Goethe's *The Sorrows of Werther*. Madame de la Roche had come to England to see the sights, which included Fanny Burney, and she was not to be put off by the strict rules of a Queen who, in spite of her beloved Miss Burney, detested novelists as much as the King disliked foreigners. Madame de la Roche could not be more unwelcome – or more insensitive to the fact. She expects to stay for dinner. It is a scene from a novel written to amuse both Nobody and Susan.

The gate-crasher at the Court of George III

Monday, 11 September 1786. I come now to introduce to you, with a new character, some new perplexities from my situation. Madame la Fite called the next morning, to tell me she must take no denial to forming me a new acquaintance – Madame de la Roche, a German by birth, but married to a Frenchman; – an authoress, a woman of talents and distinction, a character highly celebrated, and unjustly suffering from an adherence to the Protestant religion. 'She dies with eagerness to see you,' she added, in French, 'and I have invited her to Windsor, where I have told her I have no other feast prepared for her but to show her Dr Herschel and Miss Burney.'

I leave you to imagine if I felt competent to fulfil such a promise: openly, on the contrary, I assured her I was quite unequal to it.

She had already, she said, written to Madame la Roche, to come the next day, and if I would not meet her she must be covered with disgrace.

Expostulation was now vain; I could only say that to answer for myself was quite out of my own power.

'And why? – and wherefore? – and what for? – and surely to me! – and surely for Madame de la Roche! – *une femme d'esprit – mon amie – l'amie de Madame de Genlis*,' etc. etc., filled up a hurried conference in the midst of my dressing for the Queen, till a summons interrupted her, and forced me, half dressed, and all too late, to run away from her, with an extorted promise to wait upon her if I possibly could.

Accordingly I went, and arrived before Madame la Roche. Poor Madame la Fite received me in transport; and I soon witnessed another transport, at least equal, to Madame la Roche, which happily was returned with the same warmth; and it was not till after a thousand embraces, and the most ardent professions – '*Ma digne amie! – est il possible? – te vois-je?*' etc. – that I discovered they had never before met in their lives! – they had corresponded, but no more!

This somewhat lessened my surprise, however, when my turn arrived; for no sooner was I named than all the *embrassades* were transferred to me – '*La digne Miss Bourni! – l'auteur de "Cecile"? –*

d' "Evelina"? – non, ce n'est pas possible! – suis-je si heureuse! – oui, je le vois à ses yeux! – Ah! que de bonheur!' etc.

As nobody was present, I had not the same confusion from this scene as from that in which I first saw Madame la Fite, when, at an assembly at Miss Streatfield's, such as these were her exclamations aloud, in the midst of the admiring bystanders.

But soon after there entered Mrs Fielding and Miss Finch, both invited by Madame la Fite to witness these new encounters. A literary conversation was then begun, opened by Madame la Fite, and kept alive by Mrs Fielding.

Madame la Roche, had I met her in any other way, might have pleased me in no common degree; for could I have conceived her character to be unaffected, her manners have a softness that would render her excessively engaging. She is now *bien passée* – no doubt fifty – yet has a voice of touching sweetness, eyes of dove-like gentleness, looks supplicating for favour, and an air and demeanour the most tenderly caressing. I can suppose she has thought herself all her life the model of the favourite heroine of her own favourite romance, and I can readily believe that she has had attractions in her youth nothing short of fascinating. Had I not been present, and so deeply engaged in this interview, I had certainly been caught by her myself; for in her presence I constantly felt myself forgiving and excusing what in her absence I as constantly found past defence or apology.

Poor Madame la Fite has no chance in her presence; for though their singular enthusiasm upon 'the people of the literature', as Pacchierotti called them, is equal, Madame la Fite almost subdues by her vehemence, while Madame la Roche almost melts by her softness. Yet I fairly believe they are both very good women, and both believe themselves sincere.

In the midst of a warmth the most animated for whatever she could approve, how admirably did Madame de Genlis steer clear of both these extremes, of violence and of languor, and confer honour by her praise, even where most partial and unmerited, by the dignity mingled with sweetness that accompanied it!

I returned still time enough to find Mrs Schwellenberg with her tea-party; and she was very desirous to hear something of Madame la Roche. I was led by this to give a short account of her: not such a one as you have heard, because I kept it quite independent of all reference to poor Madame la Fite; but there was still enough to make a little narration. Madame la Roche had told me that she had been only three days in England, and had yet made but a beginning of seeing *les spectacles*, and *les gens célèbres*; – and what do you think was the first, and, as yet, sole spectacle to which she had been carried? – Bedlam! – And who the first, and, as yet, only *homme célèbre* she had seen – Lord George Gordon! – whom she called *le fameux* George Gordon, and with whom she had dined, in company with Count Cagliostro!

When foreigners come hither without proper recommendations, how strange is their fare! General Budé found himself so excessively diverted with this account, intermixed, at the time, with several circumstances I have now forgot, and with the novelty of hearing anything beyond a grave monosyllable from my mouth, that it surprised him off all guard, and he began, for the first time since the day of his arrival, to venture coming forward to converse with me; and though it was soon over, from that time he has never seen me without the amazing temerity of speaking a few words to me!

At night the Princess Royal came into my room, sent by the Queen for little Badine's basket. I begged her permission to carry it myself, but she would not suffer me. She stayed a few minutes, conversing chiefly upon Mrs Delany, and when, as she was going away, I could not forbear saying a word or two of the many little marks of favour she had shown me, she came back, and took hold of my hand to make me a kind answer. Charming indeed is it to see the goodness, native and acquired, of this lovely young Princess.

Sunday, 17 September. At the chapel this morning, Madame la Fite placed Madame la Roche between herself and me, and proposed bringing her to the Lodge, 'to return my visit'. This being precisely what I had tried to avoid, and to avoid without shocking Madame la Fite, by meeting her correspondent at her own house, I was much chagrined at such a proposal, but had no means to decline it, as it was made across Madame la Roche herself.

Accordingly, at about two o'clock, when I came from the Queen, I found them both in full possession of my room, and Madame la Fite occupied in examining my books. The thing thus being done, and the risk of consequences inevitable, I had only to receive them with as little display of disapprobation of their measures as I could help; but one of the most curious scenes followed I have ever yet been engaged in or witnessed.

As soon as we were seated, Madame la Fite began with assuring me, aloud, of the 'conquest' I had made of Madame la Roche, and appealed to that lady for the truth of what she said. Madame la Roche answered her by rising, and throwing her arms about me, and kissing my cheeks from side to side repeatedly.

Madame la Fite, as soon as this was over, and we had resumed our seats, opened the next subject, by saying Madame la Roche had read and adored *Cecilia*: again appealing to her for confirmation of her assertion.

'O, oui, oui!' cried her friend, '*mais la vraie Cecile, c'est Miss Borni! charmante Miss Borni! digne, douce, et aimable!* Coom to me arms! *que je vous embrasse mille fois!*'

Again we were all deranged, and again the same ceremony being performed, we all sat ourselves down.

Cecilia was then talked over throughout, in defiance of every obstacle I could put in its way.

After this, Madame la Fite said, in French, that Madame la Roche had had the most extraordinary life and adventures that had fallen to anybody's lot; and finished with saying, '*Eh! ma chère amie, contez nous un peu.*'

They were so connected, she answered, in their early part with M. Wieland, the famous author, that they would not be intelligible without his story.

'*Eh bien! ma très-chère, contez nous, donc, un peu de ses aventures; ma chère Miss Burney, c'étoit son amant, et l'homme le plus extraordinaire – d'un génie! d'un feu! Eh bien, ma chère? où l'avez vous rencontré? où est-ce qu'il a commencé à vous aimer? contez nous un peu de tout ça.*'

Madame la Roche, looking down upon her fan, began then the recital. She related their first interview, the gradations of their mutual attachment, his extraordinary talents, his literary fame and name; the breach of their unions from motives of prudence in their friends; his change of character from piety to voluptuousness, in consoling himself for her loss with an actress; his various adventures, and various transformations from good to bad, in life and conduct; her own marriage with M. de la Roche, their subsequent meeting when she was mother of three children, and all the attendant circumstances.

This narrative was told in so touching and pathetic a manner, and interspersed with so many sentiments of tenderness and of heroism, that I could scarcely believe I was not actually listening to a Clelia or a Cassandra, recounting the stories of her youth.

When she had done, and I had thanked her, Madame la Fite demanded of me what I thought of her, and if she was not delightful? I assented, and Madame la Roche then, rising, and fixing her eyes, filled with tears, in my face, while she held both my hands, in the most melting accents, exclaimed, '*Miss Borni! la plus chère, la plus digne des Angloises! dites-moi – m'aimez vous?*'

I answered as well as I could, but what I said was not very positive. Madame la Fite came up to us, and desired we might make a trio of friendship, which should bind us to one another for life.

And then they both embraced me, and both wept for joyful fondness! I fear I seemed very hard-hearted; but no spring was opened whence one tear of mine could flow.

The clock had struck four some time, and Madame la Fite said she feared they kept me from dinner. I knew it must soon be ready, and therefore made but a light negative.

She then, with an anxious look at her watch, said she feared she was already too late for her own little dinner.

I was shocked at a hint I had no power to notice, and heard it in silence – silence unrepressing! for she presently added, 'You dine alone, don't you?'

'Y-e-s, – if Mrs Schwellenberg is not well enough to come downstairs to dinner.'

'And can you dine, *ma chère Mademoiselle* – can you dine at that great table alone?'

'I must! – the table is not mine.'

'Yes, in Mrs Schwellenberg's absence it is.'

'It has never been made over to me, and I take no power that is not given to me.'

'But the Queen, my dearest ma'am – the Queen, if she knew such a person as Madame la Roche was here.'

She stopped, and I was quite disconcerted. An attack so explicit, and in presence of Madame la Roche, was beyond all my expectations. She then went to the window, and exclaimed, 'It rains! – *Que ferons nous?* – My poor littel dinner! – it will be all spoilt! – *La pauvre Madame la Roche! une telle femme!*'

I was now really distressed, and wished much to invite them both to stay; but I was totally helpless; and could only look, as I felt, in the utmost embarrassment.

The rain continued. Madame la Roche could understand but imperfectly what passed, and waited its result with an air of smiling patience. I endeavoured to talk of other things; but Madame la Fite was restless in returning to this charge. She had several times given me very open hints of her desire to dine at Mrs Schwellenberg's table; but I had hitherto appeared not to comprehend them: she was now determined to come home to the point; and the more I saw her determination, the less liable I became to being overpowered by it.

At length John came to announce dinner.

Madame la Fite looked at me in a most expressive manner, as she rose and walked towards the window, exclaiming that the rain would not cease; and Madame la Roche cast upon me a most tender smile, while she lamented that some accident must have prevented her carriage from coming for her.

I felt excessively ashamed, and could only beg them not to be in haste, faithfully assuring them I was by no means disposed for eating.

Poor Madame la Fite now lost all command of herself, and desiring to speak to me in my own room, said, pretty explicitly, that certainly I might keep anybody to dinner, at so great a table, and all alone, if I wished it.

I was obliged to be equally frank. I acknowledged that I had reason to believe I might have had that power, from the custom of my predecessor, Mrs Haggerdorn, upon my first succeeding her; but that I was then too uncertain of any of my privileges to assume a single one of them unauthorized by the Queen; and I added that I had made it the invariable rule of my conduct, from the moment of my entering into my present office, to run no risk of private blame, by any action that had not her previous consent or knowledge.

She was not at all satisfied, and significantly said,

'But you have sometimes Miss Planta?'

'Not I; Mrs Schwellenberg invites her.'

'And M. de Luc, too, – he may dine with you!'

'He also comes to Mrs Schwellenberg. Mrs Delany alone, and her niece, come to me; and they have had the sanction of the Queen's own desire.'

'*Mais, enfin, ma chère* Miss Burney, – when it rains, – and when it is so late, – and when it is for such a woman as Madame la Roche!'

So hard pressed, I was quite shocked to resist her; but I assured her that when my own sisters, Phillips and Francis, came to Windsor purposely to see me, they had never dined at the Lodge but by the express invitation of Mrs Schwellenberg; and that when my father himself was here, I had not ventured to ask him.

This, though it surprised, somewhat appeased her; and we were called into the other room to Miss Planta, who was to dine with me, and who, unluckily, said the dinner would be quite cold.

They begged us both to go, and leave them till the rain was over, or till Madame la Roche's carriage arrived. I could not bear to do this, but entreated Miss Planta, who was in haste, to go and dine by herself.

This, at last, was agreed to, and I tried once again to enter into discourse upon other matters. But how greatly did my disturbance at all this urgency increase, when Madame la Fite said she was so hungry she must beg a bit of bread and a glass of water!

I was now, indeed, upon the point of giving way; but when I considered, while I hesitated, what must follow – my own necessary apology, which would involve Madame la Fite in much blame, or my own concealing silence, which would reverse all my plans of openness with the Queen, and acquiescence with my own situation – I grew firm again, and having assured her a thousand times of my concern for my little power, I went into the next room: but I sent her the roll and water by John; I was too much ashamed to carry them. Miss Planta was full of good-natured compassion for the scene in which she saw me engaged, but confessed she was sure I did right.

When I returned to them again, Madame la Fite requested me to

go at once to the Queen, and tell her the case. Ah, poor Madame la
Fite! to see so little a way for herself, and to suppose me also so
every way short-sighted! I informed her that I never entered the
presence of the Queen unsummoned.

'But why not, my dear ma'am? – Mrs Haggerdorn went out and
in whenever she pleased.'

'So I have heard; but she was an old attendant, and only went on
in her old way: I am new, and have yet no way marked out.'

'But Miss Planta does also.'

'That must have been brought about by the Queen's directions.'

She then remonstrated with me upon my shyness, for my own
sake; but I assured her I was more disengaged, and better pleased,
in finding myself expected only upon call, that I could be in settling
for myself the times, seasons, and proprieties of presenting myself
of my own accord.

Again she desired to speak to me in my own room; and then she
told me that Madame la Roche had a most earnest wish to see all
the Royal Family; she hoped, therefore, the Queen would go to
early prayers at the chapel, where, at least, she might be beheld: but
she gave me sundry hints, not to be misunderstood, that she
thought I might so represent the merits of Madame la Roche as to
induce the honour of a private audience.

I could give her no hope of this, as I had none to give; for I well
knew that the Queen has a settled aversion to almost all novels,
and something very near it to almost all novel-writers.

She then told me she had herself requested an interview for her
with the Princess Royal, and had told her that if it was too much to
grant it in the Royal apartments, at least it might take place in Miss
Burney's room! Her Royal Highness coldly answered that she saw
nobody without the Queen's commands.

How much I rejoiced in her prudence and duty! I would not have
had a meeting in my room unknown to the Queen for a thousand
worlds. But poor mistaken Madame la Fite complained most bitterly
of the deadness of the whole court to talents and genius.

In the end, the carriage of Madame la Roche arrived, about tea-
time, and Madame la Fite finished with making me promise to
relate my difficulties to the Queen, that she might give me such
orders as to enable me to keep them any other time. And thus

ended this most oppressive scene. You may think I had no very voracious appetite after it.

QUEEN VICTORIA
(1819–1901)

A natural and prodigious writer who poured out her life in millions of words, Queen Victoria was not in need of Disraeli's arch compliment, 'We authors, Ma'am'. She was also a competent artist and a good musician. She was insistent that everything – all communications to her – should be in writing. Her journals and letters are by turn racy and homely, authoritative and naive. A part of her diary, called *Leaves from a Journal of Our Life in the Highlands, 1848–61*, was published privately in 1867 and given to a few close friends. The following year she was persuaded – somewhat doubtfully – to reissue the book for the public as its editor, Arthur Helps, realized that fragments of the private edition were sure to get into the newspapers, with gossipy results. Helps also told the Queen that nothing could better explain her bereavement to the country at large. Her husband had died from typhus seven years earlier at the age of forty-two, and there were signs of puzzlement and irritation at her protracted mourning and withdrawal from public affairs.

Under Arthur Helps's guidance – he persuaded the Queen to add parts of her diary covering journeys she had made in England, Ireland and the Channel Islands, and to dedicate the book to 'The dear memory of him who made the life of the writer bright and happy' – a bestseller emerged. 'If only Elizabeth and Anne had kept diaries!' wrote Helps in his Preface. 'There is always something in the present which has the appearance of being trivial and prosaic, but the future historian will delight in having details before him . . .' Prosaic, Queen Victoria most certainly is, but not trivial. Nor, unlike her subjects, is she class-ridden or in the least pretentious. The pleasure of her diary, with its famous style, is hard to define. It is soothing but not emollient. The detail it contains is a literary equivalent of the detail that makes old photographs so fascinating. The reader finds himself constantly attempting to define the charismatic quality of the author, but without success. The dull-interesting days follow one another in the long Victorian afternoon. So popular was the *Journal* that the second instalment, *More Leaves . . .*, was published later.

Thursday, 26 September 1864. Slept very well and was much rested. At half-past twelve I started with Louise on ponies (I on Sultan), and Jane Churchill, the Duke of Richmond, and Sir Thomas walking, rode past the stables on a good road, and then turned to the right and went up *Glenfiddich* for about four miles. The scenery is not grand, but pretty; an open valley with green and not very high hills, some birches, and a great deal of fern and juniper. After about three miles the glen narrows and is extremely pretty; a narrow steep path overhanging a burn leads to a cave, which the Duke said went a long way under the hill. It is called the *Elf House*. There is a small space of level ground, and a sort of seat arranged with stones, on which Louise and I sat; and here we all lunched, and then tried to sketch. But I could make nothing of the cave, and therefore scrambled up part of the hill with great trouble, and tried again but equally unsuccessfully, and had to be helped down, as I had been helped up, by Brown. We were here nearly an hour, and then, after walking down the steep path, we got on our ponies and rode up to the left, another very steep and narrow path, for a short while on the brink of a steep high bank with the *Fiddich* below. We emerged from this ravine and came upon moors in the hills (the whole of this is 'the forest'), and rode on a mile and a half till near the head of the *Livet* on the right of the *Sowie*, a high, bare, heathery, mossy hill; *Cairn-ta-Bruar* to the left. Here we had a fine view of *Ben Aven* and *Ben-na-Bourd*, and this was the very way we should have ridden from *Tomnavoulin*. We had a slight sprinkling of rain, but very little at this time. We saw eight stags together at a distance. Oh! had dearest Albert been here with his rifle! we rode on and back till we came to a sheltered place near the burnside, about one mile and three-quarters from *Glenfiddich Lodge*, where one of the Duke's keepers had prepared a fire and got a kettle boiling, and here we took our tea. Afterwards I sketched, but we were surrounded by a perfect cloud of midges which bit me dreadfully. The gentlemen left us, after tea, and walked home. I walked a little while, and then rode back by a quarter to seven. A beautiful mild evening, the sky a lovely colour. Dear good Sharp* was with us and out each day, and so affectionate.

A. Thomson, S. Forbes, Kennedy, and J. Stewart, the latter with the ponies, as well as the Duke's forester Lindsay, were out with us. Dinner as yesterday. Jane Churchill finished reading 'Pride and Prejudice' to us after dinner. A very clear starlight night.

Thursday, 21 October 1875. Much grieved at its being a worse day than ever for the funeral of Brown's father, which sad ceremony was to take place to-day. The rain is hopeless – the ninth day! Quite unheard of! I saw good Brown a moment before breakfast; he was low and sad, and then going off to *Micras*. At twenty minutes to twelve drove with Beatrice and Janie Ely to *Micras*. As we drove up (unfortunately raining much) we met Dr Robertson, and all along near the house were numbers of people – Brown told me afterwards he thought above a hundred. All my keepers, Mitchell the blacksmith (from *Clachanturn*), Symon, Grant, Brown's five uncles, Leys, Thomson (postmaster), and the forester, people below *Micras* and in *Aberarder*, and my people; Heale, Löhlein (returned this day from a week's leave), Cowley Jarrett, Ross and Collins (sergeant footman), Brown and his four brothers, including Donald (who only arrived last night, and went to the *Bush*, his brother William's farm), took us to the kitchen, where was poor dear old Mrs Brown sitting near the fire and much upset, but still calm and dignified; Mrs William Brown was most kind and helpful, and the old sister-in-law and her daughter; also the Hon. M. West, Mr Sahl, Drs Marshall and Profeit, Mr Begg, and Dr Robertson, who came in later. The sons, and a few whom Brown sent out of the kitchen, were in the other small room, where was the coffin. A small passage always divides the kitchen and the sitting-room in this old sort of farmhouse, in front of which is the door – the only

---

* *A favourite collie of mine.*

door. Mr Campbell, the minister of *Crathie*, stood in the passage at the door, every one else standing close outside. As soon as he began his prayer, poor dear old Mrs Brown got up and came and stood near me – able to hear, though, alas! not to see – and leant on a chair during the very impressive prayers, which Mr Campbell gave admirably. When it was over, Brown came and begged her to go and sit down while they took the coffin away, the brothers bearing it. Every one went out and followed, and we also hurried out and just saw them place the coffin in the hearse, and then we moved on to a hillock, whence we saw the sad procession wending its way sadly down. The sons were there, whom I distinguished easily from their being near good Brown, who wore his kilt walking near the hearse. All walked, except our gentlemen, who drove. It fortunately ceased raining just then. I went back to the house, and tried to soothe and comfort dear old Mrs Brown, and gave her a mourning brooch with a little bit of her husband's hair which had been cut off yesterday, and I shall give a locket to each of the sons.

When the coffin was being taken away, she sobbed bitterly.

We took some whisky and water and cheese, according to the universal Highland custom, and then left, begging the dear old lady to bear up. I told her the parting was but for a time. We drove quickly on, and saw them go into the kirkyard, and through my glasses I could see them carry the coffin in. I was grieved I could not be in the kirkyard.

Saw my good Brown at a little before two. He said all had gone off well, but he seemed very sad; he had to go back to *Micras* to meet all the family at tea. All this was terribly trying for the poor dear old widow, but could not be avoided. Already, yesterday morning, she had several of the wives and neighbours to tea. Every one was very kind and full of sympathy, and Brown was greatly gratified by the respect shown to him and his family to-day . . .

I said that the use of the Church was that it made one think of what one would not otherwise think of . . .

SIR HENRY CHANNON
(1897–1958)

'Chips' Channon belongs to the Horace Walpole/Lord Hervey/ Saint-Simon school of diarists. If his artistry could not match theirs it does at least display a greater personal charm. One can see why he gained such easy access to both the British aristocracy and the most celebrated literary and theatrical circles of the inter-war years. He was ever the enchanted *arriviste*, grateful, dazzled. He kept a diary for nearly forty years and knew its value. Enormous care was taken to see that his records, especially of the Abdication–Appeasement era, got through to posterity. When the war came the diary was buried in Kelvedon churchyard for safety, and eventually Channon himself was to lodge it in the British Museum.

He talked about the diary a lot and society must have known that it was being watched and called to daily account. 'At dinner [15 November 1945] we discussed Diaries, and Willy [W. S. Maugham] volunteered that mine would be illuminating. Other diarists, he said, would be too cautious; that Eddie Marsh was too kind, and that Harold Nicolson was not in society.' Maugham was right: Channon *is* illuminating, if somewhat in the way a correctly veneered surface is illuminating, throwing up as he does countless unguarded reflections. Although a gossip, Chips doesn't actually write in order to amuse, but to inform.

Channon was a native of Chicago who fled America in his youth, and who swiftly and easily penetrated the British establishment, becoming a friend of royalty, a Member of Parliament (where he rarely uttered a word) and the husband of Lady Honor Guinness. He lived fashionably and opulently, with a would-be Proustian eye on his adopted world. Only a small part of his diary has been published so far and the full extent of his achievement has still to be assessed. He had little or no notion of politics, but he did have a shrewd idea of what was happening and there is a steely foundation to his edifice of décor, clothes, manners, scandal, tics and traits. And he is touchingly honest: 'I . . . put my whole life's work into my anglicization, in ignoring my early life,' he wrote in 1927.

The Channon diaries are a rich hold-all of period detail and eyeball-to-eyeball observations of the Nazis, Mrs Simpson, Chamberlain (a Channon idol), Churchill, the great hostesses, and nearly every famous event and its dramatis personae. Chips has a nose for glamour and an unblushing enthusiasm for top people. He drifted from marriage to friendships with Terence Rattigan and the 'Bloomsbury boys', and was in later life torn a little between orthodoxy and the freer milieu of writers and artists. He is good on parliamentary matters and these provide some of his best portraits and tales. The Channon diaries carry Thirties chatter through to the Fifties, and although they are dominated by chic, they escape triviality.

Bognor, Whitsuntide 1935. Much gossip about the Prince of Wales' alleged Nazi leanings; he is alleged to have been influenced by Emerald (who is rather éprise with Herr Ribbentrop) through Mrs Simpson. The Coopers are furious, being fanatically pro-French and anti-German. He has just made an extraordinary speech to the British Legion advocating friendship with Germany; it is only a gesture, but a gesture that may be taken seriously in Germany and elsewhere. If only the Chancelleries of Europe knew that his speech was the result of Emerald Cunard's intrigues, themselves inspired by Herr Ribbentrop's dimple!

13 June. We dined with the Fitzgeralds for the Court Ball; Honor very resplendent in her sapphire parure, diamond tiara, and many other jewels. She looked radiant, Rubenesque and gorgeous. When we arrived at the Palace at 9.50, the ballroom was already overcrowded, the Ball may have been a respectable function but it was dam' dull. At first one saw no one one knew but gradually, like feeling in the dark, I saw familiar faces. We danced or rather pushed our way round the floor. The Duchess of Kent winked and gave us both dazzling smiles; like Honor she was dressed in dark blue to hide her pregnant figure. The Queen glittered and heaved under her jewels. I saw her send for the Begum Aga Khan and motion her into the King's throne. Maureen Dufferin sailed past on the arm of a black potentate. Emerald Cunard nearly fainted in the heat, and 'the Coalbox', dripping with Kitty Winn's diamonds, chattered and chirped to everyone. But it was not a fashionable function, though, of course, a magnificent sight to the uninitiated. As we left, we met Beaverbrook on the staircase and I said 'Oh! Prince Metternich himself' – he pinched me and passed on. The Prince of Wales seemed in a very bad temper but looked about twelve. Alfred Potocki, Lord of Lançut, told me it was a delight to see the rage of the French in Paris when they heard of his recent speech extending a friendly hand to Germany.

London, 16 June. All day long I spent alone with Bundi, who is an undemonstrative dog but always charming, until six o'clock when I went to see Emerald. She was in bed looking very seductive as she reclined in blue and lace. I sat on her bed for two hours, and we gossiped. She leaves on Tuesday to do hostess for the Prince of Wales at Fort Belvedere for his Ascot party, which, of course, includes the Simpsons – but Emerald is wobbling a little bit about Mrs Simpson because Portia Stanley so attacked her about her. In the midst of our talk Ribbentrop rang up, the arch-Hitler spy of Europe. Emerald flattered him for a few minutes and then asked him to join her at the Opera tomorrow. She then suddenly said: 'Corbin, the French Ambassador, says that you are perfectly charming.' I could hear the German's voice drop with surprise and when, a minute later, I asked Emerald whether Corbin had ever said such a thing, she laughingly admitted that she'd invented it, on the spur of the moment.

6 July. There is something classical in Mussolini's seaplane flying to Rome being struck by lightning. It would seem as if the Gods themselves were jealous of this dynamic man. Only once have I met him. It was in 1926. Gage and I were motoring through Europe and turned up at Perugia. The whole town was en fête with garlands and bands and photographers and we were told that Il Duce was arriving the next morning. At 4 a.m. next day the streets were crowded with singing, black-shirted boys and George and I leant out of our window watching them. I got tickets for a lecture Mussolini was going to give at the University, and we duly arrived and found ourselves in a small room along with 40–50 other people, the cream of Perugian society. Suddenly the door opened

... a little man, Napoleonic in stature, in a black coat, raised his right hand in a Fascist salute and advanced down the room as the audience stood up. He mounted the rostrum and spoke for an hour, very fast in flowing Italian, about Hannibal and the Punic Wars. My Italian was never very good, nevertheless I understood almost every word he said. He held the audience spellbound, and made cold chills run down my spine. It gave me more of a thrill than my interview with the Pope.

When it was over we were led up, because we were English, and introduced to him and I shook his warm big hand.

This is my only personal contact with Mussolini. Now all our Roman friends meet him often, as during the past few years he has deigned to go out into Society ...

We spent seven hours today with Monsieur Boudin from Paris. He is considered the greatest decorator in the world. He brought the plans for our dining-room: I think it is going to be stupendous. There is to be a small ante-room opening into a gallery – orange and silver like the Amalienburg; then another door, and then I hope, stupefaction – a high banqueting hall, all blue and silver. Constructing it will take six months, and Boudin is going to Munich for inspiration.

19 July. Sometimes I think I have an unusual character – able but trivial; I have flair, intuition, great good taste but only second rate ambition: I am far too susceptible to flattery; I hate and am uninterested in all the things most men like such as sport, business, statistics, debates, speeches, war and the weather; but I am riveted by lust, furniture, glamour and society and jewels. I am an excellent organizer and have a will of iron; I can only be appealed to through my vanity. Occasionally I must have solitude: my soul craves for it. All thought is done in solitude; only then am I partly happy.

Pyrford, 26 July. I feel caddish, even treacherous sometimes keeping this diary from the eyes of my wife – yet it is our only secret. She knows I keep it, but if she were to read it, and I knew she were, it would lose much spontaneity, and cease to be a record of my private thoughts. Once or twice in the past I have dictated a few harmless paragraphs to a Secretary – and they have never been the same, becoming impersonal and discreet immediately. And what is more dull than a discreet diary? One might just as well have a discreet soul.

30 July. I am bored by this Italian–Abyssinian dispute, and really I fail to see why we should interfere. Though, of course, the League of Nations will stand or fall by it. But I am a little uneasy that the destinies of countless millions should be in the exquisite hands of Anthony Eden, for whom I have affection, even admiration – but not blind respect. Why should England fight Italy over Abyssinia, when most of our far flung Empire has been won by conquest?

11. THE DIARIST *EN ROUTE*

THE REV. HENRY TEONGUE
(1621–90)

Teongue was fifty-four when, having run out of money, he abandoned his Alcester living for a riotous and prosperous career as a naval chaplain. He kept two rollicking sea diaries for the years 1675 to 1679. 'Nothing but merriment' and 'No prayers today by reason of business.' His son looked after the parish in his absence. Teongue 'gott a good summ of monys', 'spent greate part of it', and thoroughly enjoyed himself. His first voyage took him to Antioch as chaplain to H.M. 'Frigott' *Assistance*.

1675. The Arabian Lady was tall and very slender very sworfy of complexion and very thinn faced; having nothing on but a thinn loose garment a kinde of gyrdle about her middle and the garment open before. She had a ringe in her left nostrill which hung downe below her nether lipp; at each eare a round globe as bigg as a tennis ball, shining like gold, and hanging almost as low as her brest . . . She had also gold chaines about her wrists and the smalls of her naked legs. Her nayles of her fingers were coloured almost redd and her lips coloured as blew as indigo; and so also was her belly from the navill to the hammes, painted blew like branches of trees or strawberry leaves. Nor was she cautious but rather ambitious to shew you this sight . . .

We had a princelike dinner; and every health that we dranke, every man broake the glass he dranke in, so that before night wee had destroyed a whole chest of pure Venice glass.

More myrth at dinner this day than ever since we cam on board.

The wind blew very hard and we had to dinner a rump of Xante beif a little salted and well rosted. When it was brought into the cabin and set on the table (that is on the floore for it could not stand on the table for the ship's tossing) . . . we all sat closse round about the beif, some securing themselves from slurring by setting their feete against the bedd and the Captain set his back against a chayre. Our liquer was white rubola, admirable food. We also had a couple of fatt pullets, and whilst wee were eating of them a sea cam and forced into the cabin through the chinks of a port hole, which by looking behind mee I just discovered when the water was coming under mee. I soone got up, and no whitt wett, but all the rest were well washed and got up as fast they could and laughed one at the other.

THE REV. JOHN WESLEY
(1703–91)

John and his elder brother Charles were the sons of Samuel Wesley, rector of Epworth, Lincolnshire. In 1729 Charles founded a 'Holy Society' which John joined and the small group set out to fire the near-moribund Church of England with an evangelical passion which shocked its stolid adherents, who mockingly dubbed the young men 'Methodists'. Their mentor was the mystic, William Law. Both Charles and John were brilliant speakers, good poets and obsessive writers generally. John's was the greater genius and it carried him along on an ocean-tide of zeal; it was he who turned Methodism into a Nonconformist sect by ordaining a minister for America, where he knew communities were crying out for spiritual leaders. John Wesley's personality was so overwhelming that his mission overshadowed the work done by other evangelists, notably George Whitefield, who travelled to America thirteen times to John's two.

John Wesley began to write his journal while still at Oxford as the result of reading Jeremy Taylor's exquisite *Holy Living*, which made him 'take a more exact account than I had done before of the manner wherein I spent my time, writing down how I had employed every hour'. For the first fifteen years he did this quite literally, but then, in October 1735, circumstances drastically halted this self-examination. He was off to Georgia and it was a case of travel broadening the mind. It was not that the journal was less religiously orientated, but simply that action, the effect of new scenes, and energies which Wesley could never have experienced or even have imagined while preaching and tutoring at the University, were released. As with many diary-writers, the possibilities of publication began to occupy his thoughts. In 1739 he published *An Extract of the Rev. Mr John Wesley's Journal, from his embarking for Georgia, to his return to London*, and from then over the next fifty years other edited extracts appeared, to good notices in the press. His energy was prodigious and he is said to have travelled a quarter of a million miles on horseback in England alone, besides vast tours of the Continent and the New World. He often wrote as he rode.

The journal was astutely edited by the diarist himself and no one will ever know exactly what it originally contained. It was not written to entertain, but to profess, edify, reform and inspire. All the same, it remains his greatest literary achievement and an incomparable authority on the social life of the eighteenth century. Twenty-one instalments of it were issued by Wesley between 1739 and 1791, and for countless readers it held the fascination of a huge sacred novel.

Arriving in America

Sunday, 1 February 1736. We spoke with a ship of Carolina; and Wed. 4. came within soundings. About noon the trees were visible from the mast, and in the afternoon from the main deck. In the evening lesson were these words, 'A great door and effectual is opened.' O let no one shut it!

Thursday, 5 February. Between two and three in the afternoon, God brought us all safe into the Savannah river. We cast anchor near Tybee-island, where the groves of pines, running along the shore, made an agreeable prospect, showing, as it were, the bloom of spring in the depth of winter.

Friday, 6 February. About eight in the morning, we first set foot on American ground. It was a small uninhabited island, over against Tybee. Mr Oglethorpe led us to a rising ground, where we all kneeled down to give thanks. He then took boat for Savannah. When the rest of the people were come on shore, we called our little flock together to prayers. Several parts of the second lesson, Mark vi, were wonderfully suited to the occasion; in particular, the account of the courage and sufferings of John the Baptist; our Lord's directions to the first Preachers of his Gospel, and their toiling at sea, and deliverance, with those comfortable words, 'It is I, be not afraid.'

Sunday, 27 June. About twenty joined with us in morning prayer. An hour or two after, a large party of Creek Indians came, the expectation of whom deprived us of our place of public worship, in which they were to have their audience.

Wednesday, 30 June. I hoped a door was opened for going up immediately to the Choctaws, the least polished, i.e. the least corrupted of all the Indian nations. But upon my informing Mr Oglethorpe of our design, he objected, not only the danger of being intercepted, or killed by the French there; but much more, the inexpediency of leaving Savannah destitute of a Minister. These objections I related to our brethren in the evening, who were all of the opinion, 'We ought not to go yet.'

Comparative religion

Thursday, 1 July 1736. The Indians had an audience, and another on Saturday, when Chicali, their head-man, dined with Mr Oglethorpe. After dinner, I asked the grey-headed old man, 'What he thought he was made for?' He said, 'He that is above knows what he made us for. We know nothing. We are in the dark. But white men know much. And yet white men build great houses, as if they were to live for ever. But white men cannot live for ever. In a little time, white men will be dust as well as I.' I told him, 'If red men will learn the good book, they may know as much as white men. But neither we nor you can understand that book, unless we are taught by Him that is above: and he will not teach unless you avoid what you already know is not good.' He answered, 'I believe that. He will not teach us while our hearts are not white. And our men do what they know is not good: they kill their own children. And our women do what they know is not good: they kill the child before it is born. Therefore, He that is above, does not send us the good book.'

Tuesday, 20 July. Five of the Chicasaw Indians (twenty of whom had been in Savannah several days) came to see us, with Mr Andrews, their interpreter. They were all warriors, four of them head men. The two chief were Paustoobee and Mingo Mattaw. Our conference was as follows:

Q. Do you believe there is one above who is over all things?

Paustoobee answered, We believe there are four beloved things above, the clouds, the sun, the clear sky, and He that lives in the clear sky.

Q. Do you believe there is but one that lives in the clear sky?

A. We believe there are two with him, three in all.

Q. Do you think he made the sun and other beloved things?

A. We cannot tell. Who hath seen?

Q. Do you think he made you?

A. We think he made all men at first.

Q. How did he make them at first?

A. Out of the ground.

Q. Do you believe he loves you?

A. I do not know. I cannot see him.

Q. But has he not often saved your life?

A. He has. Many bullets have gone on this side, and many on that side, but he would never let them hurt me. And many bullets have gone into these young men; and yet they are alive!

Q. Then, cannot he save you from your enemies now?

A. Yes, but we know not if he will. We have now so many enemies round about us, that I think of nothing but death. And if I am to die, I shall die, and I will die like a man. But if he will have me to live, I shall live. Though I had ever so many enemies, he can destroy them all.

Q. How do you know that?

A. From what I have seen. When our enemies came against us before, then the beloved clouds came for us. And often much rain, and sometimes hail has come upon them, and that in a very hot day. And I saw, when many French and Choctaws and other nations came against one of our towns; and the ground made a noise under them, and the beloved ones in the air behind them; and they were afraid, and went away, and left their meat and drink and their guns. I tell no lie. All these saw it too.

Q. Have you heard such noises at other times?

A. Yes, often; before and after almost every battle.

Q. What sort of noises were they?

A. Like the noise of drums and guns and shouting.

Q. Have you heard any such lately?

A. Yes: four days after our last battle with the French.

Q. Then you heard nothing before it?

A. The night before, I dreamed I heard many drums up there: and many trumpets there, and much stamping of feet and shouting. Till then I thought we should all die. But then I thought the beloved ones were come to help us. And the next day I heard above a hundred guns go off before the fight began; and I said, 'When the sun is there, the beloved ones will help us; and we shall conquer our enemies.' And we did so.

Q. Do you often think and talk of the beloved ones?

A. We think of them always, wherever we are. We talk of them and to them, at home and abroad; in peace, in war, before and after we fight; and indeed whenever and wherever we meet together.

Q. Where do you think your souls go after death?

A. We believe the souls of red men walk up and down near the place where they died, or where their bodies lie, for we have often heard cries and noises near the place where any prisoners had been burned.

Q. Where do the souls of white men go after death?

A. We cannot tell. We have not seen.

The victim

Thursday, 24 March 1737. In 1733, David Jones, a saddler, a middle-aged man, who had for some time before lived at Nottingham, being at Bristol, met a person there who, after giving him some account of Georgia, asked whether he would go thither? adding, his trade (that of a saddler) was an exceeding good trade there, upon which he might live creditably and comfortably. He objected his want of money to pay his passage and buy some tools, which he should have need of. The gentleman (Cap. W.) told him, he would supply him with that, and hire him a shop when he came to Georgia, wherein he might follow his business, and so repay him as it suited his convenience. Accordingly to Georgia they went; where, soon after his arrival, his master (as he now styled himself) sold him to Mr Lacy, who set him to work with the rest of his servants, in clearing land. He commonly appeared much more thoughtful than the rest, often stealing into the woods alone. He was now sent to do some work on an island, three or four miles from Mr Lacy's great plantation. Thence he desired the other servants to return without him, saying he would stay and kill a deer. This was on Saturday. On Monday they found him on the shore, with his gun by him and the forepart of his head shot to pieces. In his pocket was a paper book; all the leaves thereof were fair, except one, on which ten or twelve verses [lines] were written; two of which were these (which I transcribed thence from his own handwriting):

> Death could not a more sad retinue find;
> Sickness and pain before, and darkness all behind!

Self-doubt

Tuesday, 24 January 1738. I went to America, to convert the Indians; but oh! who shall convert me! Who, what is he that will deliver me from this evil heart of unbelief? I have a fair summer religion; I can talk well; nay, and believe myself, while no danger is near: but let death look me in the face, and my spirit is troubled.

Sunday, 29 January. We saw English land once more, which about noon appeared to be the Lizard Point. We ran by it with a fair wind, and at noon the next day made the west end of the Isle of Wight.

Here the wind turned against us, and in the evening blew fresh, so that we expected (the tide being likewise strong against us) to be driven some leagues backward in the night; but in the morning, to our great surprise, we saw Beachy Head just before us, and found we had gone forwards near forty miles.

Toward evening was a calm; but in the night a strong north wind brought us safe into the Downs. The day before, Mr Whitefield had sailed out, neither of us then knowing any thing of the other. At four in the morning we took boat, and in half an hour landed at Deal: it being Wednesday, February 1, the anniversary festival in Georgia for Mr Oglethorpe's landing there.

It is now two years and almost four months since I left my native country, in order to teach the Georgian Indians the nature of Christianity; but what have I learned myself in the mean time? Why, (what I the least of all suspected,) that I who went to America to convert others, was never myself converted to God. I am not mad, though I thus speak; but I speak the words of truth and soberness; if haply some of those who still dream may awake, and see, that as I am so are they.

Are they read in philosophy? So was I. In ancient or modern tongues? So was I also. Are they versed in the science of divinity? I too have studied it many years. Can they talk fluently upon spiritual things? The very same could I do. Are they plenteous in alms? Behold, I gave all my goods to feed the poor. Do they give of their labour as well as of their substance? I have laboured more abundantly than they all. Are they willing to suffer for their brethren? I have thrown up my friends, reputation, ease, country; I have put my life in my hand, wandering into strange lands; I have given my body to be devoured by the deep, parched up with heat, consumed by toil and weariness ... but does all this make me acceptable to God?

JAMES BOSWELL
(1740–95)

On Monday, 16 May 1763, the youthful Boswell was having tea in the back room of Thomas Davies's bookshop in Russell Street, off Covent Garden, when Dr Johnson came in. Davies, who had been an actor before he became a bookseller, was a good mimic and had entertained Boswell with lifelike performances of Johnson holding forth in his celebrated manner which had made Boswell laugh and long to meet the great man. In the circumstances the snubbing introduction that followed had some justice on Johnson's part. Yet less than three months later the Doctor had grown so attached to this pushy law student from Scotland that he accompanied Boswell all the way to Harwich in a stage-coach in order to say goodbye to him when he sailed for Holland to continue his studies. Shortly before this, while they were sitting in the Mitre tavern and it was pouring with rain outside, Boswell asked Johnson why it was he felt so much easier with him than with his own father (Johnson was then fifty-four – a large, cumbersome, aged-looking man). It was, replied the Doctor, because 'I am a man of the world. I live in the world, and I take, in some degree, the colour of the world as it moves along. Your father is a judge in a remote part of the island, and all his notions are taken from the old world ... besides there must always be a struggle between father and son ...' A day or two later, Boswell notes,

[Johnson] recommended me to keep a journal of my life, full and unreserved. He said it would be a very good exercise, and would yield me great satisfaction when the particulars were faded from my remembrance. I was uncommonly fortunate in having had a previous coincidence with him upon this subject, for I had kept such a journal for some time; and it was no small pleasure to me to have this to tell him and to receive his approbation. He counselled me to keep it private, and said I might surely have a friend who would burn it in case of my death. From this habit I have been enabled to give the world so many anecdotes, which would otherwise be lost to posterity.

From this habit Boswell gave the world something far beyond 'many anecdotes'; a carefully created masterpiece, no less – his *Life of Samuel Johnson, LL.D.,* a biography built out of a diary. It was in a way a joint effort, for Johnson knew that he was being watched and recorded, and reacted accordingly. Boswell too knew how to provoke exciting responses from his majestic subject. Tucked into the *Life* is the entrancing travel book, *The Journal of a Tour to the Hebrides*, in which the popular travel-journal format was transmuted into art.

The full extent of Boswell's genius as a diarist was unsuspected until the publication after the Second World War of the huge cache of his papers discovered at Malahide Castle, under the editorship of the peerless F. A. Pottle of Yale University. *Boswell's London Journal, 1762–63*; *Boswell on the Grand Tour*; *Boswell in Search of a Wife*; *Boswell for the Defense* ... the swift succession of these amazing volumes shattered the Edinburgh lawyer's limited reputation for being a one-book author (he had written much more than the *Life* and the *Journals*, but these other works are forgotten), and made him a unique figure in English literature. No one, before or since, has so fully revealed himself, or with such a writer's skill. How was it that such an apparent extrovert could take such a relentless look at himself, with such power of retrieval? How is it that he continues to show each of us *our*selves? What had Johnson seen in the bumptious 23-year-old that he should tell him to 'keep a journal' which had to be 'full and unreserved'?

While they were in Edinburgh together in 1773, just before setting out for the Hebrides, Johnson left behind in Boswell's house – in an open drawer, along with a pair of pistols which Boswell assured him they would not be needing – 'one volume of a pretty full and curious Diary of his Life, of which I have a few fragments; but the book has been destroyed. I wish female curiosity had been strong enough to have had it all transcribed, which might easily have been done, and I should think the theft, being *pro bono publico*, might have been forgiven. But I may be wrong. My wife told me she never once looked into it. She did not seem quite easy when we left her: but away we went!' What is all this about? Who destroyed most of Johnson's 'curious Diary' for the public good? The uneasy Mrs B.? Johnson himself? The latter, probably. But had Mrs Boswell really not read it?

Turin, Tuesday, 22 January 1765. Needham and Gray breakfasted with me. I was quite easy and genteel. I sent to Mme. S— and begged she would return me my letter. She bid the valet say that she had thrown it in the fire. Here was the extreme of mortification for me. I was quite sunk. Worthy Needham bid me continue to lay up knowledge, and took an affectionate leave of me, hoping we should meet again.

I set out at eleven. As I went out at one of the ports, I saw a crowd running to the execution of a thief. I jumped out of my chaise and went close to the gallows. The criminal stood on a ladder, and a priest held a crucifix before his face. He was tossed over, and hung with his face uncovered, which was hideous. I stood fixed in attention to this spectacle, thinking that the feelings of horror might destroy those of chagrin. But so thoroughly was my mind possessed by the feverish agitation that I did not feel in the smallest degree from the execution. The hangman put his feet on the criminal's head and neck and had him strangled in a minute. I then went into a church and kneeled with great devotion before an altar splendidly lighted up. Here then I felt three successive scenes: raging love – gloomy horror – grand devotion. The horror indeed I only *should* have felt. I jogged on slowly with my *vetturino*, and had a grievous inn at night.

Wednesday, 23 January. I set out by four o'clock. It was cold and wet. I slept all day. My blood stagnated and I was a deplorable being. My inn was again wretched.

Milan, Friday, 26 July. Yesterday my Lord* waked you boldly and showed *erect and tall*.† Quite ludicrous this, but diverting. Drove briskly. Dined at Bergamo ... Disputes with my Lord. He said, 'I

* Lord Mountstuart, his travelling companion.
† See *Paradise Lost*, iv. 288–90.

shall always esteem you, but you're most disagreeable to live with. Sad temper,' &c. Smiled to hear this. Was in strong spirits and afraid of nothing. Before dinner Mallet said, 'The defect of hypochondriacs is that they seize upon an object so strongly from one aspect that they see none of the others. One must accustom one's self to correct that by reason – I mean, to keep one's self from always being convinced by each side of an argument in turn. Your logic is poor. It is more difficult to govern a hypochondriac than a kingdom, because one must be always starting again. You should have employment at Court, write verses, and not marry.' ... At night, Milan; curious sensations. Again dispute with Mallet ... This morning up immediately. Rinse well. Then wash feet and hands with warm water and soap, and all private parts with milk and water. Then have illustrious barber ... Have long conference with my Lord and own being in wrong, not for obstinacy but loose conduct. Say sorry, and you'll be on guard. Bid him be prudent not to say follies of you, as you've been free with him. Get Mallet to make you out character as he promised, neither keeping back bad nor good ...

Fréjus, Wednesday, 18 December. Jogged most sluggishly along. Disputed with Jacob, who said he knew me perfectly and that it was impossible for servants to live well with me, as I was not, like other gentlemen, content with external acquiescence, but would always show them clearly that they were wrong. He is very right. I am always studying human nature and making experiments on the lowest characters, so that I am too much in the secret with regard to the weakness of man in reality, and my honest, impetuous disposition cannot take up with that eternal repetition of fictitious minutiae by which unthinking men of fashion preserve a great distinction between master and servant. By having Jacob so free with me, I have felt as servants do, and been convinced that the greatest part of them laugh in their sleeve very heartily at the parade of their lords, knowing well that eating, drinking, sleeping, and other offices of nature are common to all. Jacob said, 'I believe, Sir, that you have been badly brought up. You have not the manners of a nobleman. Your heart is too open.' I confessed to him that I was two and twenty before I had a servant. Said he, 'The son of a gentleman ought to be accustomed early to command a servant, but reasonably, and never to joke with them; because each must live in his state according to his quality. You, Sir, would live just like a peasant. And you force a servant to speak in a way he shouldn't, because you torment him with questions. You want to get to the bottom of things. Sir, I do not think you should marry. At least, if you marry, you should not live in the same house with your wife; otherwise, *ma foi!* there will shortly be disputes, and a quarrel which cannot be made up. Sir, this is what you should do: marry a lady, give her a certain allowance, and let her have her house where you can go when you find it agreeable and not be inconvenienced; and you must never see your children, or otherwise they will be as badly brought up as you. I hope, Sir, you will not take this in bad part.' The fellow talked thus with so much good sense, so much truth, and with so natural an air, that upon my word I admired him; I, however, hoped that a few years more would temper all that impetuosity and remove all that weakness which now render me inconstant and capricious. At any rate, I have a singular kind of philosophy which will make me content to be whatever I shall turn out.

I came at night to a tolerable inn. I sat up too late writing, and I suppose astonished the people of the house, who are used to see their guests tumble into bed immediately after supper. By the by, the French soft feather beds are destroying me by relaxing my nerves. The inns of this light-headed nation are very seldom good, for the rooms are cold and comfortless and dirty, the sheets damp, and snuffers difficult to be found. Old England live for ever, for thy inns are more excellent than are palaces anywhere else.

London, 23 February 1766. You met at Mitre Dr Goldsmith whom you had before called upon. You both went to Mr Johnson's, who was still bad and would not come out. 'Come then,' said Goldie, 'we will not go to the Mitre tonight, since we can't have the big man with us.' But we had sent for Davies, and I insisted on going. Goldsmith said, 'I think, Mr Johnson, you don't go near the theatres. You give yourself no more concern about a new play than if you had never had anything to do with the stage.'

JOHNSON. 'Why, Sir, our tastes alter. The lad does not care for the child's rattle, and the old man does not care for the young man's whore.' GOLDSMITH. 'Nay, but Sir, your Muse was not a whore.' JOHNSON. 'Sir, I don't think she was. But as we advance in the journey of life, we drop some of the things which have pleased us; whether it be that we are fatigued and don't choose to carry so many things any farther, or that we find other things which we like better.' BOSWELL. 'But, Sir, why don't you give us something in some other way?' GOLDSMITH. 'Ay, Sir, we have a claim upon you.' JOHNSON. 'No, Sir, I am not obliged to do any more. No man is obliged to do as much as he can do. A man is to have part of his life to himself. If a soldier has fought a good many campaigns, he is not to be blamed if he retires to ease and tranquillity. Sir, a physician who has long practised in a great city may be excused if he retires to a small town and takes less practice. Sir, the good I can do by my conversation bears the same proportion to the good I can do by my writings that the practice of a physician, retired to a small town, does to his practice in a great city.' BOSWELL. 'But I wonder, Sir, you have not more pleasure in writing than not.' JOHNSON. 'Sir, you *may* wonder.' In short, Goldsmith and I could make nothing against him.

He talked of making verses. He said, 'The great matter is to know when you have made good ones. I generally have 'em in my mind, perhaps fifty at a time, walking in my room; and then write 'em, and often from laziness wrote only the half lines. Sir, I have written a hundred lines a day. I remember I wrote a hundred lines of *The Vanity of Human Wishes* in a day. Doctor, I made one line t'other day, but I made out no more.' GOLDSMITH. 'Let us hear it, and we'll put a bad one to it.' JOHNSON. 'No, Sir, I have forgot it.'

We left him, and as we were going along Fleet Street, Goldsmith very gravely said, 'Don't you think that head's failed – wearing, eh?' O fine! BOSWELL. 'No, Sir, I think he is rather more impatient of contradiction than he was.' GOLDSMITH. 'Sir, no man is proof against continual adulation.'

Friday, 25 November 1776. I went out a little fretted with some trifling dispute with my wife, saying I would not dine at home. I took myself just as I got into the street, but could not yield. I thought I would punish myself by walking in the fields and fasting; but I had not resolution, so dined at my father's. Claud was there. I drank little, and cannot say I was intoxicated; but my fretfulness worked me, and as I was coming home at five, I met a young slender slut with a red cloak in the street and went with her to Barefoots Parks and madly ventured coition. It was a short and almost insensible gratification of lewdness. I was vexed to think of it.

Tuesday, 26 November. Drank tea at Sir George Preston's. My father came out today to the Court, and was very well.

Wednesday, 27 November. Went out with Commissioner Cochrane in his chaise and dined with him. Nobody there. Somehow it happened that I drank enough to be somewhat intoxicated. I returned in the fly. Quitted it in the Canongate, and in the High Street met a plump hussy who called herself Peggy Grant. It was one of the coldest nights I ever remember. I went with her to a field behind the Register Office, and boldly lay with her. This was desperate risking. I read books at night on the subject of Dr Memis's cause.

Thursday, 28 November. I know not how, my mind was not uneasy at what happened last night. I pleaded in the Inner House against Dr Memis with much gravity and dull attention for about an hour and three quarters. I spoke as long as I decently could, to make the Lords sensible of what I thought an impropriety – making a serious cause of it. My speech was not finished today. I dined at Lord Monboddo's; a dull party; drank very little. Called on Mr Alexander Boswall, who was ill with a fall from his horse, and sat with him near two hours. The girl with whom I was last night had told me she lodged in Stevenlaw's Close, and at my desire engaged to be at the head of it generally at eight in the evening, in case I should be coming past. I thought I could not be in more danger of disease by one more enjoyment the very next evening, so went tonight; but she was not there. Had a consultation at home between eight and nine. Little Davie was now in a fine way. I was shocked that the father of a family should go amongst strumpets; but there was rather an insensibility about me to virtue, I was so sensual. Perhaps I should not write all this. I soothed myself with Old Testament manners.

Sunday, 1 December. Went out to hear Dr Webster, but was too late. Mr Alexander Boswall was now pretty well. He saw me walking in the Parliament Close, and called to me from his sister-in-law's, where he was. I went up and passed the forenoon with him and her and Major Nisbet Balfour and Lieutenant Balfour of Fernie. I was somewhat displeased with Alexander for talking too much, as it kept me from having my curiosity satisfied by the Major. They asked me to dine with them at three; or if I must dine at my father's, to come afterwards and drink. I found Dr Webster at my father's and could not well get away, so dined and drank about half a bottle of claret, and then went with Webster to his kirk and heard David Dickson's son preach. I must *confess* that I planned, even when sober, that I would in the evening try to find Peggy Grant, and, as I had risked with her, take a full enjoyment. After sermon I went to Mr Boswall's. Mr Alexander drank none. But the two Balfours and I drank a great deal. My mind was agitated by hearing General Howe's aide-de-camp talk (I am now writing on Tuesday the 3 December) of all the various incidents of war, and, seeing my keenness, tell me I should have been a soldier. I was much intoxicated. I drank tea with Mrs Boswall. About eight I got into the street and made Cameron, the chairman, inquire for Peggy Grant at a house in Stevenlaw's Close where she had told me she lived. He brought her out, and I took her to the New Town, and in a mason's shade in St Andrew's Square lay with her twice. I grew pretty sober by the time I got home, but was in a confused, feverish frame. My dear wife asked me if I had not been about mischief. I at once confessed it. She was very uneasy, and I was ashamed and vexed at my licentiousness. Yet my conscience was not alarmed; so much had I accustomed my mind to think such indulgence permitted.

JOHN BYNG
5TH VISCOUNT TORRINGTON
(1743–1813)

'Tour writing is the very rage of the times,' wrote Byng in 1782 as he jogged west on his horse Vestris, refusing to buy a newspaper from the tollgate man at Hyde Park, ignoring the threat of a storm and eventually reaching the inn at Bagshot where, two years earlier, he had stayed with his wife. He was now on his own and glad of it. For twenty more years he would ride about England to escape from her fashionable presence and from her lover William Windham. He didn't dislike her. It was simply that for him she was part of an England which was going to the dogs, she and her frippery. It was for her that he kept a tour-diary – to show her another England.

Byng made a dozen tours, the furthest of these to the North in 1792, and they all reveal a good-natured man's philosophy of the open road, plus a lasting lament for the country's moral and economic decline. His personality was that of the classic bluff, sentimental, intelligent but anti-intellectual patriot, rooted in rural tradition. He could deplore Sunday Schools which taught the common people to read and write, but his conduct towards the innumerable ordinary folk he met with on his travels is affectionate and easy-going, and wholly without snobbery. As a soldier turned civil servant, Byng considered he was unsuccessful. Straight from the regiment into the Inland Revenue office at Somerset House, that had been his fate. He rued it in a little rhyme:

> His early days were spent in Camps,
> His latter days were pass'd at Stamps.

Although he writes a great deal about his son, destined to be the Regency character 'Poodle' Byng, he is cool and reticent on his family generally. His uncle had been the unfortunate Admiral Byng who, according to Voltaire, had been executed to encourage the others. Another uncle had looked exactly like the King of Prussia, 'the same round, smooth unmeaning Face, and the same little mischievous Nose', and had brought him up, not pleasantly. At twenty-four Byng had married the wildly eccentric Julia Forrest, whose free talk shocked society, and they had produced twelve children. All the same, because of Windham, Byng was a famous cuckold.

Byng died only a few weeks after succeeding to the title. His enormous diary lay undisturbed at Yates Court in Kent until just after the First World War, when it was bought at auction and re-sold to a bookseller who stupidly disposed of the twenty-four volumes piecemeal. Volumes were found in the Bodleian Library, in various country houses, vicarages, public libraries and second-hand bookshops. Their publication in 1934 under the editorship of C. B. Andrews, in the heyday of 'open road' literature, was quite an event. Sir Arthur Bryant said that they 'left us a picture of England ... which is among the great treasures of our social history'. He saw Byng as a forerunner of the Romantic Revival, of the Oxford Movement, and of the nineteenth-century piety and scholarship that restored to England a proper realization of its noble Gothic heritage.

1782. Tour writing is the very rage of the times; it is selldom that I am in the fashion, but fashions change so quickly that I am obliged, in their round, sometimes to find myself a man of mode. Every one now describes the manners and customs of every county thro' which they pass, tho' but from an observation in a Margate-Hoy; and new Yoricks monthly improve our minds with their sentimental effusions. However whilst this description-passion continues, it may be the means of informing ignorant owners, of what treasures of antiquity they possess; and of stimulating them to the proper pride of guarding, and preserving those remaining monuments of religion, and grandeur, which have escaped the ravages of reformation, and civil wars; and the yet more barbarous neglect of tasteless masters.

I dread not the reviewers, as I shall never hazard a bookseller's window; for the grocer, do I waste so much white paper; my reviewers are in my own house; and it is from Mrs B.'s assenting nod, and the (flattering) approbation of Harriet, that I receive the bays; wishing my descriptions to be, what most of my country-women are, elegant, neat and engaging; full of decency, simplicity and fancy; not tricked out with false taste, and French trimmings: to such an imitation the pen must naturally soar, and study to adhere to the model itself proposed.

I would have desired Mrs B. to assist me in my journals, but from the recollection of a story of a sea captain, who observing (on shipboard) two boys aloft, call'd out: 'Jack, what are you doing there?' 'I am doing nothing at all,' says Jack. 'And what are you doing there, Will?' 'I am only helping Jack, Sir' . . .

Were I to publish, I should experience the same fate, that a Clerk of the Treasury did, with a tour made in six weeks to Marseilles and back; so that he had seen nothing but on the gallop . . .

Lewes, 22 August 1788. The ancient church of St John has lately undergone a destructive reparation (destructive I mean to the antiquary) for then all the brasses, stain'd glass, and any thing moveable, fall a prey to the masons, and glaziers.

The key not being to be found I saved sixpence; nor was the inside worth seeing; on the outside are placed, as the stoppers up of an archway, two old stone coffin lids, around one of which is a curious inscription to the memory of a Danish warrior: antiquity can go no further back.

Then I crossed the river, to where resides Mr Segt Kemp, (*'in a shady, cool, retreat'*,) opposite to the old small church of St Morland; when the returning rain drove me for shelter into a venerable looking cottage, with an arched stone entrance, and an iron-guarded door; wherein were a woman, and her two children – she said she was the wife of Mr K.'s huntsman; was very civil, brought me pen and ink for my journalizing, and told me that her house was supposed to belong to the fryars; and probably it might have been a cell belonging to the priory, and the large house a residence of the priors. How wretched do the miseries of a cottage appear! (and this was only of comparative distress;) want of food, want of fuel, want of clothing! Children perishing of an ague! and an unhappy mother unable to attend to, or relieve their wants, or assuage their pains; nor to allow time sufficient even for the reparation of their rags; whilst the worn-down melancholy father (perhaps a shepherd) pinch'd by cold, and pining with despair, returns at evening close, to a hut devoid of comfort, or the smallest renovation of hope: for no longer are left the fost'ring, forgiving hand of his landlord, or the once bountiful buttery of the manor house, to apply to!

All the rich and gay world, huddled together in London, on Turkey carpets, before register stoves, can but little conceive the pangs of poverty; and what mischiefs they inflict: what benefits they withold; and what true grandeur and felicities they forego; by thus sacrificing their lives, and fortunes, in the company of vitious women of quality, and rascally politicians!

Woolsthorpe, 7 June 1789. As I proceed in Tour Writing, and Print-Pasting, I get Bold and Vain, Believing that all Diaries become Valuable from Age; tho' I often Revert to some sad Diaries I have read, or heard of, as one of a punctual woman, who wrote:

> Friday.   Buried my poor dear Husband.
> Saturday. Turned my *Ass* to Grass.

and tho' this is ludicrous, yet with over Study, and devoid of Nature, what does Tour Writing or any other Writing become?

Tourists should think for themselves, and forget what they have read, for sadly do Recollection and Invention Clash. If possible, I wish to glean my own Remarks, and pick up the few ears that the rich Farmer-Tourist may have left. Descriptions should fall from the Eye upon The Heart; so that the Ignorant might feel, and the Scientific acknowledge the Truth of every Page . . .

Buxton, 17 June 1790. In the evening I took a walk to Mr Arkwrights great cotton mill, at a small distance from the town; and wou'd have enter'd it, but entrance was denied, for this (no doubt right) reason, however, odd, 'That I shou'd disturb the girls'! It is work'd from a noble pool of water; Mr A.'s house adjoins it, placed under a steep hill, with a pleasant view.

Cold ham, and cold veal pye for supper. I had no one to speak to, my writing was quickly exhausted, and so I strove to think; but I (*now*) hate thinking; I left London to avoid thinking; in youth, people won't think, and when they grow into years it is of no use! But I will think that I never was in a nastier house, or a more gloomy place; everything dirty . . .

Buxton, 18 June. One of the worst things in small inns is the being obliged to hear the odious merriment and sad singings in the kitchen. These cotton mills, seven stories high, and fill'd with inhabitants, remind me of a first rate man of war; and when they are lighted up, on a dark night, look most luminously beautiful.

Rochdale, 24 June 1792. Arrived at — Bridge upon the river (Calder) around which are numberless coalpits, for the whole country seems to be a bed of coal; crossing a common, we pass'd by the village of Accrington, where they are building rows of houses, as every vale swarms with cotton mills; some not bigger than cottages – for any little stream, by the means of a reservoir, will supply them. (Cotton mills have chosen the Old Abbey situations; in the abbies there was religion, and decency; in the cotton mills, blasphemy, and immorality. Religion might have overstretch'd her power, and intention; and was blown up: I hope the cotton trade will flourish; but it may crack! And then they must be converted into work houses? No corn is rais'd where cotton mills abound; for no hands could be found for agriculture; so all the flour is brought from a distance; and wonderful is the import of wheat, to Liverpool, from America, &c!)

We crawl'd up a stoney lane to reach the Rochdale road, which was very bad, and over a wild moor, till the hill which descends into Rochdale! The rain now came on, but I was consoled by the thoughts of a good inn. All round Rochdale they are building away – and have swell'd it from a small market town into a great city.

LORD BYRON
(1788–1824)

'This journal is a relief. When I am tired – as I generally am – out it comes, and down goes every thing. But I can't read it over; and God knows what contradictions it may contain. If I am sincere with myself (but I fear one lies more to one's self than to any one else), every page should confute, refute, and utterly abjure its predecessor . . .' So Byron the diarist on a December day in 1813. Three weeks earlier, swamped with ennui, he had written, 'Well, – I have had my share of what are called the pleasures of this life, and have seen more of the European and Asiatic world than I have made a good use of. They say "Virtue is its own reward", – it certainly should be paid well for its trouble. At five-and-twenty, when the better part of life is over, one should be *something*; – and what am I? nothing but five-and-twenty – and the odd months.'

Byron was in fact a very great deal more than just a jaded and no longer very young man. He was the author of *Childe Harold* and the toast of London, a radical genius who the previous year had rattled the House of Lords with his magnificent speech during the debate on the Frame-work Bill, and an extraordinarily handsome aristocrat-poet whose private life was so sexually honest as to compromise the existing conventions.

Like everything else he wrote, his journal was dashed down at high speed, though he declared that this did not indicate ease and facility, and that, contrary to what was believed about being able to write fast, for him it required an intense effort. The dashes and misplaced commas are not a sign of the pen lagging behind the brain but of his acknowledged difficulties with punctuation, an art which always lay beyond his grasp. So Byron's journal races on, helter-skelter, but with bite, glorious colour and the sinewy energy only to be found in a narrator of the first rank. He is reckless, audacious and tender all at once, and often wildly humorous. Idealism gleams beneath the sophistry. So do the massively romanticized landscapes of early nineteenth-century Europe. Byron has a head and a heart – and a nerve. His liveliness is infectious, his glooms either operatic or unbearably real. His short life, from his birth in a house whose site lies somewhere below John Lewis's shop in Oxford Street to his death in the marshes of Missolonghi, was turbulent and restless, fame and infamy tumbling over each other, the poetry itself a river-flood, his politics advanced and urgent, and his lovers – his half-sister Augusta, John Edleston, Countess Guiccioli the chief among many – were never absent, from boyhood on. Besides their unrivalled confession of emotion and descriptions of action, Byron's journals have a grand worldliness. They are fiercely anti-cant and they move with dramatic swiftness through various phases of freedom – freedom from a wife who wanted to cage him, from sexual restrictions, from Regency Britain and its reaction, for *la dolce vita* in Italy and, finally, freedom to fight for the liberation of Greece from the Turks. Byron's journals echo with the sound of shackles being broken. They are glittering and poignant. Byron's motto was *Trust Byron*. Trust him certainly in his 'scribblings', as he explained his dashed-down diary. It has to be read alongside his letters for its full effect.

From the Alpine Journal *written for Augusta Leigh*

19 September 1816. . . . left our quadrupeds with a Shepherd – & ascended further – came to some snow in patches – upon which my forehead's perspiration fell like rain making the same dints as in a sieve – the chill of the wind & the snow turned me giddy – but I scrambled on & upwards – *H*. went to the highest *pinnacle* – I did not – but paused within a few yards (at an opening of the Cliff) – in coming down the Guide tumbled three times – I fell a laughing & tumbled too – the descent luckily soft though steep & slippery – H. also fell – but nobody hurt. The whole of the Mountain superb – the shepherd on a very steep & high cliff playing upon his *pipe* – very different from Arcadia – (where I saw the pastors with a long Musquet instead of a Crook – and pistols in their Girdles) – our Swiss Shepherd's pipe was sweet – & his time agreeable – saw a cow strayed – told that they often break their necks on & over the crags – descended to Montbovon – pretty scraggy village with a wild river – and a wooden bridge. – H. went to fish – caught one –

our carriage not come − our horses − mules &c. knocked up −
ourselves fatigued − (but so much the better − I shall sleep). The
view from the highest point of today's journey comprized on one
side the greatest part of Lake Leman − on the other − the valleys &
mountains of the Canton Fribourg − and an immense plain with the
Lakes of Neufchatel & Morat − and all which the borders of these
and of the Lake of Geneva inherit − we had both sides of the Jura
before us in one point of view, with Alps in plenty. − In passing a
ravine − the Guide recommended strenuously a quickening of pace
− as the stones fall with great rapidity & occasional damage − the
advice is excellent − but like most good advice impracticable − the
road being so rough in this precise point − that neither mules nor
mankind − nor horses − can make any violent progress. − Passed
without any fractures or menace thereof. − The music of the Cows'
bells (for their wealth like the Patriarchs is cattle) in the pastures
(which reach to a height far above any mountains in Britain −) and
the Shepherds' shouting to us from crag to crag & playing on their
reeds where the steeps appeared almost inaccessible, with the surrounding scenery − realized all that I have ever heard or imagined
of a pastoral existence − much more so than Greece or Asia Minor
− for there we are a little too much of the sabre & musquet order −
and if there is a Crook in one hand, you are sure to see a gun in the
other − but this was pure and unmixed − solitary − savage and
patriarchal − the effect I cannot describe − as we went they played
the 'Ranz de Vaches' and other airs by way of farewell. − I have
lately repeopled my mind with Nature.

24 September. Set out at seven − up at five − passed the black
Glacier − the Mountain Wetterhorn on the right − crossed the
Scheideck mountain − came to the Rose Glacier − said to be the
largest & finest in Switzerland. − *I* think the Bossons Glacier at
Chamouni − as fine − H. does not − came to the Reichenback
waterfall − two hundred feet high − halted to rest the horses −
arrived in the valley of Oberhasli − rain came on − drenched a little
− only 4 hours rain however in 8 days − came to Lake of Brientz −
then to town of Brientz − changed − H. hurt his head against door.
− In the evening four Swiss Peasant Girls of Oberhasli came & sang
the airs of their country − two of the voices beautiful − the tunes

also – they sing too that *Tyrolese air* & song which you love – Augusta – because I love it – & I love because you love it – they are still singing – Dearest – you do not know how I should have liked this – were you with me – the airs are so wild & original & at the same time of great sweetness. – The singing is over – but below stairs I hear the notes of a Fiddle which bode no good to my nights rest. – The Lord help us! – I shall go down & see the dancing. –

25 September. The whole town of Brientz were apparently gathered together in the rooms below – pretty music – & excellent Waltzing – none but peasants – the dancing much better than in England – the English can't Waltz – never could – nor ever will. – One man with his pipe in his mouth – but danced as well as the others – some other dances in pairs – and in fours – and very good. – I went to bed but the revelry continued below late & early. – Brientz but a village. – Rose early. – Embarked on the Lake of Brientz. – Rowed by women in a long boat – one very young & very pretty – seated myself by her – & began to row also – presently we put to shore & another woman jumped in – it seems it is the custom here for the boats to be *manned by women* – for of five men & three women in our bark – all the women took an oar – and but one man. Got to Interlachen in three hours – pretty Lake – not so large as that of Thoun. – Dined at Interlachen – Girl gave me some flowers – & made me a speech in German – of which I know nothing – I do not know whether the speech was pretty but as the woman was – I hope so. – Saw another – very pretty too – and *tall* which I prefer – I hate short women – for more reasons than one. – Reembarked on the Lake of Thoun – fell asleep part of the way – sent our horses round – found people on the shore blowing up a rock with gunpowder – they blew it up near our boat – only telling us a minute before – mere stupidity – but they might have broke our noddles. – Got to Thoun in the Evening – the weather has been tolerable the whole day – but as the wild part of our tour is finished, it don't matter to us – in all the desirable part – we have been most lucky in warmth & clearness of Atmosphere – for which 'Praise we the Lord.' –

26 September. Being out of the mountains my journal must be as flat as my journey. – From Thoun to Bern good road – hedges –

villages – industry – prosperity – and all sorts of tokens of insipid civilization. – From Bern to Fribourg. – Different Canton – Catholics – passed a field of Battle – Swiss beat the French – in one of the late wars against the French Republic. – Bought a dog – a very ugly dog – but *'tres mechant'*. this was his great recommendation in the owner's eyes & mine – for I mean him to watch the carriage – he hath no tail – & is called 'Mutz' – which signifies *'Short-tail'* –he is apparently of the Shepherd dog genus! – The greater part of this tour has been on horseback – on foot – or on mule; – the Filly (which is one of two young horses I bought of the Baron de Vincy) carried me very well – she is young and as quiet as anything of her sex can be – very goodtempered – and perpetually neighing – when she wants any thing – which is every five minutes – I have called her *Biche* – because her manners are not unlike a little dog's – but she is a very tame – pretty childish quadruped. –

29 [28] September. Passed through a fine & flourishing country – but not mountainous – in the evening reached Aubonne (the entrance & bridge something like that of Durham) which commands by far the fairest view of the Lake of Geneva – twilight – the Moon on the Lake – a grove on the height – and of very noble trees. – Here Tavernier (the Eastern traveller) bought (or built) the Chateau because the site resembled and equalled that of *Erivan* (a frontier city of Persia) here he finished his voyages – and I this little excursion – for I am within a few hours of Diodati – & have little more to see – & no more to say. – In the weather for this tour (of 13 days) I have been very fortunate – fortunate in a companion (Mr H[obhous]e) fortunate in our prospects – and exempt from even the little petty accidents & delays which often render journeys in a less wild country – disappointing. – I was disposed to be pleased – I am a lover of Nature – and an Admirer of Beauty – I can bear fatigue – & welcome privation – and have seen some of the noblest views in the world. – But in all this – the recollections of bitterness – & more especially of recent & more home desolation – which must accompany me through life – have preyed upon me here – and neither the music of the Shepherd – the crashing of the Avalanche – nor the torrent – the mountain – the Glacier – the Forest – nor the Cloud – have for one moment – lightened the weight upon my heart – nor enabled me to lose my own wretched identity in the majesty & power and the Glory – around – above – & beneath me. – I am past reproaches – and there is a time for all things – I am past the wish of vengeance – and I know of none like for what I have suffered – but the hour will come – when what I feel must be felt – & the – but enough. – To you – dearest Augusta – I send – and *for* you – I have kept this record of what I have seen & felt. – Love me as you are beloved by me. –

WILLIAM BECKFORD
(1759–1844)

Beckford's travel-diaries, *Dreams, Waking Thoughts and Incidents* (1783; revised by him in 1834) and the superb *Recollections of an Excursion to the Monasteries of Alcobaça and Batalha* (1835), reveal a writer of astonishing descriptive power. He has been called the archetypal millionaire eccentric and is remembered chiefly for a strange romance entitled *Vathek: An Arabian Tale*, and for the fantastic palace which he built – and deserted – on Salisbury Plain, Fonthill. But for the modern reader to come to some comprehension of Beckford it is necessary to accompany him on his princely progress through Europe, and especially through Portugal.

Beckford was the son of a Lord Mayor of London who was a close friend of John Wilkes and who had inherited an immense fortune from the family's West Indian investments. The brother of the founder of this fortune appears in Pepys's diary as the 'slop seller', i.e. a manufacturer of baggy clothes for sailors and workmen. He was as a matter of fact a successful clothier who was knighted. The writer was only ten when he inherited a million pounds sterling, vast estates in London, Wiltshire and Bedfordshire, the Jamaican properties and some £100,000 a year – riches which in eighteenth-century terms were scarcely calculable. Brilliantly educated by tutors, with Pitt as one of his godfathers and the world before him, Beckford's future was glorious in the extreme. But a

teenage passion for a younger boy, William Courtenay (afterwards
Earl of Devon), ruined all his prospects, and there is in Beckford's
hounding from society, flight south, flamboyance and grandeur a
suggestion of Byron. Romney's portrait of Courtenay, painted
during the height of Beckford's attraction, has a teazle in the foreground.

This disaster was the making of Beckford as an artist. Unable to
proceed in the conventional way, he wrote and built. His wonderful
travel-diaries are monuments to Augustan taste, style and emotion.
They are opulent, sombre and sensuous. Beckford, miraculously,
ran through the better part of his wealth and ended up in – for
him – modest circumstances in Bath.

A dinner invitation in Portugal

Cintra, 12 September 1787. I was hardly up before the grand prior
and Mr Street were announced: the latter abusing kings, queens,
and princes, with all his might, and roaring after liberty and
independence; the former complaining of fogs and damps.

As soon as the advocate for republicanism had taken his departure,
we went by appointment to the archbishop confessor's, and were
immediately admitted into his *sanctum sanctorum*, a snug apartment
communicating by a winding staircase with that of the queen, and
hung with bright, lively tapestry. A lay-brother, fat, round, buffoon-
ical, and to the full as coarse and vulgar as any carter or muleteer in
christendom, entertained us with some very amusing, though not
the most decent, palace stories, till his patron came forth.

Those who expect to see the Grand Inquisitor of Portugal, a
doleful, meagre figure, with eyes of reproof and malediction, would
be disappointed. A pleasanter or more honest countenance than
that kind heaven had blessed him with, one has seldom the comfort
of looking upon. He received me in the most open, cordial manner,
and I have reason to think I am in mighty favour.

We talked about archbishops in England being married. 'Pray,'
said the prelate, 'are not your archbishops strange fellows? conse-
crated in ale-houses, and good bottle companions? I have been told
that madcap Lord Tyrawley was an archbishop at home.' You may

imagine how much I laughed at this inconceivable nonsense; and though I cannot say, speaking of his right reverence, that 'truths divine came mended from his tongue', it may be allowed, that nonsense itself became more conspicuously nonsensical, flowing from so revered a source.

Whilst we sat in the windows of the saloon, listening to a band of regimental music, we saw Joaô Antonio de Castro, the ingenious mechanician, who invented the present method of lighting Lisbon, two or three solemn dominicans, and a famous court fool in a tawdry gala-suit, bedizened with mock orders, coming up the steps which lead to the great audience-chamber, all together. 'Ay, ay,' said the lay-brother, who is a shrewd, comical fellow, 'behold a true picture of our customers. Three sorts of persons find their way most readily into this palace; men of superior abilities, buffoons, and saints; the first soon lose what cleverness they possessed, the saints become martyrs, and the buffoons alone prosper.'

To all this the Archbishop gave his hearty assent by a very significant nod of the head; and being, as I have already told you, in a most gracious, communicative disposition, would not permit me to go away, when I rose up to take leave of him.

'No, no,' said he, 'don't think of quitting me yet awhile. Let us repair to the hall of Swans, where all the court are waiting for me, and pray tell me then what you think of our great fidalgos.'

Taking me by the tip of the fingers he led me along through a number of shady rooms and dark passages to a private door, which opened from the queen's presence-chamber, into a vast saloon, crowded, I really believe, by half the dignitaries of the kingdom; here were bishops, heads of orders, secretaries of state, generals, lords of the bedchamber, and courtiers of all denominations, as fine and as conspicuous as embroidered uniforms, stars, crosses, and gold keys could make them.

The astonishment of this group at our sudden apparition was truly laughable, and indeed, no wonder; we must have appeared on the point of beginning a minuet – the portly archbishop in his monastic, flowing white drapery, spreading himself out like a turkey in full pride, and myself bowing and advancing in a sort of *pas-grave*, blinking all the while like an owl in sunshine, thanks to my rapid transition from darkness to the most glaring daylight.

Down went half the party upon their knees, some with petitions and some with memorials; those begging for places and promotions, and these for benedictions, of which my revered conductor was by no means prodigal. He seemed to treat all these eager demonstrations of fawning servility with the most contemptuous composure, and pushing through the crowd which divided respectfully to give us passage, beckoned the Viscount Ponte de Lima, the Marquis of Lavradio, the Count d'Obidos, and two or three of the lords in waiting, into a mean little room, not above twenty by fourteen.

After a deal of adulatory complimentation in a most subdued tone from the circle of courtiers, for which they had got nothing in return but rebuffs and gruntling, the Archbishop drew his chair close to mine, and said with a very distinct and audible pronunciation, 'My dear Englishman, these are all a parcel of flattering scoundrels, do not believe one word they say to you. Though they glitter like gold, mud is not meaner – I know them well. Here,' continued he, holding up the flap of my coat, 'is proof of English prudence, this little button to secure the pocket is a precious contrivance, especially in grand company, do not leave it off, do not adopt any of our fashions, or you will repent it.'

This sally of wit was received with the most resigned complacency by those who had inspired it, and, staring with all my eyes, and listening with all my ears, I could hardly credit either upon seeing the most complaisant gesticulations, and hearing the most abject protestations of devoted attachment to his right reverence's sacred person from all the company.

There is no saying how long this tide of adulation would have continued pouring on, if it had not been interrupted by a message from the queen, commanding the confessor's immediate attendance. Giving his garments a hearty shake, he trudged off bawling out to me over his shoulder, 'I shall be back in half-an-hour, and you must dine with me.' – 'Dine with him!' exclaimed the company in chorus: 'such an honour never befel any one of us; how fortunate! how distinguished you are!'

DAVID LIVINGSTONE
(1813–73)

Livingstone's travel-journals combine scientific records and simple decency towards his fellow men with equal splendour, and as a lesson in kindness and endurance have never been surpassed. There is something mighty about them, something unreachable by the rest of us. Factual, unpretentious, noble, they stunned the Victorians and they disturb us; especially as the last scraps of the colonial idea totter to oblivion. Livingstone was the great-great-grandson of a Highlander slaughtered on Culloden Moor while fighting for Prince Charlie. His father sold tea in a small way and the great explorer himself started work at the age of ten as a 'piecer' in a cotton-mill, educating himself with books propped up on his spinning-jenny. His childhood's few spare hours were spent searching for plants and minerals, and he was twenty before religion claimed him, when he vowed to spend the rest of his life alleviating human misery. After putting himself through a university course on a cotton-spinner's wages – and being mocked for his pretensions – he became a doctor, then a medical missionary, sailing for the Cape a little over a fortnight after his ordination. He was twenty-seven.

Thus began the epic decades of exploration, first to carry the Gospel but soon for the sake of discovery itself. The moral impetus was a desire to destroy the Boer and Arab slave trades, the emotional one to see what a white man had never seen before. The black men were entranced by him as, fearless and restless, and frequently very ill, he mapped their lands virtually single-handed. He was now more the hero of the Royal Geographic Society than the servant of the London Missionary Society, which he left in 1857.

Livingstone was a most scrupulous diary-keeper, and a 'very large Lett's Diary, sealed up' was entrusted to H. M. Stanley to bring back to England after their celebrated encounter. A year or so later the devoted Susi and Chuma made certain that not only their beloved friend's roughly embalmed corpse should reach Westminster Abbey, but the tin trunk containing the wonderful last journals should arrive home safely; the poignancy of the journals overwhelmed Victorian England. Susi, the Shupanga tribesman who was with Livingstone when he died and who had been his friend and servant, and Chuma, the lad whom Livingstone had rescued from slavery, were unable to be present at his funeral.

When Livingstone ran out of notebooks he sewed ancient newspapers together and wrote across the type in ink made from tree juices. 'It is not all pleasure this exploration,' he wrote a few days before his death. As Livingstone's body and the journals were carried to the coast, the British, French and Germans were poised to 'enlighten' Africa in the great Empire race.

From Nyassaland towards Tanganyika

18 September 1866. From Pima's village we had a fine view of Pamalombé and the range of hills on its western edge, the range which flanks the lower part of Nyassa, – on part of which Mukaté lives, – the gap of low land south of it behind which Shirwa Lake lies, and Chikala and Zomba nearly due south from us. People say hippopotami come from Lake Shirwa into Lake Nyassa. There is a great deal of vegetation in Pamalombé, gigantic rushes, duckweed, and great quantities of aquatic plants on the bottom; one slimy translucent plant is washed ashore in abundance. Fish become very fat on these plants; one called 'kadiakola' I eat much of; it has a good mass of flesh on it.

It is probable that the people of Lake Tanganyika and Nyassa, and those on the Rivers Shiré and Zambesi, are all of one stock, for the dialects vary very little. I took observations on this point. An Arab slave-party, hearing of us, decamped.

19 September. When we had proceeded a mile this morning we came to 300 or 400 people making salt on a plain impregnated with it. They lixiviate the soil and boil the water, which has filtered through a bunch of grass in a hole in the bottom of a pot, till all is evaporated and a mass of salt left. We held along the plain till we came to Mponda's, a large village, with a stream running past. The plain at the village is very fertile, and has many large trees on it.

The cattle of Mponda are like fatted Madagascar beasts, and the hump seems as if it would weigh 100 lbs. The size of body is so enormous that their legs, as remarked by our men, seemed very small. Mponda is a blustering sort of person, but immensely interested in everything European. He says that he would like to go with me. 'Would not care though he were away ten years.' I say that he may die in the journey. – 'He will die here as well as there, but he will see all the wonderful doings of our country.' He knew me, having come to the boat, to take a look *incognito* when we were here formerly.

We found an Arab slave-party here, and went to look at the slaves; seeing this, Mponda was alarmed lest we should proceed to violence in his town, but I said to him that we went to look only. Eighty-five slaves were in a pen formed of dura stalks (*Holcus sorghum*). The majority were boys of about eight or ten years of age; others were grown men and women. Nearly all were in the taming-stick; a few of the younger ones were in thongs, the thong passing round the neck of each. Several pots were on the fires cooking dura and beans. A crowd went with us, expecting a scene, but I sat down, and asked a few questions about the journey, in front. The slave-party consisted of five or six half-caste coast Arabs, who said that they came from Zanzibar; but the crowd made such a noise that we could not hear ourselves speak. I asked if they had any objections to my looking at the slaves, the owners pointed out the different slaves, and said that after feeding them, and accounting for the losses in the way to the coast, they made little by the trip. I suspect that the gain is made by those who ship them to the ports of Arabia, for at Zanzibar most of the younger slaves we saw went at about seven dollars a head. I said to them it was a bad business altogether. They presented fowls to me in the evening.

10 March 1867. I have been ill of fever ever since we left Moamba's; every step I take jars in the chest, and I am very weak; I can scarcely keep up the march, though formerly I was always first, and had to hold in my pace not to leave the people altogether. I have a constant singing in the ears, and can scarcely hear the loud tick of the chronometers. The appetite is good, but we have no proper food, chiefly maëre meal or beans, or mapemba or ground-nuts, rarely a fowl.

The country is full of hopo-hedges, but the animals are harassed, and we never see them.

11 March. Detained by a set-in rain. Marks on masses of dolomite elicited the information that a party of Londa smiths came once to this smelting ground and erected their works here. We saw an old iron furnace, and masses of haematite, which seems to have been the ore universally used.

12 March. Rain held us back for some time, but we soon reached Chibué, a stockaded village. Like them all, it is situated by a stream, with a dense clump of trees on the waterside of some species of mangrove. They attain large size, have soft wood, and succulent leaves; the roots intertwine in the mud, and one has to watch that he does not step where no roots exist, otherwise he sinks up to the thigh. In a village the people feel that we are on their property, and crowd upon us inconveniently; but outside, where we usually erect our sheds, no such feeling exists, we are each on a level, and they don't take liberties.

The Balungu are marked by three or four little knobs on the temples, and the lobes of the ears are distended by a piece of wood, which is ornamented with beads; bands of beads go across the forehead and hold up the hair.

Chibué's village is at the source of the Lokwéna, which goes N. and N.E.; a long range of low hills is on our N.E., which are the Mambwé, or part of them. The Chambezé rises in them, but further south. Here the Lokwéna, round whose source we came on starting this morning to avoid wet feet, and all others north and west of this, go to the Lofu or Lobu, and into Liemba Lake. Those from the hills on our right go east into the Loanzu and so into the Lake.

15 March. We now are making for Kasonso, the chief of the Lake, and a very large country all around it, passing the Lochenjé, five yards wide, and knee deep, then to the Chañumba. All flow very rapidly just now and are flooded with clean water. Everyone carries an axe, as if constantly warring with the forest. My long-continued fever ill disposes me to enjoy the beautiful landscape. We are evidently on the ridge, but people have not a clear conception of where the rivers run.

19 March. A party of young men came out of the village near which we had encamped to force us to pay something for not going into their village. 'The son of a great chief ought to be acknowledged,' &c. They had their bows and arrows with them, and all ready for action. I told them we had remained near them because they said we could not reach Kasonso that day. Their headman had given us nothing. After talking a while, and threatening to do a deal to-morrow, they left, and through an Almighty Providence nothing was attempted . . .

31 March and 1 April. This is the south-eastern end of Liemba, or, as it is sometimes called, Tanganyika . . .

WILLIAM CORY
(1823–92)

William Cory the poet ('Heraclitus') kept a holiday diary for those special pupil-disciples of his at Eton who, like Miss Jean Brodie's favoured girls, he intended to send out into the world with his mark, as it were. It was to be a fine, patrician, high-minded mark and it certainly was to have a lifelong influence on the future statesmen, proconsuls and churchmen who came under his spell. 'I write journals for one or two friends,' he told a new boy, 'so now I offer you, as a sign of friendship and confidence, my prose sentimentalities . . . they would, perhaps, convince you that I am not . . . a bit blasé or embittered or "torified".' After his death these young men, now beginning to run the Empire, acknowledged their debt to the patrician Cory and his complex emotional platonism, wit and charm by publishing the holiday journals he had written for them.

Born William Johnson, Cory had been teaching at Eton for nearly thirty years when the crash came. His special friendships were deplored and he had to resign. In 1878, in his mid fifties, he began to 'explore that *terra incognita*, girlhood', married a Miss Rosa de Carteret Guille and went to live in Madeira until the sad, tubercular expatriates who surrounded them drove the couple back to Britain and a few last years in Hampstead.

Cory saw his role as a civilizer of the ruling class. In 1872 Eton put a sudden check to it. Immensely buoyant, he recovered very quickly – 'I am not well; and half my time I meditate the ceremony of dying, but the other half I bud with schemes for the enjoyment of my liberty.' He left his successor an enlightened little treatise on the art of teaching. Eton scraped his name from the spines of his books, but they still sing his 'Boating Song'.

14 August 1865. They talked about the custom of sitting to drink wine after dinner, peculiar to Englishmen. The Count made me laugh with his account of Lord Malmesbury entertaining foreigners, and, as it is his habit to think aloud, saying to himself, 'Shall we go out all together or not?' Mrs Disraeli was sitting next to him, and, thinking he meant the Tory Ministry, exclaimed, clasping her hands (at least the Count clasped his), 'Oh dear, I trust to God, not!' . . .

Chartres, 10 April 1868. I left off at Chartres. We went to church with the Papists. I had a British Prayer Book. Entered by the famous and well-remembered North Transept Gate, a triple cavern peopled with big Saints. We stood meekly watching the procession: there were stout choristers in red and stout ones in black, with short surplices; there were officials with embroideries stiff and flat on their backs, like the 'sandwich' men who carry placards on their fronts and backs at a Marylebone election; there was a yellow bishop whose mitre looked uncanny, yet somewhat poetical: as they swung round a corner from south aisle to main nave going eastward, they were slovenly and even rollicking: Elliot judged them severely from the drill point of view; I compared them unfortunately with the sublime purity and slow stateliness of our white-surpliced choristers singing at midnight with torches, 'I am the Resurrection and the Life,' coiling round the Lifeguardsmen with their cuirasses flashing back the tall wax candles they held, in 1837, when William the King was buried in St George's. Even in their own line we beat the Papists.

I have seen the beloved Abbey since I was at Chartres: it is to the great French church as a peregrine falcon to a kite.

Fine as Chartres is, there is nothing to read in it: where there should be monuments there are altars, needless and tautologous. No doubt there are inexhaustible mines of iconography in the windows, but they are out of sight to any one but a student; there are forests of sculpture, but all old worn-out subjects. Far rather would I see our frieze with the life of Edward the Confessor, our relief representing André going to his death and Washington refusing to yield to the entreaties of the English flag-bearer. In France you get your flood of hagiology in one place, where no one heeds it but the archaeologist, and your torrent of history in another place, Versailles, where the patient public is driven like a flock of sheep. At the sublime shrine of England we have Christianity in the fairest form, blended with the glowing patriotism of our heroic centuries and the mournfulness of mothers robbed long ago by some fever of their Westminster scholars, young Morgans and Mansels and Cholmondeleys: 'You might know that he was of the ancient stock of the Cholmondeleys,' says the Latin of 1680; and within sound of our intelligible psalmistry is the proud lament for the Lord Aubrey Beauclerk who commanded H.M.S. *Prince Frederick* at Carthagena, and had both legs shot off, and would not give up his breath till he had told his first lieutenant how to fight it out against the Spanish forts. And after the anthem is forgotten, I listen affectionately to the country cousins and the ugly London artizans reading to one another the records of Englishmen 'who behaved themselves with honour and applause' . . .

The yellow bishop read on for ten minutes at a time quite inaudibly, whilst people were scrambling in, children fidgeting in their seats, a virago lifting out chairs to sell them elsewhere, men making gaps in chair-lines for their wives to squeeze through, other men talking aloud; no order, no kneeling, no devout standing, no visible sympathy – in the midst of it, two roughs with hats on . . .

LADY MONKSWELL
(1849–1909)

Mary Monkswell was still the Hon. Mrs Robert Collier when she and her husband arrived in the United States in the summer of 1881. She had begun her journal some twenty years earlier when she was still a child, and she continued to write it in her vigorous, tactless fashion for the rest of her life. The daughter of Joseph Hardcastle, a Suffolk M.P., she trained as an artist at the Slade and was a thoroughly independent spirit. Her husband, the 2nd Lord Monkswell, was an Under-Secretary at the War Office. As a diarist she is direct and unpretentious, and atrenchant critic of Abroad.

There seems to have been a tradition for the Victorian woman traveller to speak her mind on Abroad. Frances Trollope's unsparing *Domestic Manners of the Americans* had set the pace, and it became especially necessary to be candid about America. Mary Collier was thirty-two when the S.S. *Celtic* docked in New York and her tour West is crammed with sharp vignettes of modern America in the making. She observes it with a ruthless eye.

In old age she would be found by callers hungrily browsing through the fat journal, but never offering them a morsel from it. The later pages are filled with wonderfully fresh impressions of Queen Victoria (wearing 'very strong glasses' but 'up to everything'), Gladstone ('I have to read old Gladstone's letters five times before I can dig out what he means'), Tennyson ('What did I see – an old, old man, bent and broken, with glazed eyes and displeased wearied look'), and other celebrities. Her easy racism comes as a shock to us, but was no more than confident British Empire language to her.

Mormons, 'cow-boys' and Oliver Wendell Holmes

Tuesday, 2 September 1881. It was burning hot when we left Denver & started off in a very unsatisfactory manner. A negro, who was a sort of porter, hurried us into a train just as it was starting. When we had gone 100 yards we discovered we were in the wrong train so they actually stopped the train for a quarter of a moment & we hopped out & walked back to the station. The long compartment open to everybody is all very well when you want to sleep in the train, but it is decidedly nasty when you have to share it with miners & tramps. For 25 or 30 miles we went up Clear Creek Cañon, a roaring river down the middle & rocks quite straight up & 1,000 & 2,000 ft. high. The railway was carved out of rock like a shelf or banked up in the stream the whole way.

All the way along were disused galleries & scaffoldings, & signs of forsaken mines. The 'Clear Creek' is now as thick as possible in consequence of the mining. We got in at 7 just as the sun set, & went to a nice little inn called Beebee House. Such a relief after the heat, noise & smells of the half dozen hotels we have been in since we landed. This is almost like a Swiss inn, wooden floor *salle-a-manger*, no bells, 3 tidy girls to bring the meals, & such good bread & butter, milk & venison steaks. My spirits went up at once.

Sunday, 4 September. Bob got up about 6 & went forth to find his much desired warm swimming bath (which made his cold 50 times worse). We had been coaching up Appleton's guide & ordered a buggy with two horses & one more tied on behind to take us to Chicago Lakes, 14 miles up in the mountains. This is the most wonderful day I have had since we started, the first I have really enjoyed. The buggy was hardly more than a truck with two seats across it, high & thin wheels, &, to judge by the jolting it endured, the most wonderful springs in the world. The splinter bars were very wide so as to give the horse plenty of room. We started at 9, a lovely morning, down a most beautiful valley, the hills on each side of us one to two thousand feet & covered – where the American could not get at the trees to cut them down which he never fails to do if it is at all possible – with fir trees & some poplar & maple, & a sort of willow. The Autumn colours have begun altho' it is so early. The road was pretty bad for the first 3 miles, it then became perfectly execrable. Without doubt it is the worst road in America, which is saying a good deal.

Monday, 19 September. So sorry to leave Manitou, where I have really got better. Got to Denver at 12. Very tired. About 10 p.m., when I was trying to get to sleep, I heard a big bell & thought it must be for the President's death. The next morning I learnt that poor President Garfield, after lingering about ten weeks, had died last night of his wound. [He had been badly wounded by a would-be assassin on 2 July.]

Tuesday, 20 September. We got up about 5.30, oh lor! & began our long journey to Salt Lake City. We saw the range of the Rocky Mountains very well, particularly Long's Peak. At Colorado Junction, a little station consisting of one shed, we joined the main line. Two enormous engines & about ten compartments. They were hung with black for the poor President. We passed Sherman's, the highest point, about 3. For 15 or 20 hours we passed along the dreariest country, sage grass & grey earth, & sometimes great battlements of rock. Our fellow travellers were rather nice, a pretty actress & a most amusing old woman all going to New Zealand.

Thursday, 22 September. [At Salt Lake City.] Bob went off before daylight, & before I could get myself anything like awake, on an expedition with Mr Bryce. [This was Mr Bryce the historian; later Lord Bryce, and British Ambassador at Washington.] I had a very quiet & pleasant day quite by myself. I took a drive for two hours in a charming victoria with two very handsome chestnut horses, & I don't think I ever had more variety of extraordinary sensations. This place looks so like any other rising American town, the half occupied streets, the atrocious roads, the nice detached houses in gardens, the really beautiful & complete workmen's cottages, & the usual allowance of huts, that I could not believe that the people here live under a moral code as different to ours as if we were at Constantinople. It was soon brought home to me by the driver, who seemed to be the very thing I wanted, a discontented & perhaps 'apostate' Mormon. He pulled up before a very nice house & said, 'This is where Brigham Young used to live & where his widows live now.' Opposite there was a really very nice house indeed; 'That is "Amelia House", he built it for his favourite wife.' Then at another very good house – 'This house he built for Eliza Jane his 19th wife, who brought him into such trouble; she is away now lecturing on polygamy in the States.' Over & over again we stopped before some nice house & he said, 'This belongs to John

311

Smith, he has 4 wives, he lives with one here, & the others live in those 3 houses.' I could not believe my ears – that women should be such arrant fools as to marry a man on the understanding that he may discard them when he pleases & leave them unprovided for. I don't know what the women can be made of. To go no further than the poor old chambermaid who has just made my bed – she is the wife of a Mormon who has taken another wife, & has gone away to some distant farm to live with her. I asked her if he had made any provision for her & her 2 or 3 children, she said nothing except this that he kindly offered to let her come & live with him & the new wife, which she of course refused to do. She poured forth to me a most dreadful tale of wrong about one of her daughters, who has two children & whose husband has forsaken her. This brave old lady gets 14 dollars a month as chambermaid.

The driver took me to see the Tabernacle, a most hideous building, all roof. I went inside, there was a sort of stage & an organ, & the roof was hung with festoons of dead evergreen, which had been up there for 10 years. They say 12,000 people can sit there; it has a gallery all round. A very dreary place I thought.

Quite close to it is the Temple, half-built. The driver told me they had been building it for 28 years, & he considered it the greatest swindle. Twenty years ago they collected money in Liverpool for its windows, & nothing more has been heard of that money. Then he took me round & showed me the great Brigham's grave – 'There's 13 tons of granite on there.' He made no bones at all of saying, 'He was a clever thief.'

Thursday, 29 September. San Francisco is rather like Manchester or Liverpool, &, if it had a cloudy sky instead of this everlasting blue, it would be almost as smoky. We understood it better when we drove about this afternoon. It is built on steps cut up a steep hill. Its roads surpass any American roads I have yet felt, which is saying a good deal. Large round boulders or rotten planks at a most dangerous incline – one cannot go much further. We took a very jolly drive in an open brougham, if such a thing can be – along two miles of streets, then through the public park, which seemed to have no natural conclusion but began with thick plantations of fir trees, & some lawns & flower beds & a sort of crested partridge walking about, & then lost itself in boundless sand hills, & then some cliffs, a narrow beach, & the great misty Pacific . . .

We thought our character would be quite gone if we did not see something of the celebrated Chinese quarter, so we told the driver to take us through for us to see what we could. There are plenty of Chinamen anywhere in San Francisco, but, bless my soul! I never saw such crowds. There seemed to be hundreds & hundreds of them, the pavement was thick with them as they came crowding in from their work. They all looked to me exactly alike with their mild *female* faces & blue clothes. The San Francisco-ites hate them like poison; our driver turned up his nose at them, & spoke of them as the scum of the earth. The shops were hung with queer & horrible looking things to eat, the very street smelt of Chinese stuffiness. They were most of them exceedingly poor looking & dirty, but the only two women we saw looked clean & well combed. We saw only one little child & one baby. A little visit to the Chinese goes a long way . . .

Sunday, 16 October. There was some fear we should have to stay at Deming, which was a very lively place by reason of the 'cow-boys'. The other day a cow-boy being mad drunk *rode* into the inn, which is one of the two houses of which the place consists, on his horse with a loaded pistol. The sheriff was also there & his pistol was also loaded so he shot the cow-boy. Mr Flint said, 'If we do have to stop at Deming I'm glad to know that that cow-boy has been shot.' After an hour's delay we were fastened on to the other end of that freight train & shoved it on for 4 miles when it was put on a siding & we then passed it. At Deming (10.30) we changed into another train, & immediately went to bed. After this we go North, so I hope & pray that we are escaping from my great enemy the heat. I never appreciated before what a cruel giant the heat is.

Monday, 17 October, and Tuesday, 18 October. We stopped at Santa Fé. I was as usual very seedy. Monday in bed all day. A most dreadful journey starting Wed. morning 19 Oct. from Santa Fé, & getting into St Louis at 8 o'c. on Saturday morning, after a delay of 12 hours at Kansas City. We stayed 5 days at St Louis, I chiefly in bed. I was doctored by a nice Dr Carson who did me a great deal of good. On Wed. evening, 27 Oct. I was considered well enough to

The Penguin Book of Diaries

travel, & had another journey I should like to wipe out of my memory, to Boston, where we arrived on Friday morning, 28th Oct. I am not ill now, only very weak & absurdly nervous. We are in clover here (Revere House).

Saturday, 29 October. After my resting comfortable breakfast in bed this morning the porter returned from the post bringing 35 letters. Most, most delicious. I remained up to my ears in letters all day, & have not half taken them in even now. Later on we took a fly & drove round the town to leave our cards & letter of introduction on the following people: – Mr & Mrs Holmes [Dr & Mrs Oliver Wendell Holmes], Mr & Mrs Oliver Holmes – his son, Mr & Mrs Winthrop, Mr & Mrs Charles Perkins, Mr & Mrs Cabot Lodge, & Mr & Mrs Augustus Lowell. We had not to wait long for response. On Sunday afternoon 30 Oct. in walked Mr Charles Perkins. I had not seen a gentleman since we left the Valley, & I would not have believed what an amusement & pleasure it was to talk in good English to this man, who much resembled Villiers Lister. He took a great interest in us directly he discovered that we knew about Italy, where he had lived for some years. He stayed quite half an hour, &, no sooner was he gone, than Mr Oliver Holmes was announced – a tall handsome most agreeable young man. He was as friendly as it is possible to be, & as he lives in lodgings with his wife immediately asked us to dine with his father. His father is a well-known (to every one but me) literary man, a sort of small king in Boston, so we thought the desire to be hospitable could not go much further, & we hoped that Holmes *père* would like the arrangement.

On Monday 31 Oct. I was not very well so Bob went to the Holmes' to ask about a doctor. The trouble they took; – if both my legs had been broken they could not have been kinder. A Dr Warren was produced without much difficulty who, I think, is sharp eno' to see that what is the matter with me is railway journeys. About 11 o'c. came an inviting looking box, I opened it & found about 15 *lovely roses* sent by dear Mr Holmes, & *'Uncle Remus'*, & the last *Punch*. We are not used to such kind attentions. About 1 o'c. old Dr Holmes called with his wife. I never saw such a jolly old fellow, with a face like a little old boy, & such a merry

314

laugh. Although I was only in my dressing gown I was obliged just to come out & speak to him. We were talking of phrases & language, & he said, 'there are many degrees amongst us beginning with Daniel Webster & going down to the Choctaw Indians; it just depends where you strike the spectrum' . . .

Little old Dr Holmes is the best-known literary man in America besides Longfellow, &, I imagine, he has always cut out Longfellow by the extraordinary brilliancy of his conversation. (He said about Longfellow, 'We love him but not intensely.')

JAMES AGATE
(1877–1947)

Ivor Brown maintained that Agate deliberately set out to be the diarist of his epoch when, in 1935, he began to publish his *Ego*, nine volumes in all of 'wit in causerie', club talk, theatre and literary criticism and social comment. The model was William Hazlitt, but *sans* his passionate politics – or politics of any kind. Agate concealed certain aspects of his personality which would have been condemned at the time under a cloak of horsiness and the manners of a gentleman farmer. Beneath the bluster was a sensitive and erudite soul, considerable intellectual vigour, and a style which was to make him the most sought-after newspaper and radio critic of his day. 'He was a hedonist,' wrote Brown, 'in the best sense, seeking pleasure of the senses to the end; but his hedonism was mitigated by discernment.' Agate was also a Francophile and French culture influenced his journalism. His *Ego* volumes had a great but brief popularity – the best diaries are not conceived as bestsellers – but they still provide a racy comment on Agate's cautious bohemia.

Monday, 26 April 1937. The *Sunday Times* has been dangling America before me! *Pour-parlers* are now finished, and I leave on the *Bremen* on Wednesday. The idea is to write about the New York scene, with the theatre as pivot. I was a little nervous about this until in Borrow's *Celebrated Trials* – my present bed-book – I came across this: 'It is no easy thing to tell a story plainly and distinctly by mouth; but to tell on paper is difficult indeed, so many snares lie in the way. People are afraid to put down what is common on paper; they seek to embellish their narratives, as they think, by philosophic speculations and reflections; they are anxious to shine, and people who are anxious to shine can never tell a plain story.' Jumping at the tip, I have decided to treat the whole thing as a diary.

Tuesday, 27 April. A jolly doctor friend of mine comes with me. As B. [Ralph Baker] looks like a Jewish Traddles, I have asked the shipping company whether there will be any Nazi nonsense on board. The clerk replies that the company does not allow politics to interfere with business. An admirable Jewish maxim!

Thursday, 29 April. . . . As we cast off the band strikes up *Eine Seefahrt die ist Lustig.* Lots of telegrams, and a letter from John Gielgud in his exquisite, absurdly tiny handwriting, telling me all the things I should do and the people I must meet: 'The nicest person of all is Lillian Gish.' The boat is about half full, with nobody on board I have ever heard of except Max Schmeling, the boxer. The food is excellent beyond belief. For lunch we have the most decorative hors-d'œuvres, including a delicious, velvety herring known as 'Swedish Appetiser', langouste, and a German family dish of chopped beef. A good bottle of Eitelsbacher Sonnenberg at 4 marks. Am struck not so much by the extreme attentiveness of the stewards as by their spick-and-spanness, and above all their noiselessness. This is dream waiting. The lazy man need never trouble his pockets; when he wants matches there is always a silent presence to put the box into his hand, like the ghost in the story. A bandbox smartness pervades the ship. The lift-boys in their white uniforms suggest tap-dancers in revue; the stewardesses have the rectitude of hospital nurses.

Leaving Cherbourg, we meet the *Queen Mary* coming in. She left Southampton two hours after us, but is faster by three knots. I ought to be able to calculate when she will catch us up, but even at

school could never do this kind of sum. And now I have not the
vaguest idea how to employ the time. I have put on an Elia-like
quality of superannuation. I am Retired Leisure. I am to be met
with on trim decks. I grow into gentility perceptibly. I am like a
dog which, having been on a leash for years, is suddenly liberated
and has forgotten how to frisk . . .

Just received a radio-telegram from Sam Eckman, the London
head of Metro-Goldwyn-Mayer. 'Hope Neptune will be as kind to
you as you will be to us.' That's just it. I have always found
Americans enchanting, while rather boggling at their country. This
is probably because it frightens me; I am afraid of its slang,
efficiency, bustle and stark cruelty. No English critic would want to
write, and no English editor consent to print, Robert Benchley's
notice of a new play in the current number of the *New Yorker*:
'There must have been a play called *Bet Your Life* which opened
last week, for I have it on my list. However, as I can't find it
anywhere in the advertisements and nobody seems to know anything
about it now, we might as well let the whole matter drop.' Against
this my reason suggests that the American hurly-burly may conceal
an inferiority complex. But does that help? What about mine? Can
there be anything more dangerous to mutual understanding than a
clash of inferiority complexes?

And on what, pray, do I base my prejudices? On some Sunday-
school Longfellow, sickly Hawthorne, priggish Emerson? A handful
of modern novels, some plays, all the Hollywood nonsense? The
only American book I have ever really liked is Louisa M. Alcott's
Little Women. Or am I worried by the lack of great dramatic and
singing poets? Walt Whitman has written sound sense about this.
His first point is America's *material* preoccupation, which in any
new country must come before the arts. His second point is about
Shakespeare and Tennyson. He calls the plays 'the very pomp and
dazzle of the sunset' while the poetry is 'feudalism's lush-ripening
culmination and last honey of decay'. Just before sailing I threw
into my bag W. W.'s *Complete Prose*. 'Meanwhile democracy
(meaning American democracy) waits the coming of the bards in
silence and in twilight – but 'tis the twilight of the dawn.' A fine
passage which ought to put the English visitor to the States on his
guard against uppishness.

Thursday, 6 May. Called on Mrs Patrick Campbell, who is living at a clean little hotel in West 49th Street. Took her to lunch at a place she insisted was called the Vendôme, but which turned out to be Voisin's. Didn't notice what we ate or drank, and don't remember paying. Probably very good. After lunch went for a drive across Washington Bridge. This also I dare say is very nice, but my attention was entirely taken up by Mrs Pat, who radiated quicksilver. Saw the *Hindenburg* nosing majestically between the skyscrapers on its way to Lakehurst, and had the taxi turn round so as to follow it and get a better view. By the time we had rounded a block it had disappeared, and we couldn't catch it again. This made Mrs P. pretend it had never been there, and that I needed psychoanalysing. I think I have never been in contact with a mind so frivolous and at the same time so big. She talked a great deal about 'flight' in acting as being the first quality of a great actor. For four hours I listened to chatter about everything, from Moses to Schnabel. About the former: 'He probably said to himself, "Must stop or I shall be getting silly." That is why there are only ten commandments.' She described Schnabel's playing of Beethoven as being 'like the winds of the air and the waves of the sea, without shape'. As she said this I heard again the crooning of Mélisande.

Of a well-known English novelist: 'He has never met a great actress. No actress could be great in his presence. He has a worm in his brain. He lives in hell and likes it.' About an American actress: 'She has a Siamese forehead and a mouth like a golosh.' About another actress: 'She is the great lady of the American stage. Her voice is so beautiful that you won't understand a word she says.' About the same actress: 'She's such a nice woman. If you knew her you'd even admire her acting.' With a smile, about *Ego*: 'I did so enjoy your book. Everything that everybody writes in it is so good.' About Washington Bridge: 'The world's greatest piece of architecture after *Hedda Gabler*.' About Hedda: 'You have always been right. I never could play her because I could never get the Latin out of my blood. I have had Swedish masseuses who were ten times better Heddas.' About herself: 'Many people say I have an ugly mind. That isn't true. I say ugly things, which is different.' And again: 'My voice at least has not gone, and Brenda can always make me another face.' About her future: 'I don't think I want to return to London. They seem quite satisfied with Miss B.' The whole of this was punctuated with stories of her white Pekinese, Moonbeam, and melodious altercations with the taxi-driver, who failed to convince her that a certain monument was not Grant's Tomb. About Sarah Bernhardt she said: 'I toured with her for five months, sat on her bed till five o'clock in the morning, and never heard her say a word to which a child could not have listened.' She told me how she dined with Sarah three nights before she died. Sarah was wearing a dress of pink Venetian velvet with long sleeves, sent for the occasion by Sacha Guitry. Knowing that she had not long to live, she sat there with a white face eating nothing and infinitely gracious. Her son Maurice was at the table, paralysed, and fed by his wife. At the end of the meal Sarah was carried upstairs in her chair; turning the bend of the staircase, she kissed one finger and held it out. Both knew they would not meet again.

When I got back to the hotel I found I was holding a velvet geranium which, on one of the altercations with the taxi-driver, had become detached from Mrs Pat's headgear. We had chattered and chunnered for four hours.

Wednesday, 26 May. Nathan called this afternoon to take me to tea with Lillian Gish. She came into the room looking exactly as she did in *Way Down East*. A sad, pinched little face, with woebegone eyes looking out from under a hat like a squashed Chinese pagoda. A trim, tiny figure very plainly dressed; the whole apparition strangely reminiscent of Vesta Tilley. Since she left films she has played Shakespeare, Tchehov, and Dumas *fils*: 'I came from the theatre, and I am glad to go back to it,' Nathan has a theory that acting has nothing to do with the film or the film with acting, and that the proper function of the screen is to exploit the exuberant vitality of the Robert Taylors and Loretta Youngs, and discard all players as soon as they cease to exuberate. He thinks Lillian was the last screen-actress. I talked a bit about her old pictures, and she seemed to like it. Anyhow she sat there silently, nodding like some grave flower.

SIR STEPHEN SPENDER
(b. 1909)

If there has to be, or could be, any solution to what many have found the puzzling business of why such an essentially private person should have spent his life largely in public places, it could only be found in Spender's journals. These are capacious, one of the great hold-alls of British, German and American cultural experience from the Thirties on. In them the poet's solitude is made doubly obvious by his being so much in the thick of things. He is engaged in his times – especially, of course, during the Fascist period, when he made his reputation. His involvement then had an extra edge because of his being half German. Since the last war Spender has been among the least parochial of British writers; both his European-ism and his long spells at American universities have taken him out of most of the usual brackets; a broader perspective which could be judged by his co-editorship of magazines like *Horizon* and *Encounter*. His poetry apart, he might be called an intellectual in the non-English sense.

Spender kept a journal chiefly for two reasons: to work out, or write out, private crises, and as background material for future books, articles and lectures. His remarkable autobiography *World Within World* (1951) witnesses to the fact that a Life can be far more eloquent than the daily notes used to construct it. So why, at long last, publish the journals themselves? Spender give his reply thus:

> I think that the journal writer, like the poet, is haunted by the ghost of a reader; but a ghost is very different from some palpable flesh-and-blood reader whom the writer imagines looking over his shoulder with his expectations, standards and demands. The writer of the journal need only set down what is interesting to himself, his own truth, and much of this will conform to no standards of publication that he is aware of at the time. Much of it will be, indeed, unpublishable.

Posterity and the market would decide the latter; also the laws of kindness and libel. Spender is famously unhidden and vulnerable among his contemporaries. He is less deliberate in his self-revelation than his friends Isherwood and Auden because from his youth he has failed to master the customary self-protection. His politics (always engaged) are idealistic in the old progressive way, and feature strongly throughout the journal.

Nashville, Holiday Inn, 5 January 1979. I seem to myself a very different person from even five years ago. Because five years ago, though conscious some of the time of my age – a lot of the time I was not conscious of it. If I bought a diary for 1975 I felt that I would be the same person at the end of it – 31 December – as I was at the beginning – 1 January. Now I can just about feel I'll be the same at the end of 1979 – but to look at a diary for this year haunts me with the idea of another diary – ten years hence perhaps – at the end of which I shall be, in one way or another way, finished.

7 January. Sitting at the window of my tenth-storey room, I look over a large parking lot and beyond it the side of a baseball stadium, and, to the right of that, the redbrick longitudinal block of a church surmounted by a diminutive tower which looks like a little triangular hat. The dull snow with wiry branches of trees interrupting it, posts trailing wires, and in the background a woody hillside. The weather looks as if it will stay the same for at least three months. I think I should buy galoshes. No one has communicated with me for two days. I think with equal dread of going on like this and of the classes, the academic invitations, the interviews which lie ahead of me, and I remember really far worse days at Charlottesville where I had an apartment in a tiny house that seemed made of matchwood and which was stifling with the smell of talcum powder and deodorants; and Houston where I stayed at the University Hotel on the campus looking out on an immense area of buildings like railway sheds, with beyond them, miles away, a view of some immensely expensive-looking skyscrapers, sprouting like a ring of toadstools out of the plain. It seems to me quite ridiculous I should spend so much of my life in such desultory circumstances, at my age when I ought to be surrounded by family, troops of friends, and a little honour. One can fill a blank time like this with some self-realization. But I think I have learned my lesson already: that I

simply have to try, in the little time left me, to do work which will
make up for the waste of so many years.

I am reading David Jones's *The Dying Gaul*. David Jones is
different from other modern writers in that he is not really to be
reckoned as a writer out of a literary situation. He writes firstly out
of his own life which is that of a private soldier among other
soldiers in the First War, a Welshman not quite fitting into Wales,
but passionately identifying with his Welshness, an artist who feels
that to be a modern artist is to be a kind of outcast from a time to
which he in his most intimate being feels he belongs, when all men
were creative. He is also a religious man, a devout Catholic, who
feels that his every action should be sacramental, depriving himself
of worldly goods not just because he has nothing to do with the
utilities of the manufacturing world (well, he did have, I think, a
creaky old gramophone on which he played very old and worn
recordings of plainsong).

In one of his essays he writes that a real object is worth any
number of descriptions of it. His contact with the past – of Rome,
of Wales and of Ireland chiefly – is through objects, is archaeological
rather than literary. This gives his self-identification as artist with
the past a kind of authority which is questionable in Eliot and other
modern writers whose connection with the past is through literature,
the works of tradition.

18 January. Still here after ten days without anyone in Nashville
having invited me even for a drink, except the lady along the
corridor who gave me a general invitation to breakfast each day
and did give me breakfast yesterday. Realizing this morning I
should not count on this, I did not knock at her door. She rang at
ten and explained that she was now going to travel in Europe
earlier than expected, so every table in her room was covered in
income-tax papers. This cancelled all breakfasts and also the prospect of dinner one night, which she had held out. However, would I
like her to send her son along with a pot of tea and toast? I said I
would be glad of this and a bespectacled spotty boy with an
incipient moustache arrived with tea and hung around till I asked
him to sit down. He then explained he was interested in me because
I was a poet. He did not like poetry which had metre and rhythm

to it but nevertheless he had been moved by the poetry of Sylvia Plath, which made him think that perhaps if he was a poet it would help him to solve the problems he was having with his identity.

He said that next time he came he would bring along some of his poems for me to look at.

A thing about the room I now have is that it has a kind of grating near the ceiling through which voices in the next room come magnified.

At four today a man visited the old lady in the next apartment. (She is hard of hearing.) For a time I thought the voice of the man, interrupted by inaudible gurgles from the old lady, was of a character in a TV soap opera. He had a horribly unpleasant voice raised to a shout to penetrate the old lady's deafness, and rising to a scream at times. As this stopped me working, I started writing down odd sentences:

'Tell me who you trust. Is there anyone you trust?'

'The first law is my survival – unless you want me to kill myself.'

'You never once slapped your father's face? Did you ever once slap your father's face?'

'If you can choose an easy or a hard way to do it, you'll choose the hard way.'

'You're an old woman. Why should anyone love you?'

'You make a federal case out of being a mother.'

'I never did want my mother around. If I did want my mother around I'd be sick. Sick, sick, sick, sick.'

I tried to visualize the man, but I could not do so. His sentences seemed to spring up like brown water from some underground pipe in cities where people speak with an undisguised brutality, which is the ugly side of intimacy. There is a kind of basic unkindness, lack of charity here, and I recognize something of myself in it, wondering at the same time whether this kind of callousness towards others is not peculiar to some Americans. It links up with something Frank Kermode wrote to me, that in this country the really nice people (and they are extraordinarily nice) have an air of being dazed and lost, as though they did not know how they got here.

DERVLA MURPHY
(b. 1931)

A journey taken for no other purpose than to make a book out of it can be a false journey, though far from being so in the case of Dervla Murphy, who, in the dreadful winter of 1963, set off on her bicycle named Roz to ride from Ireland to India. The result is one of the most illuminating and best-written travel-diaries of the post-war years. Presents of a bicycle and an atlas when she was ten had set the plan in motion, but she was thirty-one before she could leave, inspired by Robert Louis Stevenson's dictum: 'For my part I travel not to go anywhere but to go. I travel for travel's sake. The great affair is to move, to feel the needs and hitches of our life more nearly, to come down off the feather-bed of civilization and find the globe granite underfoot and strewn with cutting flints.'

Full Tilt, Dervla Murphy's diary, which she kept from March to July 1963, from Teheran to New Delhi, is amused, brave and unencumbered with the fashionable guru-seeking trek notions of her contemporaries. She is an Irish convent girl whose father has suffered many years' imprisonment for his republican activities and she possesses a keen eye and an ear for the solitudes of freedom. Her diary is also a valuable record of an Iran not yet taken over by the mullahs and an Afghanistan still awaiting the Russians. Most of all, it is the diary of a cyclist, of a woman pedalling across the East on a man's Armstrong Cadet to challenge its vaunted rules of hospitality.

Goosheh, 1 April 1963. It's very funny – around here the idea of a woman travelling alone is so completely outside the experience and beyond the imagination of everyone that it's universally assumed I'm a man. This convenient illusion is fostered by the very short haircut I deliberately got in Teheran, and by a contour-obliterating shirt presented to me at Adabile by the U.S. Army in the Middle East, who also donated a wonderful pair of boots – the most comfortable footwear I've ever had and ideal for tramping these stony roads. The result of the locals' little error of judgement is

that last night and tonight I was shown to my bed in the gendarm-
erie dormitory. These beds consist of wooden planks with padded
sleeping-bags laid on them and I have the bed of one of those on
night-patrol. There are no problems involved as 'getting ready for
bed' consists of removing boots, gun and belt and sliding into a
flea-bag so I simply do likewise and that's that! Incidentally, these
barracks are kept spotlessly clean.

Herat, 9 April. During one of these pauses in a tea-house a man,
whom I had never seen before and will never see again, silently
approached, laid a packet of cigarettes beside me and vanished
before I even had time to thank him; I couldn't help thinking then
of my kind European friends who had warned me so often of the
dangers of being a woman and a Christian in Muslim countries.

Strolling through the bazaar I was delightedly conscious of the
fact that when Alexander's soldiers passed this way they must have
witnessed scenes almost identical to those now surrounding me –
bakers cooking flat bread in underground ovens, having spread the
dough on leather cushions stuffed with straw and damped with
filthy water; blind-folded camels walking round and round churning
mast in stinking little dens behind their owner's stalls; butchers
skinning and disembowelling a sheep and throwing scraps to the
yellow, crop-eared dogs who have been waiting all morning for this
happy event; tanners curing hides, weavers at their looms, potters
skilfully firing pitchers of considerable beauty, cobblers making the
curly-toed, exquisitely inlaid regional shoes and tailors cutting out
the long, fleece-padded coats which when thrown over the shoulders
of an Afghan makes him look like a fairy-story king.

On my way back to the hotel I observed hens importantly
leading their excited broods to unrevealed destinations, tiny boys
sitting cross-legged on the pavement meticulously cleaning oil-
lamps, diminutive, anxious, furry donkey-foals who had temporarily
lost their mothers, and youths squatting in doorways preparing
hookahs for the men to smoke. It's unlikely that the other Afghan
cities will be equally attractive; Herat is now so cut off from
everywhere on every side that it's just gone jogging along happily
while the rest of the country is being modernized by the U.S. and
the U.S.S.R.

Herat, 10 April. I slept very well last night in my roadside tea-house, curled up in a corner of the one-roomed building, with moonlight streaming through the door-way that had no door and the 'proprietor' curled up under his camel-hair rug in another corner, rifle and turban to hand. He was a dear old boy, who seemed quite shocked when I attempted to pay him before leaving at 5.30 a.m.

It took me four and a half hours to cover the thirty miles to Herat but I enjoyed the wide silence of the desert in the cool of the morning.

This is a city of absolute enchantment in the literal sense of the word. It loosens all the bonds binding the traveller to his own age and sets him free to live in a past that is vital and crude but never ugly. Herat is as old as history and as moving as a great epic poem – if Afghanistan had nothing else it would have been worth coming to experience this. Even the loss of my wallet containing over £12 hasn't been able to depress me today. (It was not stolen but just slipped out of my pocket somehow, as I was exploring.) Of course I'd feel worse about such a loss in Europe; the fact that every Afghan I've seen so far obviously needs £12 even more than I do is quite a consolation. During a long trek some disaster of the sort is inevitable.

Kabul, 4 and 5 May. Living in the West, it's now impossible for most of us to envisage our own past by a mere exercise of the imagination, so we're rather like adults who have forgotten the childhood that shaped them. And that increases the unnaturalness of our lives. So to realize this past through contact with a people like the Afghans should help us to cope better with our present – though it also brings the sadness of knowing what we're missing. At times during these past weeks I felt so *whole* and so at peace that I was tempted seriously to consider settling in the Hindu Kush. Nothing is false there, for humans and animals and earth, intimately interdependent, partake together in the rhythmic cycle of nature. To lose one's petty, sophisticated complexities in that world would be heaven – but impossible, because of the fundamental falsity involved in attempting to abandon our own unhappy heritage. Yet the awareness that one cannot go back is a bitter pill to swallow.

Kabul, 6 May. Today I met a twenty-five-year-old American boy in the Museum who was typical of a certain category of youngster – European, Commonwealth and American – I've met all along the route. To them, travel is more a *going away from* rather than a *going towards,* and they seem empty and unhappy and bewildered and pathetically anxious for companionship, yet are afraid to commit themselves to any ideal or cause or other individual. I find something both terrifying and touching in young people without an aim, however foolish or even wrong it may be. This young man was pleasant and intelligent but wasting himself and resentfully conscious of the fact. He doesn't want to return home in the foreseeable future, yet, after two years of it, is weary of travelling, probably because he always holds himself aloof from the people he travels among – not through hostility or superiority but through a strange unconsciousness of the unity of mankind. Is this something else our age does – on the one hand make communication easier than ever before, while on the other hand widening the gulf between those who are 'developed' and those who are not? . . .

At mid-day I went asleep for about half-an-hour on a mountain-side, having been up since 5.30 a.m., and woke to find myself in a *tent.* I had decided that I was still asleep and dreaming when a filthy old man of the Kochi (nomad) tribes appeared and explained by signs that they'd noticed me going to sleep with no shade, which they thought very bad, so he erected one of their goat-hair tents over me – without loosening a pebble, they move so very stealthily. The moral here is that the basis of a successful psychological approach to Afghans is *not* to be afraid of them. Yet it's literally true that the same old man would think nothing of murdering his own daughter if she ran away and married into an enemy tribe. It does take a while to sort out the fact that such people don't want to murder *you!*

This city is full of Sikhs, who are undoubtedly the most forth-coming people on my route since Bulgaria. They told me that I could stay as long as I like in their Golden Temple at Amritsar, where a bed and three meals a day are given free to all travellers of every colour, class and creed – one of these religious 'things'. The complexity of Eastern religions is quite beyond me – when you think of how Sikhs and Muslims massacred each other in '47–'48!

Yet it's absolutely true that once you leave Europe you could, if you were stingy enough, live entirely free on the generosity of people with about a twentieth of the average European income. The other day in a tea-house I made a casual remark to a total stranger about the postal rates here and he immediately offered to pay all my stamp bills – a man with no shoes to his feet!

12. THE DIARIST IN DESPAIR

TRIALS, REMEDIES AND RESOLUTIONS

Elias Ashmole, antiquary (1617–92)

This night about one of the clock I fell ill of a surfet occasioned by drinkinge water after venison. I was greatly oppressed in the stomach and next day Mr Saunders the Astrologian sent me a piece of Briony root to hold in my hand and within a quarter of an hour my stomach was freed of that great oppression.

I took early in the morning a good dose of Elixir and hung three spiders about my neck and they drove my ague away.

Sir William Brereton (1604–61)

The sluttishness and nastiness of this people [the Scots] is such that I cannott ommitt the particularizing thereof though I have more than sufficiently often touched upon the same. Their houses and halls and kitchens have such a noysome taste and savour and that soe strong as itt doth offend you, soe soone as you come within their walls, yea sometimes when I have light from my horse, I have felt the distaste of itt before I have come into the house; yea, I never came into my own lodgings in Edinburgh, or went out butt I was constrained to hold my nose or to use warme-wood or some such sented plant. Their pewter I am confident is never scowred, they are afraid it should too much weare and consume thereby, only sometimes and that but seldome they doe sleightly rubb them over with a filthy dish clowte dipped in most sluttish greasy water ... To come into their kitchen and to see them dress their Meate and to behold the sinke (which is more offensive than any jakes) will be a sufficient supper and will take the edge off your stomach.

Adam Eyre, gentleman (b. 1614)

I went to Bordhill to see a match played at the foot ball between Peniston and Thurlston but the crowd hindered the sports so that nothing was done . . .

This morne my wife began after her old manner to braule and revile me for wishing her to weare such apparrell as was decent and comly and accused mee of treading on her sore foot with curses and others, which to my knowledge I touched not, nevertheless she continued in that extacy til noone.

The Rev. Henry Newcombe, Presbyterian minister (1627–95)

Alas I must endeavour to walke closer with God or I cannot keepe cart on wheels.

I resolve to let this tobacco alone and to studdy to forget it for it doth me no good . . . I doe see my slavery with this tobacco . . . But sometimes to deny it when it is so desired were but a small degree of self denial.

Oliver Heywood, Presbyterian minister (1630–1702)

On Saturday morning my sons not having made their latin in expectation to goe to Halifax were loath to goe to schoole yet I threatened them, they went crying, my bowels workt and I sent to call them back and I went into my study and fel on my knees and found sweet meltings – if God set in a little they will occasion much good.

Aug. 24 [1671] called black Bartholomew day I resolved to keep a fast and because I came home but last night and could get no more company I kept it with my family, the forenoon we spent in prayer beginning at youngest Eliezer prayer first very sensibly, the short, John prayed both a long time and exceedingly pertinently and affectionately, weeping much. I admired at it, God helped my maid, my wife and myself wonderfully – oh what a melting duty and day it was.

Ralph Thoresby, antiquarian and topographer (1658–1725)

Went to bed with wet cheeks.
Rivers of tears issued from my eyes.
Lord, discover my naughty heart more and more to me.
I am a useless unprofitable cumber-ground . . .

GEORGE CRABBE
(1754–1832)

In 1780, when he was twenty-six, and after 'starving as an apothecary in a little venal borough in Aldborough Suffolk', as he put it in a begging letter to Lord Shelburne, Crabbe fled to London, there to starve in earnest. His diary of the three months preceding his being taken up by Edmund Burke (one of literature's classic instances of patronage), and called *The Poet's Journal*, is full of fear. He is broke. His appeals to peers, publishers – and pawnbrokers – are harshly dealt with. The Gordon Riots are in progress and sights worse than anything seen in Aldeburgh are met with whenever he leaves his lodgings. He is a gauche genius in tatters and needs help badly. He fawns on the great and remembers other young hopefuls who drowned themselves or, like Oliver Goldsmith, were forced to do menial tasks because the world rejected them. He gets more and more desperate and worried, and pours it all out to his fiancée, Sarah Elmy, whom he calls his 'Mira'. His son found this anxious diary after Crabbe's death and published it in its entirety in his *Life of Crabbe* (1834), one of the finest biographies in the language. To understand the diary one has to recall the humiliation which the poet has already suffered, and also the near impossibility of a man such as himself being able to clamber out of his 'condition' without somebody believing in him and giving him a leg up. Burke took him into his own house. This is how Crabbe's son described the fairy-tale change of fortune:

> He went into Mr Burke's room, a poor young adventurer, spurned by the opulent, and rejected by the publishers, his last shilling gone, and all but his last hope with it; he came out virtually secure of almost all the good fortune that, by succes-sive steps, afterwards fell to his lot – his genius acknowledged by one whose verdict could not be questioned . . .

12 May 1780. Perhaps it is the most difficult thing in the world to tell how far a man's vanity will run away with his passions. I shall therefore not judge, at least not determine, how far my poetical talents may or may not merit applause. For the first time in my life that I recollect, I have written three or four stanzas that so far touched me in the reading them, as to take off the consideration that they were things of my own fancy. Now, if I ever do succeed, I will take particular notice if this passage is remarked; if not, I shall conclude 'twas mere self-love – but if so, 'twas the strangest, and, at the same time, strongest disguise she ever put on.

You shall rarely find the same humour hold two days. I'm dull and heavy, nor can go on with my work. The head and heart are like children, who, being praised for their good behaviour, will overact themselves; and so is the case with me. Oh! Sally, how I want you!

16 May. O! my dear Mira, how you distress me: you inquire into my affairs, and love not to be denied – yet you must. To what purpose should I tell you the particulars of my gloomy situation; that I have parted with my money, sold my *wardrobe*, pawned my watch, am in debt to my landlord, and finally, at some loss how to eat a week longer? Yet you say, tell me all. Ah, my dear Sally, do not desire it; you must not yet be told these things. Appearance is what distresses me: I *must* have dress, and therefore am horribly fearful I shall accompany Fashion with fasting – but a fortnight more will tell me of a certainty.

18 May. A day of bustle – twenty shillings to pay a tailor, when the stock amounted to thirteen and three-pence. Well – there were instruments to part with, that fetched no less than eight shillings more; but twenty-one shillings and three-pence would yet be so poor a superfluity, that the Muse would never visit till the purse was recruited; for, say men what they will, she does not love empty pockets nor poor living. Now, you must know, my watch was mortgaged for less than it ought; so I redeemed and repledged it, which has made me – the tailor paid and the day's expenses – at this instant worth (let me count my cash) ten shillings – a rare case, and most bountiful provision of fortune! ...

It's the vilest thing in the world to have but one coat. My only one has happened with a mischance, and how to manage it is some difficulty. A confounded stove's modish ornament caught its elbow, and rent it halfway. Pinioned to the side it came home, and I ran deploring to my loft. In the dilemma, it occurred to me to turn tailor myself; but how to get materials to work with puzzled me. At last I went running down in a hurry, with three or four sheets of paper in my hand, and begged for a needle, &c., to sew them together. This finished my job, and but that it is somewhat thicker, the elbow is a good one yet.

These are foolish things, Mira, to write or speak, and we may laugh at them; but I'll be bound to say they are much more likely to make a man cry, where they *happen* – though I was too much of a philosopher for *that*, however, not one of those who preferred a ragged coat to a whole one.

On Monday, I hope to finish my book entirely, and perhaps send it. God almighty give it a better fate than the trifles tried before!

Sometimes I think I cannot fail; and then, knowing how often I have thought so of fallible things, I am again desponding. Yet, within these three or four days, I've been remarkably high in spirits, and now am so, though I've somewhat exhausted them by writing upwards of thirty pages ...

BENJAMIN ROBERT HAYDON
(1786–1846)

'I acquired in early life a great love of journals of others, and Johnson's recommendation to keep them honestly I always bore in mind . . . I have kept one now for thirty-four years. It is the history, in fact, of my mind.' So wrote Haydon in his autobiography, a fine work which drew heavily upon an even finer, his journals. His sister had sent him their father's diary, which made him laugh because of the way in which the wind blew through its pages: 'Poor Mrs Burgess died in childbed, poor Tom Burgess much afflicted: Wind W.N.W.' A terrible windiness was to inflate Haydon the artist and make it inevitable that he should eventually go off with a bang, but when it came to Haydon the writer, what a telling difference there was! He wrote his autobiography up to the age of thirty-four, filling it out with chunks from his journal. The autobiography breaks off in 1820 and from then onwards until his death at sixty it is the journal alone. There is nothing comparable to it in its irony. In his compelling need to explain and justify himself as a painter, he proves to the world that he is really a writer. An apology for determinedly treading the wrong path was never more grandly expressed, and the pistol-shot which brought a bloody end to a wrong direction, like Hedda Gabler's, continues to ricochet through the imagination.

If only those literary friends whose faces he put into his pictures – Keats, Hazlitt and the rest of them – could have convinced Haydon of his error and persuaded him to write novels, what masterly tales we would still have been reading! Yet had it not been that his frustrated, blind ambition to become England's major history-painter generated his narrative and descriptive powers, there would have been little literary drive. Being a middling artist was what made Haydon a great diarist and potentially great writer of anything he cared to tackle, had he been capable of thinking in such terms. For years critics have belaboured him for being too vain to recognize what he was, Aldous Huxley most of all. But Haydon's error has to be seen in the context of the pressures of his day, which included for him the heroic climate of the Napoleonic Wars, aristocratic patronage, the debtors' prison and his wife's ceaseless confinements. His journal is that of a desperate being turning this way and that to find a solution for the problems common to many London-based artists.

Just before he killed himself on 22 June 1846 he sent his journal, all twenty-six 'bulky, parchment-bound, ledger-like folios', to Elizabeth Barrett in Wimpole Street, at the very moment when Robert Browning had appeared to persuade her to abandon her invalidism and her father for marriage and Italy. It was published a few years later, as Haydon had intended it to be, to add a memorable dimension to the tragedy of self-deception. He is the only diarist whose magnificence equals his wretchedness. How could somebody who was made exultant by the bombast of history-painting ('have been like a man with air balloons under his armpits and ether in his soul. While I was painting, walking, or thinking, beaming flashes of energy followed and impressed me') write with no sign of such inflationary notions? His literary perceptiveness and style are astonishing. Incident after incident carries with it a kind of cinematic vividness, and there are endless instances to choose from. Here is a typical observation of a little scene when he and David Wilkie the artist were in Paris the year before Waterloo:

> Beyond the Pont Neuf, near a building close to the Seine, I saw, as I passed, women and girls playing battledore and shuttlecock. I went in, and to my horror found two dead bodies, half green, lying dead behind a glass partition. It was the well-known Morgue. Every time the shuttlecock dropped the women and children entered the place, gratified their heartless curiosity and then began their game again.
>
> And yet everything, however abominable, was done by the women with such grace and sweetness, that residence among them would soon have rendered me as insensible as themselves ... A little beggar bored Wilkie for money; he rather pettishly repulsed him. In London the boy's pride would have fired up ... but the little fellow in Paris made a bow, saying, *'Pardon, Monsieur, une autre occasion.'*

There were fleeting moments towards the end when Haydon,

flinching, recognized his *métier*: 'The truth is I am fonder of books than of anything else on earth. I consider myself, and ever shall, a man of great powers, excited to an art which limits their exercise. In politics, law, or literature, they would have had a full and glorious swing . . .'

The following extracts show Haydon badgering politicians in his extremity, first Henry Brougham, and then Lord Melbourne. Both men receive the artist wearily, having clearly listened to him on previous occasions. But Haydon is desperate and beyond caring that they think him a nuisance. The old Houses of Parliament have burned down and he wants the government to commission him to decorate the new buildings with history-paintings which, he believes, will establish him as a great artist. Both Melbourne and Brougham give him the brush-off. From then on until 22 June 1846, when he both cuts his throat and shoots himself in his studio, it is downhill all the way.

1 March 1831. I have not sold the Mock Election. I have no orders – no commissions. After all the public sympathy of last year, I am still without employment. The exhibition of the picture gets me a bare subsistence, and that is all.

'Non sum qualis eram.'

What to do I am at a loss. Brougham is chilled, and the state of the finances renders any expectation of a Government vote for the higher walk of Art a vain delusion. My admission into the Academy is out of the question. It has turned out as I predicted to Lord Egremont it would. I begin at last to long to go abroad, family and all. Had I been single, after leaving prison for the first time, I would have gone back to my stripped house and finished the Crucifixion; but here my wife shrank, and I loved her too well to pain her.

To have finished the Crucifixion without a bed to lie on, or a chair to sit on, without casts or prints, because the world thought it impossible, was to my mind a cause of fiery excitement. I would have gloried in doing it, and would have done it. But by painting lately only paltry things I have ceased to excite the enthusiasm I once lived in, because I have ceased to feel it myself. How all this will turn out God knows – for though I do not pray to Him as I used, I trust in His mercy, as I ever shall. I dread blindness in my old age, but I hope my God will spare me this calamity. His will, not mine, be done.

2 April. I got up melancholy in the extreme, and sallied forth to call on Brougham, in order to come to some conclusion. I saw him in the passage. His carriage was at the door; a gentleman was eagerly talking; Brougham had his foot on the stairs, and could not get up for the importunity of this man. Brougham's hand was full of papers, and his whole appearance was restless, harassed, eager, spare, keen, sarcastic and nervous. The servant did not hear me ring, and the coachman called from his box in a state of irritable fidget, 'Why, George, don't you see a gentleman here? He has been here these five minutes.' Up came George, half dressed, and showed me right in. The moment Brougham saw me, he seemed to look, 'Here's Haydon – at such a moment – to bore me.' Brougham never shakes hands, but he held out his two fingers. 'Mr Haydon, how d'ye do? I have no appointment with you. Call on Wednesday at half-past five. I can't spare you two minutes now.' I never saw such a set out. The horses were not groomed. The coachman not clean. The blinds of the coach were not down, and gave me the idea as if inside the air was hot, damp, foul and dusty. There the horses were waiting, half dozy; the harness not cleaned or polished; their coats rough as Exmoor ponies; and inside and outside the house the whole appearance told of hurry-scurry, harass, fag, late hours, long speeches and vast occupation. Since I saw him last he seems grown ten years older – looks more nervous and harassed a great deal. He tried to smile, by way of saying, 'Don't be hurt'; but I never am hurt by such things. When a man calls on another in that way, he must expect the consequences of breaking in. I wish anybody was as considerate for me.

Haydon tries to persuade Melbourne that he could go down in history as a patron of the arts:

19 October 1834. 'A new House must be built. Painting, sculpture, and architecture must be combined. Here's an opportunity that never can occur again. Burke said it would ultimately rest on a Minister. Have you no ambition to be that man?' He mused but did not reply. 'For God's sake, Lord Melbourne, do not let this slip; for the sake of Art – for your own sake – only say you won't forget Art. I'll undertake it for support during the time I am engaged, because it has been the great object of my life. I have qualified myself for it, and be assured, if High Art sinks, as it is sinking, all Art will go with it.' No reply. 'Depend on my discretion. Not a word shall pass from me; only assure me it is not hopeless.' Lord Melbourne glanced up with his fine eye, looked into me, and said: 'It is not.'

There will be only a temporary building till Parliament meets. There's time enough.

9 November. Sent down in the morning to know if Lord Melbourne could see me. He sent me back word he would receive me at one. At one I called and saw him. The following dialogue ensued: 'Well, my Lord, have you seen my petition to you?' 'I have.' 'Have you read it?' 'Yes.' 'Well, what do you say to it?' He affected to be occupied, and to read a letter. I said: 'What answer does your Lordship give? What argument or refutation have you?' 'Why, we do not mean to have pictures. We mean to have a building with all the simplicity of the ancients.' 'Well, my Lord, what public building of the ancients will you point out without pictures? I fear, Lord Melbourne, since I first saw you, you are corrupted. You meet Academicians at Holland House. I am sure you do.' He looked archly at me and rubbed his hands. 'I do. I meet Calcott. He is a good fellow.' 'Good enough: but an Academician.' 'Ha, ha,' said Lord Melbourne. 'Now, my Lord, do be serious.' 'Well, I am: Calcott says he disapproves of the system of patrons taking up young men to the injury of the old ones; giving them two or three commissions and letting them die in a workhouse.' 'But if young men are never to be taken up how are they to become known? But to return. Look at Guizot. He ordered four great pictures to commemorate the barricades for the government. Why will not the Government do that here? What is the reason, Lord Melbourne, that no English Minister is aware of the importance of Art to the manufactures and wealth of the country? I will tell you, my Lord; you want tutors at the universities' – I was going on talking eagerly with my hand up. At that moment the door opened and in stalked Lord Brougham. He held out his two fingers and said: 'How d'ye do, Mr Haydon?' While I stood looking staggered, Lord Melbourne glanced at me and said: 'I wish you good morning.' I bowed to both and took my leave.

I cannot make out Lord Melbourne, but I fear he is as insincere as the rest. The influence behind the curtain is always at work, and if he meets Academicians at Holland House, their art playing on his comparative ignorance chills him.

28 November. Called on Lord Melbourne and found him as hearty as ever. We had a set-to about Art. He advised me to try Peel, which I shall do. He would not open his lips about politics. Lord Melbourne said he had talked to several artists about a vote of money, and they all said it had better be let alone. 'Who?' said I. 'Portrait painters in opulence. Why do you not give me an opportunity to meet these fellows? The fact is,' said I, 'you are corrupted, you know you are, since I first talked to you. Calcott after dinner at Lord Holland's has corrupted you, sneered you out of your right feelings over your wine.' He acknowledged there was a great deal of truth in this, and laughed heartily.

He advised me to attack Peel, and told me how to proceed to get a sum in the estimates. This is exactly Lord Melbourne. He has no nerve himself; he seemed ashamed, and now, willing not to lose some of the credit, pushes me off on Peel. We shall see.

.

A year passes and Haydon visits Melbourne again:

13 October 1835. Called on Lord Melbourne, and had an hour's interview. 'Is there any prospect, my Lord, of the House of Lords being ornamented by Painting?' 'No,' he thundered out, and began to laugh. 'What is the use of painting a room of deliberation?' 'Ah,' said I, 'if I had been your tutor at college you would not have said that.' He rubbed his hands again, looking the picture of mischief, and laughed heartily. I then said, 'Let me honour your reign.' He swaggered about the room in his grey dressing-gown, his ministerial boxes on the table, his neck bare – and a fine antique one it was – looking the picture of handsome, good-natured mischief. 'Suppose,' said he, 'we employ Calcott.' 'Calcott, my Lord, a landscape painter!' said I. 'Come, my Lord, this is too bad.' He then sat down, opened his boxes and began to write. I sat dead quiet, and waited till his majesty spoke. 'What would you choose?' 'Maintain me for the time, and settle a small pension to keep me from the workhouse.' He looked up with real feeling. 'Let me,' said I, 'in a week bring you one side as I would do it.' He consented, and we parted most amicably. God knows what will come of it.

16 October. Worked very hard, and delightfully. Make a sketch of one side of the House of Lords, as I propose to adorn it, with a series of subjects to illustrate the principle of the best government to regulate without cramping the liberty of man:

Anarchy	Banditti.
Democracy	Banishment of Aristides.
Despotism	Burning of Rome.
Revolution	La dernière charette.
Moral Right	Establishment of Jury.
Limited Monarchy	King, Lords and Commons.

God grant this victory at last.

Nothing comes of all this. Other artists are given the task of decorating the new Houses of Parliament. Haydon's journal reflects the savagery of his times. The Duke of Wellington, now old and retired at Walmer, tells him that 'the natural state of man is plunder. Society is based on security of property alone.' What a man grabs he keeps.

A decade or so later the would-be high-flying painter kills himself. His first editor, Tom Taylor, sets the scene. 'On a table near was his Diary open at the page of the last entry, his watch, a Prayer-book open at the Gospel for the Sixth Sunday after the Epiphany, letters addressed to his wife and children, and a paper, headed "Last thoughts of B. R. Haydon, half-past ten"':

18 June 1846. O God, Bless me through the evils of this day. Great anxiety. My landlord, Newton, called. I said 'I see a quarter's rent in thy face; but none from me.' I appointed to-morrow night to see him, and lay before him every iota of my position. 'Good-hearted Newton!' I said, 'don't put in an execution.' 'Nothing of the sort,' he replied, half hurt.

I sent the Duke, Wordsworth, dear Fred's and Mary's heads, to Miss Barrett to protect. I have the Duke's boots and hat, and Lord Grey's coat, and some more heads.

20 June. O God, bless us all through the evils of this day. Amen.

21 June. Slept horribly. Prayed in sorrow, and got up in agitation.

22 June. God forgive me. Amen.

Finis
of
B. R. Haydon.
'Stretch me no longer on this rough world.' – *Lear.*

JANE WELSH CARLYLE
(1801–66)

Thomas Carlyle married Jane Welsh when he was thirty and for ten years they lived in great solitude and austerity, partly at her little farm in Dumfriesshire. She was the daughter of a laird who had become a doctor. In 1834 the testy couple set up house in Cheyne Row, where he wrote the book which was to make him famous, his *French Revolution*, and she ministered, with little thanks or consideration, to his genius. This took him into the society of Lord and Lady Ashburton and left Jane to cope with a fringe existence as best she could. 'She had married him against the advice of her friends,' wrote J. A. Froude, 'to be the companion of a person whom she, and she alone, at that time, believed to be destined for something extraordinary. She had worked for him like a servant, she had borne poverty and suffering. She had put up with his humours . . . He had risen beyond her highest expectations . . . and she dreaded that she might be a "mere accident of his lot".' She was fiery and he stubborn, and there were many disputes.

Jane's closest friend, Geraldine Jewsbury, stated flatly that 'She was miserable: more abidingly and intensely miserable than words can utter . . . The lines on which her character was laid down were very grand, but the result was blurred and distorted and confused . . . He gave her no human help nor tenderness . . . She did not falter from her purpose of helping and shielding him, but she became warped.'

When J. A. Froude edited Jane's *Letters and Memorials* in 1883, nearly twenty years after that poignant death during a carriage drive round Hyde Park, and two years after Carlyle's own death, he released a much less oppressed wife to the world. The mutual flintiness produced many heart-warming sparks. Like Thomas Hardy and his Emma, Carlyle fell in love all over again with his dead wife. Editing her letters and diary was a task which became for him as 'sad and strange as a pilgrimage through Hades'. Both letters and diary are strong and buoyant, neither the product of a broken spirit and a contrite heart, but of a tart wit and a capable soul.

A visit to the tax-man

21 October 1855. I remember Charles Buller saying of the Duchess de Praslin's murder, 'What could a poor fellow do with a wife who kept a journal but murder her?' There was a certain truth hidden in this light remark. Your journal all about feelings aggravates whatever is factitious and morbid in you; that I have made experience of. And now the only sort of journal I would keep should have to do with what Mr Carlyle calls 'the fact of things'. It is very bleak and barren, this fact of things, as I now see it – very; and what good is to result from writing of it in a paper book is more than I can tell. But I have taken a notion to, and perhaps I shall blacken more paper this time, when I begin quite promiscuously without any moral end in view.

20 November. I have been fretting inwardly all this day at the prospect of having to go and appeal before the Tax Commissioners at Kensington tomorrow morning. Still, it must be done. If Mr C. should go himself he would run his head against some post in his impatience; and besides, for me, when it is over it will be over, whereas he would not get the better of it for twelve months – if ever at all.

21 November. *O me miseram!* not one wink of sleep the whole night through! so great the 'rale mental agony in my own inside' at the thought of that horrid appealing. It was with feeling like the ghost of a dead dog, that I rose and dressed and drank my coffee, and then started for Kensington. Mr C. said 'the voice of honour seemed to call on him to go himself'. But either it did not call loud enough, or he would not listen to that charmer. I went in a cab, to save all my breath for appealing. Set down at 30 Hornton Street, I found a dirty private-like house, only with Tax Office painted on the door. A dirty woman-servant opened the door, and told me the Commissioners would not be there for half-an-hour, but I might walk up. There were already some half-score of men assembled in the waiting-room, among whom I saw the man who cleans our clocks, and a young apothecary of Cheyne Walk. All the others, to look at them, could not have been suspected for an instant, I should have said, of making a hundred a year. Feeling in a false position, I stood by myself at a window and 'thought shame' (as children say). Men trooped in by twos and threes, till the small room was pretty well filled; at last a woman showed herself. O my! did I ever know the full value of any sort of woman – as woman – before! By this time some benches had been brought in, and I was sitting nearest the door. The woman sat down on the same bench with me, and, misery acquainting one with strange bedfellows, we entered into conversation without having been introduced, and I had 'the happiness', as Allan termed it, 'of seeing a woman more miserable than myself'. Two more women arrived at intervals, one a young girl of Dundee, 'sent by my uncle that's ill', who looked to be always recapitulating inwardly what she had been told to say to the Commissioners. The other, a widow, and such a goose, poor thing; she was bringing an appeal against no overcharge in her individual

343

paper, but against the doubling of the Income Tax. She had paid the double tax once, she said, because she was told they would take her goods for it if she didn't – and it was so disgraceful for one in a small business to have her goods taken; besides it was very disadvantageous; but now that it was come round again she would give up. She seemed to attach an irresistible pathos to the title of *widow*, this woman. 'And me a widow, ma'm,' was the winding up of her every paragraph. The men seemed as worried as the women, though they put a better face on it, even carrying on a sort of sickly laughing and bantering with one another. 'First-come lady,' called the clerk, opening a small side-door, and I stept forward into a *grand peut-être*. There was an instant of darkness while the one door was shut behind and the other opened in front; and there I stood in a dim room where three men sat round a large table spread with papers. One held a pen ready over an open ledger; another was taking snuff, and had taken still worse in his time, to judge by his shaky, clayed appearance. The third, who was plainly the cock of that dungheap, was sitting for Rhadamanthus* – a Rhadamanthus without the justice. 'Name,' said the horned-owl-looking individual holding the pen. 'Carlyle.' 'What?' 'Car-lyle.' Seeing he still looked dubious, I spelt it for him. 'Ha!' cried Rhadamanthus, a big, bloodless-faced, insolent-looking fellow. 'What is this? why is Mr Carlyle not come himself? Didn't he get a letter ordering him to appear? Mr Carlyle wrote some nonsense about being exempted from coming, and I desired an answer to be sent that he must come, must do as other people.' 'Then, sir,' I said, 'your desire has been neglected, it would seem, my husband having received no such letter; and I was told by one of your fellow Commissioners that Mr Carlyle's personal appearance was not indispensable.' 'Huffgh! Huffgh! what does Mr Carlyle mean by saying he has no income from his writings, when he himself fixed it in the beginning at a hundred and fifty?' 'It means, sir, that, in ceasing to write, one ceases to be paid for writing, and Mr Carlyle has published nothing for several years.' 'Huffgh! Huffgh! I understand nothing about that.' 'I do,' whispered the snuff-taking Commissioner at my ear. 'I can quite understand a literary man does not

---

* The son of Jupiter who was made one of the judges of the infernal regions.

always make money. I would take it off, for my share, but (sinking his voice still lower) I am only one voice here, and not the most important.' 'There,' said I, handing to Rhadamanthus Chapman and Hall's account; 'that will prove Mr Carlyle's statement.' 'What am I to make of that? Huffgh! we should have Mr Carlyle here to swear to this before we believe it.' 'If a gentleman's word of honour written at the bottom of that paper is not enough, you can put me on my oath: I am ready to swear to it.' 'You! you, indeed! No, no! we can do nothing with your oath.' 'But, sir, I understand my husband's affairs fully, better than he does himself.' 'That I can well believe; but we can make nothing of this,' flinging my document contemptuously on the table. The horned owl picked it up, glanced over it while Rhadamanthus was tossing papers about, and grumbling about 'people that wouldn't conform to rules'; then handed it back to him, saying deprecatingly: 'But, sir, this is a very plain statement.' 'Then what has Mr Carlyle to live upon? You don't mean to tell me he lives on that?' pointing to the document. 'Heaven forbid, sir! but I am not here to explain what Mr Carlyle has to live on, only to declare his income from literature during the last three years.' 'True! true!' mumbled the not-most-important voice at my elbow. 'Mr Carlyle, I believe, has landed income.' 'Of which,' said I haughtily, for my spirit was up, 'I have fortunately no account to render in this kingdom and to this board.' 'Take off fifty pounds, say a hundred — take off a hundred pounds,' said Rhadamanthus to the horned owl. 'If we write Mr Carlyle down a hundred and fifty he has no reason to complain, I think. There, you may go. Mr Carlyle has no reason to complain.' Second-come woman was already introduced, and I was motioned to the door; but I could not depart without saying that 'at all events there was no use in complaining, since they had the power to enforce their decision'. On stepping out, my first thought was, what a mercy Carlyle didn't come himself! for the rest, though it might have gone better, I was thankful that it had not gone worse. When one has been threatened with a great injustice, one accepts a smaller as a favour.

13. THE DIARIST AND DEATH

ELLEN BUXTON
(b. 1848)

Ellen kept her diary between the ages of twelve and sixteen. She was the second child of a large and prosperous Quaker family who lived at Leytonstone, Essex. Her grandfather was known in the family as 'the Liberator', having been a leader in the campaign to abolish slavery. Her grandmother was one of the Gurneys of Earlham and sister to Elizabeth Fry, the prison reformer. While children's deaths were a staple of the Victorian novel, as well as being a disaster from which few homes escaped, the way in which brothers and sisters had to deal with what was a common occurrence has never been better described than in this little diary. The year is 1861 and the diarist is thirteen.

4 Feb. 1861. Lisa's birthday Poor little Leo died this morning at 4 o'clock, he had been ill since thursday morning. I will give a description of it:

On Saturday Jan. 26th, we took Leo to Ham House to see Aunt Buxton, with Papa, Mamma, Lisa and I, and the boys, we went on the ice poor little Leo tumbled down and cried but I do not think he hurt himself much, he got onto a chair and I pushed him about for a long time . . .

Sunday 27. Dear Leo quite well except looking very white as he always did Timmy (who had scaled herself) quite happy in her little bed in the Bow room: Leo went out for a walk in the garden with us before church as usual.

Monday 28. This morning Timmy seemed very dull and low indeed, she would not eat nor play. But dear Leo was quite well. In the afternoon we took Leo with us for a walk to Aunt Barclay's we took Derry without a saddle for him to ride: When we got to the gravel pits we left Arthur Geoffrey and Alfred to try and catch lizards in the little ponds while Lisa Papa Mamma and Myself went on to Aunt Barclay Leo rode Derry almost all the way there; how little we thought that he would never ride again! When we got to Aunt Barclays we found Mrs Carter and Mrs Harrison there with their babies they admired Leo so very much and called him 'like a little Angel' he was very much pleased with the beautiful blue and white hyrsenths. As we came home Leo complained of being tired and rather cold when we got in he had forgotten to take off his galoshes in the hall so when he got to the stairs he sat down and said to Lisa, 'you can pull them off because they are not very dirty'.

Tuesday. Leo came down this morning to reading and sat by Papa on the sofa he looked so lovely by him with his very pale face Timmie is still very poorly, she looks feverish and is very low indeed. In the afternoon Leo went out into the garden and he was sorry to see all the Barley for the chickens spilt upon the ground so he stayed for a long time picking them up.

Wednesday. Leo quite well ... In the afternoon Leo went out of door Miss Smith met him and Sarah and Janet at the pond watching the boys skating and sliding, Miss Smith went on but Leo called out to her to stop for him. She took him with her and as they were coming round the garden he found a stick which he said would do for some poor woman.

Jan. 31. This morning Leo had a bad earache he had had it all night and cried a great deal with it, he did not look at all well, poor little boy, but we did not think it was anything. After breakfast Doctor Ansle came we had all been to see Timmie that morning, he told us that she had scarlet Tina, but only slightly: and then we were quite sure that she had had it all Wednesday.

Dr Ansle told us that dear Leo had it also but so very slightly; he had only a little rash under his arms and legs. That morning at ten o'clock (before Dr Ansle had come) dear Leo had been sitting with

us while we were at lessons and bible reading we gave him a pencil
and paper to draw, he drew very nicely and when Lucy brought
Arty and I our Codliver oil she said she would go and get dear Leo
some orange for to eat while he drew; which he enjoyed very much
he looked very pale indeed, all over his face except one little spot
on his right cheek, which was very red.

Friday, Feb. 1st. This morning Leo was not very ill, neither was
Mamma at all anxious about him, but Emily was much worse than
he was, he had hardly any rash. At dinner time Papa took up Emily
a choice peice of pheasant with breadsauce and potatoe, but she
refused the pheasant and would only eat the breadsauce and potatoe, so Papa took it in to dear Leo which he ate ravenously, it was
the last thing he ate that he enjoyed.

Saturday. Today is dear Emily's sixth birthday Leo rather worse he
has very bad swellings on his glands and very little rash; in the
afternoon he got much worse he could not swallow and hardly
spoke and Mamma says he was in great pain till he died. In the
evening she began to be quite anxious about him. Emily is much
the same, though she is very ill.

Sunday. Dear Leo very ill indeed Mamma and Papa are very
anxious about him ... Aunt and Uncle Barclay came on their way
to meeting and Papa told them how ill Leo was. We did not go to
church at all for fear of infection.

Monday Feb. 4. This morning when we went in to Mamma she
told us that dear Leo had died in the night; we were all very sorry
indeed she told us he had died about 4 o'clock in the morning, and
that he had been in great pain before. We all stayed with Papa and
Mamma till reading time in their room, then we went down to
prayers and Papa read the first part of the XVIIIth chapter of
Matthew with the text in it 'There angels do always behold the face
of my Father'. After breakfast Aunt Buxton came and talked
with Mamma and Papa, we settled with Miss Smith as usual at
10 o'clock but we did not do regular lessons, Lisa and I went to be
with Mamma part of the time, to walk in the garden with her and
Aunt Buxton.

6th. This morning Mamma told us that she wanted us to go and see dear Leo before he was put into his little coffin; Lisa Johnney and I went with Papa and Mamma after breakfast; he was lying in the large bed, and he looked so beautiful and so perfectly at rest; but he did not look at all like himself when he was alive, he was so changed I should not have known him I am sure and so exactly like Papa he looked much older than he really was, and so very handsome, his lips were very dark purple nearly black, and he had a sort of yellowish hue all over his face; his hands were under the sheets so we did not see them, there was a handkerchief tied round his face because Mamma said it wanted support. Papa told us to remember his dear face all our life and to look at him intently he did indeed look lovely and just as though he were asleep; because his beautiful brown eyes were shut.

Feb. 7. Today is dear Leos funeral; Cousin John Paterson is coming to bury him. There are to be a great many people all the Aunts and Uncles and cousins are coming . . . At 12 o'clock we began to walk to the churchyard Mamma and Papa went first then came Lisa and I, and then followed all the others, we first went to the churchyard where Cousin John Paterson met us reading some beautiful texts when we went into the church where we read some part of the service, then we went to the little corner in which the grave was dug, by the side of the little twins and Aunt Buxton's little boy. Then we came away and walked home, when we got home Aunt Barclay and everybody else that had come went to Aunt Barclay's and left us all alone.

DORA CARRINGTON
(1893–1932)

Dora Carrington, an enigmatic woman on the periphery of the Bloomsbury circle, lived with Lytton Strachey from 1915 until his death in 1932, and then shot herself because life was intolerable without him. He was homosexual, she hated being female and understood only friendship. Their friendship by turns baffled, amused and irritated Bloomsbury. Carrington, as she was always known, had studied at the Slade and had become part of the circle which included John and Paul Nash, Stanley and Gilbert Spencer, Mark Gertler and David Bomberg. Her close friend at the Slade was Christine Kühlenthal, who married John Nash in 1918. The common attitude shared by all these young artists and writers was founded on their wholehearted repudiation of the nineteenth-century values of their bourgeois homes, and on a completely free exploration of their emotions. They saw themselves as liberated moderns, and Strachey himself cut the Victorian gods and heroes down to size. Carrington and the other girls cropped their hair and some of them lived with men outside marriage.

Carrington was a dazzling letter-writer; she was also a good home-maker, and when she and Strachey moved to Ham Spray House a decade of enchantment was to follow. What passion she ever possessed seems to have died with her brother Edmund, killed on the Somme in 1916, and all she had left – it was a big all – was a capacity for companionship. Gertler fell in love with her, and so did John Nash; she disastrously married the handsome war hero Ralph Partridge, though the marriage was brief. She was not beautiful and few among the brilliant people who surrounded her thought of her work as remarkable, yet she can now be seen as an excellent artist. Her personality too has become more dominant and intriguing since her death, and her tragedy more perplexing and overwhelming. Her diary is wonderful, and the final pages describing her decision to kill herself are among the few really great statements on suicide. Before she died, having borrowed a shotgun on the pretext that she wanted to shoot rabbits from the window, she copied out the epitaph written by Sir Henry Wotton in 1627:

> He first deceased, she for a little tried
> To live without him, liked it not and died.

20 January 1932. On Wednesday afternoon the 20th Jan. at a quarter to three, there was a change in his face.* I suddenly noticed

---

* Lytton Strachey died in his sleep on Thursday, 31 January, at half past two in the afternoon, without pain.

his breathing was different although he did not wake up. And I thought of the Goya painting of a dead man with the high light on the cheek bones. I ran and called nurse MacCabe, as he had a slight attack of hiccups, she at once asked me to ring up Dr S. S[mith] and ask how much strychnine she could give him. I saw Pippa and James at the top of the stairs just going out. Pippa said 'what is it?' I didn't tell her. I ran back after telephoning and held his arm bare while nurse MacCabe injected 30 grains. Then his breathing became less short. I ran and told James and asked Pippa to come – at that moment it became clear to me he could not live. Ralph returned from a picnic with Gerald at quarter to four. Dr S. S. arrived and gave another injection. I saw from his face he had no hope. He slept without any discomfort or pain. A hatred for nurse Phillips came on me. I cannot remember now anything except watching Lytton's pale face and his close shut eyes lying on the pillows and Pippa standing by his bed. Sleeping with his mouth open. Ray arrived. Cars came backwards and forwards on the gravel. 'There must be nightwatches. Pippa will stay with him till 12 o'clock. Then I till 3 o'clock. Ralph till 6 o'clock and then you after 6 o'clock.' At 3 o'clock I saw James outside on the landing. I had not slept. I went in and asked nurse Mooney if there was any chance of his living, she said: 'Oh no, I don't think so now.' I gave him a kiss on his cold forehead, it was damp and cold. I gave Ralph a kiss and asked him not to come and wake me. I saw him sit by the fire, and sip some tea in Lytton's room. James went downstairs. I walked very quietly down the passage and down the back stairs. It was half past three. The house was quiet and outside the moon shone in the yard, through the elms across the barns. The garage door was stuck open I could hardly move it. Every movement seemed to screech through the still night air. At last I got the doors closed. Then sitting in the car I touched the horn, and my heart stood still, for I felt R[alph] must have heard, as the landing window was open. I stood in the yard watching for a light to go on in the passages. After some time I crept back again and made every preparation, all ready that I could start up the car directly the milking engine started in the farm yard. But not a sound outside. It was very cold in my dressing gown, I thought the milkers started at 4.30. It was 4.30 by the car clock and still nobody stirred. I longed to go round the garden but I

351

feared to be too far from the garage to run back, so I stood under the beech tree by the back door. On the edge of the gutter on the roof, perched 6 pigeons asleep silhouetted against the pale dawn sky. The moon sunk lower. The faint noise of a wind blowing up came across from the trees in the garden. I thought how different one feels everything to what one usually does. As if one was almost transparent, so without any emotion. I was only terrified the cowmen had overslept and that it would be 6 o'clock before they would start. The moon disappeared behind a cloud. I went indoors and drank a whiskey in a tea cup in the dining room. The house was very warm after outside. I went back to my watch under the trees. Suddenly I heard sounds across the yard and movements in the milking shed. I ran to the garage and shut the doors. I got in the car. I started it up one minute after the milking machine which was half past five by the car clock, but that is ten minutes fast. I was terrified by the noise. Once it nearly stopped so I had to turn on the petrol more. There seemed no smell. I got over in the back of the car and lay down and listened to the sound of the crying below me, and the noise of the milking machine puffing way outside. At last I smelt it was beginning to get rather thick. I turned on the light in the side of the car and looked at the clock. Only ten minutes had gone. However Ralph would probably not come exactly at 6 o'clock. The windows of the car looked foggy and a bit misty. I turned out the light again, and lay down. Gradually I felt rather sleepy, and the buzzing noise grew fainter and further off. Rather like fainting I remember thinking. And now what Ellie had told me about a pain in one's throat. I thought of Lytton, and was glad to think I shouldn't know any more. Then I remember a sort of dream which faded away.

Suddenly, long after, waking up in my bed with a buzzing in my ears, and Dr Starkey Smith holding my arm and injecting a syringe. I cried: 'No, no, go away,' and pushed him and his hand away and saw him vanish like the Cheshire cat. Then I looked and saw my bedroom window and it was daylight, and Ralph was there. Ralph held me in his arms and kissed me and said: 'How could you do it?' I felt *angry* at being back after being in a very happy dream. Sorry to be awake again. A buzzing in my ears and something wrong with my eyes. I couldn't see my hands, or focus on anything. Ralph asked me if I'd have some tea. I asked for some water. He was very upset and I felt he was angry with me at first; perhaps he wasn't. I had no idea of the time. Then Tommy came in, but perhaps that was much later and talked to me. I felt rather far away and my eyes were still queer. James came and talked to me. I felt no remorse. I must confess I felt defrauded and angry that fate had cheated me in such a way and brought me back again. I got up at 12 o'clock and went into Lytton's room. He was still sleeping, breathing very deeply and fast. Pippa sat in a chair. I went and sat in the chair and watched him. 'So this is death,' I kept saying to myself. The two nurses moved about behind the screen. Ralph came and sat on the floor. I felt completely calm. His face was very pale like ivory. Everything seemed to be transfixed. The pale face of nurse MacCabe standing by his bed, in her white clothes. Pippa watching with those sweet brown eyes, all tear stained and her face mottled. The noise of the electric light machine outside. I sat there thinking of all the other mornings in Lytton's room and there was 'Pride and Prejudice', that I had been reading the afternoon before still on the table. It seemed as if time had lost all its properties. As if everything was marked by Lytton's [heart] beating, not by the ticks of the clock. Suddenly I felt very sick, and ran out to my bedroom and was violently sick into the chamberpot. I remember watching the yellow water pour out of my mouth and thought it is the same as what is in the pot already. Then Ralph came with a basin but I had finished being sick by then. I saw as I walked down the passage, Tommy talking to James in the library. I went back to Lytton's room and sat on the chair. About 2 o'clock or 1.30 Lytton grew worse and his breathing became shorter. I stood holding Pippa round the waist. Lytton never opened his eyes. I could not cry. I felt if he woke up we must be there not depressing or melancholy. James came in and stood behind us with Ralph. I felt like a Russian soldier holding Pippa against my body. Nurse MacCabe stood against the wall, alternately watching us and Lytton, sometimes taking his pulse. Nurse Philipps suddenly came forwards and said: 'I think you ladies had better go, and sit down, you can do no good here.' I was furious and hated her. Ralph brought me some glasses of brandy and some sal volatile to drink. A blackbird sung outside in the sun on the aspen. We stood there. I do not know for how long. Sometimes his breathing almost stopped. But then he breathed again fainter.

Tuesday, 16 February. At last I am alone. At last there is nothing between us. I have been reading my letters to you in the library this evening. You are so engraved on my brain that I think of nothing else. Everything I look at is part of you. And there seems no point in life now you are gone. I used to say: 'I must eat my meals properly as Lytton wouldn't like me to behave badly when he was away.' But now there is no coming back. No point in 'improvements'. Nobody to write letters to. Only the interminable long days which never seem to end and the nights which end all too soon and turn to dawns. All the gaiety has gone out of my life and I feel old and melancholy. All I can do is to plant snow drops and daffodils in my graveyard! Frankie [Birrell] sent me some old letters to read. I read them at tea. Now there is nothing left. All your papers have been taken away. Your clothes have gone. Your room is bare. In a few months no traces will be left. Just a few book plates in some books and never again, however long I look out of the window, will I see your tall thin figure walking across the park past the dwarf pine past the stumps, and then climb the ha-ha and come across the lawn. Our jokes have gone for ever. There is nobody now to make 'disçerattas' with, to laugh over our particular words. To discuss the difficulties of love, to read Ibsen in the evening. And to play cards when we were too 'dim' for reading. These mourning sentinels that we arranged so carefully. The shiftings to get the new rose Corneille in the best position. They will go, and the beauty of our library 'will be over'. – I feel as if I was in a dream almost unconscious, so much of me was in you.

And I thought as I threw the rubbish on the bonfire 'So that's the end of his spectacles. Those spectacles that have been his companions all these years. Burnt in a heap of leaves.' And those vests the 'bodily companions' of his days now are worn by a carter in the fields. In a few years what will be left of him? A few books on some shelves, but the intimate things that I loved, all gone.

And soon even the people who knew his pale thin hands and the texture of his thick shiny hair, and grisly beard, they will be dead and all remembrance of him will vanish. I watched the gap close over others but for Lytton one couldn't have believed (because one did not believe it was ever possible) that the world would go on the same.

17 February. In the Library. I dreamt of you again last night. And when I woke up it was as if you had died afresh. Every day I find it *harder* to bear. For what point is there in life now? I read all your letters this afternoon. Because I could not bear the utter loneliness here without you. If only I had believed my fears and had never left you for a day. But that would have meant 'encroaching' on your liberty, and breaking the 'laws'. What is the use of anything now without you? I keep on consulting you. But for what purpose? For I can no longer please you. I look at our favourites I try and read them, but without you they give me no pleasure. I only remember the evenings when you read them to me aloud and then I cry. I feel as if we had collected all our wheat into a barn to make bread and beer for the rest of our lives and now our barn has been burnt down and we stand on a cold winter morning looking at the charred ruins. For this little room was the gleanings of our life together. All our happiness was over this fire and with these books. With Voltaire blessing us with up-raised hand on the wall. It was all for you; I loved you so utterly and now there is nothing left to look forward to. You made me so absolutely happy. Every year had grown happier with you. It is impossible to think that I shall never sit with you again and hear your laugh. *That everyday for the rest of my life you will be away.* No one to talk to about my pleasures. No one to call me for walks to go 'to the terrace'. I write in an empty book. I cry in an empty room. And there can never be any comfort again. 'You can't get away from the fact that Lytton is dead,' he said.

SOURCES

The diary extracts that appear in this book have been reprinted from the following sources:

AGATE, JAMES *Ego III*, Harrap, 1938

AITKEN, JAMES *English Diaries of the XVI, XVII and XVIII Centuries*, Penguin Books, Harmondsworth, 1941

ALLINGHAM, WILLIAM *A Diary*, edited by H. Allingham and D. Radford, Penguin Books, Harmondsworth, 1985

ASHMOLE, WILLIAM *The Diary and Life of William Ashmole*, edited by J. T. Gunter, O.U.P., 1927

ASQUITH, LADY CYNTHIA *Diaries, 1915–18*, Hutchinson, 1968

BARBELLION, W. N. P. *The Journal of a Disappointed Man*, Chatto & Windus, 1919

BARBELLION, W. N. P. *A Last Diary*, Chatto & Windus, 1920

BECKFORD, WILLIAM *The Travel Diaries of William Beckford of Fonthill*, edited by Guy Chapman, Constable, 1928

BENNETT, ARNOLD *The Journals of Arnold Bennett*, selected and edited by Frank Swinnerton, Penguin Books, Harmondsworth, 1954

BLAIKIE, THOMAS *Diary of a Scotch Gardener at the French Court at the end of the Eighteenth Century*, edited by Francis Birrell, Routledge, 1931

BOSWELL, JAMES *Life of Johnson*, Murray, 1866

Boswell on the Grand Tour, Italy, Corsica and France, 1765–66, edited by Frank Brady and Frederick A. Pottle, Heinemann, 1955

BRERETON, SIR WILLIAM *Diary, 1634*, Chetham Society, 1844

BROWNING, ELIZABETH BARRETT *The Barretts at Hope End: The Early Diary of Elizabeth Barrett Browning*, edited with an Introduction by Elizabeth Berridge, Murray, 1974

BRUCKSHAW, HORACE *The Diaries of Private Horace Bruckshaw*,

Royal Marine Light Infantry, 1915–1916, edited and introduced by Martin Middlebrook, Scolar Press, 1979

BURNEY, FANNY (F. D'ARBLAY) *Diary and Letters of Madame d'Arblay*, edited by her niece, 7 vols., Colburn, 1846

BUTLER, LADY ELEANOR Journal, in *Life with the Ladies of Llangollen* by Elizabeth Mavor, Viking, 1984

BUXTON, ELLEN *Journal, 1860–1864*, arranged by her granddaughter, Ellen R. C. Creighton, Geoffrey Bles, 1967

BYNG, JOHN, VISCOUNT TORRINGTON *The Torrington Diaries*, edited by C. B. Andrews, Eyre & Spottiswoode, 1954

BYRD, WILLIAM *The London Diary, 1717–1721 and Other Writings*, edited by Louis B. Wright and Marion Tinling, O.U.P., 1958

BYRON, GEORGE GORDON, LORD *So Late into the Night: Byron's Letters and Journals*, edited by Leslie C. Marchand, Murray, 1976

CARLYLE, JANE WELSH *Letters and Memorials of Jane Welsh Carlyle*, prepared for publication by Thomas Carlyle and edited by James Anthony Froude, 3 vols., Longmans, Green, 1883

CARRINGTON, DORA *Letters and Extracts from her Diaries*, chosen and with an Introduction by David Garnett, Cape, 1970

CHANNON, SIR HENRY *Chips: The Diaries of Sir Henry Channon*, edited by Robert Rhodes James, Penguin Books, Harmondsworth, 1970

CLARK, REV. ANDREW *Echoes of the Great War: The Diary of the Reverend Andrew Clark, 1914–1919*, edited by James Munson, O.U.P., 1985

CLIFFORD, LADY ANNE *Diary*, with an Introductory Note by V. Sackville-West, Heinemann, 1923

CORY, WILLIAM *Extracts from the Letters and Journals of William Cory*, selected and arranged by Francis Warre Cornish, Oxford, 1897

CRABBE, REV. GEORGE *Life of Crabbe*, 1834

DARWIN, CHARLES *A Journal of Researches*, Ward Lock, 1914

DEE, JOHN *The Private Diary of Dr John Dee, 1577–1601*, edited by J. O. Halliwell, Camden Society, 1842

EDWARD VI, KING *Literary remains of King Edward the Sixth*, edited from his autograph MSS., with historical notes and a biographical memoir by John Gough Nichols, 2 vols., Roxburghe Society, 1857

EVELYN, JOHN   *Diary*, edited by E. S. de Beer, O.U.P., 1956

EYRE, ADAM   'Diary of Adam Eyre' in *Yorkshire Diaries*, edited by A. J. Morehouse, Surtees Society, 1875

FOTHERGILL, ROBERT   *Private Diaries: A Study of English Diaries*, O.U.P., 1974

FROUDE, R. H.   *Remains of the Late Reverend Richard Hurrell Froude, M.A.*, 4 vols., London, 1838–9

GORDON, C. G.   *Khartoum Journals of General Gordon*, with an Introduction by A. E. Hake and notes by Sir Henry Gordon, 1885

HALL, JOHN VINE   *Diary*, edited by Newman Hall, London, 1865

HARDY, FLORENCE EMILY   *The Early Life of Thomas Hardy*, Macmillan, 1928

HAYDON, BENJAMIN ROBERT   *The Autobiography and Memoirs of Benjamin Robert Haydon, 1786–1846*, edited from his *Journals* by Tom Taylor, 2 vols., Peter Davies, 1926

HEYWOOD, OLIVER   *Diaries*, edited by J. Horsfall Turner, Brighouse and Bingley, 1882–5

HOPKINS, GERARD MANLEY   *The Journals and Papers of Gerard Manley Hopkins*, edited by Humphrey House and completed by Graham Storey, O.U.P., 1958

JACQUIER, IVY   *The Diary of Ivy Jacquier*, Gollancz, 1960

JAMES, ALICE   *The Diary of Alice James*, edited by Leon Edel, Hart Davis, 1964

JEFFERIES, RICHARD   *Nature Diaries and Notebooks*, edited by Samuel L. Looker, Grey Walls Press, 1948

JOHNSON, SAMUEL   *Diaries, Prayers and Annals*, edited by A. T. Hazen and J. H. Mitzendorf, Yale, 1958

JONES, THOMAS   *A Diary with Letters, 1931–1950*, O.U.P., 1954

JOSSELIN, REV. RALPH   *The Diary of Ralph Josselin, 1616–1638*, edited by Alan Macfarlane, O.U.P., 1976

KILVERT, REV. FRANCIS   *Kilvert's Diary, 1870–78: Selections from the Diary of the Rev. Francis Kilvert*, chosen, edited and introduced by William Plomer, Cape, Vol. 1 1938, Vol. 2 1939

LAKE, DR EDWARD   *Diary, 1677–78*, Camden Miscellanies, 1838

LEES-MILNE, JAMES   *Ancestral Voices: Diaries 1942–3; Prophesy-*

ing Peace: Diaries 1944–5; Caves of Ice: Diaries 1946–7, Chatto & Windus, 1975, 1977, 1983

LIVINGSTONE, DAVID   *The Last Journals of David Livingstone in Central Africa from 1865 to his death*, edited by Horace Waller, 2 vols., Murray, 1875

MANNINGHAM, JOHN   *Diary, 1602–3*, Camden Society, 1868

MANSFIELD, KATHERINE   *The Journal of Katherine Mansfield*, edited by J. Middleton Murry, Constable, 1928

MATTHEWS, WILLIAM   *British Diaries: An Annotated Bibliography of British Diaries Written Between 1442–1942*, C.U.P., 1950

MONKSWELL, M.   *A Victorian Diarist: Extracts from the Journals of Mary, Lady Monkswell, 1873–1895*, edited by the Hon. E. C. F. Collier, Murray, 1944

MUNBY, ARTHUR   *Munby, Man of Two Worlds: The Life and Diaries of Arthur J. Munby, 1828–1910* by Derek Hudson, Murray, 1972

MURPHY, DERVLA   *Full-Tilt: Ireland to India with a Bicycle*, Murray, 1965

NEWCOMBE, REV. HENRY   *Diary, 1661–3*, edited by T. Heywood, Chetham Society, 1849

NICOLSON, SIR HAROLD   *Diaries and Letters, 1930–1964*, edited and condensed by Stanley Olson, Penguin Books, Harmondsworth, 1984

NIN, ANAÏS   *The Diary of Anaïs Nin, 1931–47*, edited by G. Stuhlmann, Peter Owen, 1966–71

PARTRIDGE, FRANCES   *A Pacifist's War*, Hogarth Press, 1978

PEPYS, SAMUEL   *The Diary of Samuel Pepys, Vol. I, 1660*, edited by Robert Latham and William Matthews, Bell, 1970

RUTTY, DR JOHN   *A Spiritual Diary and Soliloquies*, 2 vols., 1776

SASSOON, SIEGFRIED   *Diaries, 1920–1922*, edited and introduced by Rupert Hart-Davis, Faber and Faber, 1981

SLINGSBY, SIR HENRY   *Diary, 1638–49*, edited by D. Parsons, London, 1836

SMITH, ELIZABETH   *The Irish Journals of Elizabeth Smith, 1840–1850*, selection edited by David Thomson and Moyra McGusty, Clarendon Press, Oxford, 1980

SPENDER, SIR STEPHEN   *Journals 1939–1983*, edited by John Goldsmith, Faber and Faber, 1985

STOVIN, CORNELIUS *Journals of a Methodist Farmer, 1871–1875*, edited by Jean Stovin, Croom Helm, 1982

STURT, GEORGE *The Journals of George Sturt, 1980–1927*, a selection edited and introduced by E. D. Mackerness, 2 vols., C.U.P., 1967

SWIFT, JONATHAN *Journal to Stella*, edited by H. Williams, 2 vols., O.U.P., 1948

TEONGUE, REV. HENRY *The Diary of Henry Teongue, 1675–9*, edited by G. E. Manwaring, Routledge, 1927

THOMAS, EDWARD *Diary of Edward Thomas, 1 January–8 April, 1917, Anglo-Welsh Review*, Autumn, 1971

THOREAU, HENRY D. *Works*, with an Introduction by T. Watts-Dunton, World's Classics, O.U.P., 1906

THORESBY, RALPH *Diary*, edited by Jos. Hunter, 2 vols., 1830

TURNER, THOMAS *The Diary of Thomas Turner, 1754–1765*, edited by David Vaisey, O.U.P., 1984

VAUGHAN, KEITH *Journal and Drawings*, Alan Ross, 1966

VICTORIA, QUEEN *More Leaves from the Journal of Our Life in the Highlands*, edited by Arthur Helps, Smith, Elder, 1884

WAUGH, EVELYN *The Diaries of Evelyn Waugh, 1911–1965*, edited by Michael Davie, Penguin Books, Harmondsworth, 1979

WEBB, BEATRICE *Beatrice Webb's Diaries, 1912–1924*, edited by Margaret Cole, Longman, 1952

WELCH, DENTON *The Journals of Denton Welch*, edited by Michael De-la-Noy, Allison & Busby, 1984

WESLEY, REV. JOHN *The Journal of the Reverend John Wesley*, 4 vols., Dent, 1913

WHEATLEY, EDMUND *The Wheatley Diary: A Journal and Sketchbook kept during the Peninsular War and Waterloo Campaign*, edited with an Introduction by Christopher Hibbert, Longman, 1961

WHITE, REV. GILBERT *Journals*, edited by Walter Johnson, Routledge, 1931

WOODFORDE, REV. JAMES *The Diary of a Country Parson, 1758–1802*, edited by John Beresford, O.U.P., 1924

WOOLF, VIRGINIA *The Diary of Virginia Woolf*, edited by Anne Olivier Bell, Hogarth Press, 1977–84

WORDSWORTH, DOROTHY *The Journals of Dorothy Words-worth*, edited by W. Knight, London, 1904

ACKNOWLEDGEMENTS

The author and publishers wish to thank the following for permission to use copyright material:

The British Academy for extracts from *The Diary of Ralph Josselin 1616–1638*, edited by Alan Macfarlane, Oxford University Press, 1976

Cambridge University Press for extracts from *The Journals of George Sturt 1890–1927*, edited by E. D. Mackerness, 1967

Jonathan Cape Ltd for extracts from *Kilvert's Diary*, edited by William Plomer, 1938–9; on behalf of the Estate of David Garnett with A. P. Watt on behalf of the Estate of David Garnett and the Sophie Partridge Trust for extracts from *Dora Carrington: Letters and Extracts from her Diaries*, chosen and introduced by David Garnett, 1970

Century Hutchinson Ltd for an extract from *Diaries 1915–18* by Lady Cynthia Asquith, 1968

Chatto & Windus Ltd for extracts from *A Pacifist's War* by Frances Partridge, 1978; *Prophesying Peace: Diaries 1944–5* by James Lees-Milne, 1977; and on behalf of the Executors of the Virginia Woolf Estate for extracts from *The Selected Diaries of Virginia Woolf*, edited by Anne Olivier Bell, The Hogarth Press, 1977

Collins Publishers for extracts from *Sir Harold Nicolson's Diaries and Letters*, edited by Stanley Olson, 1980

Constable Publishers for an extract from *The Travel Diaries of William Beckford of Fonthill*, edited by Guy Chapman, 1928

Croom Helm for extracts from *Journals of a Methodist Farmer 1871–1875*, edited by Jean Stovin, 1982

Faber and Faber Ltd for extracts from *Siegfried Sassoon: Diaries 1920–1922*, edited by Rupert Hart Davis, 1981; and *Sir Stephen Spender: Journals 1939–1983*, edited by John Goldsmith, 1985

The Penguin Book of Diaries

Victor Gollancz Ltd for extracts from *The Diary of Ivy Jacquier* by Ivy Jacquier, 1960

William Heinemann Ltd for extracts from *The Autobiography and Memoirs of Benjamin Robert Haydon 1786–1846*, edited by Tom Taylor, Peter Davies Ltd, 1926, and *Diary* by Lady Anne Clifford, introductory note by V. Sackville West, 1923; and on behalf of The Yale Editions of the Private Papers of James Boswell for extracts from *Boswell on the Grand Tour: Italy, Corsica and France 1965–66*, edited by Frank Brady and Frederick A. Pottle, 1955

David Higham Associates Ltd on behalf of the University of Texas Press for extracts from *The Journals of Denton Welch*, edited by Michael De-la-Noy, Allison & Busby, 1984

London Magazine Editions for an extract from *Journal and Drawings* by Keith Vaughan, 1966

The London School of Economics and Political Science for extracts from *Beatrice Webb's Diaries 1912–1924*, edited by Margaret Cole, Longman, 1952

Longman Group Ltd for an extract from *The Wheatley Diary: A Journal and Sketchbook kept during the Peninsular War and Waterloo Campaign*, edited by Christopher Hibbert, 1961

Methuen for extracts from *The Torringham Diaries* by John Byng, edited by C. B. Andrews, Eyre & Spottiswoode, 1954

John Murray Ltd for extracts from *The Barretts of Hope End: The Early Diary of Elizabeth Barrett Browning*, edited by Elizabeth Berridge, 1974; *Munby: Man of Two Worlds: The Life and Diaries of Arthur J. Munby*, edited by Derek Hudson, 1972; *A Victorian Diarist: Extracts from the Journals of Mary, Lady Monkswell 1875–1895*, edited by E. F. C. Collier, 1944; with Harvard University Press for extracts from *So Late Into the Night: Byron's Letters and Journals*, edited by Leslie C. Marchand. Copyright © 1976 by John Murray; with The Overlook Press for extracts from *Full Tilt: Ireland to India with a Bicycle* by Dervla Murphy. Copyright © 1965 by Dervla Murphy

Peter Owen Ltd and Harcourt Brace Jovanovich, Inc. for extracts from *The Diary of Anaïs Nin 1931–47*, edited with an introduction by Gunther Stuhlmann. Copyright © 1966 by Anaïs Nin

Oxford University Press for extracts from *The Journals and Papers of Gerard Manley Hopkins*, edited by Humphry House and Graham Storey, 1958; James Woodforde's *Diary of a Country Parson 1758–1802*, edited by John Beresford, 1924; Jonathan Swift's *Journal to Stella*, edited by Harold Williams, 1948; *A Diary with Letters 1931–1050* by Thomas Jones, 1954; *The Irish Journals of Elizabeth Smith 1840–1850*, edited by David Thomson and Moyra McGusty, 1980; *The Diary of Thomas Turner 1754–1765*, edited by David Vaisey, 1984; *Echoes of the Great War* by Andrew Clark, edited by James Munson, 1985; and *The Diary of John Evelyn*, edited by E. S. de Beer, 1956

Penguin Books Ltd with Curtis Brown on behalf of Elizabeth Mavor for extracts from *The Ladies of Llangollen* by Elizabeth Mavor. Copyright © 1971 by Elizabeth Mavor

Peters, Fraser and Dunlop Group Ltd for extracts from *Ego III* by James Agate, Harrap Ltd, 1938, 1976

Routledge & Kegan Paul for extracts from *The Journals of Gilbert White*, edited by Walter Johnson, 1931

Unwin Hyman Ltd with The University of California Press for extracts from *The Diary of Samuel Pepys Vol. I*, edited by Robert Latham and William Matthews. Copyright © 1970 by G. K. Bell and Sons

A. P. Watt Ltd on behalf of Mme V. Eldin for extracts from *The Journals of Arnold Bennett*, edited by Frank Swinnerton, Penguin Books, 1954

George Weidenfeld & Nicolson Ltd for extracts from *Chips: The Diaries of Sir Henry Channon*, edited by Robert Rhodes James, Penguin Books, 1970; with Little Brown and Company for extracts from *The Diaries of Evelyn Waugh*, edited by Michael Davie, Penguin Books, 1979. Copyright © 1976 by The Estate of Evelyn Waugh

Yale University Press for extracts from *Diaries, Prayers and Annuals of Samuel Johnson*, edited by A. T. Hazeh and J. H. Mitzendorf, 1958

By Ronald Blythe

Akenfield

A huge bestseller, Ronald Blythe's close-up of a Suffolk village has, for most readers, justified C. P. Snow's forecast that it would become a classic of its kind. Only a man born and bred in the county could, one feels, have extracted the confidences and revelations that fill these pages as a soldier, a farm labourer, a district nurse, an ex-army officer and other typical figures tell their personal stories.

'One of the most absorbing books that I have read in the last ten years. A penetrating, extraordinarily unprejudiced, yet deeply caring account of modern rural life in England' – Angus Wilson

'The fatalism, dissenting spirit, and the imponderables of the East Anglian character are drawn, with patience and subtlety, from people who live on the heavy soil . . . completely fascinating' – *The Times*

'One of the most poignant and moving books which I have read in years' – J. H. Plumb

'It seems to possess an appeal far beyond its immediate subject matter for a variety of readers' – *The Times Educational Supplement*